From Discussion to Writing

Instructional Resources for Teaching

Prepared by

Valerie Duff-Strautmann
Jeffrey Ousborne
Gregory Atwan

From Discussion to Writing

Instructional Resources for Teaching

America Now

Short Readings from Recent Periodicals

From Discussion to Writing

Instructional Resources for Teaching

America Now

Short Readings from Recent Periodicals

Ninth Edition

Edited by

Robert Atwan
Emerson College

Prepared by

Valerie Duff-Strautmann

Jeffrey Ousborne
Suffolk University

Gregory Atwan

Bedford/St. Martin's Boston ♦ New York

Manufactured in the United States of America.

6 5 4 3 2 1
f e d c b a

For information, write: Bedford/St. Martin's, 75 Arlington Street, Boston, MA 02116 (617-399-4000)

ISBN: 978–0–312–60265–9

Contents

A Rhetorical Table of Contents

America Now includes numerous examples of rhetorical strategies that aid us in expressing ourselves clearly, cogently, and convincingly. Listed below are eight of the most common rhetorical categories with a brief account of how they are generally used in both verbal and visual texts. Nearly every selection in the book relies on more than one category, so you will find that several selections appear multiple times. The selections listed are those that most effectively demonstrate—either in whole or in their various segments—a particular strategy. Page numbers refer to the textbook.

R. A.

1 *NARRATION* Some uses: telling a story; reporting or summarizing a sequence of events; constructing a historical chronology; recounting a biography or autobiography; detailing how something is done or comes about; breaking down a process into a sequence of events.

2 *DESCRIPTION* Some uses: creating a picture in word or image; making information more clear or vivid; reporting objective details.

3 *EXEMPLIFICATION* Some uses: providing a "for instance" or "for example"; illustrating ideas; making something abstract more concrete; representing a larger concept or event by a single incident or image.

4 *DEFINITION* Some uses: clarifying key terms; reflecting on the significance of a word; enlarging or restricting a term's meaning; eliminating confusion or ambiguity; challenging conventional meanings and euphemisms.

5 *CLASSIFICATION AND DIVISION* Some uses: dividing a subject into several key parts; organizing material into categories; making distinctions; constructing outlines; arranging ideas in the most appropriate order; viewing an issue from its various sides.

6 *COMPARISON AND CONTRAST* Some uses: finding similarities among different things or ideas; finding differences among similar things or ideas; organizing material through point-by-point resemblance or disparity; forming analogies; expressing a preference for one thing or position over another.

7 *CAUSE AND EFFECT* Some uses: identifying the cause of an event or trend; examining how one thing has influenced another; looking at the consequences of an action or idea; assigning credit, blame, or responsibility.

8 *ARGUMENT AND PERSUASION* Some uses: convincing someone that an opinion is correct; defending or refuting a position; gaining support for a course of action; making proposals; resolving conflicts to reach consent or consensus. (At the end of the following list, you will find a collection of the Debates in *America Now*.)

DEBATES

Preface

Using America Now *in Developmental and Composition Classes*

With its strong focus on current issues and its thought-provoking assignments, *America Now* is ideal for both developmental and composition classes. Many of the questions and writing assignments in the book will give students the practice they need to pass basic skills examinations. At the same time, these questions allow students to work within a real context, and all levels of writing classes might use them to practice writing skills, promote discussion, and prepare for take-home essay assignments. Though some questions and writing assignments in the book ask students to focus on just one selection, others require them to synthesize varying opinions and to come to their own conclusions about an issue, drawing on readings and their own observations for support. These more complex assignments might be more appropriate for composition classes or the latter part of developmental classes.

Because *America Now* presents readings on some of today's most important issues and provides all the help students need to understand, discuss, and write on the topics presented, it actively engages the interest of students from a range of courses and skill levels. This book is an excellent choice for developmental students, who need to know more than just where to put a comma or how to handle verb tenses. They need to read critically, to make connections among an author's various points, and to juxtapose these points with those of other authors. They also need to be able to engage in thoughtful classroom discussion and to express and support their own opinions in their writing. Most students can meet these challenges, and instructors report that developmental students effectively analyze texts far more complex than those found in many readers. Their students often say that they can think, but they need advice on how to write in a way that is accepted in academia. Often such students write best when they are asked to discuss topics meaningful to them, and *America Now* and this manual provide contexts for such meaningful expression.

Using This Instructor's Manual

The comments and suggestions that follow invite you to use the ninth edition of *America Now* to expand your students' reading and writing abilities. Each writing class is unique, and labels often do not adequately characterize the abilities, interests, and perspectives of a particular group of students. Therefore, the questions and activities in *America Now* and the suggestions provided here include a variety of options that may be adapted for students with a wide range of reading and writing experiences. We invite you to choose those that best suit your classes, those that best fit your particular teaching style, and those that work best within the curriculum for the specific course you are teaching. We hope that these materials will encourage students to read and write more thoughtfully and critically, challenge them to think about reading and writing in increasingly sophisticated ways, and make planning and organizing classroom activities more manageable for instructors.

This manual is organized to parallel the structure of the student edition of *America Now*. Each chapter begins with a brief introduction to the themes and selections offered in that chapter. Following the introductory material are suggested answers to questions in the text. These suggested answers correspond to the question sets that follow each selection in the student edition—Vocabulary/Using a Dictionary; Responding to Words in Context; Discussing Main Point and Meaning; Examining Sentences, Paragraphs, and Organization; Thinking Critically; In-Class Writing Activities—and those that follow each chapter: Preparing for Class Discussion; From Discussion to Writing; and Topics for Cross-Cultural Discussion. These suggested answers are meant to anticipate possible student responses, to raise further questions for discussion and writing, and to help you better use *America Now* as a tool for classroom discussion and more effective student writing.

Obviously, few classes will be able to read and work with all of the selections in the text in one semester. You may want to focus on thematic groupings of units, or you may prefer to select units that are of particular interest to your students. Some instructors may allow students to choose selections; others will be more comfortable making these selections or taking turns with the class. As an alternative approach, you might ask a group of students to select a unit for the class to read; then the group of students in charge would be responsible for the discussion and the activities in which the class participates.

However you use this manual, we hope that it will help you and your students use the text fully and thoughtfully, think critically about the issues and readings, and consider how these readings fit within the larger context that is America now.

Introduction: Writing and the Art of Discussion

by Robert Atwan

> I enter into discussion and argument with great freedom and ease, inasmuch as opinion finds in me a bad soil to penetrate and take deep roots in. No propositions astonish me, no belief offends me, whatever contrast it offers with my own. There is no fancy so frivolous and so extravagant that it does not seem to me quite suitable to the production of the human mind.
>
> —Michel de Montaigne,
> *Of the Art of Discussion* (1588)

> However unwillingly a person who has a strong opinion may admit the possibility that his opinion may be false, he ought to be moved by the consideration that, however true it may be, if it is not fully, frequently, and fearlessly discussed, it will be held as a dead dogma, not a living truth.
>
> —John Stuart Mill,
> *Of the Liberty of Thought and Discussion* (1869)

Students often begin their college writing courses with a popular misconception. They think that writing is an isolating activity demanding extraordinary inner resources. They picture writers as sitting alone at their desks or computers anxiously staring at a blank page or screen until inspiration strikes. Indeed, this romanticized image of anxious solitude followed by a burst of creativity has for centuries served as a powerful model of how literature is produced. But for the average student, who has little understanding of how real writers work and has perhaps never observed people writing professionally, this popular image can lead to a distorted view of writing and the role writing plays in a person's intellectual development.

Most writers work within a lively social context, one in which issues and ideas are routinely discussed and debated. They often begin writing on topics that derive directly from specific professional situations: a journalist covers a murder trial; a professor prepares a paper for a conference; a social worker writes up a case study; an executive reports on a business meeting. Usually, the writer consults with friends and coworkers about the task and solicits their opinions and support, sometimes even asking them to comment on a draft of the work. If the work is to be published, the writer almost always receives additional advice and criticism in the form of editorial comment, copyediting, proofreading, and independent reviews. By the time the work appears, it has probably gone through numerous drafts (for some writers as many as ten or twelve) and has been subjected to a rigorous sequence of editorial support, from fact checking to stylistic fine tuning.

Nearly all the published work a student reads, with the possible exception of work published on the Internet, has gone through this process. Even the most ephemeral article in a magazine has probably been revised several times by several people before publication. But, of course, none of this is visible in the final product. Students have little knowledge of all the various levels of work and collaboration that have gone into a piece of writing—the author's often extensive reading and research; the time spent traveling, interviewing, and discussing; the organization of the information; the composing of several drafts; and the concerted effort of editors and publishers. Unlike a film, a piece of writing shows only the author's name and seldom everyone else who helped make the published work possible (though some books include an acknowledgments page).

The point about student writing should be clear: Students write in a much narrower professional environment than do experienced people whose writing is a significant part of their work. Too often, the student writes in an intellectual vacuum. He or she may feel only minimally engaged by an assigned topic—which may seem to have come out of nowhere—and may not know anyone with whom the topic may be seriously and intelligently discussed. Unlike the professional writer, the student usually sits down alone and tries to write with little intellectual provocation or encouragement. No wonder students find it so hard to begin a paper. Instead of knowing they are writing for a group of interested people, they often feel that their writing will be read by only one other person—the instructor, who will read it not for further discussion but for immediate evaluation.

America Now is designed to help writing students avoid the intellectual and emotional vacuum that confronts them when they begin to write. Two of the biggest problems in composition, finding something to say and getting started, are in large part due to the student's lack of a vital connection with what other people have to say about an issue or idea. The basis of many student writing problems, I believe, is not so much grammatical or rhetorical as social. At their worst, these problems are clearly reflected in the writing, in a disjunctive prose that sounds oddly cut off from most public discourse.

The art of writing and the art of discussion are closely linked. Experienced writers invariably write in a climate of discussion. Their writing is usually embedded in a context of others' ideas and opinions. Many writers, especially in the academic community, are directly responding to other writers—a scientist reexamining the experimental procedures of other scientists; a literary critic taking exception to a prevailing method of interpretation; a sociologist offering an alternative explanation of a colleague's data; a historian participating as a respondent at a conference. Such people are not writing in a vacuum. Their ideas often originate in discussion, their writing is a response to discussion, and their papers are designed to stimulate further discussion.

The Art of Discussion

Discussion is one of those commonly used words from speech and rhetoric—like *essay* and *style*—that remains difficult to define precisely. The word has a long and complex history. It derives from a Latin verb (*discutere*) meaning "to dash, scatter, or shake out," and it gradually came to take on the legal and, later, the rhetorical sense of "breaking" a case or a topic down into its various parts for investigation. Though the word is ordinarily used today to mean "to talk over" or "to consider carefully," it still retains a rhetorical sense of sifting a topic into separate parts for close examination.

It is easier to say what discussion is not: It is neither conversation nor debate. Unlike conversation, discussion is purposefully conducted around a given topic. Unlike debate, it is not formally organized into two competing points of view. Think of discussion as a speech activity that falls between the informalities of conversation and the formalities of debate. For the purpose of this book, discussion is defined as the free and open exploration of a specified topic by a small group of prepared people. The goal of such discussion is not to arrive at a group decision or a consensus, but to investigate as many sides of a topic as possible.

To keep discussion from rigidifying into a debate between two competing sides or from drifting into aimless conversation, a discussion leader or moderator is usually required. The discussion leader may adopt an active role in the discussion or may choose to remain neutral. But regardless of the extent of the leader's role, he or she will ordinarily introduce the topic, encourage participation, maintain an orderly sequence of responses, and ensure that the group sticks to the topic. With its regularly scheduled sessions, its diversified members, and its academic purpose, the typical college composition class of fifteen to twenty-five students makes an ideal discussion group.

It should be noted that there are many different kinds of discussion groups and techniques. Instructors who would like to read more about various discussion groups and methods may want to consult such standard texts as Ernest G. Bormann's *Discussion and Group Methods* or Mary A. Bany and Lois V. Johnson's *Classroom Group Behavior: Group Dynamics in Education.* These and similar texts on discussion can usually be found in the education and psychology sections of most college libraries.

Like writing, discussion is a learned activity. To be adept at group discussion requires the development of a variety of skills—in speaking, listening, thinking, and reading. By encouraging students to participate in group discussion, you can help them become more intellectually mature and better prepared for professional careers. Since participation in group discussion is almost always voluntary, your students can improve their discussion abilities by observing a few ground rules. They should (1) be willing to speak in public,

(2) be willing to listen, (3) be willing to examine all sides of a topic, (4) be willing to suspend judgment, and (5) be willing to prepare. These rules are explained further in the introduction for students, "The Persuasive Writer," on page 1 of *America Now.*

Generating Classroom Discussion

Many college teachers in the liberal arts feel that a particular class has gone well when they've been able to generate discussion. This is not surprising. Lively class discussion surely indicates a healthy level of student interest in the course; it also minimizes the burden and monotony of classroom lecturing. I find that even teachers who conduct large lecture courses are pleased when students ask questions and raise relevant points. Anyone who has ever given a public lecture knows how awkward it can be when the moderator invites questions and no hands are raised. Many people instinctively measure the success of a lecture or talk by the number of questions from the audience.

Yet my talks with college instructors in many disciplines indicate that, though they invite class discussion, they don't expect to generate much. "These kids have nothing to say. They just sit there," a professor complained of his introductory European history course. "I do get some students to discuss the reading," a literature teacher told me, "but it's always the same two or three talking every class. The rest are silent." "At the end of class," a writing teacher remarked, "I'll ask, 'Does anyone have any questions about the assignment?' No hands. As I dismiss class and prepare to leave, I notice five or six students gathered around my desk. Each one has a question about the assignment." These experiences, it appears, are quite typical.

Every year hundreds of thousands of college students walk into classrooms throughout America with little knowledge of how to participate in intelligent, informed discussion. One can only speculate about why this is so, but there are clearly several contributing factors: the average student's native shyness and lack of training in extemporaneous speech; an overreliance on lecturing in classrooms; the dismal models of discussion found in the media, especially on radio and television talk shows; and the decline of family conversation as people have less leisure time and as family life grows more fragmented.

One important obstacle to discussion has grown directly out of a seriously misguided educational trend. As schools concentrate more and more on the mastery of isolated and "testable" skills, they leave less and less room in the curriculum for the tentative and exploratory discussion of complex topics. This trend can easily be seen in the growing importance of college and graduate school entrance examinations, which reduce all educational achievement to the "question-answer" level. Such educational instruments not only eliminate discussion and exploration entirely; they foster a mental attitude that is directly opposed to the free and open discussion of ideas: Their rigid format implies that for every question there is always one and only one correct answer.

All of these factors add up to silent college classrooms. In composition courses, lack of discussion can be especially counterproductive to education, since most writing instructors expect their classes to respond to reading assignments and participate in workshop sessions. Few college courses, in fact, are more dependent on class discussion than first-year composition. This often puts a special strain on the instructor, who, in addition to handling a semester's worth of writing assignments, must normally engineer ways to stimulate the discussion of each class's reading material. In more than twenty years of speaking with writing teachers about their teaching, I've noticed how frequently they define a "good class" as one in which the students talk.

The ninth edition of *America Now*, like its predecessors, is specifically designed to get students talking in class. The apparatus following each unit makes it clear to students that the readings are *meant* to be discussed. More important, it gives them questions to consider and small preparatory writing tasks that will help you get class discussion started. The material in this manual is directly linked to the student exercises in the book. The possible "answers" provided here are intended to anticipate student responses to the questions following the selections, and to provide some suggestions for using *America Now* in your course. We hope they will also offer you several ideas for building on what students have prepared and for moving the class discussion of the topic toward the writing assignment.

The book and manual are so directed toward improving class discussion that I'd like to offer a few practical suggestions for generating discussion and using it as a basis for writing. These suggestions are based on the trial and error of my own experience, and on the observations of other instructors and their reports. But because class discussion is so often spontaneous and unpredictable —and is rarely the subject of systematic educational inquiry—I'd like to remind instructors that these suggestions are largely the result of impressions (mine and others') of what works and what doesn't in a classroom. I hope that this book and manual will stimulate the further study of discussion techniques in the field of composition.

Here are a few suggestions designed to generate class discussion and direct it toward the primary goal of the course—student writing:

1. *Emphasize the Importance of Discussion.* Inform students from the start of the course that class discussion is an essential ingredient of the program and that you will be counting on full participation. Remind students that both speaking well and writing well are important factors in anyone's career (it is difficult to think of any profession in which participating in discussion meetings is not essential). Remind students, too, that discussion is neither systematic debate nor aimless conversation but is the free and open exploration of an agreed-upon topic. Since most students are naturally shy, the exploratory nature of class discussion should be emphasized: Questions should be freely asked and points raised without anyone being made to feel stupid.

2. *Create a Climate of Discussion.* Free and open discussion cannot exist in a tense or anxious atmosphere. From the start, therefore, try to know who your students are (learn their names as quickly as possible) and help them become familiar with each other. You might ask your students to stand up and introduce

themselves one by one to the entire class and to say something about themselves (where they're from; their major; what they want to be, and so on). This procedure helps break the ice and gets students talking in class. Remember: Productive classroom discussion is not a matter of students talking only to their instructor; they must also talk to each other.

You may have students suggest questions that they believe would make an interesting interview—what they would like to know about a person. Then divide the class into pairs and have students use those questions as a framework for interviews with each other. The students should write down each other's responses (if a class doesn't pair off evenly, a student can do two interviews or two students can handle one). This interview is then read by the interviewer as a way to introduce the other student. Clearly, this method takes the burden off individuals who would feel shy about introducing themselves in front of the class; it also gets the students writing as they learn about each other.

To create a relaxed atmosphere for discussion, it is important to avoid an overbearing manner or a sarcastic tone. Many students are dreadfully afraid of appearing stupid in front of their peers, and an adversarial or sarcastic style of teaching—though it may appeal to a few "knowing" students—may easily lead diffident students to retreat into the safety of silence. A teacher who wants to maintain a lively atmosphere of discussion will also need at times to restrain the sarcasm of the other students toward irrelevant or "stupid" comments. This is easily done by reminding everyone of the exploratory nature of this discussion and the ground rule that no one need be afraid to say anything. I've found that many disarmingly blunt comments or "off-the-wall" questions that I tended to dismiss proved later to be quite good. Questions that sounded ill-informed were merely ill-formed. Many students have not yet learned the art of posing questions, and everything possible should be done to encourage them to do so.

3. *Beware of the Socratic Method.* So many instructors were themselves taught by this method that they often resort to it instinctively in their classrooms. If conducted in the proper dialogic spirit, the method is, of course, a superb tool for both instilling knowledge and creating intellectual drama. But too often it becomes a question-and-answer game in which instructors ask a series of questions for which they possess definite answers. Often, these questions are posed as though the instructor didn't know the answer, but it becomes evident as answer after answer is rejected that this is a pretense of inquiry, that the process is simply leading to the answer the instructor wants. The apparent inquiry is merely a disguised lecture. Students see through this game quickly. Many are put off by it and refuse to play; a few others, adept at reading the instructor's mind, soon become the class's dominant participants. One of the dangers of this type of Socratic method is that it leads to classes in which discussion is limited to the instructor and several "star" pupils.

Quite clearly, some question-and-answer procedures are necessary to generate and direct discussion. But instructors are encouraged to expand class participation by asking more open-ended questions that invite a variety of "right" answers. The topics and instructional apparatus of *America Now* contain many questions designed to elicit more than one answer.

4. *Set Up Collaborative Tasks and Small-Group Activities.* People like to work together—consider how many composition texts are coauthored and coedited. A good way to broaden class participation is to get students working together in small groups. Most composition classes have from fifteen to twenty-five students. Though groups of this size can accommodate lively general discussion, it is sometimes useful to divide the class into several subgroups (preferably four to five per group) to work on specific tasks. These smaller groups can work together to brainstorm ideas, to consider subdivisions of a topic, or to prepare in-class reports.

Another way to expand participation and to organize discussion is the use of panel sessions or forums. These can take a variety of forms, ranging from the delivery of finished papers to brief statements of positions. One of the most practical ways to conduct panel sessions in the classroom is to divide the class into several groups of four to five students to discuss the various subdivisions of a topic. Either in or outside class, each group collaborates on a written response to the topic or takes a position on it. Each group then selects one of its members to participate on a panel in which papers from all the groups are read for open discussion. Panels introduce students to more organized methods of discussion and expose the class to a wider range of viewpoints. Panel sessions—even very informal ones—take time, however. Instructors who use them should be sure to schedule assignments carefully; a well-constructed panel could take up as many as three class periods.

Though setting up formal debates involves procedures that are outside the scope of this book (and of most composition courses), class discussion can also be enlivened by informal debates. Many topics in *America Now* suggest provocative issues for opposing points of view. If a class is not too large (fifteen students or fewer), it can be divided into two groups for debating purposes; larger classes may need to form smaller groups that come together as teams. As in the panel sessions, each group should select a member to represent its position. If the topic is one students are quite conversant with, impromptu informal debate can be arranged in class. With less familiar topics, outside preparation should be scheduled.

Panels and debates often involve the practical problem of seating arrangements. The most efficient way to set up small groups is to have students cluster their desks together in tight circles. For panel formation and informal debates, several students can bring their desks to the front of the classroom. The average composition classroom, with its instructor's desk set imposingly in front, is perhaps better designed for lecturing than for open discussion. Instructors who want to broaden student participation and interaction may want to experiment with different seating styles. Some instructors, for example, feel that sitting with students at one of their desks facilitates discussion. Others may ask the students to form a large circle of seats and then sit among them. If a class is relatively small and a seminar table is available, its use will generally enhance discussion.

5. *Keep Discussion Linked to Writing.* Though lively group discussion can be an end in itself, the agenda of *America Now* is to use class discussion as a

basis for writing. This agenda works two ways: (1) it encourages students to get the composition started in the classroom, and (2) it encourages students to use class discussion as a stimulus and a context for writing.

As you direct class discussion, keep in mind how the discussion can bear directly on the writing assignment. You might want to point out ideas that contain the germ of interesting papers, a tactic that also helps student writers learn how to see ideas emerge. Another way is to periodically focus attention on specific writing strategies as the reading material is discussed. Students almost always want to discuss topics and subjects, rarely techniques and strategies. It is therefore a good idea to initiate discussion by focusing on topics and gradually turn to a consideration of how the writers handled these topics.

From Discussion to Writing

As they prepare to write for college courses, students often confront difficulties that have less to do with the routine tasks of composition—spelling, punctuation, correct grammar—than with the deeper problems of finding something to say and establishing a context in which to say it. It is not uncommon for beginning students to turn in papers that contain few serious errors yet lack intellectual substance and a clear orientation. Using group discussion as a basis for composition can help remedy these problems. Group discussion can serve as a stimulus for an individual's ideas and provide a meaningful context in which to express them. Furthermore, as we will see, the art of discussion can function in many ways as an important model for the art of writing.

Finding something to say about a topic always ranks high on lists of student writing problems. It is the main reason that the blank sheet of paper or computer screen so often triggers a set of anxious questions: "What can I say?" "Where do I begin?" For many, intellectual panic sets in as the page or screen remains blank, the mind remains blank, and the entire writing process suddenly seems to exist in a total vacuum.

Exploratory discussion offers a solution to this dilemma. Years ago, an advertising executive, Alexander F. Osborn, developed a group method of generating ideas that became enormously popular in many fields. With typical advertising savvy, Osborn gave his technique a memorable name—*brainstorming*. Osborn's goal was to stimulate creativity by presenting a small group of people with a problem topic and then encouraging them to toss off as many ideas about it in as short a time as possible. Speed, spontaneity, and free association were essential to his method. But the most important part of his brainstorming procedure was a complete absence of criticism. No one in the group was allowed to criticize or disagree with any idea, no matter how silly or farfetched it seemed. This absence of criticism, Osborn found, kept ideas flowing since people were not afraid to sound ill-informed or just plain stupid.

This brainstorming technique can clearly help students come up with ideas to write about. It could be done in the composition classroom for a brief period, or small groups of students could profitably conduct brainstorming sessions on their own. Moreover, most exploratory discussion—if it is free, open, and relaxed—will contain some degree of spontaneous brainstorming in which ideas can sprout and grow. Students who take note of these ideas will find that when they sit down to write, they will not be starting out in a vacuum but will have a context of discussion out of which their composition can take shape.

An alternative type of brainstorming can also help students move from class discussion to writing. In this type of brainstorming (sometimes referred to by communication researchers as *nominal* brainstorming), each person, instead of vocalizing ideas in a group, works alone, silently jotting down a brief list of ideas. Afterward, all the lists are compared, and after some culling and combining, individual ideas are listed on a blackboard. This brainstorming method is very useful at the start of a class session in opening up various avenues of discussion. The written list also serves as a tangible source of ideas for individuals to pursue later in their papers.

If exploratory discussion can help reduce the anxiety students face in trying to develop ideas for papers, it can also alleviate another major writing problem—the student's alienation. Thinking and writing alone, with little awareness of an actual audience or of a practical situation, the beginning student often composes papers that sound hollow, disembodied, and disengaged. Ideas seem to come out of nowhere; transitions and connections are missing; conclusions that should grow out of the development of an idea are instead little more than blunt, unearned assertions. Though such papers are common, instructors find it difficult to pinpoint precisely what is wrong with them, since the problems are vague, not easily isolated, and therefore hard to identify by the usual marking symbols. The real problem with such papers is not in the writing but in the orientation of the writer. It is not one of style, structure, or content, but of overall *context.*

Experienced writers, as mentioned earlier, invariably work with a clear sense of audience and occasion. For example, a literature or composition teacher working on a critical article is writing within a clearly definable context: He or she has a sense of who the audience will be, where the article could be published, and—most important—why it is being written. No matter what its subject or point of view, the article will be intellectually oriented to a community of readers presumed to be aware of the topic and attuned to the various points of view involved in its discussion. That so many academic papers are first prepared for delivery at professional conferences underscores the vital importance of a concrete audience and situation.

As students discover the connections between discussion and composition, they will also find their bearings as writers. Their writing—no matter what the topic—will be oriented toward response. Their writing will be not only a response to an assigned topic but, more important, a response made in the context of a continuing discussion of that topic. The student, in other words, writes as an active participant, responding, as she or he would in group discussion, to the actual or anticipated responses of others. This texture of mutual response is what so often gives professionally written essays and articles their mature tone and clear orientation. Instructors might further encourage this climate of response by inviting students to cite comments by other class members in their papers.

Once your students see writing as a form of response, they will become more conscious of their social and intellectual attitudes as writers. Are they closed off to other opinions? Are they overbearing in their attitudes? Do they try to see all sides of an issue? Are they patient with complexity? Do they oversimplify difficult problems? Do they skirt issues? Do they base too much on personal experience? These are all considerations learned in group discussion that directly carry over into composition.

As your students work through *America Now*, they will observe how participation in group discussion is relevant to all kinds of writing tasks. It is perhaps easy to see how an awareness of conflicting opinions can play an important part in critical, analytical, and argumentative writing. But personal essays can also profit from exploratory group discussion. By discussing their personal experiences, your students can begin to view them from a broader social perspective and to understand them within a context of divergent human experiences.

Composition that is closely linked to lively group discussion reminds students that they are writing not in a vacuum but as part of a group, part of a community. In a written work, as in discussion, someone is always speaking and someone (or some group) is always being addressed. *America Now* encourages your students to view their writing as an extension of group discussion, to see writing as public, not private, behavior, as a social act rather than a solitary one. To think of writing as an extension of discussion, however, students need to reimagine themselves as writers. When they sit down to write, they should do so not as isolated individuals anxiously awaiting inspiration but as active participants in a process of communication with others. Students then will not expect ideas for writing to "come out of the blue." Rather, they will expect to find their ideas where they are most likely to originate—out of their considered responses to the ideas of others.

Forming Forums: Student Presentations to Encourage Research, Discussion, and Better Writing

by Liz deBeer

"The forums give a chance for students to participate verbally and not just listen to the teacher."

"Forums enabled students to get to know each other as they worked in groups."

"Forums made people get up in front of class and talk who otherwise didn't talk during class discussion."

"The forums presented lots of good information that I think I would not have learned anywhere else. They provided lots of discussion, and I think that was the best part. The class got a chance to communicate about their cultures and share their experiences or anecdotes, which made the class a much better place to be at 8:30 in the morning."

"Forums: Keep doing this!"

As the student evaluations above reveal, many students seem to enjoy my classes and learn the most when they are asked to work in groups and share their ideas with their peers. Panel presentations or forums help give students authority in the classroom and motivation to write in steps. Perhaps just as important, forums motivate teachers like me to listen more to their students. Even students who feared forums because they didn't like the idea of talking in front of the class acknowledged that they benefited from them, as one student wrote: "I found the forums to be very informative and interesting even though I hated speaking in front of the class."

Forums require students, working in small groups, to research a topic, make presentations, and lead classroom discussion. Forums motivate students to explore topics by interviewing experts, preparing surveys, and analyzing trends, just as many of the writers whose essays appear in *America Now* did. This type of research allows students to observe the controversy implicit in most of the topics in the text and prepares them for writing papers that go beyond clichés. On the first day of class, I tell students that forums allow them to teach part of the class; this comment always gets their interest.

Why Bother? The Value of Forums

After my first few years of teaching composition, I realized that I was doing more research than my students to prepare for my classes. Exhausted and overwhelmed, I decided to create a course where the students were responsible for much of the research and, later, the presentation of it. Although several students balked at the idea of speaking in front of their peers, all followed through, which created the most successful composition classes I had ever taught. In fact, previous students accosted me in the hall demanding to know why we hadn't done forums when they took the course.

There is much research to support the use of collaborative work like forums. Lev Vygotsky's emphasis on collaboration has been well documented; he asserts that students learn from working with others: "With assistance, every child can do more than he can by himself. . . . What a child can do in cooperation today he can do alone tomorrow" (187–88). Douglas Barnes and Frankie Todd reflect on a thirteen-year-old who wonders why the teacher can't just write all the questions and answers on the board so that the students can memorize them. The authors comment that "such students need opportunities and challenges that will enable them to see learning as constructing an understanding, not as reflecting and repeating ready-made formulae whose implications they have not grasped" (14). Talk is the antidote, according to Barnes and Todd, particularly talk that is student-centered, where students can "try out new ways of thinking and reshape an idea midsentence, respond immediately to the hints and doubts of others, and collaborate in shaping meanings they could not hope to reach alone" (15). Forums provide students with time to talk about their projects, reconsider their ideas, and listen to new ideas; forums also hold students accountable for their talk, because the forums eventually involve presentations and term papers, both of which are graded.

Additionally, talk in forums is genuine, unlike much classroom "discussion" where the teacher is searching for someone who can "reproduce what the teacher has presented to them" (Barnes and Todd 15). Jeffrey Wilhelm, reflecting on his own practice and why so many students dislike reading, notes, "If we take the theoretical stance that reading is, in fact, producing meaning, then the way reading education is traditionally practiced in schools must be rethought. . . . [Teachers] must take responses beyond boilerplate questions and 'correct' answers" (10). Wilhelm uses drama and art to teach literature as an active enterprise between students and text; I suggest using forums as an active enterprise between students and *America Now*. Forums rarely disappoint me in my main goal, which is to learn something new—related to the curriculum—from each student, for forums often involve students researching areas beyond the teacher's own knowledge. For example, in past years, students have done forums on immigration and have interviewed people whom I had never met, presenting information that opened my eyes. Other students shared their own stories, such as one student who included an anecdote about how she traveled to the United States from Vietnam on a tiny fishing boat.

Forums also challenge teachers to look differently at the common complaint about lack of resources (Moll). Forums motivated me to embrace the community as a resource, a means to reach out of the classroom door and windows—which are usually shut in college classrooms—and connect student worlds to the texts. Luis Moll calls this "mobilizing funds of knowledge" (231). Although he is referring to a program where community members physically enter the classroom to teach their special skills, forums use students as facilitators of these "funds of knowledge" through their research, which often involves surveys and interviews. For example, in past years, forums on parenting resulted in students presenting research on parenting in other cultures, much of which was unfamiliar to me.

Research strongly suggests that group work can increase tolerance among groups of diverse students, assuming the group work has "highly valued goals that could not be obtained without cooperation" (Schofield 13). However, research also suggests that if group work is not well planned and valued by the teacher, students may not take the tasks seriously (Weinstein). In fact, many teachers suggest that they do not use group work for fear of losing order (Weinstein). I have never experienced difficulty with classroom management when using forums, mainly, I believe, because so many students preferred them to lectures. Moreover, since the group work led to graded work, students knew that if they were unproductive during group work, they might not have a successful forum or a strong paper.

Steps: Preparing Students

Because forums follow the philosophy behind process writing, there are several steps involved. Four major writing activities are involved throughout the semester. First, students brainstorm in small groups for ideas and strategies for researching and presenting information effectively, writing ideas on the sign-up sheet and in their notebooks. Then, they write a two-page paper that summarizes and analyzes the student's individual topic, which is handed in the day of the presentation and is summarized for the student's forum presentation. (Time limits may be necessary.) Each presenter should also prepare a discussion question on the subtopic being presented.

Students who are not presenting must hand in a one-page critical response to each forum other than their own, due the class following each forum. This should evaluate the effectiveness of each presentation — not summarize it. This is excellent practice for students to hone their listening skills and discern the most important aspects of a talk. Recently, I have also asked students to write a one-sentence positive response, telling the presenter what they liked best about the presentation. I do this to help the class feel more like a community; I have found students with eyes brimming upon hearing positive comments from their peers, some telling me that this is the first time they realized anyone was actually paying attention to what they had said in class.

Finally, students in composition classes must write a research paper based on the data gathered for their forum presentation. (Basic skills instructors may choose to eliminate this step.) This paper should involve more sources, more analysis, more detail, and better editing than the two-page paper. After the presentations are all completed, instructors can explain the traditional research paper and how the students' presentations can be revised into longer, more scholarly works.

A typical syllabus for my Composition 101 class, which meets for one semester, includes four or five forum topics, so that about five or six students are members of each group. I organize my syllabus by beginning with a few lectures in which I describe my goals and allow students time to research and prepare their projects. I spend several class periods preparing students for these forums at least two weeks before the first group's topic is due. We spend one class period working on interviewing skills, usually based on a topic from *America Now*. For example, using past editions of the text, I might begin the semester with "Are our news media reliable? Why or why not?" and ask students to conduct an interview of another person about his or her opinions on the objectivity and quality of journalism and television news. Then, I would have students write an essay using a few quotes from the subject of the interview, perhaps also using one essay from *America Now* as a supplement to the paper. Because many of the students interview an expert for their forum presentation, I like to assign one interviewing project well before the forum projects are due.

I schedule one week (or two class periods of eighty minutes each) for each forum topic. For the first class, students are asked to read the unit in *America Now* that covers the assigned topic, and we then analyze the articles and write on each topic in our notebooks. The second class is a student forum based on the same topic. The entire class period is devoted to presentations and discussion led by about five students who are in charge of that topic. I organize my syllabus so that students are working on their projects at the same time. I usually reserve a class period in the middle of the projects for an in-class exam. We spend the rest of the semester concentrating on peer reviews, punctuation, writing, reading and test-taking skills, and work on other small projects like the ones described in units of *America Now*. Usually, I reorganize the order of the table of contents to meet the needs of my syllabus.

I choose forum topics based on which issues I believe will most interest students and create the most compelling forum presentations. Since the material in *America Now* addresses current events, many students are already thinking about the issues they are being asked to write about. Instructors should capitalize on students' interests and concerns when choosing the broad topics for the forums. If students are concerned about obesity or consumerism, then these are good topics for forums. If the issues of social networking, the environment, immigration, or racial conflict have been debated regularly on the news or in the campus paper, then these topics will have special appeal. Much of this evaluation of topics depends on a school's geography and demographics. I rely on past students' essays and discussion to gauge popular topics. Although all topics in *America Now* will interest most students, the ideal forum topic is one that students will be compelled to spend more than one class period discussing. I also avoid topics that are too polarized, such as abortion, which people tend to view as either inherently wrong or right. The topic should be broad enough that several students can explore different angles and should be covered by accessible research sources.

At the beginning of the semester, I write on the board four or five forum topics chosen from issues addressed in *America Now* and ask that each student pick one. Through this process, the small groups are formed. For example, the students who pick the topic obesity will work together on a forum for that topic. Because groups should be approximately the same size to allow for different angles to be addressed on each issue, instructors should limit the number of students allowed to pick each topic.

When groups have been formed, I hand each one a sign-up sheet with the chosen topic written on top. Then, each group member picks a subtopic or angle that relates to the general topic and lists some possible sources that will be used to research it. Students should be reminded that their research may require them to alter the proposed topic or sources.

Although I encourage students to create their own ideas for topics and sources, I provide each small group with some ideas to model how to create a specific topic from a broad one as well as some sources that might be applicable to the general topic. I usually give each group a separate handout along with the sign-up sheet. Examples of my ideas for approaching topics appear at the end of this essay.

At this point, I dedicate a whole class period to reviewing forums so that students know what I expect. Although I have already defined forums briefly before they picked their topics and subtopics, I define them in more detail once students know what area they will be researching. I also make a model presentation to show students the kind of work I expect. I include a visual aid and speak, without reading in a monotone, from my notecards. I pick a topic that is relevant to *America Now*. For example, I once made a presentation on patriotism, for which I interviewed instructors from the political science and journalism departments about their views regarding the role of patriotism in relation to the government, the media, and the public in America today. Students then evaluated my presentation orally as I wrote my expectations on the board; the students themselves provided excellent tips for each other. My use of model presentations has helped my classes improve their presentations over years past. It also reminds me of all the steps students need to take to be prepared for their presentations.

Next, I review how students should prepare their research, presentations, and class discussion. I discuss the importance of asking questions that elicit thoughtful responses and of asking follow-up questions, both during their research and during presentations. I explain how I evaluate forums based on whether presentations — and written reports — are focused and informative, and I discuss the value of current sources. Since students have usually begun to work on their projects, they are encouraged to ask specific questions.

At the next class period, groups meet for the second time so that students can discuss their plans for research and their overall strategy. Instructors should visit each group to learn of individual concerns and should discuss wider concerns with the whole class. Often, group members discuss their fears of talking in front of others. I try to point out the value of speaking skills and sometimes encourage students to participate in later forums so that they can see other students do presentations before they take a turn. Given that many high schools require oral presentations as part of their graduation requirements, many students are already knowledgeable about the basics of preparing forums.

After their second group meeting, students must conduct their research and prepare their presentations. I ask that they write a two-page (typed, double-spaced) report on their forum topic that includes at least one source other than *America Now.* Those sources may include books, magazines, interviews, or even personal experience. If students use personal experience as a source, they must also use one other source. To document their sources, I require a typed "works cited" page. Students may read from their papers, but they may not read the whole paper or they will go over their allotted time. It is imperative to save time for class discussion. Remind students not to use names of people interviewed if the topic involves personal material, as might be the case in a presentation on stereotypes, for instance.

Letting Go: Letting Students Learn

Perhaps instructors' greatest challenge in working with forums is allowing students to research and explore topics on their own and to work in groups during class time. This doesn't *feel* like teaching, but it is. If we want students to actually say something meaningful, as Berthoff suggests in *The Making of Meaning*, we must leave them alone to make their own discoveries. As Bartholomae and Petrosky write in *Facts, Artifacts, and Counterfacts*, "A course in reading and writing whose goal is to empower students must begin with a silence, a silence the student must fill" (7). When students conduct interviews, research their forum topics, or lead class discussion, they are literally filling the silence. Forum projects allow students to think for themselves, to take risks. All this, of course, leads to better writing.

Usually, students ask for little help. Most of them are eager to interview people they know or to find their own sources. Occasionally, students panic and ask me to help with library research, particularly those with limited library experience. (I usually arrange an on-campus library tour before the forums begin.) However, once I have given them enough pointers to get started, I try to leave them alone. Often, during such periods of silence, I observe students working together. Such collaboration confirms my belief that students learn not only from me and from sources but also from each other.

Other experiences have reinforced my belief in the value of forums and have helped me get through the waiting and worrying period. One student, who appeared to be half asleep during much of the class time preceding the forums, became so involved and excited by interviewing his Vietnam-veteran uncle for a forum on the gun-control debate that he suddenly sparkled, waking up enough to complete and pass the course. Similarly, a student from a local subsidized housing development admitted to me later that he planned on dropping my class because of an overloaded schedule. Instead, he stuck it out, comparing and contrasting attitudes about guns from ten men from "the projects" who did not attend college and ten men who did attend college, drawing conclusions about guns and lack of hope. He admitted that the reason he stayed in the course was because he felt impelled to work on his forum project and felt his background and insights were valued in the class.

Teacher as Listener

I like to start with a forum on an accessible topic such as body image because it makes students think critically about something with which they are already familiar. Although (or because) students' experiences vary, these topics should prompt a lot of class discussion. Students who are in these forum groups may interview campus counselors or social workers. One student might survey two generations' attitudes about body image and compare results or split the survey into two social or cultural groups.

Some students may resent it if their group has to present first, but others actually like to "get it out of the way." Once, when a student in the first forum group was unable to finish his research, I moved him to a different topic that was due toward the end of the semester. However, I discourage such behavior by telling the class that I will give an F to students who do not perform on the due date, unless they can be excused because of an extreme circumstance. Only once did a student miss the deadline without an excuse; I allowed her to hand in her written paper, and I averaged the F for the presentation with the written project.

On the day of the presentation, I take attendance and sit in the back of the class. Then, the group presenting moves to the front of the room and presents its reports. At this point, the class asks questions only for clarification so that there is time for everyone to present. Students who are not presenting should be taking notes for their one-page written response to the forum. Instead of a simple summary, I ask students to follow a formula that includes what the main idea was, what they liked best about the presentation, and what they learned. (Students don't have to write such a paper on their own forum topic or on anyone else's in their group. When all the students have presented, I average all of the critical responses of each student to equal one paper grade. Usually everyone who hands in the written response gets a high grade; the only way to fail is to cut class and not hand in any of these papers.)

After all the students in the group have finished their presentations, the rest of the class may ask questions. Sometimes, presenters need to ask the class a question to prompt discussion. I prefer to keep quiet and let the presenters lead the discussion, but sometimes I'll intervene when I feel it's necessary. Often, I have to remind myself to let the students talk, to let them fill the silence. I usually learn from these discussions. In one class, a student from Nigeria responded to a parenting forum presentation about how divorced American men are fighting to get custody of their children. The Nigerian student commented that in his country it is the norm for divorced men to have custody of the children. This led to a discussion of cultural issues concerning gender roles.

Occasionally, students make poor presentations. In the weakest one I have seen, a bright woman simply chatted for a few minutes without presenting material from any source. Another student twisted data about rape so that it sounded like the violence was justified by the victim's flirtatious behavior. In both instances, the students learned from their peers' responses and my commentary on their short papers, and their final research papers reflected their understanding. Much of this learning process occurs during the discussion following the presentations. Even a blunt comment like "Why do you always call the rape victim 'she'?" can lead to discussion about improving writing.

It is common for students to present too much general information without specific examples, to make rough transitions, or to analyze data inadequately. These problems can also be remedied with helpful commentary from fellow students and the instructor. Because the forum project involves writing in steps, I rarely receive plagiarized or sloppy papers. Before I used the forums, students often had only one chance to write their final research papers and no time to learn from their mistakes. By presenting their ideas and research orally before writing a final research paper, students have time to think and rethink. They learn to value their audience by striving to be clear, concise, and original. Since the projects are staggered, I can spend more time on the two-page papers, offering advice about revising for the final research paper.

When students write critical responses to their peers' presentations, they learn to analyze. One student commented that "I tended to . . . learn more from the people who analyzed their information rather than the ones who dictated the information to the class." Another wrote that "when [presenters] read off a sheet of paper, they were boring. . . . I feel you must get the audience involved." These comments reveal that students were able to learn important writing lessons from the oral presentations.

Other students' comments revealed that they enjoyed the forums. One wrote: "Forums are an excellent learning device. . . . Students taught students about what they had researched." Another reported that "the forums . . . forced the speakers to really know their topics. . . . I feel that a majority of the people got really involved in their subjects, enabling them to learn more about it than if they just read it out of a book. Also, the forums showed that how you say your information is important. You must try to catch the interest of your audience."

These remarks show how eager students are to fill the silence of the classroom, as long as we instructors are willing to give up some of our control. If we empower our students, they can provide the classroom with much more knowledge than any one person alone can.

Works Cited

Barnes, Douglas, and Frankie Todd. *Communication and Learning Revisited: Making Meaning through Talk*. Portsmouth, NH: Boynton/Cook, 1995. Print.

Bartholomae, David, and Anthony Petrosky. *Facts, Artifacts, and Counterfacts: Theory and Method for a Reading and Writing Course*. Portsmouth, NH: Boynton/Cook, 1986. Print.

Berthoff, Ann E. *The Making of Meaning*. Upper Montclair, NJ: Boynton/Cook, 1981. Print.

Moll, Luis. "Literacy Research in Community and Classrooms: A Sociological Approach." *Theoretical Models and the Process of Reading*. 4th ed. Ed. R. B. Ruddell, M. R. Ruddell, and H. Singer. Newark, DE: IRA, 1994. 211–44. Print.

Schofield, Janet W. *Black & White in School: Trust, Tension or Tolerance?* New York: Teachers College Press, 1989. Print.

Vygotsky, Lev. *Thought and Language*. Cambridge, MA: MIT Press, 1987. Print.

Weinstein, Carol S. *Secondary Classroom Management: Lessons from Research and Practice*. New York: McGraw-Hill, 1996. Print.

Wilhelm, Jeffrey D. *"You Gotta Be the Book": Teaching Engaged and Reflective Reading with Adolescents*. Urbana, IL: NCTE, 1995. Print.

1

What's in a Name?

"What's in a name?" asks Juliet in Shakespeare's famous play, and as we know from the play's ending, much is at stake. So, too, the authors in this chapter agree that names matter. Names for all kinds of things must be decided upon: for children, for trucks, for sports teams, for time periods, for countries. Among other things, names create our identity, they affect self-esteem, and they help establish our place in the world.

With nods to Shakespeare in her essay as well, Rebecca Mead's "What Do You Call It?" raises the dilemma of naming to a new level. What do we do when a name doesn't fit? When we seem unable to encapsulate a time period with a name (in this case, the first decade of a new century)? Mead shows how, post-9/11, our history feels like it is spinning out in new directions and how the decade we've just passed through did not live up to what we might have expected, "since this turned out to be the decade in which there were no good answers."

Patrick Olsen's "Does Your Pickup Truck Have a Nickname?" offers a different tone, but examines the question of naming as well. Certain people feel even their trucks need a name, and the naming is no light matter. Brittany Bergstrom agrees, as she follows the debate over the proposed name change for the University of North Dakota's athletic teams and notes how passionately some argue for the sake of the name "Fighting Sioux" despite the controversy over keeping it. "The Fighting Sioux: The End of a Legacy?" is more of an examination of the love of a name than of the damage it might do as a stereotype.

Two essays about whether a family should share a surname (take a mother's or father's last name) come from Liz Breslin and Laura Williamson. Breslin argues for the cohesiveness of the family under one name and suggests that her argument is not antifeminist. Williamson follows her own family story, with a focus on another woman in the family who disagrees with her point of view—her mother-in-law—and makes the case that the "family is more than a single surname."

The chapter ends with "America Then . . . 1507: Who Named America?" It might be surprising to find out how America was "misnamed," and that the name that stuck was established not by an explorer but a mapmaker. The detail from the map included shows how names and places can change in the minds of those who help discover and shape them. Following the history of a name sheds light on just how complicated this naming process can be.

Patrick Olsen

Does Your Pickup Truck Have a Nickname?

[*Cars.com*, September 22, 2009]

Vocabulary/Using a Dictionary

1. A *survey* is a poll, and in this essay people are *surveyed* to get their opinions on their pickup trucks. *Survey* can also be used as a verb and means to appraise or inspect.
2. When something is *hauled* it is drawn or pulled by someone or something else. The body of a pickup truck is built for the carrying or *hauling* of materials.
3. A *percent* is also called a *per centum* (Latin), or one one-hundredth part. The abbreviation of *per centum* is "per cent," and the words have since been joined to form *percent*. A *percentage* is a proportion, and this article deals with surveys and the comparison of those surveys' numbers.

Responding to Words in Context

1. An *age gap* refers to a disparity in ages. In this case, it simply means that the owners who give their pickups names are not usually the same age as the ones who don't care to name them.
2. The *truck bed* is the open rear cargo area of the truck.
3. The data may affect or worry the automakers. In this instance, *concern* is being used as a verb. If the automakers were concerned, they would be troubled or anxious.

Discussing Main Point and Meaning

1. The article suggests that most pickup truck drivers claim to love their pickups as much as they love family members. An intimate relationship, perhaps seemingly odd to some outsiders, is established between owner and vehicle, marking it as a special piece of property—the owner bestows a name on the truck, sleeps in it, values it as highly as a spouse or a house.
2. According to the data collected here, younger truck drivers are not as loyal to U.S. brands as are older drivers. Younger drivers feel more completely identified with the truck as a reflection of their personality and are more likely to have slept in their truck beds.
3. The statistic about drivers in the West sleeping in their trucks suggests that owners from that part of the country are more likely to view their truck as an extension of their home. Or perhaps it just indicates something about the region and its vast spaces lending itself to the use of the truck as a makeshift abode, either due to travel or the desire to experience the "great outdoors."

Examining Sentences, Paragraphs, and Organization

1. Students may say that the article reads like an advertisement because throughout it presents the pickup as a highly desirable object. The poll is of pickup drivers only and suggests that they value their vehicles tremendously. The lack of negative presentation in the article (which stops just short of saying "Go out and buy a truck!") is very much in line with an advertisement for pickups.

2. Many people find themselves defined by their material possessions, where they live, or other external factors. It does not mean that their trucks are serious, funny, outgoing, or any other facet that one associates with individual personality. Owning a truck might be a reflection of one's eagerness to travel or a choice to live outside the confines of a city (where one is less likely to need to use a truck on a regular basis). *Personality* can refer to such visible qualities, as referenced in this article, or it could refer to one's psychology.

3. The numbered points clearly outline the importance of trucks to their owners, and highlighting them in this way adds to the surprise of the response (many said a spouse, house, or sex were less important than their pickup). Olsen gives the results of his surveys throughout the article, but setting these responses apart near the end of the article creates greater effect.

Thinking Critically

1. Students may or may not be surprised at how excited truck owners are by their vehicles. Depending on how students view physical possessions, they might not understand why drivers are so in love with them (it doesn't seem strictly about their utility) or they may have a similar feeling about something they own or drive.

2. A discussion of numbers may be helpful—Olsen reveals that 1,068 truck owners age eighteen and up were questioned about their trucks. Ask students if they would be more convinced if a wider poll had been taken. How would they view the information if the pool of interviewees were smaller? Students may have wanted more personal or anecdotal information in the article or they may say the statistics give a more concise view of how pickup drivers feel about their trucks.

3. Answers will vary based on what vehicles students gravitate toward or have experience with. The question can be considered by examining each point made in the article about naming a vehicle, choosing one that is U.S.- or foreign-made, how they use their vehicle, and its importance in their lives.

In-Class Writing Activities

1. Students should consider how this article might have differed (or stayed the same) if it had not been found in an advertising supplement. They should make note of how "informational" articles are similar to or different from articles that push certain brands (in this case, the pickup

truck). Students should note how the push or "plug" for an item is phrased in these supplements or where they lack objectivity.

2. Responses to this question will vary from student to student. Students may choose a car or something similar and describe why it is so important to them, or they may choose something more unique and personal. Students should consider the nature of a "relationship" with something other than a person and what that relationship consists of, given Olsen's findings about pickup truck owners.

3. Students' answers will vary based on their research. Specific details should be included about one brand vs. another and the advantages and disadvantages for various people. They may choose to look at the truck-owning population in terms of age or region as Olsen does, or they may choose a different way of categorizing their information. Students should feel free to speculate about the appeal of trucks in general based on what they discover about various types.

Rebecca Mead

What Do You Call It?

[*The New Yorker*, January 4, 2010]

Vocabulary/Using a Dictionary

1. When one is *overwrought*, he or she is excited to the point of agitation or distress. It is, in fact, the past participle of *overwork*. To be *wrought* is to be pushed into a certain shape. *Over* can mean excessive (as when one is *overly* excited about something).

2. *Sobriquet* is a French word. One might be familiar with similar words that come from the French language like *bouquet* or *tourniquet*. Its etymology may be apparent by its dictionary pronunciation. The word means "nickname."

3. Something *comprehensible* is understandable. The root comes from the verb *comprehend*. When one *comprehends*, one understands or knows something. Whatever one is trying to grasp is then *comprehensible*.

Responding to Words in Context

1. When one *infringes*, one violates or trespasses upon something (infringement of copyright, infringement of privacy). Civil *liberties* are one's rights as a citizen. *Civil* in this case has to do with citizenship, like the word *civic*. A *liberty* is a freedom.

2. *Intractable* means not easy to control, difficult to manage. *Irresolvable* means not solvable. Both adjectives suggest a certain amount of difficulty or an impossibility of resolution.

3. *Omniscience* refers to unlimited knowledge or perception; *omnipotence* means unlimited power. *Omni* comes from Latin, meaning "all." *Omniscience* means "all-knowing" and *omnipotence* means "all-powerful."

Discussing Main Point and Meaning

1. The decade is problematic because no one has been able to pin a name on it, and before Mead discusses the years 2000–2010, she mentions that it turned out to be "the decade in which there were no good answers." The events of the decade that are mentioned were often catastrophic (9/11, Katrina, the economic downturn) or at the very least unsettling to the status quo (the United States had its first African American president and things like Facebook drastically changed the way we share information with each other). The events are presented as negative or as unusual enough to disturb past perceptions of ourselves and our world. Mead suggests that because of this, perhaps we'd rather not name the decade after all.

2. *Aught* is a corruption of the archaic word *naught*, which means "nothing" or "zero." *Naught* makes sense given that these are the years beginning with zero. The actual definition of *aught* is "anything." *Naught* and *aught* both suggest a void, which is how Mead paints the decade and our general feelings about it.

3. Mead finds it fitting that no name has emerged, suggesting that we would rather set this period of time adrift nameless after all of its disappointments and chaos.

Examining Sentences, Paragraphs, and Organization

1. The inclusion of the "alternate decade of fantasy" in which Al Gore ("forever slim and with hairline intact") becomes president, ratifies Kyoto, and avoids September 11 provides a stark contrast to the way events really unfolded in history. It underscores her view of the decade as a terrible, possibly preventable, tragedy. By putting her imagined decade in parentheses, she downplays its importance—it is simply her wish for what might have happened—but it also calls attention to an alternative to what did in fact happen.

2. The first references are to the zeros that follow as the year changes from 1999 to 2000. "Zero" suggests nothing, leading to "the zips" and "the nadas" ("nothing" in Spanish). "The naughties" follow that, possibly referring to "naught" and/or suggesting disobedience or something "not nice." All names suggest the absence of something. Mead makes each name in the list a sentence fragment and uses question marks, highlighting the fact that no consensus exists on a name.

3. Mead begins with a look at the words under consideration for the decade and then examines the most likely candidate: the "aughts." She gives reasons why this name feels appropriate and examines the decade, event by disastrous event. She mentions the dramatic change that took place, possibly because of those earlier events, with the election of Barack Obama. She ends with some of the odder inventions that came about during that time.

Thinking Critically

1. 9/11 is the turning point, as Mead sees it, for the new century and new decade. One might argue that the change that took place in our under-

standing of terrorism and safety in this country was vast enough to mark the previous decade as "reassuring" or "comprehensible" in retrospect. The nineties were also years of conservatism that appeared to be placid and ordinary on some level although they may have led directly to events that followed.

2. The main defining event that she points to is September 11, 2001. One might argue that 9/11 was the defining event because one can look at the other political and economic events she mentions (Katrina, war, and the fluctuations in the marketplace) as coming about as a direct result of the events of and reactions to that day. (She does mention that she sees 9/11 as a direct result of the earlier election.)

3. Consider names that encapsulate a group of people or a time period (Generation X, the Roaring Twenties). Those names label a particular group or time, forever coloring one's view of them. Names provide people with a way of speaking about something based on a general perception (not everyone in Gen X was aimless or hopeless, and not everyone in the Roaring Twenties lived a fast life, yet those names ellicit certain assumptions based on them).

In-Class Writing Activities

1. Students may begin their essays with a defense of the "aughts" or they may side with Mead. If they disagree with her, they should include examples from the decades not mentioned in the article that show the time period in a more positive light. Or they may expand upon the rise of Barack Obama to the presidency, exploring the message of hope brought by his campaign. If they agree with her, they may discuss war or the general perception of the U.S. abroad at the turn of the century, changing of weather patterns due to the greenhouse effect, the discovery of lead in myriad toys manufactured in and imported from China, the identification of the H1N1 virus in Mexico and its global spread, or any other events not mentioned in the article.

2. Students may focus on the fact that Obama is the first African American president of the United States. They may discuss how his campaign and policies differ from the Bush administration's or from any of the other 2008 presidential candidates. They may focus on Mead's quotation from the Nobel acceptance speech or explore reasons why Obama might have been nominated for and then received such a prize.

3. Answers will vary depending on the student. Students should be able to compare their event and how it defines the time with examples from Mead's essay.

Brittany Bergstrom (student essay)

The Fighting Sioux: The End of a Legacy?

[*The Spectrum*, University of North Dakota, September 29, 2009]

Vocabulary/Using a Dictionary

1. A *logo* is a representation or trademark that often accompanies a brand name (or in this case, the name of a sports team). A *nickname* is substituted for a proper name. A *mascot* is also something that represents a group (in this case, the sports team is represented by a fighting Indian).
2. A *rival* is a competitor. Sometimes people romantically interested in the same person are called *rivals* for his or her affection. Students may also be familiar with the term *sibling rivalry*.
3. A *connotation* is a suggestion or association. A *denotation* is the explicit meaning of a word.

Responding to Words in Context

1. The words *divide* and *unify* are opposites. When something is divided, it is separated into parts. If things are unified, they are made into a single unit.
2. An *alumnus* is a graduate of a particular school, college, or university. It is a Latin masculine noun. It can change to other forms such as *alumna*, a female graduate of a particular school, college, or university, or *alumni*, the plural form of *alumnus*.
3. *Race* refers to classifications of people by common descent or heredity. Physical characteristics (such as skin color), common history, and genetic similarity help determine a person's race. *Ethnicity* relates to a group of people sharing a common and distinctive culture, religion, or language. Race and ethnicity share much in common; however, race often refers mostly to one's skin color and ethnicity has more to do with common shared culture.

Discussing Main Point and Meaning

1. Opponents of the name object to the name itself, apart from the school team's history. They object on racial/ethnic grounds and feel that the characterization of the "Fighting Sioux" reflects badly on Native Americans as a people.
2. The nickname might harm people of the Sioux tribe who feel it characterizes them as a violent people. The image of the "Fighting Sioux" that accompanies the logo may not reflect the modern Sioux people or it creates a negative impression of their ancestry.
3. The history she is referring to is not the history of the Sioux people. She is talking about the school's history of a vibrant, determined, successful sports team.

Examining Sentences, Paragraphs, and Organization

1. Bergstrom writes in a journalistic style, includes many quotations, and is not particularly arguing her personal "side." However, the quotes she includes are overwhelmingly on the side of keeping the name "Fighting Sioux," and she does not interview any of the Sioux representatives in the lawsuit, nor does she expound upon the "harmful" aspects of the name "Fighting Sioux." Her final quote suggests that problems will not immediately be solved if the nickname is removed ("a new nickname may not be implemented for some time, if at all").

2. Bergstrom interviews former and current UND and NDSU students and faculty. The article would have changed to show more of the opposition if she had included some quotations from the tribes in question.

3. The quotations give the article an objective feeling because it is not an article presented in the writer's voice trying to persuade. In her selection of quotations, Bergstrom seems to believe that the evidence supports the continuation of "Fighting Sioux" as a nickname—she does present some mild opposition or questioning of the name, but no one vehemently opposed is quoted.

Thinking Critically

1. It is difficult to discover the opposition to the name in this article, since no one demanding a name change is interviewed. However, the article alludes to the controversy and states that "critics view the nickname as racially offensive." The Sioux were subjugated and have experienced prejudice in this country. The name could affect (or be perceived as harmful by) those who do not attend UND.

2. Native American peoples lost a good deal of their freedoms in this country as settlers arrived and moved west across the United States. Ultimately, native peoples were placed on reservations as their lands were given to pioneers by the U.S. government. Today, they are achieving more of a voice as laws against discrimination are passed.

3. Sports are very important to the faculty and students of UND. The Fighting Sioux are a popular and successful athletic body. This information comes across in the overwhelmingly positive quotations from students very proud of their school's teams. The construction of the Engelstad Arena is a good example of this.

In-Class Writing Activities

1. The arena is a fabulous and expensive construction, and after it opened, attendance at Fighting Sioux hockey games skyrocketed. Engelstad was a goalie on the UND hockey team and played as a "Fighting Sioux." Students may discover other details about Ralph Engelstad that shed light on his relationship to the university and to the name "Fighting Sioux."

2. A legacy is something handed down from generation to generation. A legacy could be financial or it could be something less tangible—a sports

legacy, a political legacy, a unique family legacy. Students' answers will differ based on their personal experience.

3. It will be easy for students to research the history of Native Americans, and they will come to this question with preconceptions. They may discuss the Battle of Little Bighorn or Wounded Knee and examine the outcomes for the Sioux. They may discuss historical events like the Trail of Tears and the removal of Native Americans to reservations.

Liz Breslin

Debate: Does a Family Need to Share a Surname? Yes

[*Brain, Child,* Winter 2009]

Vocabulary/Using a Dictionary

1. A *feminist* is someone who advocates for women's rights. *Paternal* means "relating to the father." In this essay, Breslin is engaging in a debate over the traditional use of the man's surname by his family. One assumes a feminist would be interested in the right of the woman to give her child her surname instead of using the paternal surname.
2. *Exclusion* comes from the verb *exclude*, which means "to shut or keep out." Other words that share the root are *exclusive* and *exclusivity*. Students may have heard of an "exclusive" club, or they may be more familiar with the opposite word: *inclusion* (*inclusive*, etc.).
3. An *assumption* is something taken for granted. Assumptions are suppositions, whereas facts have proof behind them.

Responding to Words in Context

1. A *default setting* is the setting set by a manufacturer or user that a computer returns to. A mother could be seen as a default setting because she is the parent (or "setting") her children instinctively choose for comfort.
2. A family might be considered exclusive because they shut out others to a certain extent. It is inclusive because it is all-embracing within the family unit. A single surname would add to a family's exclusivity as well as its inclusivity.
3. *Double-barrelling* literally means having two barrels mounted side by side. One may have heard of a "double-barrelled shotgun." When someone double-barrels a name, he or she usually hyphenates a couple's surnames to make one name. The double barrels are the two names side by side.

Discussing Main Point and Meaning

1. Breslin identifies herself as a feminist, but her argument rests on the statement that a single name—and in keeping with her family's choice, her husband's name—is best for her family. Students may still note a

discrepancy between her being a feminist and the argument that her husband's name is the best for the family, but Breslin says she is less concerned with the feminist side of this question and more concerned with the unification of her family.

2. In Breslin's mind, there is no doubt of the strength of the bond between herself and her children because she is the mother. Because of this intangible but indestructible bond, she is happy to choose to give her kids her husband's surname.

3. The world has a preference, it seems, for the consistent use of a surname. Historically, that name has been the father's. For those who take the mother's name or a new name, it may be difficult to prove a link to one's family if there is a need to prove identity. Breslin cites schools, doctors' offices, and immigration offices as places where the use of a different surname could be problematic.

Examining Sentences, Paragraphs, and Organization

1. The use of questions throughout shows that Breslin has anticipated her audience's challenges to her position. It makes the essay feel more like an interview and less like an argument. The questions provide a structure for the essay, and as a device they allow her to have a conversation with the reader instead of simply hammering a point home.

2. Breslin's use of questions followed by answers shows that she has considered the other side of the argument. She mentions in the early paragraphs that she discussed surnames with her partner early in the pregnancy and that she may even have entertained the opposing position at one time (para. 4) before giving it a good deal of thought. Her thoughts are what follow in the essay.

3. The father's position on surnames is mentioned both early and late in the essay. Breslin notes his early objection to the possibility of not using his surname, which led her to look at the question more closely. She ends by mentioning his pride in sharing his name and reiterates that her decision was a choice made by both of them for the good of all family members. Students may feel the essay ends too abruptly on that note without much talk about how they "chose" this together, but most may say that bringing the father back into the discussion helps round out her argument about the experience of the family as a whole (not just her decision).

Thinking Critically

1. Answers will vary depending on students' experiences. They may refer to religious or cultural traditions, or they may have more unique family traditions. Reasons for accepting or rejecting certain traditions will also vary depending on personal, cultural, and familial values.

2. Students may believe Breslin is a feminist because she clearly considered the question of surnames before assuming her husband's name. They

may also note that she doesn't come from a traditional marriage, and that may have some reflection on her feelings about traditional roles and women's rights. There is a question at the end about whether Breslin "chose" to give herself and the kids her husband's name or if she "let" him do it because he didn't want to give them her name. The discussion at that point is very brief and some may not be convinced without more explanation of their mutual decision (he seemed distressed at the beginning that she might not take his name). What, for example, would it have meant, given her argument, if they had all taken her name (husband included)? Or if they had all legally changed to a "double-barrelled or blended" name?

3. Students' answers will vary depending on which side they take in the argument. Some may agree with the need for a shared name while others will question whether it's necessary for a unified family. Expect students to form their responses around specific points brought out in the essay when they take on or side with her argument. Other reasons for deciding for or against a shared name may have to do with the configuration of the family or particular beliefs grounded in more traditional expectations or a more feminist perspective.

In-Class Writing Activities

1. The history of taking the male surname is not the focus of Breslin's essay, so it may be helpful for students to research traditions and expectations of married couples either via the Internet or personal research involving their own families. Students might explore the legal aspects of marriage and how it affects the family and women's struggles for rights in the past. They should consider the traditional role of the man as the sole breadwinner, or head of household, and how that role has altered (or not) in recent history.
2. Names have been very important to identity—not just for individuals, but for identifying land, for identifying property, and for establishing a family's heritage. Scottish clans were made up of relatives within a family, and they were associated with particular areas of Scotland that they controlled. Today, people with certain names can try to identify the clan they have descended from and learn more about their particular genealogical history. People settling in certain areas (the "small-towners" referred to) gave names, often their names, to streets, rivers, mountains, and towns, in order to make their mark on the world. A family name could stretch through time that way.
3. Holiday traditions may first spring to mind when students approach this writing assignment. Or they may think about traditions around life events (births, weddings, deaths). Some may choose to write about traditions that spring from their ethnic or religious background. Answers will vary, but students may also discover traditions unique to their families as they consider the question.

Laura Williamson

Debate: Does a Family Need to Share a Surname? No

[*Brain, Child,* Winter 2009]

Vocabulary/Using a Dictionary

1. A *sucker punch* is a blow that comes without warning. (It's slang, and it's derived from the verb form of *sucker punch*.) The term is a phrase used in boxing.
2. Williamson questions the statement that the surname is the male's *prerogative*, or special right—she feels it makes no sense that men automatically control the child's last name.
3. Quite literally, to *underwrite* means to write under or at the end of something. Williamson, in this instance, means that one assumption directly follows another. Students may have heard of sponsors providing the *underwriting* for a project or a television show, but in that case the word has to do with the guarantee of financial support for that project or show.

Responding to Words in Context

1. At immigration checkpoints, people are stopped and documentation is checked to confirm identity and citizenship. Often these checkpoints are at a country's borders (for example, one might encounter an immigration checkpoint on the border between the United States and Mexico). A difference in surname within a family might cause some confusion because a common surname easily establishes connection between members of a family.
2. Williamson is referring to the confusion caused by the assumption that paternity is bound up with a shared surname. The "pressures" are not weighty burdens, but instead revolve around the difficulties of having to explain a family's decision about names.
3. The word *gnaw* has negative connotations (as opposed to neutral words like *chew* or *suck*). Pregnancy and breastfeeding are often viewed as wonderful and natural events without any consideration given to the mother's possible struggles and pains. Williamson wants to convey the difficulties (and painful nature) of breastfeeding that one might not have considered.

Discussing Main Point and Meaning

1. In Williamson's opinion, families are not about names alone. Families are about the memories and histories that are created together, and they are about love that goes beyond measure. She also understands that families exist in many configurations and are not simply made up of the traditional mother-father-child unit.
2. The mother-in-law explains the couple's decision to others as best she can and then goes on to discuss her grandchild without dwelling on the

decision about his name. Williamson says that love in families runs deep, and her mother-in-law loves her grandchild because he's her grandchild—not because of the name attached to him.

3. Williamson speaks about the discomforts of pregnancy, such as swollen ankles and the need to be careful about everything she puts in her body. She also talks about the deep connection between a woman and the fetus inside her and how unfair it seems that the intense connection seemingly disappears after birth. To her, the sharing of her name feels like a natural progression from the pregnancy.

Examining Sentences, Paragraphs, and Organization

1. The essay opens with the information that Williamson's mother-in-law's "first grandchild had been born." She keeps her child gender neutral at certain points in the essay. Other times, she refers to her son or the grandson. It might make a difference to some that the child is a boy (and should take his father's name), and perhaps she avoids such an immediate reaction from the reader by not naming gender. Also, the taking of a surname is a gender-charged issue, and she diffuses this somewhat by leaving the child's gender ambiguous.

2. The question about the husband is interjected because of course another person has a say in the naming of the child. The question shows that Williamson is considering the other side of the argument (not just reacting to it), and its use keeps the essay from sounding too defensive (as it might have if the next paragraph simply began "My husband agreed with me").

3. The anecdotal information about the mother-in-law creates an intimate tone. She relates the story with some humor, and it cushions the argument within a personal narrative. Williamson very carefully begins and ends her essay on that note and shows the evolution of her mother-in-law's opinion of her position as well.

Thinking Critically

1. People who go against majority opinion often encounter dissent or ridicule—even within their own families. They also must face obstacles presented by the world at large (Williamson mentions "the dentist's office, immigration checkpoints, and PTA meetings" [para. 9]). Williamson finds that many other women support her decision, although they may not feel up to following in her footsteps. She draws support from her family as well, mentioning her husband's understanding of her position and her mother-in-law's eventual acceptance. Different ways of being in the world can become more acceptable in society, but it often takes time for change to feel normal.

2. Students may agree that Williamson would respect her son's decisions about parenting out of love; similarly, she hopes her mother-in-law will respect her decisions. However, she may hope that her son shares her values, since families live by a shared set of values (para. 14). Students may

wonder what the essay would be like if Williamson's husband had disagreed with her desire to use her surname, or they may speculate on what might happen if her son wants his child to take his name.

3. The question of surnames is a charged one, since the norm is for the child to take the father's name (based on a history that has seen women struggle for rights at home and in society). Students may fall on the pro-woman or pro-man side of the question, or they may feel that families have changed so much over the last century that the question is more about how to define a family and less about a power struggle between men and women.

In-Class Writing Activities

1. Both women discuss their relationships and their pregnancies, but they take very different approaches. Breslin mentions the "growing, nurturing, breastfeeding times," the closeness to her children which makes her feel that giving them her name would not create additional intimacy. Williamson, however, feels that giving her child her name allows her to maintain that intimacy now that he is through that stage, which was often quite a bit of work for her alone. Students may bring in other examples from the essays to compare and contrast.
2. Students' answers about what constitutes a family will differ based on their personal experiences and values. Their answers about what surname to give a child may vary depending on whether they have experienced only the typical family unit or one of the configurations Williamson mentions.
3. Students will find that women have gained many rights regarding citizenship, their names, and even their own bodies over the last several decades. Essays will be concerned with social and personal changes, and students may remark on Williamson's position in light of their findings. The feminist movement has encountered opposition from its very beginnings, and even today students may have experienced disagreement or backlash against it in one form or another.

Discussing the Unit

Suggested Topic for Discussion

You may want to discuss with students the outcome of the Fighting Sioux battle and talk about their opinions on the lawsuit. Why does a name mean so much, and why was it being challenged? Regarding Mead's piece, your students might have some ideas about what to name the decade in which they primarily grew up—see if they agree with Mead's arguments about 9/11 and its aftermath. It is possible that these students, many of whom remember very little of life before 9/11, have an entirely different perspective on the decade and therefore disagree with her conclusions.

Preparing for Class Discussion

1. Students can draw from Williamson's and Breslin's essays for the first question. They might consider Mead, Olsen, and Bergstrom for the second question. In all essays, students should note the sifting of evidence and examination from all sides that go into the choice of a name.

2. In "America Then . . . 1507," America is named by a European mapmaker, but it had a different name before that. In "What Do You Call It?" Mead offers a variety of names to choose from, all of which have some connection to the time, but none of which encapsulate the decade. Williamson discusses her mother-in-law's difficulties with her grandchild not having her son's name, but the child is more than the name (and perhaps legally the child is named Williamson, but in her heart, her mother-in-law thinks of him as whatever her son's surname might be). There are many ways in which a name changes, even as we fight so hard to make it one thing.

From Discussion to Writing

1. Students may look at the issue of gender that arises in the Breslin/Williamson essays. They could consider the power of public opinion and politicians in Mead's essay, or the roles of different people such as explorers and mapmakers in other times.

2. Comparisons in these essays will vary depending on which ones students decide to pair.

Topics for Cross-Cultural Discussion

1. Answers will vary, but students might consider essays like Bergstrom's or "America Then . . . 1507" or the ones about surnames (Breslin and Williamson). They might notice the lack of race/gender as a category in Olsen's essay. They could consider Mead's gender as the author of "What Do You Call It?" if they can make a case for it as an influence on the naming process. They might also consider Mead's references to Obama and consider whether his race influences the naming of the first decade of the twenty-first century.

2. Students might consider the danger of investing power in one particular group if only one is in charge of naming people and places and things. Examples from both essays can be discussed when thinking about the dangers or harm done by the dominant naming group. Examples of shifts include changes to schools and street names to represent a minority's choices, and holidays instituted to celebrate names previously uncelebrated in American history.

2

Happiness: Can It Be Defined?

Americans often seem to be on a track to find happiness, but what that happiness consists of is open for debate. Does happiness lie in the material world (can it be bought)? Is it an internal satisfaction or self-knowledge? Many people feel more familiar with its antithesis—unhappiness, anxiety, failure. But still, everyone strives to be happy.

Fear puts one of the greatest dampers on happiness. Daniel Gilbert writes about fear and uncertainty and its effect on feelings of happiness in his essay, "What You Don't Know Makes You Nervous." In it, he makes the bold statement that "people feel worse when something bad *might* occur than when something bad *will* occur," stressing that anxiety has a more pronounced effect on our happiness than does the reality of something awful happening. The uncertainty protracts unhappiness; those who know their bad circumstances can deal with it and move on—hopefully to a happier condition.

Even when success is achieved, people still struggle with happiness. Adriana Barton's "If You're Happy and you Know It, You're in Third" shows us that even successful athletes grapple with happiness. The triumph of a medal is diminished depending on expectations—a second-place winner is less likely to feel positively about his or her achievement than a third-place winner. Barton focuses on the contrasting reactions of skiers Shannon Bahrke and Jennifer Heil as they received their medals in the Vancouver Olympics.

Walter Mosley identifies the unhappiness of many Americans and then invokes the Declaration of Independence to assert our "right" to pursue happiness. In "Get Happy," he suggests that Americans may need to set up a government agency to safeguard that right. How else will they keep up with a mood "cultivated under a sophisticated understanding of a rapidly changing world" (para. 6)?

"Learning from Tison" by student Tom Hewitt compares the happiness of a young American with the happiness of a ten-year-old Indonesian burn victim. Somehow the privileged person from the technologically advanced country experiences less happiness than the burned child from the developing nation. Hewitt draws his lessons about happiness from this juxtaposition.

Daniel Gilbert

What You Don't Know Makes You Nervous

[*The New York Times*, May 21, 2009]

Vocabulary/Using a Dictionary

1. A *breadline* refers to a line of people waiting to receive free food from an agency or charity.
2. *Fin de siècle* literally translates from the French as "end of the century."
3. A *dearth* refers to a scarcity or lack, so someone experiencing a "dearth of dollars" would be in need of money.

Responding to Words in Context

1. A dais is a raised platform. An *inaugural dais* would be a platform used during an inauguration. One might guess what it is from context because Gilbert mentions that President Roosevelt "took to the inaugural dais" to make a speech.
2. Psychologists study the science of the mind and behavior, and economists study how people use their resources and how wealth and production of goods are manifested within countries. Both psychologists and economists would have an interest in how the happiness of people is affected by wealth.
3. *Unremitting* means incessant; it is an adjective.

Discussing Main Point and Meaning

1. FDR was president during the Great Depression and World War II, when times were tough and very little money was available for most Americans. One of Roosevelt's most famous quotations is "The only thing we have to fear is fear itself." Gilbert explores the effect of money on happiness. He acknowledges that having little money is a problem, but that the most important influence on happiness is "fear" or "uncertainty."
2. People who were certain to receive a shock experienced less anxiety than people who were unsure about what sort of shock they were to receive. This practical data supports Gilbert's claim that people fare better or are "happier" knowing that something bad will happen instead of wondering if it will.
3. Gilbert explains that when we know the worst will happen, we experience the pain, fear, or sorrow over whatever will happen, and then we cope as best we can with the knowledge. When we are living in uncertainty, we are unsure of what to prepare for and unable to go on with life. In effect, we are paralyzed by the uncertainty.

Examining Sentences, Paragraphs, and Organization

1. Gilbert is saying that those who don't believe "material" goods are important have never experienced hardship (such as experiencing a

scarcity of food). The play on words (the echo of the words *material* and *immaterial*) harkens back to the FDR quote, "The only thing we have to fear is fear itself."

2. Again, Gilbert is harkening back to the rhetorical devices of Roosevelt, repeating words for effect. One is used to hearing the phrase "insufficient funds" when referring to money. He creates an effect by referring to "insufficient certainty." We may think our problems and unhappiness stem from not having enough money, when in fact the problem is that we must deal with economic insecurity and other uncertainties that affect us more.

3. By referring to fundamental needs such as shelter, sustenance, and security as "quaint assets" that "enhance happiness" (para. 3), Gilbert is being sarcastic. It goes without saying that someone who has no food, no place to live, no feelings of being safe would be unhappy indeed. These needs go beyond quaint and useful qualities—they are the basis of fundamental happiness.

Thinking Critically

1. Some students may disagree that they would be happier in the long run knowing they will develop a disease like Huntington's. They may argue that there is greater happiness in uncertainty about something like that vs. uncertainty about something like shocks in an experiment or fluctuations in the stock market. Others will agree that there is a peace that comes with not having to worry about whether something even as grave as Huntington's would occur. Students may talk about what they would want to know about vs. what they would not.

2. Some of the issues Americans are concerned about are brought up in the article: economics, illness, etc. Since the age of the atomic bomb, we live in an increasingly uncertain society, and 9/11 has furthered that uncertainty for Americans. We are uncertain of the state of our planet with increasing global warming and overpopulation. We are uncertain of our marriages given the growing divorce rate. We are uncertain of our jobs, our homes, and our finances thanks to the recession and bank crisis.

3. Students may feel that there are things they want that would make them happy. They should consider the degree of happiness that those things would bring in light of other kinds of nonmaterial happiness.

In-Class Writing Activities

1. Answers will differ, but most of the symptoms raised in Gilbert's essay will be mentioned: increased heart rate, perspiration/clammy palms, stomach ache, sleeplessness, fear. Students should consider what sort of relief comes even with an unfavorable response to the uncertainty, and whether living with that answer is better than the anxiety of not knowing.

2. Students may look at the state of the world, wars Americans are/were engaged in, financial stability, the state of technology, and other issues that could affect one's general anxiety. Students may compare and

contrast the situations of Americans at the turn of the twentieth century vs. Americans at the turn of the twenty-first century. They should feel free to agree with or argue with Gilbert's statements.

3. Students will find that many people didn't cope during the Great Depression, or barely made it through the great hardship and anxiety of the time. They may find stories of those who managed their anxieties and flourished through such difficult times. One person to look at is FDR, who is mentioned in the essay, and who had to guide a country through the Great Depression.

Adriana Barton

If You're Happy and You Know It, You're in Third

[*The Globe and Mail,* February 18, 2010]

Vocabulary/Using a Dictionary

1. A *mogul* is a bump or mound of hard snow on a ski slope.
2. The root of the word *objectively* is *object*. An object is a visible thing. If something is objective (as opposed to subjective), it is more about the object than about the perception of the viewer. The word *objectively* is an adverb.
3. If you *disconnect* something, you sever or interrupt a connection. The word *disconnect* is used here as a noun and refers to a lack of connection.

Responding to Words in Context

1. To *counter* something is to oppose it. *Factual* refers to facts, or truths. If something is *counterfactual*, it goes against observable facts. Counterfactual thinking is thinking that runs contrary to the facts at hand.
2. If something is *controversial*, it often engages people in debate. A *controversy* is a dispute.
3. *Footage* refers to a length of film or videotape.

Discussing Main Point and Meaning

1. Barton says third-place winners are often simply happy to have a medal (they came very close to not having one), while people who come in second can only think that they came close to winning but did not.
2. Jennifer Heil is a Canadian in an Olympics held in Canada. Many had pinned their hopes on her to win the first gold medal for the Canadians in this Olympics.
3. Barton cites the pressures of sponsors, teammates, and fans as influences on how an athlete may feel at the end of a competition. Media attention and advertising can create certain expectations that are also upheld or let down depending on the outcome.

Examining Sentences, Paragraphs, and Organization

1. Barton writes about the day in Vancouver when the competition takes place. She mentions the weather conditions and adds that Bahrke was able to see not the "silver lining" (a phrase that refers to seeing the good in what's happening around you) but the "bronze lining" in reference to her positive outlook about winning the third-place bronze medal.

2. Students' answers will differ on this question. Most will see that the quotations add depth to the discussion of events. They offer direct insight or add weight to the data offered.

3. The fact that Ms. Bahrke is soon to marry a man named Happe ("happy") and that she sees herself as becoming "Mrs. Happy" sheds light on her personality and the way she perceives her athletic win. It provides some personal detail that doesn't directly affect the argument, but gives the reader a more complete picture of the person being discussed. It also refers directly back to Barton's title, "If You're Happy and You Know It, You're in Third."

Thinking Critically

1. Barton mentions that Bahrke was much younger when she won the silver and that she was not expected to win any medals in Vancouver. Student opinions may differ on the value of a bronze medal vs. a silver or gold, but they can look back at the many details about Bahrke's personality and her career as a skier to answer this question.

2. Athletes who win silver can have a variety of feelings, both positive and negative, but the overriding thought brought out in this article is a feeling that winning the silver is more about missing the gold. Coming closer to winning, but not quite making it, can make the silver medal seem somewhat disappointing.

3. Bahrke is described as "bubbly." Since she had not expected to win a medal at all, she says she is honored just by being on the podium. At the time of her third-place win, she was considering retiring from her sport in order to focus on marriage. Not much personal information is given about Heil, but the writer makes it clear she had been hoping for a gold medal and had experienced a good deal of pressure from outside sources to win first place. Her disappointment is felt throughout the article, as she is described as "crestfallen" and "blunt with reporters."

In-Class Writing Activities

1. Students' answers will differ based on what they focus on about the two athletes. Essays should compare and contrast Bahrke and Heil. The conclusion should incorporate the argument in Barton's article in some way.

2. Students may agree or disagree with Barton's argument as they reflect on their own experiences. When writing about this question, students should discuss material from the article and use examples from it in addition to exploring their own feelings and experiences.

3. Students may or may not have much experience watching the Olympics. They may believe the Olympics has changed based on modern advertising and corporate sponsorship. They may document changes in the experiences of early athletes vs. modern ones, or they may note that competition in sports remains in some ways very much the same.

Walter Mosley

Get Happy

[*The Nation*, October 5, 2009]

Vocabulary/Using a Dictionary

1. *Domination* is mastery or control. Students may be familiar with *dominate, dominion, dominatrix, domineer, predominate.*
2. *Codify* means to reduce to a code or systematize. *Codify* is a verb.
3. A *subset* is a division within a set. *Sub-* means under, beneath, or below. A *subset* is smaller and more specific than a larger *set.*

Responding to Words in Context

1. A *barren* landscape is a sterile landscape. The *tropics* is an area that's hot and humid, where tropical plants grow.
2. *Urban sprawl* is a way of describing the spread of urban development into surrounding areas. In this context, it refers to the cities and outlying regions that are filled with pollution from cars.
3. *Consensus* is general agreement. It is achieved when people come to an agreement or abide by the majority of opinion.

Discussing Main Point and Meaning

1. Americans, according to Mosley, are driven by an all-too-fast-moving technology, are insatiable consumers, have "untreated physical and psychological ailments" (perhaps due to lack of health care), and are hard-pressed to find meaning in their lives.
2. While Mosley acknowledges that happiness often has a connection to wealth, he believes that happiness is a state of mind affected by the pace and conditions of the world that surrounds one.
3. Our capitalistic, consumer society is well-identified as a source of our unhappiness. The constant and rapid change we are undergoing as our world changes is another source. But our unhappiness is as complex as our society, and our happiness seems to be as complex as well.

Examining Sentences, Paragraphs, and Organization

1. The passage from the Declaration frames the essay, giving us the "pursuit of happiness" as an unachieved goal and an elusive right. Mosley

can refer back to it throughout the essay, and it directs him to a government agency that would help secure that right for us.

2. The questions in paragraph 15 are some of the more fundamental requests that we as a people would ask for in order to secure happiness—food, health, help with childcare, education, land, and knowing that our government is concerned for our welfare. Most people feel they are on their own in securing these paths to happiness or they are at a loss as to how to secure them. Mosley explains these are large undertakings and they are as complicated as our current society.

3. In this essay, Mosley puts forth some strong opinions about the happiness and unhappiness of the American people. By nodding to those who may feel happy with their lot as Americans, he admits that some may disagree with him. He phrases it in such a way that it makes anyone who disagrees seem privileged and out of touch with most Americans, however ("I certainly do not wish to bring unhappiness to anyone who feels they fit into this world like a pampered foot into a sheepskin slipper" [para 8]), and in paragraph 9 he speaks of the "many of us" who are unhappy in the current state of society.

Thinking Critically

1. Mosley may or may not believe that any such agency can be formed; however, he begins by discussing the branches of government formed to uphold the rights established in the Declaration of Independence and the Constitution. By suggesting that we need such an agency, he underscores the fact that most Americans feel unable to hold on to their right to the "pursuit of happiness."

2. Mosley mentions that the "pursuit of happiness" usually refers to the pursuit of property or financial success. Despite that, he widens the definition of pursuit of happiness to a general happiness in society and happiness within the boundaries of an ever-changing world. Money, he says, can influence happiness, but it can't secure it.

3. The rapidity of changing technology, values, and experiences has an effect on how we experience the world around us. Mosley describes the speed of the changes as disorienting. He raises the pointed question, "How can a normal person be happy with herself in this world, when the definition of the world is changing almost hourly?" (para. 13).

In-Class Writing Activities

1. The executive, legislative, and judicial branches refer to the President, the Congress, and the Supreme Court. The three branches were established for checks and balances when our government was formed, so that no one branch held too much control. There are ways in which a government that equalizes itself in this way might lead to its citizens having more happiness. But Mosley makes the case that the pursuit of happiness is much more elusive as a right than the right to life and liberty. Answers may differ.

2. Students may agree with Mosley's idea for a central agency that helps citizens achieve and maintain happiness, or they may feel that there is no real way a government agency could be entrusted to handle a pursuit of something so unclear. Essays should address ways in which the government can help rectify or redirect problems that cause our unhappiness, or they should propose ways in which other specific methods or ideas could be implemented.

3. Answers will vary. Statements by Mosley include the blurring of truth in our society, our use of drugs even while we fight a "war on drugs," our poor lifestyle choices, our anxiety about health and money, our desire to get rich quickly, our love affair with things, our need to wage wars, and our dwindling integrity in our relationships.

Tom Hewitt (student essay)

Learning from Tison

[*The Sun Star*, University of Alaska Fairbanks, December 15, 2009]

Vocabulary/Using a Dictionary

1. A *documentary* is a film or broadcast of some kind that presents its subject in a factual and informative way.
2. *En route* comes from the French and means "on the way."
3. *Terrain* is land or earth. It comes from the word *terra*, which is Latin for "land" or "earth."

Responding to Words in Context

1. A clinic can refer to a group that meets to tackle a particular problem (for example, a speech clinic), but in general clinics are connected to hospitals and offer treatment to people on an outpatient basis. Hewitt mentions that Tison is a child and a burn victim, which indicates that he is receiving medical treatment (and is probably part of a burn clinic).

2. When something is reconstructed, it is rebuilt or re-created. Reconstructive surgery is sometimes called plastic surgery, which is a branch of surgery concerned with restoring the form or functionality to various parts of the body.

3. To measure something, you gather its dimensions or extent by comparing it to a standard (a standard measurement). You make a judgment by comparing one thing with something else. In paragraph 11, Hewitt is talking about measuring people by seeing how they respond to a given situation.

Discussing Main Point and Meaning

1. Tison is a ten-year-old Indonesian burn victim. Hewitt is filming him because Tison will be flown from Indonesia to Fairbanks, Alaska, for

reconstructive surgery. Hewitt's paper is based in Fairbanks, so the story has local resonance.

2. Hewitt lives in Alaska and writes for a paper. He describes his "stress level," which is high because he is missing school and has many papers to complete. The Indonesian villagers lack most of the privileges and opportunities Hewitt's life provides. They live in shacks and have to cross a local river on rafts in order to get to a field for a soccer game. The simple fare of cold water and baked bananas is a tremendous treat for the teams.

3. The lives of the people of the village are much harder than the lives of most Americans. A soccer game provides a diversion and a chance to relax and enjoy other people that most Indonesians don't get when they are working daily to survive in poverty. Perhaps their lifestyle allows them to view a soccer game as the opportunity that it is, while most Americans would be focused on competition and more material concerns.

Examining Sentences, Paragraphs, and Organization

1. Hewitt chooses to begin at the "end" of his story, mentioning that he's been in Jakarta and is preparing to return to Alaska. By beginning in this way, he grabs his readers' attention and creates a little suspense by then stopping ("Let me back up") and starting again with the details the reader needs to know about Tison and his project.

2. Students may wish they had more details about Tison. Hewitt makes the claims about his "cheery" personality, but the reader might want more of a picture of Tison—the sort of picture they would see in a documentary. Hewitt states that "life isn't fair" (para. 9) and then says, "The Indonesians know that, but it doesn't stop them from finding fulfillment" (para. 9). Students may want more information on how that fulfillment manifests itself (beyond the details of the soccer game), or they might want to see more of the contrast between the Indonesians' needs and life experience with Americans' needs and life experience (or, at least, Hewitt's).

3. The reader knows Hewitt is a journalist and that he's willing to travel great distances for his work. In paragraph 5, he mentions the stresses in his life, which provide clues to his personality. He also states in paragraph 10 that the burn victim, Tison, is "several times cheerier than I am in the best of times."

Thinking Critically

1. Hewitt focuses on the villagers' happiness in the face of their extreme poverty. He portrays their experience in paragraphs 6 through 8 and makes the statement that despite the hardships they endure, they still manage to find fulfillment in simple experiences and pleasures.

2. Tison's situation is described, but we don't get much of a picture of his daily life or the pain he experiences (although we know he has burns over 40 percent of his body). We gather he is able to play soccer and

even endure some travel to do so, but we don't know the circumstances of his injuries or how he is able to travel to Alaska for surgery. Students may wish to be "shown" how Tison is cheerier than Hewitt instead of being "told."

3. One might expect a person who isn't "spoiled" by the advantages of the modern world to be happier in his/her life because he/she has more of a connection to community and family or to the land he/she lives on. He/she may be less distracted by technology and more focused on simple human actions and happinesses. However, Tison isn't just poor—he is a burn victim. The reader may want to know how Tison has come to cope with his burns and have a better sense of what support network he has in his village in order to understand his happy outlook. Some may feel that the conditions of Tison's life might indicate he would be less happy or even unable to find happiness in his life.

In-Class Writing Activities

1. Answers will vary depending on the country chosen. Most students will identify the similarity of basic human needs and perhaps a similarity in what is needed to create a satisfying or fulfilling life. Differences will include the value of money or at least the prevalence of it, and the differences between life in a modern "technological" world vs. a developing country in which people must be self-sufficient without modern conveniences. Whether or not students find similarities or differences in models of family and community depends on the student and the country.
2. Soccer is a team sport, so there is a sense of bonding together with one's teammates at a game in addition to competition with the opposing team. Because teams have joined to play the same sport, there is an element of camaraderie overall. Students should do some research on soccer, a game that is played in many developed and developing countries, and consider why this sport brings so many people together. Teams are a source of great pride in many places.
3. There are times when a journalist might want to comment on the story being told, but most journalists are asked to present news objectively. Students may feel that reporters today show their biases in the work, and they should explore how this bias might come across in the writing. They might use examples from current news stories or they might explore the difference between an article about Tison and an article that comments on Tison.

Discussing the Unit

Suggested Topic for Discussion

Students may want to discuss the differences between some of the conclusions drawn in these articles. Does money affect happiness and, if so, to what extent? As many of the authors do, the students will want to relate this idea of happiness to personal experience—have they had a moment of realization akin to that of Hewitt or a sense of frustration for their current situation like Mosley? Discuss the factors they think lead to happiness that do not appear in any of these selections and see if it is possible for the class to come to some sort of consensus.

Preparing for Class Discussion

1. Consider Hewitt's essay, which compares his happiness with Tison's. Other essays compare degrees of happiness of others—those who think something bad might happen with those who know something bad will happen (Gilbert) and the winners of first, second, and third place in a sporting event (Barton). Mosley assumes he is a spokesperson for the happiness of Americans, so he is drawing from his experience in the essay. Some may trust the objective consideration of happiness over the subjective one, although they might find the use of personal definitions of happiness to be more persuasive.

2. Answers will vary. It is important for students to be able to articulate the argument in the essay they gravitate toward, and they should use examples from that essay to support their own position.

From Discussion to Writing

1. Tison's story is useful when considering this question, because Tison has had something bad happen to him and has plenty to fear, but he continues to be quite happy. Fear of failure or the fear in Barton's essay—of not winning—affects our happiness. Fear of an ever-changing modern world, or fear of a lack of definition of happiness (Mosley), is also a factor that keeps us from achieving happiness.

2. Students must isolate the thesis statement of two of the essays in this chapter in order to effectively tackle this assignment. Then they must present examples from both essays and compare and contrast them.

Topics for Cross-Cultural Discussion

1. Some of these essays deal exclusively with the happiness or unhappiness of Americans. The question of knowing or not knowing if something bad will happen (or simply accepting that something bad could happen) is more universal. The question of the American mindset might be explored, given what's presented in these essays. The one essay that clearly offers a cultural distinction is Hewitt's essay about Tison, the Indonesian boy.

2. Some discussion about what constitutes Jefferson's definition of "happiness" in the Declaration might be in order, in addition to a consideration of what rights were available (or not) to nonwhites and immigrants over the course of American history. Students should be able to compare that information with the argument and definition of happiness that Mosley offers (as well as his suggestion of how to safeguard a right to happiness).

3

Is There an Ethics of Eating?

Decisions we make about the food we eat are no longer simple. The days of finding healthy foods grown on the local farm are gone. Most of the food we find in the store is imported, and we wonder whether it is treated with pesticides. Our lives are made simpler by fast food, but our bodies suffer. All the essays in this chapter consider the choices we must make about what we eat and how we eat now that we are so far removed from where and how our food is grown.

In "The Rich Get Thinner, the Poor Get Fatter," Warwick Sabin examines why people from poorer regions of the country like the South struggle with obesity and food-related health issues more than people in other regions of the country. Regional cuisine may be a reason for the rates of obesity, but it is now extremely hard for people in the South to buy some of the healthier foods the region is known for. Sabin shows us how the production and distribution of food has changed in the South and elsewhere.

This change extends to how we eat at restaurants. As Amy Domini points out in "Why Investing in Fast Food May Be a Good Thing," "fast food is a way of life" (para. 3). The days of eating a slowly prepared meal made from fresh foods are a thing of the past. Instead of fighting the fast food movement, which has an effect on our general health much like the one Sabin writes about, Domini suggests that we change the industry from within. In this way, we can improve what fast food chains offer and reduce their negative impact on the environment.

Like Domini, Brian Jay Stanley does not call for an end to our consumption, since we are "consumers by essence." In his essay "Confessions of a Carnivore," he speaks of our ability to have a conscience about what we eat, but suggests that the answer is to "destroy with respect." Domini asks the fast food industry to maintain an awareness of its behavior, and Stanley asks that we as individuals stay aware of what we eat and of our subsequent effect on the earth.

Jacob Swede, in "Remembering Johnny Appleseed," reminds us of the legacy of Johnny Appleseed. Appleseed was very aware of both the growing of food and the conservation of the earth. Swede says that in forgetting Appleseed's legacy, we have also forgotten our connections to the earth and to food. Swede doesn't have the faith that Domini and Stanley have in the growers and purchasers of food—in his account, food ignorance has become a problem for consumers and producers alike.

Warwick Sabin

The Rich Get Thinner, the Poor Get Fatter

[*Oxford American*, #68, March 2010]

Vocabulary/Using a Dictionary

1. The root of *ensnared* is the word *snare*. *Snare* is both a noun and a verb. As a noun it refers to a trap. The verb form means "to entangle." The prefix *en* means "to confine" or "to cause to be in."

2. *Processed* foods are prepared in a certain way by machinery, while fresh foods are items like vegetables and fruit from a garden or meat that is directly from the farm (with no extra additives or other manipulation).

3. An *epidemic* is something that spreads rapidly and usually refers to disease. An "obesity epidemic" refers to the exponentially growing numbers of people who suffer from obesity—almost as if it were spreading like an illness.

Responding to Words in Context

1. An "obesity rate" is the percentage of people in a given area who are considered obese, or extremely overweight. It might also be called an obesity trend.

2. *Cuisine* is derived from the French word for "kitchen." A Southern cuisine refers to the style of cooking and ingredients used that one would find in the South. A regional cuisine refers to the style of cooking and ingredients that one would find used in any particular region.

3. The word *corporate* refers to an organization or body of employees created by a group of shareholders. Corporations are usually large institutions, and they would handle the creation and distribution of foods much differently from the local farms and grocery stores that used to provide food to the general public. A *homogenizing force* is one that makes things more alike—the variety of choices in our foods would disappear under such a force.

Discussing Main Point and Meaning

1. The South has been, traditionally, a poor region of this country. Foods grown and prepared there would have been intentionally high in calories because of scarcity or poor economic conditions. The calories would have served people well if they only were able to grow or purchase small amounts of food.

2. The poor people of a hundred years ago did not have the enormous corporate supermarkets that are found across the country today. They would not have been familiar with the fast food chains that offer cheap "meals." Today those supermarkets and fast food chains provide sustenance for many of the nation's poor in the form of high-calorie, high-fat, low-nutritional-value foods.

3. Because of how food is mass produced and distributed today, the food grown in local, rural areas might be shipped far away to other chains or have inflated prices because of demand in other areas.

Examining Sentences, Paragraphs, and Organization

1. The bulk of the essay is written in third person and feels objective; however, the essay begins and occasionally reverts to first-person plural (we). In the second paragraph, it changes to second person (you). Using *we* includes the reader in the general argument being made. Using *you* is noticeable because it directly involves the reader in the issue at hand. (Will you eat that fatty food or not? Why?)
2. Economics deals with financial considerations. If once-cheap foods are now mostly available to the wealthy, then the economic shift makes no sense—the general rules have been turned upside down.
3. The writer made a reference earlier to Marie Antoinette who famously said of the French poor: "Let them eat cake." This statement refers directly back to that allusion, but also highlights the insensitivity of an economy that dooms its poor to foods, like cake, that provide little nutrition but make them fat. "Little Debbie" is a brand name that would be familiar to anyone in the packaged desserts aisle of an ordinary supermarket.

Thinking Critically

1. Students might go further than Sabin and outline some of the types of jobs that are in place now (sedentary computer jobs and the effect of technology on our ability and desire to burn calories). They might mention the prevalence of fast food and advertising. They might look at their own consumption of sodas and candy bars that Sabin mentions later.
2. Answers to this question will differ based on where students are from and what sorts of markets they choose. Many students may never have noticed that most foods are "from" somewhere. Choices may be affected by background, financial and time considerations, or other factors.
3. Because small farms have been dwarfed by big chain suppliers and supermarkets, a local food movement might seem quite radical in some areas. Consider what it would take to get such a movement off the ground. Students may have some familiarity with Fair Trade and farmer's markets or other groups that provide local foods, and they can comment on whether these groups constitute a form of protest.

In-Class Writing Activities

1. The South has always been an agriculturally based area of the country; many of its people have experienced poverty (and still do). Students may look at the beginnings of agriculture and industry in the United States, or they may look at the Civil War and Reconstruction. They may look

at how the poorer states in the South are represented. Then they can look at the sort of foods Sabin mentions (and others based on research) and discuss why those foods are grown and eaten in the region.

2. Answers may vary depending on whether or not students believe that choices for the poor are as limited as Sabin claims. They may argue other reasons for the obesity epidemic in this country. Essays should include some of Sabin's examples as touchstones, whether they are agreed with or refuted.

3. Students may be aware of the CDC because of disease epidemics they've encountered in their lifetime. Going to the CDC Web site will familiarize students with the scope of the CDC's work and give them a better idea of whether obesity and food are worthy of the CDC's attention.

Amy Domini

Why Investing in Fast Food May Be a Good Thing

[*Ode Magazine,* March 2009]

Vocabulary/Using a Dictionary

1. An *advocate* is someone who supports something. When used as a verb, "to advocate" means to support or urge by argument.

2. *Ailment* and *illness* are often interchangeable terms, but an ailment often refers to an illness that is chronic in nature. In this essay, it refers to the chronic conditions of diabetes, high cholesterol, and high blood pressure.

3. To *eliminate* something is to remove it.

Responding to Words in Context

1. A *phenomenon* is an observable fact. A global phenomenon is an observable fact that is apparent across the globe. Fast food is a global phenomenon because it exists almost worldwide.

2. A *consumer* is a person who consumes (or uses) something. In this case, it refers to consumers of fast food, but it could refer to anything anyone purchases or eats or uses in modern society.

3. If paper is *diverted* from a landfill, it is rerouted. In this case it is diverted in order to be recycled.

Discussing Main Point and Meaning

1. Slow Food is a movement started in reaction to the proliferation of fast food. It attempts to support small family farms, crop diversity, and the idea that food can be prepared slowly and intentionally so as to promote health and environmental consciousness. Fast food refers to an industry that took off in post–World War II America. Most food found in fast food restaurants is precooked and packaged in such a way that it can be delivered to the consumer within minutes.

2. Most Americans eat fast food at some point. It exists almost everywhere and is available at a relatively low price. Fast food chains are very much a part of American culture.

3. Domini points out the health issues involved with fast food (fast food's connection with the rise of diabetes, high cholesterol, and high blood pressure, now found even in children) and the issue of packaging, which causes forest destruction and an increase in waste.

Examining Sentences, Paragraphs, and Organization

1. The inclusion of information on the Dogwood Alliance adds strength to Domini's argument and illustrates how some companies come to "move in the right direction and listen to their critics" (para. 2). Dogwood Alliance shows the reader that there are groups in place to help "guide" companies to make supportable decisions.

2. The bulleted points stand out and show very specifically how companies are taking steps to reduce the amount of paper waste they generate.

3. Domini establishes herself as a supporter of Slow Food, which is important because she is trying to sway an audience that might view fast food as an evil industry. By aligning herself with Slow Food, yet finding a way to support investing in fast food, she manages to create a connection with the readers she is hoping to convince. Including that information again at the end serves as a reminder to those readers.

Thinking Critically

1. Student answers will differ based on their feelings about fast food's connection to unhealthy eating and environmental issues. Some may share Domini's opinion that investing in the fast food industry will have an impact on health and environment, but others may believe investing in fast food perpetuates a destructive industry. And still others may not feel fast food companies are responsible for health or environmental problems.

2. The companies Domini would invest in have taken steps to become more health and environmentally conscious. They might be dogged by watchgroups that keep them in line with certain standards or they might be run by people who have decided that healthier, more environmentally sound choices help promote a better business. Students may agree or disagree with Domini's statement about there being no "perfect" companies.

3. The idea of a "movement" is brought up at the beginning of this essay. Students may look at different movements and organizations that have influenced the way companies run their businesses. As environmental and health issues become more noticeable, individuals begin to voice their opinions and groups begin to form to take a stand against company policies that affect their lives.

In-Class Writing Activities

1. Students can research Dogwood Alliance and other watchdog groups on the Web. They may know of smaller groups that have a more local influence on companies, or they may look at the effect of larger, more well-known groups (such as Greenpeace) and discuss how they protest company policies or effect change.

2. Answers will vary. Some students may recycle; some may not. Some may have participated in the process of recycling and know what happens to the materials that get carted away. Answers about what could be recycled that generally isn't may be creative and surprising.

3. Fast food has taken off in many nations, including some (Greece is mentioned in this article) that previously had no significant difficulties with obesity and food-related ailments but now do. Some countries continue to resist Americanization and the incorporation of fast food in daily life. If students want to write an essay that examines the influence of fast food in several countries, they may do so; if they wish to stick to one particular country (such as Greece, Japan, or France), that essay will work as well.

Brian Jay Stanley

Confessions of a Carnivore

[*The North American Review*, September/October 2009]

Vocabulary/Using a Dictionary

1. *Nonchalance* is cool indifference or lack of concern. It is derived from French.

2. A *smorgasbord* is a buffet meal made up of a variety of foods. It is a Swedish word that translates as "sandwich table."

3. A *quadruped* is an animal that has four legs (*quadru-* meaning "four" and *ped* meaning "feet" in Latin).

Responding to Words in Context

1. A *proboscis* is the protruding mouth part of an insect, which is sometimes called the beak. *Proboscis* also refers to an elephant's trunk and is sometimes used to refer to a human nose.

2. When something is *callused*, it is hardened. In this context, it refers to cattlemen and their outlook on life. *Callused* is an adjective. A *callus* (noun) is a hardened or thickened part on the skin.

3. One has doubts or second thoughts about eating meat if one has *misgivings* about it.

Discussing Main Point and Meaning

1. Insects and animals seem to accept that killing and being killed are natural processes, while humans have the reaction of horror, fearing death in

any form. It is impossible to know how animals "think" about these things, if they even do, but Stanley is reporting from observation.

2. Humans seem to have a hand in the deaths of animals either directly or indirectly, whether they eat meat or not. If they don't eat meat, they still use resources that affect the lives of animals and demand goods that may entail the death of an animal or the destruction of its habitat.

3. Stanley offers few solutions, since the problem seems to be one of simply being human. He does suggest being aware of one's actions and their effects as a way of being less insensitive to the world around one.

Examining Sentences, Paragraphs, and Organization

1. Stanley's confessions are infused with a semireligious feeling or at least an acknowledgment of a certain sacredness to existence. The writing in this sentence alludes to the story of Christ and raises the impact of eating meat by doing so. Much of Stanley's writing is hyperbolic in this way, exaggerating his experience of daily occurrences for effect.

2. Stanley's paragraphs are fairly long and often go on for half a page. His style is somewhat verbose, and the reader can tell he enjoys going deeply into each story. Long paragraphs accommodate this style of writing and allow him to include great detail and emotion.

3. Stanley lets meaning unfold from narration in this essay. He might have started with the statement, but it would change his style of "show, don't tell" that runs through the essay, because he would first tell and then follow up with the example.

Thinking Critically

1. Stanley was speaking of the arribada in Costa Rica in which most of the tiny sea turtle hatchlings are devoured by other creatures as they make their way to the sea. He asks the question, "What five-star chef ever went to such trouble preparing a meal?" (para. 5). By saying "death is the stock in the soup of life" (para. 5), he continues the metaphor—there is no separating death from the "soup" that is life. They exist in an inextricable cycle.

2. Humans consume everything—food to make their bodies go, water to keep from dying of thirst, resources to create their homes, and their possessions, and so on. Often people don't consider how much they are taking and using every day to keep themselves alive and happy and well.

3. While Stanley feels a good deal of guilt and shame over how much he affects the life of the planet, causing the death of animals that he eats, or removing vital resources from the earth for his daily life, he realizes that there isn't much for him to do besides acknowledge these feelings (or "confess" them). By living "appreciatively," he can be aware of the great impact he has on other creatures and the planet as a whole.

In-Class Writing Activities

1. Annie Dillard begins much of her stories and nonfiction with anecdotes from the natural world, just as Stanley does here. She has an appreciation of her impact on the world as well and a similar religious or spiritual reverence for daily things and for nature. She often lets images from the natural world stand as metaphors in her writing, just as Stanley does. Students should include any examples they may find from Dillard's writing as points of comparison with Stanley's.

2. Students may agree or disagree with the idea that they are "fat emperors ruling a kingdom of inanimate serfs" (para. 11), and they should provide evidence as to why they do or do not see themselves in this light. Some may feel Stanley overdoes his argument about the effect humans have while some may feel swayed by the way he has presented his case.

3. Students can choose from a variety of problems Stanley presents here. They should be able to describe themselves as "consumers" much as he does in the essay and explore their effect on the world from one particular angle. They may be able to include information on how to slow or stall the negative impact by choosing to behave in a certain way or engage in any sort of beneficial activity.

Jacob Swede (student essay)

Remembering Johnny Appleseed

[*The Minnesota Daily*, University of Minnesota Twin Cities, March 10, 2010]

Vocabulary/Using a Dictionary

1. A *legacy* is something that gets handed down from an ancestor or predecessor. In this essay, Johnny Appleseed's legacy, the story of his planting of apple orchards, is honored on Johnny Appleseed Day.

2. An *ecosystem* refers to an environment in which organisms interact, an ecological community that functions as a unit. Words that begin with *eco-* usually deal with the environment or nature. A *system* is a combination of things functioning as a whole.

3. If something is *rampant*, it is unchecked or widespread. In this essay, Swede refers to the use of cheap labor as rampant in poorer countries.

Responding to Words in Context

1. A *critique* is a criticism or comment on something. In this case, the critique is of modern life—Johnny Appleseed's legacy points out the ways in which people today have grown disconnected from the land and what they eat.

2. Swede means that what we don't know about our food can hurt us—physically. Our bodies suffer from our lack of knowledge—we can

quickly become obese and suffer myriad health problems that come as a result of obesity.

3. *Land degradation* is the spoiling of the environment as a direct result of human activity. *Degradation* is the reduction or breaking down of something. As a geographical term, it often refers to erosion.

Discussing Main Point and Meaning

1. Swede points out that the American public views food only as it is presented to them on the grocery shelf or a plate and that we have little or no idea of where it comes from, what it is treated with (in terms of chemicals), the effects of farming on our world, or even of the nutritional values of different foods (fast food vs. fresh). This ignorance is dangerous to our environment, to our physical well-being, and to our sense of ourselves in the world (our relationship to the land and to food—the very things that sustain our life).

2. Land degradation due to current food production practices is the main environmental concern voiced in the essay. Land degredation destroys ecosystems, which in turn creates an economic concern for those who work in those ecosystems. Poor working conditions and poor pay are other economic concerns, since cheap labor often supports the production and distribution of imported foods.

3. The example of "the apple at breakfast, the half-price turkey on Russian rye you had for lunch" illustrates that most people know no more about their food than the fact that it somehow gets put in front of them. People know where they buy their food, but they have lost their connection to where the food *really* comes from. At one time people grew their own food or at least knew where it was grown and by whom.

Examining Sentences, Paragraphs, and Organization

1. Johnny Appleseed was someone who traveled the countryside planting orchards. As Swede points out, Johnny Appleseed Day is a largely forgotten holiday in the United States. The point is made in the essay that just as people have forgotten a man who was so connected to the land he lived on and who could help sustain people by growing food, so too have they forgotten their own relationship to the food they eat. Not many of us could grow food ourselves—we have become entirely dependent on unseen forces to create food and feed us. Swede would like us to remember a time when food was much more important and fathomable to us.

2. The Appleseed reference is made in the introductory paragraph and at the end of the essay. The body paragraphs deal largely with our ignorance of the food we eat and the undesirable effects of that ignorance. Students may feel the Appleseed reference is necessary to the essay and a good way to present the information that follows; others may feel it is extraneous to the point being made about our lack of relationship to the food we eat. If more information had been brought out about Appleseed

and tied into the body paragraphs, students might feel the reference is more important to the essay.

3. "Americans have forgotten what Johnny Appleseed achieved and that forgetting has led to a lack of connection to farming in general" is one attempt at a rewrite using simpler language. Answers will vary.

Thinking Critically

1. Consumers no longer know what they put in their bodies—they don't know which foods are healthy. Producers no longer care about producing healthy foods, and the way they produce destroys the land instead of maintaining it for production.
2. Some may agree with Swede's claim that our relationship to the food we eat has become so disjointed, but some may feel that bad food choices also have to do with lifestyle choices and apathy instead of ignorance.
3. Students may think Johnny Appleseed Day has to do with awareness, or with self-sufficiency, or with conservation and a more intimate pretechnological relationship to the earth.

In-Class Writing Activities

1. Students can research the life and legacy of Johnny Appleseed and discuss their familiarity with the man and the holiday. Their writing about why it is a neglected holiday should both echo and enhance the information found in Swede's essay.
2. Depending on what they eat and where they buy, students may or may not know what countries their foods came from or what companies packaged them or what each food's nutritional values are. They may or may not know what farming practices were used and what type of labor was employed.
3. Students should pick one of the topics and stick to it through this brief essay. Focusing on one topic will challenge students to go deeper than Swede in terms of their responses, since he tackled a variety of issues in one essay.

Discussing the Unit

Suggested Topic for Discussion

There is a growing trend to pay more attention to what we consume, but you may want students to explore whether or not this has had any effect on their eating habits. Did any of these articles make them rethink what they eat on a daily basis? In addition to the advice given by the authors of these articles, what do the students think would make a difference in our relationship with food?

Preparing for Class Discussion

1. Good food is harder to come by because of the changes in the farming industry (the move to agribusiness, as Sabin mentions), which has left the poor of this country, particularly, with the difficult choice of paying much more for simple, healthy food. Swede looks at similar problems that stretch across economic lines. Stanley discusses how we have become divorced from the understanding of our own needs—because we are in a consumer society, we eat without thinking, "constantly eating, and for contradictory reasons." Domini has hope for the fast food industry, but she thinks the fast food tradition is too entrenched for us to get around it.

2. Most of these essays show us to be consumers in a consumer-driven society. Based on our choices about how we eat and how we grow our food, we seem to have little interest in or respect for the world we live in and the people we live with. Domini has hope for how we can change the fast food industry, but the damage is already being done, socially and environmentally (Swede points out similar actions and damage in his essay). Stanley speaks of our conscience and calls for a deeper awareness of what we eat and what we do.

From Discussion to Writing

1. Answers will vary depending on what essays students choose to compare.

2. The history provided by most of these authors highlights the contrast between how we used to view food and how we view it now. They show the gulf in our knowledge of food production and what foods are good for us that would not have been the case for someone in another time. The rise of agribusiness and fast food is made manifest, as are the differences between the situation and needs of our ancestors and our own.

Topics for Cross-Cultural Discussion

1. Students should consider what sorts of choices about food Hispanics bring from their original countries, or people of Asian or African descent. Then examine the cultures of particular regions of this country. Students should take into account not only regional and cultural differences, but also the role of economics when answering this question.

2. The role of the United States in the world post–World War II (when products like fast food came into being) should be discussed. The role of technology and advertising as influences on our choices and the choices of the rest of the world should also be discussed. Students may want to think about how globalization affects food and consider how our choices about food are influenced as well.

4

Photography: Can We Believe What We See?

In "This Photo Is Lying to You," Rob Haggart writes, "The old trope 'The camera never lies' is, in fact, backwards—the camera *always* lies." Each of the essays in this unit explores the relationship between photography and truth. Haggart focuses on the common practice of manipulating and enhancing photographs. He begins with a discussion of photographer Ed Freeman, who uses Photoshop to create striking—and unrealistic—pictures. Haggart concedes that photographers have always tampered with their work, going back to nineteenth-century "pictorialists." But he argues that the prevalence and acceptance of such practices now is "screwing up our concept of reality." He ends on an optimistic note: All this artifice has created a "growing hunger for truth"—and a growing number of photographers in pursuit of it.

Jed Perl writes in the context of a photographic and political controversy: the Obama administration's decision not to release more photographs of prisoner abuse at Abu Ghraib. Perl agrees with the administration's position in his essay "Picture Imperfect." His argument touches upon the idea of photographic "truth" as a "particular kind of truth," as well as the ways in which pictures can "skew the truth" or "collapse a complex story into an image that, however horrific, is only one piece of evidence in a story that is even more terrible." Perl's case is subtle and counterintuitive; he argues that truth might be better served by suppressing photographs than by releasing them. As he writes, "information does not always advance knowledge . . ."

For Elizabeth Svokos, digital photography has removed spontaneity, excitement, and imperfections from picture-taking. In "Head to Head—Print Photographs," she laments the loss of all her photographs after her computer crashes. The occasion leads her to consider the differences between digital and print photography—and argue in favor of the latter. Not only does she like the red eyes, blemishes, and spontaneous "bad" photographs captured by film cameras, she also prefers the experience of handling weathered pictures: "life captured in those imperfect and beautiful photographs with their smudge marks and rips on the edges from passing them around so much."

Rob Haggart

This Photo Is Lying to You

[*Outside*, September 2009]

Vocabulary/Using a Dictionary

1. The prefix *Franken-* derives from Mary Shelley's novel *Frankenstein*, which features a fictional monster pieced together from human body parts. The word connotes both artificiality and monstrosity. Haggart uses it to describe Freeman's photographic creation as an unnatural hybrid.
2. A *trope* can be any literary or rhetorical device, such as a metaphor, simile, or irony; it may also refer generally to a turn of phrase. The word comes from the Greek *tropos* (turn, direction, figure of speech). It shares this origin with terms such as *trophy* and *tropical.*
3. The term comes from the Latin *verus* (true). *Veracity* means conformity to truth or fact.

Responding to Words in Context

1. The phrase often appears as a euphemism for unintended damages, injuries, or deaths caused by a military operation, especially civilian casualties. Haggart uses it to refer to the unintended and negative consequences that artificial or composite photographs have on both photography and our "sense of reality" (para. 5).
2. *Hallowed* usually refers to places, objects, or people who are regarded as holy or sacred. In the context of Haggart's essay, however, the word suggests certain curators and photographic images are venerated and revered.
3. The quotation marks highlight the word's double meaning for Haggart. In one sense, photographers and photo editors "tweak" images—darken skies, adjust coloring, sharpen the contrasts—to make their pictures more appealing and compelling. But for Haggart, such tampering degrades the practice of honest photojournalism, as well as the viewers' trust.

Discussing Main Point and Meaning

1. *Migrations* appeared four years after the introduction of Adobe Photoshop. Wolfe was an "early adopter of digital tools" and used them to "enhanc[e] images" as a painter would (para. 10). These deliberately altered pictures "started a stampede of accusations" that such work would break the trust "between nature photographers and viewers" (para. 11). According to Wolfe, however, these practices have become so common that "nobody would bat an eye" if the book were released now (para. 12).

2. In Haggart's view, people are "finally fed up with all the tampering" (para. 23). He also sees the professional photographic community "policing" photographs (para. 23). Haggart cites a *New York Times Magazine* portfolio of altered images, which was spotted by viewers and ultimately pulled by the magazine's editors. He sees this as evidence of a "growing hunger for truth" (para. 24).

Examining Sentences, Paragraphs, and Organization

1. The detail signals Freeman's distance from his subject and suggests the inauthenticity of his photographs. At the same time, Freeman's justifications—that he was capturing "how surfing feels to me," as opposed to "how it is"; that he's an "artist" who "couldn't care less" if the images were "'real' or not"—set up Haggart's main points about the value of truth in photography.
2. In this section, Haggart demonstrates that "truth in photography has always been fuzzy" (para. 6). He provides a brief but evocative account of photographic deceptions, from fake images of Abraham Lincoln to altered photographs of the Kent State massacre. These paragraphs provide historical context. They also demonstrate that dishonest photography is not a recent development.
3. Haggart begins the essay with specific examples of photographic dishonesty; he then moves to the long history of photographers manipulating or altering images. But after examining the present "crisis" and placing it in historical context, he closes the essay by arguing that tampering has led to healthy skepticism and a "growing hunger for truth" (para. 24). You might note how this is a corollary to the "collateral damage" Haggart refers to earlier in the essay. In this case, though, the unintended consequences—a "more savvy public," photographers looking to "pursue truth"—are a benefit, not a problem.

Thinking Critically

1. Freeman raises provocative questions about the relationship between photography and reality, as well the one between art and reality. He concedes that his goal is to represent how "surfing feels to me," rather than produce "sports photography" (para. 1). Students may agree that he can alter his photos, but only on the condition that he disclose that they have been altered. That way, "our concept of reality" (para. 5) is not affected.
2. Haggart could have chosen to make a more general argument, supported with specific examples of altered photography. He might have merely summarized the counterarguments of photographers like McLean. Instead, Haggart quotes their own language, which gives his own argument a grainy specificity. The choice demonstrates his good faith in letting people explain themselves: Haggart takes their point of view seriously and addresses it honestly, even though he largely disagrees with them. The choice also suggests Haggart's trust in his readers to draw their own conclusions.

3. Haggart hopes and suspects that we are fed up with simulation and tampering: "Too many published photographs are unhinged from reality, morphed by a few mouse clicks into slick advertisements for perfect moments in time." There may be a case to be made for artifice over "reality." Students might also broaden the context to question assumptions about "truth" or "authenticity" that Haggart may take for granted.

In-Class Writing Assignments

1. Answers will vary depending on students' choice of image.
2. Students might consider how images from the media, advertising, movies, or popular culture affect our sense of "reality." Models in magazine ads are probably the most obvious example, but even more straightforward photojournalism may create iconic images of people and places that are "unhinged from reality" (para. 24).
3. While Wolfe is writing about the world of photography, the notion of being a "purist" is applicable to innumerable contexts—music, food, movies, hobbies, traveling, sports, fashion, religion, politics, etc. Purists can be seen as uncompromising, honest, and devoted; they may also appear stubborn, close-minded, and dogmatic. Haggart's essay concerns matters of "taste" (as he makes explicit in the final paragraph), and students can use this prompt to examine their own tastes.

Jed Perl

Picture Imperfect

[*The New Republic*, June 17, 2009]

Vocabulary/Using a Dictionary

1. *Propaganda* is information, images, ideas, or rumors spread deliberately to help or harm a person, group, movement, cause, institution, or country. The word originates from the Latin *propago* (that which produces offspring) and *propagare* (to breed plants); the origin suggests dissemination. The term *propaganda* was originally used by the Catholic Church in the seventeenth century for its missionary organization, the Congregatio de Propaganda Fide or "congregation for propagating the faith."
2. In this context, the word *grotesque* suggests that the photographs are unnatural, fantastically ugly, absurd, distorted, and bizarre. It comes from the Italian *grotta* (cave) and *grottesco* (of a cave); it was first used to describe paintings found in the basements of Roman ruins during the sixteenth century, with a connotation of the fantastic or fanciful.
3. The word *sadism* derives from the Marquis de Sade (1740–1815), a French writer infamous for the cruel sexual practices he described in his novels and short stories. It denotes the tendency to derive pleasure or sexual gratification from inflicting pain or emotional abuse on others.

Responding to Words in Context

1. Perl elaborates in the next part of his sentence on the "ability to comprehend horrors we have not ourselves experienced or for which there is little or no documentation." The term "moral imagination" is related to both empathy and sympathy: our capacity to imagine ourselves in the circumstances of others. In the context of philosophical ethics, the "moral imagination" may also refer to our ability to imagine various possible actions and evaluate the possible consequences—harmful or helpful—of those actions.
2. These words—both French—are often confused. A *cache* is a hiding place or a stash of hidden goods; it is pronounced like the word "cash." In contrast, *cachet* refers to a mark of prestige, distinction, or superior status; it is pronounced with a long *A* sound in the second syllable.
3. *Pathological* refers to disease: Perl sees the perpetrators' behavior as sick and disturbed. He worries that placing such actions in the context of sociology (as well as art history and psychology) will explain away the ugliness of the behavior, frame it as a sociological symptom, or even "make it all seem somehow interesting, the material for a novel or a movie" (para. 7).

Discussing Main Point and Meaning

1. Perl argues that photographs can only "represent an aspect of the truth," even when they are accurate, unaltered, and unedited (para. 3). If the images are made public, a photograph that "represents a single act of brutalization" will be distorted by repetition in the media—repetition that is a "form of editorializing" (para. 3). Ultimately, "Islamic militants" will exploit these "true" images to "create lies about the United States" (para. 3).
2. Some social and cultural observers have tied the Abu Ghraib photographs to the prevalence of online pornography; others have compared them to the work of Robert Mapplethorpe; still others have connected the images to works by Picasso, Goya, and the ancient Greeks. Perl resists these comparisons. He argues that they dress up an "ugly truth" and bestow "catchet" (para. 7). For Perl, the images are "evidence of particular, terrible things done by particular men and women at a particular moment" (para. 8). Associating them with art only diminishes their meaning and horror.
3. In addition to its distortion-by-repetition (para. 7), TV news is "always looking for the next flashpoint": the medium demands sensational stories. But as a result, TV news "can collapse a complex story into an image that, however horrific, is only one piece of evidence in a story that is even more terrible, if understood in its entirety" (para. 7). This problem is related to Perl's idea of "photographic truth" (para. 3).

Examining Sentences, Paragraphs, and Organization

1. Students may point to specific examples of this strategy. For example, Perl begins by asking: "What is there to say about photographs we have not seen?" (para. 1). The deceptively simple question introduces the broader themes and issues in his essay—especially because he argues that these images should remain unseen by the public. In paragraph 2, he asks: "So is the Obama administration standing in the way of truth? If we do not see these photographs, are we being denied some information that we need to have now?" These questions allow Perl to frame his argument in his own terms: For example, he can answer the first one (as he does in the next paragraph) by explaining that photographic truth is a "particular kind of truth" (para. 3).

2. The writer's long, carefully developed paragraphs match the complexity and graininess of his arguments. In paragraph 8, for example, Perl discusses his resistance to those who make connections between the Abu Ghraib photographs and "various works of art." The length of the paragraph gives him room to include examples of these connections; but it also gives him time and space to reflect on them—as in his ambivalent response to Stephen F. Eisenman's book *The Abu Ghraib Effect*. Obviously, paragraph length is relative. You might point out to students, however, that all the sentences in this paragraph support and extend the topic sentence. Magazines like *The New Republic* provide an opportunity to examine complex issues in ways that briefer news stories or television reporting cannot. Notice that the writer presumes his reader is familiar with the Abu Ghraib prisoner abuse stories and images, as well as with artists like Francisco Goya and Robert Mapplethorpe.

3. Perl acknowledges opposing viewpoints: "The arguments of the American Civil Liberties Union and other organizations that support release cannot be taken lightly" (para. 2). In paragraph 4, he writes: "The argument has been made that the wide distribution of torture photographs helps to concentrate the public's imagination, rendering ideas of brutality and suffering concrete." Yet, you might point out the lack of specificity about the ACLU's claims, as well as the passive voice in the previous sentence ("The argument has been made . . ."). Perl summarizes opposing views in his own words, as opposed to citing specific language. He seems to do so fairly, even to the point of conceding the merits of some of his opponents. However, his framing of these counterarguments allows him to respond to them in ways that further his own case.

Thinking Critically

1. Perl wants to focus on the particularity of the photographs—images of "terrible things done by particular men and women at a particular moment" (para. 8). He makes a measured, almost bland statement about the possibility of "violent power relationships" being "appealing to certain individuals" (para. 7). But he equates attempts to provide any larger meaning or context with "amelioration" (para. 8). This seems

like a problematic stance. Even his own claim against psychological analysis is undermined when he refers to the "pathological behavior" at Abu Ghraib, which implies a psychological disorder. Students may connect the images to history, culture, sociology, and psychology to attempt to understand the reasons for such behavior.

2. Students' answers will vary depending on whether or not they agree with Perl. Those who do agree with him may use examples such as Obama's defense of the photos depicting torture (para. 3) and explain that these photos cannot possibly tell the whole story of the war, nor can they be sufficiently contextualized. Those that disagree may state that as long as a photo is unedited, it captures a moment of truth, and therefore cannot be disputed. Students on both sides may want to discuss media manipulation of an image, although those who agree with Perl's statements may say that the ability to manipulate images is a good reason to keep them secret; those who disagree may say that the image cannot be blamed for the subsequent manipulation and should not be withheld regardless.

3. Students' answers will vary depending on their stance, but both sides may see similar connections to knowledge, information, and democracy. It would seem that a well-informed society has a better chance of being a successful democracy, but Perl's idea that "information does not always advance knowledge" complicates that theory (para. 9). Perl seems to argue that knowledge is more important than information in creating a successful democracy, and therefore withholding information does not always negatively affect the voting public.

In-Class Writing Activities

1. While most students will define propaganda in the most historical political sense, or even equate it with "lying," students might also choose other examples: advertising, college brochures, cover letters and resumes, anti-drug campaigns, movies or TV shows with a "message," political punditry, etc. Students will most likely say that their chosen example of propaganda is ineffective, perhaps because it is too easily identified as pushing an agenda and not conceding merit to any opposing views. Propaganda is often so radical it may be hard for students to imagine it being effective.

2. Students should use this prompt to examine their own assumptions and ideas about information, knowledge, photographic truth, and the need for an informed public in a democracy. Students might respond to a specific aspect of Perl's argument—e.g., his points about "photographic truth"—if the scope of the assignment seems too broad.

3. For this assignment, students may want to consider the way they control the dissemination of their own images—on Facebook, for example. They might even look at photographs of family or friends that conceal something, or create a false impression.

Elizabeth Svokos (student essay)

Head to Head—Print Photographs

[*The Bi-College News*, Bryn Mawr College/Haverford College, November 18, 2009]

Vocabulary/Using a Dictionary

1. In the context of computers and cameras, the word *digital* refers to devices that can generate, record, receive, transmit, or display information that is represented and processed in numerical form. *Digital* derives from the Latin *digitus* (finger or toe); it took on a numerical connotation because numbers were counted on fingers.

2. The word derives from the Latin *monstrum* (monster, misshapen creature, omen, portent) and the root *monere* (warn). *Monstrosity* carries the connotation of something unnatural, abnormal, and hideous. The word seems better chosen than "deformity" or "horror," for example, which do not evoke the comic overstatement of "monstrosity." But the synonym *atrocity* might be suitable to Svokos's tone and purpose.

3. In its broadest meaning, *technology* refers to all the ways that social groups create the material objects of their civilization by drawing on subjects like engineering, the industrial arts, and applied science. It originally comes from the Greek *tekhne* (art, skill, craft) + *logos* (word, speech, discourse, theory, thought).

Responding to Words in Context

1. The word *weathered* is usually associated with objects like stone or wood, which are worn, disintegrated, discolored, or otherwise affected by exposure to weather. Svokos adapts it here to imply that old photographs are worn and seasoned.

2. In the context of her overall purpose, she wants the reader to understand the word ironically: Svokos does not think that photographs—and our experience of photographic images generally—are improved by alteration, retouching, editing, or the instant gratification that digital picture-taking allows. The quotation marks signal her detached and ironic attitude. Students might discuss whether this kind of irony can be overused.

3. The phrase *second nature* describes a habit or way of behaving so long practiced that it seems natural or innate. It can have a positive connotation when referring to a skill (driving in bad weather, for example). However, Svokos's use implies that our newer habits of mind toward photography reduce the pleasure of anticipation.

Discussing Main Point and Meaning

1. Svokos begins the essay with a literal loss: Her computer crashes and she loses all her photographs. But she moves to other kinds of losses: the

loss of entertainingly "bad" pictures in the pursuit of perfection; the loss of "weathered" physical objects—old photographs—which get passed through hands or saved in tins; a loss of spontaneity and excitement around picture taking, the "one-shot chance you get with a film camera" (para. 5). She argues that digital photography diminishes our sense of delayed gratification and anticipation.

2. According to Svokos, the bad photos—even a "monstrosity"—can become the most beloved and revealing in hindsight: "But isn't the best picture in your family album the one of your uncle looking constipated?"(para. 3). Such images result from the spontaneity and playful risk involved with printed pictures: "you just go for it, giggling, and hope no one's finger is blocking the lens" (para. 5).

3. The writer associates digital photography with false ideas about "enhancement," sterile perfectionism, instant gratification, and misplaced trust in technology. She associates print photography with authentic familial and social ties, spontaneity, the pleasures of anticipation, the bonds between generations, and the beauty of imperfection.

Examining Sentences, Paragraphs, and Organization

1. In this sentence, Svokos correctly uses the semicolon to join two independent clauses without a coordinating conjunction or a conjunctive adverb. She could have ended the first clause with a period and started a new sentence with the second clause, but the punctuation—and the breathless single sentence—help capture the spontaneity of her subject.

2. It does not matter if we know who Reyes is, specifically. Svokos presumes we can infer the subtext: Reyes is a friend of the writer's; readers can identify her as a type because we may all recall embarrassing photographs of friends. Similarly, when Svokos says she would use a bad picture of Juliana "as blackmail someday," we know that the writer was not planning a criminal act. Rather, she means the word "blackmail" in a friendly, playful way that matches the overall tone of the article.

3. Svokos begins with personal experience—her computer crashing, her memory of passing old photographs around, her decision to buy a film camera. She also ends her essay on a personal note, with the image of her mother's old photographs. But she uses this personal material to reflect on larger issues: how our relationship to photography has changed; our "world of instant gratification" (para. 4); the ways in which advances in technology do not always mean improvement. You might point out the value of connecting autobiographical information to larger themes and issues, rather than merely narrating anecdotes without reflecting on them and their larger significance.

Thinking Critically

1. Svokos writes in a style that is conversational, informal, even confessional. Most obviously, she drops into the second person: "Didn't you grow up looking at old pictures of your family and friends?" (para. 2).

She presumes complicity and intimacy with her reader: "But isn't the best picture in your family album the one of your uncle looking constipated?" (para. 3). She deliberately leaves some things unexplained, counting on her audience to understand: "Oh, that night! Where did we find a kiddie pool?" (para. 4).

2. Svokos means that we have grown accustomed to having exactly what we want immediately, without the pleasure of anticipation or the satisfaction of delayed gratification. She sees digital photography as an example of this. Students might discuss examples other than photography to support their agreement (or disagreement) with Svokos's statement.

3. The writer seems skeptical about technology, at least in her attitude toward digital photography. She implies that it severs our connection to other people—and even to cherished objects: "But now that we can't physically hold photographs, they are entirely in the hands of technology. They can be altered, enhanced, touched up, and even lost forever" (para. 7). Students may react in different ways to her skepticism about technological progress, generally, and digital photographs, specifically. Some might point out that people have been suspicious of photography itself since its invention (e.g., painters worried that photography would make them obsolete).

In-Class Writing Activities

1. For this prompt, students may argue from personal experience (as Svokos does). They could also take a more detached point of view and focus on the advantages of digital photography (or disadvantages of print photography). Svokos is nostalgic and even sentimental about the past. Students could begin with their own skepticism about her nostalgia—and about her suspicion of new technology.

2. This exercise should get students to consider not only the content or specific image, but the context around—or story behind—a favorite photograph.

3. This prompt should get students to consider technological advances more thoughtfully and skeptically, especially because our culture tends to place so much value on new technology. The examples are innumerable: cellphones, the Internet, iPods, text-messaging, etc. Students might focus on paradoxes like ways in which new devices both connect us and separate or isolate us.

Discussing the Unit

Suggested Topic for Discussion

Students may take this time to confess that they do not objectively analyze every image that they see. Perhaps they can cite an instance when photos of friends were posted on Facebook and taken out of context. Students may not have even thought about this question before because, as these sayings and "conventional wisdoms" point out, photos have long been thought to be the great truth-purveyors. And some students might still think they are. For example, in the Elián González photo, students might argue that it doesn't matter who the gun was pointed at, but simply that it was there—and the photograph is definite proof of that.

Preparing for Class Discussion

1. Of course, most people would claim to have a "hunger for truth": We do not generally see ourselves as eager consumers of dishonesty or artificiality. However, students might consider how that hunger is—or is not—reflected in their own lives, habits, and tastes. These considerations could go beyond photography—to film, television, video games, the Internet, etc. Perl suggests that we may understand the truth of the Iraqi prisoner abuse scandal better if we do not see more pictures—especially given the warping effects of the media. Svokos seems hungry (or nostalgic) for a particular kind of photographic truth, one that is best captured by imperfect print photography.

2. You might raise the question of "photographic truth" in the context of the González photograph. The image distorts and overpowers the facts behind the story, but does it capture and convey anything truthful? Or does it support Perl's claim that "information does not always advance knowledge, and photographic information in its raw form can mean many different things"? Despite the cliché about a picture being worth a thousand words, written language—used in good faith—can often provide a less visceral, more nuanced and accurate explanation of events.

From Discussion to Writing

1. There are many examples from history: the famous flag-raising photograph on Iwo Jima during World War II, Dorothea Lange's "Migrant Mother," Arthur Sasse's photograph of Albert Einstein sticking out his tongue, Eddie Adams's picture of a Saigon police officer shooting a Vietcong prisoner, the "Tank Man" image from the 1989 Tiananmen Square uprising, etc. Students may also consider why a particular image became so enduring and iconic.

2. Many students are immersed in contemporary technology. This prompt should get them to reflect on high-tech devices in the same way that Svokos does in her essay. The goal should not be to turn students into neo-Luddites, of course. But Svokos notes the way that our habits around technology can become unexamined "second nature," and this exercise should get students to think about those assumptions. You might even encourage them to consider these questions in the context of "retro" appeal—the renewed interest in vinyl records, for example.

Questions for Cross-Cultural Discussion

1. The prisoner abuse photos not only provided material for explicit propagandists and terrorists, they also sparked outrage more generally in the Arab and Muslim world. Similarly, after the September 11, 2001, attacks in New York, there was outrage when American television news networks showed Palestinians celebrating in East Jerusalem. Might a Cuban person look at the photograph of Elián González differently from an American? In all these cases, images shaped public perceptions. If the media will often "collapse a complex story into an image," the resulting distortions become even more complicated when they cross cultural borders. Ask students how they make sense of images of current events in other countries. Are they more skeptical? Do they notice a lack of context? Have they ever experienced a misunderstanding or misrepresentation of their own cultural or national background?

2. While such customs may be second nature, most of us are aware of unstated rules about photography. For example, we do not generally take pictures at funerals. If you wish to take a picture of someone, it is customary to ask that person first. This etiquette can become even more complicated when people travel. Have any students ever gotten in trouble for taking a picture? What were the circumstances? Did the rules seem sensible? Why would there be etiquette and customs around the practice of photography?

5

What Do We Fear?

International terrorism, massive economic downturns, flu outbreaks, an increasing national debt, global warming: We must face these problems and many more. But how can we react to them without giving into panic and hysteria? The essays in this unit address the problem of overreaction and fear in our culture. While their diagnoses and prescriptions overlap, the authors approach the problems from different vantage points.

In "What Should You Worry About?" Steven D. Levitt and Stephen J. Dubner begin by establishing that human beings are "quite bad at assessing risk." The writers present several "topics about which our fears run far out of proportion to reality," such as the "Summer of the Shark" in 2001, when the media overhyped the risk of shark attacks. Levitt and Dubner place real crises —like global warming—in historical context: Every generation has seemingly insolvable problems, from horse manure on the streets of nineteenth-century New York City to polio to global warming. The authors balance their dim view of our abilities to assess risk with their optimism about human ingenuity in the face of true threats: "A band of clever, motivated people—scientists usually—find an answer."

Irwin Savodnik takes a darker view than Levitt and Dubner. In "All Crisis, All the Time," he argues that Americans are addicted to overreaction. But rather than seeing overreaction as a common human impulse, he interprets it as a symptom of deeper cultural and social problems. Americans are in "retreat from reality"; they are succumbing to overemotional "mythical thinking," a practice usually "found in children, tribal cultures, and dreams." Savodnik also sees our addiction to crises as a moral problem: Increasingly, we are "acting in bad faith."

College student Erica Zucco writes as a self-diagnosed hypochondriac who's fed up with America's "Culture of Fear." Her immediate topic is the swine flu and her college's reaction to possible outbreaks. But she makes a broader argument about our tendency to "fear things we shouldn't" and not "fear the things we should." She advocates exercising good judgment, finding good sources of information, and ignoring the media's inclination to exaggerate crises.

The essays in this unit could be paired usefully with selections from Chapters 2, 8, 11, and 12. You might consider general overreaction in the context of specific issues: How does our ability to assess potential risks compare with our ability to predict our own future happiness? Do our strategies for preventing terrorists attacks seem sensible and effective, or do they suggest our addiction to crises?

Steven D. Levitt and Stephen J. Dubner

What Should You Worry About?

[*Parade*, October 18, 2009]

Vocabulary/Using a Dictionary

1. *Flu* is a short form of *influenza* (an acute epidemic, a viral disease), which comes from the Latin *influere* ("to flow into"). It is related to the word *fluent* (flowing, easy) as well as to *influence*, a French astrological term that originally referred to the presumed power that stars had over the character and destiny of human beings.
2. The word *hysteria* denotes an uncontrollable outburst of emotion or fear, characterized by crying, irrationality, laughter, or other unmanageable behavior. It derives from the Greek *hystera* (womb, uterus), which reflected the Greek belief that such disturbances were characteristic of women and originated in the uterus.
3. *Paralysis* comes from the Greek *paralusis* (loosening or disabling) from *para* ("beside" or "on one side") + *luein* (untie, release).

Responding to Words in Context

1. Levitt and Dubner do not mean that global warming is a problem in the Bible or a supernatural occurrence. Rather, the word suggests a disaster or catastrophe on a biblical scale or of an enormous size—such as the Old Testament flood.
2. The writers put seemingly intractable problems in the context of other "impossible" historical challenges, such as polio or even horse manure in nineteenth-century New York City. The quotation marks suggest that we take the word ironically: These "unsolvable" problems were ultimately "solvable."
3. Their point is that despite media hysteria (i.e., the "Summer of the Shark"), a more dispassionate analysis reveals that the number of shark attacks did not increase by much in 2001. These statistics, especially in comparison with the number of shark attacks in other years, provide the context necessary for people to accurately assess—and respond to—risks. The writers' bland headline illustrates the disparity between sensational media coverage and more empirical assessments of reality.

Discussing Main Point and Meaning

1. According to Levitt and Dubner, "economics" offers "powerful ideas and tools, along with huge piles of data, to understand topics that aren't typically associated with economics" (para. 2). The writers argue that their professional discipline provides a way to analyze data and determine real risks in more objective and realistic ways than, say, typical news coverage of issues. They also see such analysis as a corrective to our emotional responses—"fear, blame, paralysis"—in the face of crises or potential threats.

2. The authors imply that our responses to uncertainty may be hard-wired: "Uncertainty also has a nasty way of making us conjure the very worst possibilities" (para. 15). But the authors also highlight how the media shapes our responses—and not just with the sensational coverage described in their opening paragraphs. In addition to the media, our own fear can "distort our thinking" (para. 13) to the point that we can no longer distinguish between a relatively harmless "threat" and an imminent one.

3. Nearly "every unsolvable problem we've faced in the past has turned out to be quite solvable" (para. 22). According to this historical "script" (or storyline), a "band of clever, motivated people—scientists usually—find an answer" (para. 22). The writers offer an optimistic view of science and progress: The "best minds in the world" can "focus their attention" and come up with solutions to problems like global warming.

Examining Sentences, Paragraphs, and Organization

1. The writers use fragments and one-word sentences for emphasis and for transitions. For example, they ask: "So how can we find out what's truly dangerous? Economics" (para. 2). The single word heightens the sense that this answer is both surprising and certain in its claim of truth. Paragraph 2 ends with a fragment that allows Levitt and Dubner to shift from the merits of economics to the topic of shark attacks. Later in the essay, they discuss the amount of manure produced by horses: "In New York, that added up to nearly 5 million pounds. A day" (para. 19). The two-word sentence adds to the sense that this is an enormous amount of horse manure. You might note here that these writers are choosing to use these fragments deliberately. Such choices depend on the writing occasion and the audience. For example, economists can write more informally for a publication like *Parade* than they can for scholarly journals in their field.

2. In paragraph 5, which quotes the lead paragraph from a news article on shark attacks, Levitt and Dubner demonstrate how such stories heighten anxiety and encourage fears "far out of proportion to reality" (para. 10). It supports the writer's argument by showing how the media influences our fears.

3. The writers see global warming as the seemingly "unstoppable" threat to this generation, in the same way that plague or polio appeared intractable to earlier generations. Before they examine approaches to global warming, however, Levitt and Dubner first establish that human beings are bad at assessing risk and tend to worry about the wrong things, generally. The authors ultimately concede that climate change is "an incredibly large and challenging problem" (para. 23), but the overall effect of their argument suggests that people may be panicking or responding in a way that is disproportionate to the threat. You might ask students how the essay would be different if the writers began with a more direct approach to global warming.

Thinking Critically

1. Strictly speaking, the writers are unconcerned with the production, distribution, and consumption of goods and services, which is the primary focus of economics as a social science. Instead, they want to encourage certain practices and habits of mind associated with their discipline: a preference for numbers and "huge piles of data," as opposed to subjective responses or human intuition. Students will most likely see this approach as a departure from their more traditional view of economics.

2. Students' answers will vary. Many may have difficulty believing that the horse manure problem is a fair comparison to global warming, simply because the negative effects of each are disproportionate. Some students, however, may see validity in an argument like this, especially if they are predisposed to thinking that global warming is somewhat overstated in the media. The authors attempt to downplay global warming by calling it the "problem" that our generation is faced with—just like the plague, polio, or manure (para. 14). The severity of these other "problems" however, may seem small compared to global warming and its potential effects.

3. While Levitt and Dubner think people are prone to irrationality and emotional reactions, the writers take an extremely optimistic view of human beings and human progress: "human ingenuity" will trump "large and challenging" problems (para. 23). The writers especially value groups of "clever, motivated people" and scientists (para. 22). Students' answers on whether they agree with this vision of people will vary.

In-Class Writing Assignments

1. This assignment should give students an opportunity to consider not only their own concerns, but those of others: Levitt and Dubner write in the context of generational problems. Students may find other issues more pressing: economic, political, educational, etc. They might also write about misplaced fears or priorities, which would build on one of the main points of "What Should You Worry About?"

2. Students may also use this prompt to consider the "media" more generally than just news stories. Levitt and Dubner note that our perceptions can come from other forms, like movies (para. 9). The assignment should encourage them to be self-conscious about how media shapes our perceptions. Point out that the authors cite specific language ("Summer of the Shark," a paragraph from a news story) to demonstrate how writing can be part of this distorting process. Students may mention specific examples such as global warming, terrorism, plane crashes, and natural disasters, among others.

3. You might note that Levitt and Dubner are the authors of *Freakonomics: A Rogue Economist Explores the Hidden Side of Everything* (2005) and *Superfreakonomics: Global Cooling, Patriotic Prostitutes, and Why Suicide Bombers Should Buy Life Insurance* (2009). Their work brings economic approaches, principles, and research methods to a broad

range of social and cultural issues. Students may consider the study of economics opaque and difficult, even as they are aware that their own lives will be shaped by economic realities.

Irwin Savodnik

All Crisis, All the Time

[*The Weekly Standard*, November 2, 2009]

Vocabulary/Using a Dictionary

1. *Animated* means full of life, action, or spirit; its root is the Latin *anima* (life, breath). *Animated* is related to words such as *animal* and *animus*.
2. A *mutation* is the process of change, especially a sudden change, in the context of genetics and inheritable characteristics. It may also refer to the individual or new species that results from such a change or departure. Mutation derives from the Latin *mutare* (to change). Words such as *mutant* and *immutable* share the same root.
3. *Volatile* comes from the Latin *volare* (to fly). In its literal sense, *volatile* means evaporating quickly or passing off regularly in the form of vapor. In Savodnik's context, it suggests something flighty, explosive, and quickly passing.

Responding to Words in Context

1. The term, which comes from construction and architecture, is most often used in geology; it refers to shifts and forces that move the Earth's crust. Savodnik uses the word figuratively to refer to major, fundamental historic changes that had widespread effects.
2. Savodnik is drawing a sharp contrast between reasonable, civilized, and enlightened adults, who use logic and empiricism, and primitive people who childishly rely on myth, emotion, dreams, and superstition. Students might find his usage condescending in this context or they might think it represents an important and valid distinction.
3. The phrase *bad faith* has several related definitions and connotations. It means that a person acts or speaks with the premeditated intent to deceive. "Bad faith" may also suggest that one acts knowingly and recklessly in a way that is inconsistent with accepted facts. It connotes self-deception, too: In existential philosophy, "bad faith" refers to people who deceive themselves about their choices and authentic identities. In this context, to act "in bad faith" means to reject the premise that we can make conscious decisions and shape our own lives. Savodnik's use of the term draws on all of these meanings.

Discussing Main Point and Meaning

1. Savodnik's thesis is that Americans are overreacting to events and turning them into "crises," which draw upon our illogical and emotional

responses. He introduces his main claim in the first sentence, as well as the first two paragraphs. Savodnik spends the rest of the essay supporting, unpacking, and refining this basic argument. You might ask students about the advantages of positioning the thesis at the beginning of an essay: Would the essay be less effective if, for example, Savodnik began with his discussion of the worldwide swine flu epidemic?

2. For Savodnik, *overreaction* is defined by "its reliance on emotion, its episodic time frame and, ultimately, its retreat from reality" (para. 4). He acknowledges that issues like widespread Attention Deficit Disorder or climate change do have "substance" and should not be ignored. But he aims to distinguish between reasonable responses to real problems, and overemotional reactions to "strings of events vying for crisis status" (para. 2).

3. The writer refers to a number of contemporary events and issues, including the "Great Depression" of 2009, the increasing prevalence of ADD, and global warming (para. 1). But his primary examples are an overreaction to a measles vaccine in 1998 and the responses to the recent worldwide swine flu pandemic. The example of the measles vaccine allows him to look at several aspects of overreaction (e.g., the role of the media), as well as the ways such responses can make problems worse rather than resolve them.

Examining Sentences, Paragraphs, and Organization

1. The gerund phrase "denying the value of either" as the object of the preposition "about," the repetition of "is," the strange word order—all make this an awkward short sentence. You might use it as a chance to talk about style and syntax. Would it be better as: "Those who overreact deny the value of both"? Or: "When we overreact, we deny the value of both"? "Overreaction denies the value of both"? Which choice is best, and why?

2. In paragraph 3, Savodnik examines the word *crisis*, which literally means "separation, and involves a break with the past by supplanting the existing order with a new one." He then gives examples of historical changes that meet this definition, such as the French and Russian Revolutions. In contrast, the credit card "crises" or education "crises," while "substantive concerns," do not merit the label in the "strict sense of the term." In the context of his overall argument, the paragraph demonstrates that we are overreacting to circumstances that are not "real" crises.

3. Savodnik builds his argument around a series of dichotomies. For example, he contrasts real examples of "crises" (on one hand) with events or "substantive concerns" (on the other) (para. 3). He makes a distinction between "overreaction" and a "forceful response" to the swine flu pandemic. But the writer uses these oppositions to discuss more fundamental contrasts: reason vs. emotion; science vs. mythical thinking; mature responses vs. childish ones; enlightened and civilized approaches vs.

primitive or "tribal" thinking; subjectivity vs. objectivity; reality vs. dreams. In each case, Savodnik's value judgment is clear: Science is superior to myth.

Thinking Critically

1. The writer discusses the controversy around a 1998 *Lancet* article about vaccinations and autistic enterocolitis. While the article itself caused little notice, a remark by one of the authors "ignited a furious reaction that caught the imagination of the media" (para. 7). Savodnik implies that the media is prone to such overreaction; it privileges "imagination," emotion, and "crises" over the less sensational aims of scientists, who value logic, fact, and "premises that are true" (para. 7). You might ask students if they can recall their own examples of "overreaction."

2. He considers "mythical thinking" a way of "embodying our emotions and impulses in tales of our fears, vulnerabilities, and guilt in strange, often colorful, stories" (para. 9). This "regressive" view helps us deal with our dread of being powerless and allows us to "concoct magical cures for our weakness" (para. 9). For Savodnik, mythical thinking is overemotional, childish, and primitive. It is also a "flight from reality" (para. 9). But you might ask how this applies, specifically, to contemporary problems. For example, Savodnik claims that Americans have overreacted to the economic crisis of the last two years. What is "mythical thinking" in this context?

3. For Savodnik, our tendency to overreact is not an unavoidable human reflex or an unfortunate-but-excusable result of contemporary culture. Rather, it is a matter of right and wrong: "We are not mere mythmakers. We know that fairy tales don't solve the problems that plague us" (para. 10). Our knowledge that there is a clear "right" choice and a clear "wrong" choice gives the problem of overreaction a "moral dimension." To knowingly revert to childish or mythical thinking in the face of serious problems is morally wrong. Students' answers about whether a moral dimension exists in this context will vary.

In-Class Writing Assignments

1. To get started, students may want to choose a problem (current or historical) that draws a range of responses. They may also want to challenge Savodnik's stark distinction between the two approaches.

2. Students' answers will vary, but almost all students should be able to easily describe a situation in which they overreacted. Students may want to test their specific examples against Savodnik's claims about "mythical thinking." They can also use this prompt to consider a time when they underreacted, or remained unaware of the seriousness of a particular problem or crisis.

3. Savodnik makes enormous generalizations here, even as he describes his conclusions as "self-evident" (para. 11). Students might argue that the

Internet and other new media forms can connect people and make them less "alienated." They should measure his account against their own experiences and observations.

Erica Zucco (student essay)

Quit Living in Swine Fear

[*The Maneater*, University of Missouri Columbia, September 4, 2009]

Vocabulary/Using a Dictionary

1. The word originally derives from the Latin *sanus* (healthy, sane). It shares this root with the English words *sanity* and *insane*.
2. The word comes from the Latin *quattuor* (four) and *quadraginta* (forty). It derives its modern meaning—the practice of isolating people to prevent the spread of disease—from the fifteenth-century Venetian custom of keeping ships from plague stricken countries waiting in the port for forty days.
3. *Stress* is a shortening of the Middle French *destresse* (distress). It originates in the Latin *stringere* (draw tight). Words like *strain, stringent,* and *strict* share the same root.

Responding to Words in Context

1. A *hypochondriac* is a person who is excessively preoccupied or worried about his or her health. Zucco's self-diagnosis—even if she means it lightheartedly—is important because her fear of becoming ill is heightened even further by a "culture of fear."
2. Traditionally, *hysterics* referred to fits of weeping or laughing ("hysteria"). Now, the word includes more general outbursts of unrestrained emotion or fear. *Hysterical* now has the connotation of something funny or comical, but Zucco does not mean hysterics in that sense. She could have used the words *panic, madness,* or *frenzy*, among others.
3. Zucco chooses a slangy term, which fits with the informal, conversational style of her writing. Alternatives include "panicking" and "being frightened by," although the second choice does not carry the same connotation of a loss of control. Students might suggest that her wording here makes her essay seem less serious. They might also discuss the benefits and drawbacks of slang.

Discussing Main Point and Meaning

1. Zucco blames the "Culture of Fear" (para. 3). In the writer's view, the "interaction of the media, public policymakers and corporations, sometimes by accident and at other times on purpose, constantly issue widespread reports of danger" (para. 4). People tend to ignore more likely threats while they worry about sensational—but more improbable—dangers. Panic over the swine flu is only the latest example.

2. According to the writer, the media will overemphasize a "hot-issue story even if it wasn't really that newsworthy or a huge danger" (para. 4). The government may confirm these threats, and then companies find ways to exploit public fear.

3. She advises readers to "think about all of the realistic things we could be doing instead of preparing for the worst" (para. 6). She suggests avoiding the media when they create an "overblown threat" (para. 6). People should also use their own judgment and rely on trustworthy people to "discern between the actual and the exaggerated" (para. 6). She proposes that we try to avoid overreacting to overblown or irrational threats and focus on things we have control over.

Examining Sentences, Paragraphs, and Organization

1. The writer chooses a deliberately informal, conversational tone: She seems to be talking directly to the reader. Zucco's style implies her honesty and common sense amid a "Culture of Fear." Her diction is appropriate in the context of a college newspaper column. Ask students how the style might be different if Zucco was writing this essay for a media studies, sociology, or anthropology class.

2. In paragraph 5, she cites Marc Siegel's *False Alarm: The Truth about the Epidemic of Fear*. Zucco uses his thesis to support her own argument, but she does not include any specific language from the book. Her point would be strengthened if she integrated quotations from Siegel's work.

3. Zucco includes her professional background because it lends credibility to her statements about media sensationalism. Note that she uses the verb *reported* to indicate that she has experience gathering and presenting news.

Thinking Critically

1. The writer is referring to the panic and dire predictions that accompanied the turn of the century in 2000. In hindsight, the danger was overhyped. Her point might be strengthened, however, if she provided more specific evidence or examples of the overreaction to "Y2K," particularly as the media, the government, and businesses stoked public anxiety.

2. Ask students if their view is as skeptical as Zucco's. The media, in particular, has an interest in viewers and readers who are anxious or fearful: These people are likely to continue consuming media that plays upon these anxieties. Corporations can sell products (in Zucco's example, bottled water) by exploiting fear. What might the government's motive be? To increase control? To create consent or public support for certain policies? To get particular officials elected to office?

3. This question should provoke a range of responses. Students might discuss which crises, threats, and dangers fall under the purview of government responsibility: H1N1, terrorism, food safety, environmental issues,

national disasters, economic problems, etc. Is the government effective in its role? Ineffective?

In-Class Writing Activities

1. Zucco focuses on the swine flu as evidence of a "Culture of Fear." For this prompt, students will come up with their own examples that resemble Zucco's.
2. Zucco acknowledges that we "ignore the threat of more probable dangers" (para. 5). Students must discuss large threats—economic, environmental, political, medical, military, etc.—that people should be concerned about but are not. They could focus on what qualities make a threat newsworthy, or why some real dangers fail to capture the public's interest.
3. For this essay, students can choose from innumerable cultural and societal tendencies: consumerism, apathy, selfishness, patriotism, optimism, instant gratification, heroism, irresponsibility, etc. Encourage them to go beyond the obvious. They should support their generalization with specific examples. If students focus on negative qualities or problems, they should also provide possible solutions, as Zucco does in "Quit Living in Swine Fear."

Discussing the Unit

Suggested Topic for Discussion

These essays show that there are great costs for overreaction—Zucco shows the more personal side of these potential costs with her confessions about the swine flu, and Savodnik implies that we are becoming less able to reflect logically on events around us, which is actually affecting our ability to deal with threats. Students may offer ways such as critical analysis or logical reasoning to combat the sensationalized crises the media latches onto.

Preparing for Class Discussion

1. Zucco's suggestion may be appealing to some, but others may find it unrealistic. We are surrounded by media, in any case. This prompt should get students sharing their ideas and standards about what constitutes a trustworthy source of information. You might also ask if there are significant distinctions between "traditional media" (radio, newspapers, television) and newer media, like the Internet, in this context. For example, rumors and misinformation can spread much more quickly on the Web.
2. Savodnik and Levitt and Dubner take different approaches to the same general argument: that Americans are overreacting to relatively nonthreatening events and situations. Levitt and Dubner provide an example-based, economic approach to the situation, trying to logically illustrate—with figures and data—that the most feared events, like shark attacks and plane crashes, are generally not worth worrying

about. Savodnik takes a more philosophical approach, showing the absurdity and overuse of the word "crisis" in American media, and highlighting the necessity for logical thinking and reasoning, something that overreaction tends to quell. The major difference in the articles comes at their conclusion: While Levitt and Dubner have faith in human ingenuity, Savodnik seems to think that we may not be capable of coming back from this state of overreaction.

From Discussion to Writing

1. Students' answers will vary depending on their position.
2. Students' answers will vary. If they agree with Savodnik, it may be because they have experienced this increased alienation due to popular forms of entertainment. Some students may disagree with Savodnik and argue that modern entertainment actually offers quite a bit of socializing: With massively multiplayer online role-playing games and social networking sites, personal entertainment has actually become a social activity.

Questions for Cross-Cultural Discussion

1. In the case of H1N1, many countries, like Japan and Mexico, seemed to react to the "crisis" in an even more exaggerated way than America—people there wore masks and stayed away from other people—but they were also reported to have been more severely affected. It is difficult, however, to accurately analyze these events when you are seeing them all through the same American media lens. There are crises, superstitions and overreaction all over the world, but exactly what you are afraid of and how you react are most certainly shaped by your individual culture.
2. Students' answers will vary depending on their views of how "overblown" the fears surrounding cultural differences are. Many may point out that the biggest problem with creating fear of an entire culture is that it leads to stereotyping and, in many cases, racial profiling. Savodnik's idea that we are overreacting to the situations we are faced with may also fit here: There may be an immigration problem, but does that mean that immigrants are bad? And Islamic fundamentalism is behind many terrorist acts, but does that mean that Muslim communities should be persecuted? Some students may think that these connections are, in fact, warranted, and that the fear does not need to be alleviated, but others may suggest that we apply the logical analysis that Savodnik mentions in order to avoid conflict based on cultural differences.

6

How Is Today's Media Altering Our Language?

We are in the midst of a literary revolution, according to Andrea Lunsford, a writing and rhetoric professor at Stanford University. She is one of the experts quoted in Clive Thompson's essay, "The New Literacy," which argues that our writing now taking place largely online isn't changing for the worse, just changing. The writers in this chapter go back and forth on that statement. For some, the Internet has created a climate that redefines our writing and our understanding in positive ways; for others, the Internet has come between us and our ability to write well—and our ability to absorb information in an informed, educated manner.

Clive Thompson makes the case that our writing today is all about audience, similar to the Greek tradition of argument. Knowing one's audience, in his mind, holds the writing to a standard that academic writing might lack. It creates an enthusiasm and a focus previous generations never had.

Thompson would say Erin McKean is taking full advantage of the revolution taking place in the new media. Her essay, "Redefining Definition," describes how definitions and dictionaries come to be, and argues that the expansiveness of the Web can be channeled to broaden our understanding of the words we use. Her online dictionary, Wordnik.com, is already in place to begin this process. What a dictionary is will change to "involve more curation and less abridgment, less false precision and more organic understanding," all thanks to the seeming limitlessness of technologies now in place.

Rounding out the chapter, "How to Write an Incendiary Blog Post" by Chris Clarke turns the reader's attention to another facet of Internet writing: blogging. Aprille Hanson's student essay, "Stop Relying on Bloggers for News," covers the same issue. Clarke, a blogger himself, takes a look at how blogs appear to the general reader. His satirical essay points to the structures and subjects covered in a weblog, a phenomenon that has sprung up all over the Internet. Hanson chastises readers for taking the blogger's word as truth, providing data that shows the public now relies on blogs as trusted news sources. Today's media has changed the public's perception so much it would rather hear a satirist's delivery of the news than a seasoned journalist's.

Clive Thompson

The New Literacy

[*Wired*, September 2009]

Vocabulary/Using a Dictionary

1. Something *asynchronous* is out of sync, or doesn't occur at the same time. Something *synchronous* is something simultaneous, occurring at the same time.
2. *Rhetoric* comes from Greek. A *rhetorician* in ancient Greece would have been an expert in the art of rhetoric. Today, a rhetorician usually is someone who teaches rhetoric.
3. *Collaboratively* means jointly, and it is an adverb. When people *collaborate*, they work with each other on something.

Responding to Words in Context

1. The meaning of *bald* in this context is plain, or unadorned.
2. A *narcissist* is someone who loves himself (particularly his own body). Narcissus, in Greek mythology, fell in love with his own reflection in a pool of water.
3. This phrase refers to the amount of writing now devoted to the discussion of various topics on the Internet. Thompson uses the examples of "sprawling TV-show recaps to 15,000-word videogame walkthroughs." Anyone can write about anything at any length now on the Internet, no matter how ordinary.

Discussing Main Point and Meaning

1. According to the essay, we now write much more than we used to, largely because of the ease of writing on the Internet.
2. Because of technology today, Thompson says, people are writing more than ever. The Internet has created a public forum for anyone who wants to write, in the form of blogs, e-mail, and social networking sites. The resulting writing is perhaps less considered and more brief (consider status updates and e-mails vs. the letter writing that happened before the advent of the Internet), but Thompson claims more people are writing, and writing more frequently, than in the past.
3. The focus of writing happening today (outside the world of academic prose) is on audience and intention. A suggestion is made that it is a good thing that more people are writing than ever before. In the essay, this occurrence is described as a "literacy revolution."

Examining Sentences, Paragraphs, and Organization

1. Many people feel technology is destroying "good" writing. But Lunsford is an expert in her field (professor of writing and rhetoric at Stanford

University), and she is taking an unusual stance for an academic—suggesting that the writing that is taking place on the Internet does not detract from the study and practice of good academic writing in any way. Making this information evident at the beginning puts some weight behind Thompson's thesis. Lunsford's research runs through the essay to support the position that there is a "new" literacy.

2. *Kairos* is defined in the essay as "assessing their [students'] audience and adapting their tone and technique to best get their point across." Thompson states that the writing that is happening via technology today is becoming honed in a different way than ever before, with a focus on audience and the intention behind the writing. The use of the Greek word *kairos* is also relevant because of Lunsford's claim that "we're in the midst of a literacy revolution the likes of which we haven't seen since Greek civilization," connecting the dramatic changes that happened to thought and writing then with those that are happening now.

3. Midway through the essay, in paragraph 6, Thompson notes that Lunsford found that the writing taking place on the Internet shows an understanding of its audience since it is often directed to particular individuals and conversational in nature. The next paragraphs look at the students' perception of whom they are writing for and how that writing doesn't seem to have suffered any ill effects from a shift in medium. Thompson outlines some of the benefits of this writing: concision, the opportunity to write at length, and the ability to write in a collaborative way.

Thinking Critically

1. Students may believe that these forms of writing count as literacy and in fact promote literacy since so many people can participate. Others may disagree and feel that texting or other online writing is careless, encouraging writers to lose sight of the elements of "good" writing.

2. Students can imagine an audience for academic papers, and the assumed audience can help shape the tone and direction of the paper. Thompson examines the idea that writing today is shaped by the audience, because it is so public and often so directed (on a site like Facebook, for example).

3. Concise writing briefly expresses what the writer intends. It is possible that writers who text and update statuses are concise, and they could become that way with practice. However, it is possible to argue that texting and status updating, while brief, do not always cover what the writer intends, or do not cover that intention well, in so few words.

In-Class Writing Activities

1. Students will gather a good deal of varied information from Facebook. They may get a sense of a theme from some of the writing. They may believe they get a sense of the person from the writing—and it would be useful to try to describe that person based on status updates and other writing. The next step would be to try to describe the audience the person is writing for, using examples from the site. Students may disagree

that Facebook writers have a sense of their audience, and they may use examples to defend that position as well.

2. The preparation and revision students write about may be internal or may take place on paper. The essay will give students a chance to consider their academic writing and to what standards that sort of writing is held.

3. Technology is changing at an incredible pace and is changing the way we write and read. Students should research the pace and change felt by the ancient Greeks, and compare what is happening in our world with the Internet, rise of cell phones (and texting), and other technological advances. They should consider the literacy of the ancient Greeks and how they view the literacy Thompson describes in our current society.

Erin McKean

Redefining Definition: How the Web Could Help Change What Dictionaries Do

[*New York Times Magazine*, December 20, 2009]

Vocabulary/Using a Dictionary

1. When something is *primed*, it is prepared in some way or supplied with information.

2. A *lexicographer* is someone who writes, edits, or compiles a dictionary. The word *lexicon* comes from the Greek and refers to a dictionary (usually of Greek, Latin, or Hebrew).

3. The word *dissimilitude* means unlikeness. It shares its root with *dissimilarity* (noun) or *dissimilar* (adj.), both of which have to do with difference.

Responding to Words in Context

1. A *reputation* refers to how one is viewed by others and the opinion or esteem others have of one. A dictionary's reputation is established by how the words are defined and how helpful it is.

2. A book that is *abridged* is shortened in a way that still retains necessary information. Dictionaries are sometimes abridged.

3. McKean is working on an online dictionary. A colleague is an associate or partner, so McKean's colleagues would be people working together as editors, writers, and researchers on the online dictionary.

Discussing Main Point and Meaning

1. The child misuses the word in a sentence because the definition is given without context. There is a misunderstanding because the child constructs the sentence based on his understanding of the strict definition.

2. Definitions, in this essay, are shown to be limited without appropriate context. Meanings change depending on when the word is used and

how. Science implies some sort of laws or facts that govern the definitions, while poetry implies a freer, more associative or contextual way of looking at them.

3. The need to "cling to definitions" will change because the Internet provides lexicographers with more space to give examples of word use in addition to the definitions that have filled the pages of print dictionaries.

Examining Sentences, Paragraphs, and Organization

1. The examples of words and definitions clearly show the reader the power and limitations of words out of context. Without these examples, the discussion of "definition" would be too abstract. At times, McKean offers the definition first and then shows how the mind doesn't immediately jump to the word being defined. She also shows how definitions can be misconstrued. The reader is provided with concrete examples and context for the argument.
2. McKean is trying to say that words and their definitions are not meant to be seen as authoritative statements. We have come to treat dictionary definitions as "scientific pronouncements" or exact statements that somehow capture the word's "essence" or basic nature, and she wants to show another way of thinking about what definitions are and can do.
3. The phrase "According to *Webster's*" sets *Webster's* up as the overriding authority—it invests *Webster's* with a great formal power. She goes on to say that the lexicographer resists this sort of pronouncement because she knows that definitions alone should not hold that power.

Thinking Critically

1. Students may feel McKean's optimism about the Web and its "limitlessness." Or they may prefer the containment of dictionary definitions and want to argue from that position. They may have more ideas than the essay provides about how the Web can be used to build understanding of words and their meanings, or they may feel that "limitlessness" can create more ambiguity and confusion.
2. The definitions of words come from their use in context, which is something many people might not consider when they open a dictionary and look up a definition.
3. An Internet dictionary, as McKean points out, can make use of "infinite space" because of the lexicographer's ability to link to other sites and provide other ways of experiencing words without the boundaries created by paper. It can provide a more thorough experience of words and their meanings by providing contexts not physically possible in a print dictionary.

In-Class Writing Activities

1. Students can look at the format of wordnik.com and explore it. They may feel that the site is much more comprehensive than a dictionary, and they can explain why. They may also come up with ideas to expand

the site for even better word comprehension. Points of comparison and contrast with print dictionaries should be included, and examples of words and definitions via wordnik.com will vary.

2. Some students may never have used a "print" dictionary, but they may have used online dictionaries (www.merriam-webster.com or www.dictionary.com). These online versions can be used for the discussion. Most likely, students have used dictionaries for schoolwork, but perhaps some have used them in other situations. Responses will vary if students prefer to use resources that are not dictionaries. Some may try to find the words in context somehow, instead of looking up dictionary definitions.

3. Students may offer some history of the dictionary, reaching back to ancient times, but it would be useful in regard to this essay for them to examine a more recently established dictionary such as *Webster's*. They can examine Noah Webster's life and goals, the many revisions that the dictionary has gone through, and what about it has been lasting and important—what rules it established and what it includes.

Aprille Hanson (student essay)

Stop Relying on Bloggers for News

[*The Echo*, The University of Central Arkansas, April 7, 2010]

Vocabulary/Using a Dictionary

1. A *priority* is something given special attention or is highest in importance.

2. *Liberal* and *conservative* are political terms. A liberal favors progress or reform, and a conservative prefers traditional approaches and limited change.

3. *Professionalism* refers to the approach taken by someone with skill or experience in a certain field. In Hanson's mind, journalists are *professionals*, and their methods and knowledge are what creates a certain *professionalism* when they work.

Responding to Words in Context

1. *Spin* is a slang term that refers to a certain bias. When someone "spins" the news, he/she is influencing the news report in a certain direction.

2. "Platform of mistrust" is a metaphor Hanson created. She states that journalists have been placed in one area (a platform) that government finds itself on (since no one has trusted government since the Watergate scandal). She has grouped them together on a "platform of mistrust," which simply means that no one believes in what they say, as a group, anymore.

3. When someone or something is *credible*, it is believable. Something *incredible* is hard to believe or unbelievable. The words are opposites.

Discussing Main Point and Meaning

1. Hanson points out that journalists are trained for their work. while anyone can be a blogger. Journalists are required to be informed and objective about what they are reporting, while a blogger may or may not be.

2. Jon Stewart is an entertainer and not a trained journalist. In the poll taken, he comes out ahead of seasoned journalists as the most trusted newscaster in America. It is not surprising in some ways, though, because Americans have become less trusting of journalists and more likely to find their news from other sources. Stewart is also known for turning his sarcastic eye on most stories, no matter what the subject; a viewer might feel he provides a more objective viewpoint since he approaches all his work in this way.

3. Hanson says anyone can be a blogger. Journalists learn AP (Associated Press) style, interviewing techniques, how to do research, how to be objective, and are held to a standard of truthful reporting. They are accountable to people within the news organization for their work. Bloggers answer to no one but their readers.

Examining Sentences, Paragraphs, and Organization

1. Hanson offers two rhetorical questions in the final paragraph, asking the reader directly about whom we would rather trust for our news. The choices are an untrustworthy blogger vs. an informed journalist. She then states, "the answer is obvious, but the choice is yours," giving the reader the freedom to make an informed decision based on her argument.

2. The percentages highlight the startling choice that's being made between journalists and entertainers for news—Jon Stewart comes out ahead by 44 percent. The number acts as a sharper detail to bring the picture Hanson is painting into focus.

3. Hanson does not offer many examples of blogs and their lack of good information, but she does stress the difference between the potential blogger and the trained journalist. If anyone can be a blogger, the leap of faith involved in trusting him or her as a news source gets wider and more complex, just as it would if a nonsurgeon were to perform surgery. She describes the person who may be blogging the news as a "middle-aged man," unemployed, offering his latest thoughts instead of being a knowledgeable researcher and reporter.

Thinking Critically

1. Students may be able to find and cite blogs as valuable news sources, but they must offer some evidence that the bloggers are knowledgeable and/or objective about their subject matter. Others may also argue that blogs are not credible, but they, too, must provide evidence that the bloggers may not be trustworthy sources of news (the lack of credentials or an obviously biased approach may be enough to make their case).

2. Comedians can find what's funny about any subject. While comedians may be biased and poke fun only at one side of a story, they can still identify a "truth" about an event by using humor. The humor is what reveals a particular "truth" about a situation.

3. Journalists, unlike bloggers, must pass their stories through editors and "higher-ups" for review before the stories go to print or on the air. The stories can be examined for objectivity (or lack thereof) and the journalist can be questioned about his or her work *before* the general public reads it as news. A publisher or newspaper owner can create a set of guidelines for his/her journalists to look to, or create a standard for them to follow.

In-Class Writing Activities

1. Students may believe that bloggers are of more interest as news sources since the Web has made a proliferation of viewpoints easier to access. People may trust bloggers more because recent current events handled by "trusted" journalists have been communicated in ways that have eroded public trust. Examples should be provided to support whatever reasoning the student wants to follow. The examination of a particular "reporter," whether it is a trained journalist or not, should offer a picture of that person's background and field of interest as well as a description of their handling of newsworthy material.

2. Cronkite was a trusted reporter, and commentary will differ from student to student depending on what area of his reporting is looked at. Some information on the time period Cronkite was working in and a sense of the American public will be needed in this essay.

3. Students should look at topics covered, writing style, a sense of objectivity in the writing, and general layout of the newspaper for this assignment. They should make a case for whether or not it is Pulitzer-worthy (and if it isn't, perhaps give a sense of what kind of reporting would be Pulitzer-worthy).

Chris Clarke

How to Write an Incendiary Blog Post

[*Boston.com*, February 14, 2010]

Vocabulary/Using a Dictionary

1. The word *blog* is short for *Weblog* and refers to an online diary or personal thoughts of any nature published on a Web page.

2. Clarke speaks of those who have seen the *folly*—that is, the foolishness or lack of understanding—of people who disagree with the thesis of the blog post.

3. An *iconoclast* is someone who attacks traditional or strongly held beliefs (often religious beliefs). An *iconoclastic approach* would be one that goes against what is expected.

Responding to Words in Context

1. A *non sequitur* is something that doesn't follow from a premise. (It is Latin and translates as "does not follow.")
2. "To curry favor" is an idiom and means to try to gain favor through flattery.
3. Ironic words convey a meaning the opposite of the word's literal meaning. Words that are sincere are earnest or true.

Discussing Main Point and Meaning

1. Students' reactions to the writing itself may be enough to make them feel Clarke has indeed written an incendiary blog post. The examples used in the essay may be familiar enough for students to feel they know what an incendiary blog post is and how one puts it together.
2. This essay reflects on how people express themselves on the Internet, how others react to the blog posts, and how the dialogue is continued. Internet acronyms are particular to Internet writing and conversation conducted through new technology.
3. The writing in this essay is meant to call attention to itself. It is taking a hard look at how Internet writing is expressed and generalizes about that writing in a way that might make some people uncomfortable. Sentences like "This sentence is a wildly overgeneralized condemnation of one or more entire classes of people phrased in as incendiary a fashion as possible which claims to be an obvious corollary to the thesis and non sequitur" (para. 7) are examples of ones that are generalizations used to create a reaction.

Examining Sentences, Paragraphs, and Organization

1. The author calls attention to the writing and to his thought process by organizing sentences in this way. The writing feels highly structured and stylized. It creates distance between the writer and writing and between the writer and audience.
2. Students may be very confused by the self-referential nature of the sentences in this essay. The fact that each sentence begins with "this sentence" may be confusing (students will be looking for something more concrete from the writer). The sentences progress in a somewhat linear fashion, but there are leaps from thought to thought, and they often change course sentence to sentence and paragraph to paragraph.
3. The writer creates a structure for the writing that is followed through the entire essay. Readers must fill in for themselves what "this sentence" refers to. It can mean "this sentence that you are reading," but it must also connect to the sentences before and after it.

Thinking Critically

1. The writing here is abstract, but the writer uses occasional concrete examples to illustrate his points.

2. In the midst of all of the intellectual or abstract discussion of what makes an incendiary blog post, the writer must give readers something accessible and not just self-referential in the discussion. The references are to things that one might in fact find on the Internet, as over the top as they may seem. And they are things to which readers might have a strong reaction, as either funny, absurd, or offensive, in the discussion.
3. Blogs are open to public response. An "incendiary blog post" is bound to provoke response, but the author is trying to illustrate the irony of writing a post specifically for the purpose of sparking an uncontrollable response, and then trying to control that response. It shows the hypocrisy inherent in many of the blog posts Clarke is attacking, and concludes the piece on a humorous note.

In-Class Writing Activities

1. A student may better understand the purpose of the essay knowing that it first appeared as part of a blog. It may be hard to understand the writer's intent in writing the piece otherwise. The student may feel that the writing of this essay is an attempt to get a response from the reader (to find out if an incendiary blog post has indeed been written), and those responses would have appeared on the blog after the piece was published.
2. Student responses about the uses of a blog will vary and, depending on each individual's experience, the information covered in a blog will vary, too. Students may discuss the use of a blog to provoke a reader response. In this way, it is similar to other kinds of writing, but different in that the Internet provides a public forum for those responses.
3. The audience for this essay is made up of people who read Internet writing and for critics of that kind of writing. There may be others that students pinpoint as part of Clarke's audience. Students should be able to point to various examples in the essay that would appeal to such an audience. They should include that evidence in their essay.

Discussing the Unit

Suggested Topic for Discussion

You may want to ask students where they go for their news—do they agree with Hanson's assertion that they are ignoring traditional journalism in favor of a partisan agenda? What do they think makes a news source credible? How many news sources do they read on a daily basis? You can use this idea to discuss the new literacy discussed in Thompson's piece. If they get their news online, do they comment on the text? Interact with the author or blogger? If there are bloggers or Web sites that they trust more than others, have them name specific criteria as to why they trust those sites over others.

Preparing for Class Discussion

1. The writers in these essays describe bloggers as ignorant and bored, as predictable, as invested in their audiences, as people interested in creating a different version of tools like dictionaries. Answers will depend on which essays students draw from.

2. Many will feel the Internet is crucial to how they conduct their lives and may point to Thompson's arguments about the proliferation of writing on the Internet or McKean's discussion of the Internet dictionary in their essays. Others may refer to Clarke to show how blogs are unremarkable or expected. They may use Hanson to show how most people gravitate to the Internet and to blogs for their information and "truths," whether this is a wise choice or not.

From Discussion to Writing

1. Thompson and McKean are good examples to bring into this kind of essay because they support how the Internet can be used for knowledge. Students might use examples from Hanson, whether they agree that blogs are valuable sources of news or not—she shows how much we have come to believe in them as news sources. Clarke shows what we might find in blogs and looks at how we respond to them.

2. Thompson holds that writing for an audience is an example of "good" writing—and that writing standards don't necessarily vanish just because we are writing more online. Clarke exposes the writing of a blog as something we can anticipate and poke fun at. Hanson makes the distinction between the writing of trained journalists and the writing of the middle-aged, unemployed blogger. McKean reveals that dictionary writers are not simply people who have all the answers—definitions come from a variety of uses and contexts, and the Web can help further our understanding of words. Essays will vary depending on how students define "good" and "bad" writing and incorporate the authors' theses into their arguments.

Topics for Cross-Cultural Discussion

1. Students today, according to Thompson, define good writing as a way to persuade and organize and debate, no matter what they are writing about. Those who go to the print dictionary rather than the Internet dictionary might feel a lack of trust over the often faceless people who put the definitions together similar to the way Hanson distrusts the faceless people who put blogs together as a news source. People who loved Cronkite valued the person who was offering the information based on his credentials and track record while those who go to blogs for information might hope for subjectivity or a particular style (like satire) or a certain personality that comes across. (Followers of Cronkite may have been influenced by personality, too, and students should discuss how that personality might have come across.)

2. The question is whether it is subject matter and a knowledge of one's audience or something else that creates a good piece of writing. A Hispanic audience may have interests that differ from the interests of an African American audience. A Jewish audience might have different interests from a Christian or Muslim audience. Because Americans come from a variety of ethnic and racial backgrounds, interests in what's being written for the public will differ. Differences will also be apparent for those of different political and economic backgrounds.

7

Gender Roles: Should Women Act More Like Men?

In "Swagger Like Us," Ann Friedman writes, "Ever since women began making serious workplace gains in the 1970s, there has been a debate about the best way for them to climb the professional ladder." But the significance of gender roles transcends women in the contemporary workforce—and debates about the relative places of men and women (as well as their relative strengths and weaknesses) go all the way back to classical antiquity. No doubt, women have made enormous strides both socially and economically in the last several decades. Barriers remain, however. As Friedman notes, women comprised only 6.3 percent of corporate top earners in 2009. Each essay in this unit focuses on gender roles, especially conventional views of women. How can women achieve equality? In what ways do the biological differences between men and women matter? How should men and women treat each other in romantic relationships? How should women behave in the professional world?

Clay Shirky argues that women need to act more like men. In "A Rant about Women," he identifies self-aggrandizement, self-promotion, and even con artistry as distinctively masculine qualities. Shirky sees his proposal as part of a long-standing practice of crossing gender lines, as when men are encouraged to be more sensitive or women take self-defense classes: "I sometimes wonder, what would happen . . . if my college spent as much effort teaching women self-advancement as self-defense." In her essay, Friedman takes issue with Shirky's proposal, noting that women have faced a false choice for decades: Suit up in shoulder pads and be aggressively masculine or "embrace the idea that women promise to be different, somehow, from powerful men." According to Friedman, women's progress has stalled because of a "broad, cultural problem," not because of some innate biological difference between men and women. Her remedy is to "push back" against the gender dynamics that limit female advancement rather than participating in them.

In "Romance Novel Titles Reveal Readers' Desires," Tom Jacobs summarizes and discusses a study from the *Journal of Social, Evolutionary, and Cultural Psychology*. Researchers analyzed the titles of Harlequin Romance novels, hypothesizing that the language might "reflect mating preferences that have evolved over the millennia." The results suggest that "long-term commitment and reproduction are important to readers." Jacobs's tone is lighthearted, but he provides a good example of the summary form. His article should provoke lively class discussion as well.

Kim Elsesser's essay should also be provocative. In "And the Gender-Neutral Oscar Goes To . . . ," she proposes that Academy Awards should eliminate separate categories for men and women. Elsesser compares the different awards for "actor" and "actress" with the practice of racial segregation. She also argues that the separate awards have wider implications as well, as they "perpetuate the stereotype that the differences between men and women are so great that the two sexes cannot be evaluated as equals in their professions."

Shannon Morgan, a student columnist for the Boise State University *Arbiter Online*, focuses on gender roles in a more domestic sphere. She argues that we should bring a gender-neutral chivalry into the twenty-first century, a code that would "apply to any sexual orientation" and "cross cultures" as well. For Morgan, such chivalric ideals could help men and women cultivate compassionate, courteous, and committed relationships on an equal basis.

Clay Shirky

A Rant about Women

[*Shirky.com*, January 2010]

Vocabulary/Using a Dictionary

1. A *pseudonym* is a made-up or false name. It comes from the Greek *pseudes* ("false") + *onuma* ("name"). The prefix *pseudo* usually denotes falseness.
2. A *narcissist* is a person with excessive self-love or vanity. The term comes from Greek mythology: Narcissus was a beautiful young man who fell in love with his own reflection in a pool of water (there are various versions of the story from Greek and Roman antiquity).
3. A *con artist* is a person skilled at lying, dishonest persuasion, and self-serving talk; it is also synonymous with the term "swindler" or "rip-off artist." The word *con* is short for "confidence": Con artists operate by gaining the confidence of their victims, then deceiving them.

Responding to Words in Context

1. Shirky uses *gatekeeper* to label his professor as someone who controls access to something important or desirable. In this case, Warfel could facilitate Shirky's access to the college's theater program—and, indirectly, opportunities in Shirky's chosen profession. Warfel's status is essential to understanding the writer's lie. Shirky does not lie indiscriminately or aimlessly; rather, he knew that his professional future required him to get through his professor's "gate": "I can't say my ability to earn a living in a fickle profession was because of my behavior in Bill's office, but I can say it was because I was willing to do that kind of thing" (para. 12).

2. A *one-sided market* is one in which you have the autonomy to weigh options and then, as you balance "your preferences and your budget," make a choice: what to eat, where to live, etc. In a *two-sided market*, you weigh your options, but "those options are also weighing you" (para. 17). For example, your choice of where to go to college or what company to work for depends both on your own preferences and the preferences of the university or company. The distinction is important because in two-sided markets, self-promotion is a virtue—and perhaps even a necessity.

3. Shirky is using the word *lousy* to describe women's inability to act like "arrogant self-aggrandizing jerks" (para. 5). It is meant to be a bit playful—who wouldn't want to be bad at being a jerk? Shirky doesn't seem to think that it's necessarily a negative thing to not be able to act this way, but it does have a negative effect on women's abilities to succeed in the workforce.

Discussing Main Point and Meaning

1. Shirky worries that women are not as good at promoting themselves as men are. But he makes an important distinction: "This worry isn't about psychology; I'm not concerned that women don't engage in enough building of self-confidence or self-esteem. I'm worried about something much simpler: Not enough women have what it takes to behave like arrogant self-aggrandizing jerks" (para. 5). He may highlight this contrast because "self-confidence" and "self-esteem" are generally considered "good" qualities. He wants to shift the emphasis to personality traits that are necessary for success—but are not necessarily appealing or encouraged.

2. Hampton lies his way into restaurants, clubs, and affluent social circles—all the while realizing that he was taking an enormous risk. Shirky lies to get into Bill Warfel's theater design course. The writer sees the distinction as one of degree, not kind: "The difference between me and David Hampton isn't that he's a con artist and I'm not; the difference is that I only told lies I could live up to, and I knew when to stop" (para. 12). In Shirky's view, we all must occasionally take risks and behave like con artists to succeed in two-sided markets.

3. According to Shirky, it is now common to cross gender lines in this way. Colleges spend time and money teaching self-defense to women; men are asked to be better listeners or "more sensitive partners" (para. 14). You might ask if students agree with the writer that men are better than women at being "arrogant, self-aggrandizing jerks" and that women should strive to emulate their male counterparts. Does Shirky's analogy between learning self-defense and learning self-promoting behavior seem accurate or persuasive?

Examining Sentences, Paragraphs, and Organization

1. This section of the essay illustrates and exemplifies a concept that may be difficult for some readers to accept or understand: A certain kind of

lying is often necessary for personal and professional advancement. Shirky also qualifies his endorsement of temporary con artistry. He uses an example from his own life that illustrates the proper and necessary use of controlled dishonesty.

2. The writer begins his essay with a specific example of stereotypically male, self-promoting behavior. The third paragraph—and perhaps much of Shirky's essay—depends on readers recognizing that the former student is a male. If students did not guess the gender immediately, they may note that their trust in Shirky was undermined and therefore his argument was not as effective as it could have been.

3. The term *rant* implies that Shirky is writing in an exaggerated, extravagant, wild, or even violent way. But his style and tone are not "wild"; he presents arguments, makes a case, and proposes that women learn to be as good at self-promotion as men are, even if doing so requires them to become temporary con artists. He places the "rant" disclaimer at the end of the essay, reminding readers that he is only ranting; but the placement allows him to present all his ideas, and then distance himself from defending them. Ask students how the article might have been different had Shirky begun the essay by claiming he had "no idea how to fix the thing being ranted about."

Thinking Critically

1. Students may have different reactions. We generally think of lying as immoral or "wrong," but are there degrees of dishonesty or con artistry, as Shirky suggests? Does he frame his choice in moral terms? Is lying acceptable when you can "live up to" the lie (para. 12)? Some students may see Shirky's dishonesty as a necessary part of personal, educational, and professional advancement.

2. From Shirky's point of view, achieving, getting ahead, getting what you want, changing the world—all require narcissism, ego, self-promotion, and perhaps even dishonesty. Students might want to think of specific examples from history, politics, or entertainment that support Shirky's claim. Or they may find counterexamples. Students may discuss whether Shirky's statements apply to their own lives and ambitions. Is it impossible to be "forceful and self-confident without being arrogant or jerky," as he argues (para. 21)?

3. For this prompt, students may want to evaluate Shirky's stereotyping; that is, do they agree with him that women are less skilled at self-promotion, more risk averse, and overly concerned with what people think? We may think of sexism as something open and obvious. Yet, Shirky describes a subtler form, which is connected to gender tendencies: Women "wait for others to recommend them" rather than speaking for themselves; women are less assertive about raising their hands, etc.

In-Class Writing Activities

1. Encourage students to draw on their own experiences—job interviews, cover letters, college admissions interviews, applications to internships, etc. How does one play up strengths without sounding egotistical or even boorish? How does one downplay or cover over faults? They may also consider the line between honest self-promotion and lying, especially in the context of Shirky's essay.

2. In all likelihood, students have not encountered (or participated in) large-scale cons or scams. But they may have had the experience of being "taken" or lied to on a smaller scale, especially in their personal lives. They might consider how they felt or how, exactly, they were manipulated and "set up." Similarly, many students have probably engaged in minor forms of con artistry—exaggerating the symptoms of an illness to stay home from school, wheedling with their parents, trying to persuade a teacher to grant an extension, etc. What were their motives? What techniques did they use? Do they consider such behavior "wrong"?

3. Students' answers will vary depending on whether they felt Shirky successfully made his case or not. It will also probably depend on whether the student in question is a man or a woman. It is possible that students will take offense to Shirky's argument—he puts men and women into two distinct categories that students may not agree with—and if that is the case, he will have no effect on their behavior.

Ann Friedman

Swagger Like Us

[*The American Prospect*, March 2010]

Vocabulary/Using a Dictionary

1. A *mediator* is someone who settles disputes, brings about agreement and compromise, and removes misunderstandings between people or groups. The word derives from the Latin word *medius* ("middle"). *Mediator* shares its origins with words such as *media* and *intermediate*.

2. *Virtue*, which refers to excellence in conduct and morality, derives from the Latin *virtutem* ("moral strength, manliness, worth, valor"). The stem *vir* is Latin for "man" (see "virile"). These origins reveal how ostensibly gender-neutral language can carry a historical bias.

3. The word *uppity* denotes a self-important or presumptuous person who acts above his or her position in society. The first recorded use of the word is in Joel Chandler Harris's *Uncle Remus* stories, a collection of African American folktales published in 1881. *Uppity* still carries racial connotations from the post–Civil War, Reconstruction era.

Responding to Words in Context

1. Most students will be unfamiliar with *The Mary Tyler Moore Show*, a TV comedy from the 1970s. The program focused on a single, independent career woman in her thirties—a groundbreaking primary character for the time. The sentence is a line from the show's theme song. The lyric highlights the "serious workplace gains in the 1970s," even as it suggests the naivete of optimism about professional women today. You might use this example to discuss allusion more generally.

2. Friedman refers to "shoulder pads" literally; the suit of a stereotypical professional woman includes padded shoulders. The visual effect minimizes femininity. At the same time, the writer evokes the image of a football player in shoulder pads, trying to gain yardage or cross into the end zone against determined opposition. Both meanings reflect the idea that women have tried dressing and behaving like men in the workplace.

3. You might ask students how else she could have worded this. Would the sentence be as effective if she had written: "The idea that your sexual organs determine your management style is nothing new"? Friedman's wording is surprising, informal, and direct; it seems neither clinical nor precious. It also highlights the absurdity of this common assumption.

4. The phrase is from Christina Hoff Sommers, whose book Friedman quotes. Although Friedman characterizes Hoff Sommers as an "antifeminist crusader," the phrase "responsible femininity" (para. 4) sounds promising: an approving way to characterize the talents and skills of women in the workplace—and in the world. Later in the essay, however, Friedman writes, "When was the last time you saw 'responsible femininity' among desired qualities in a job listing?" (para. 6). Here, in the context of a real job search and the "real" business world, the phrase sounds naive and overly idealistic.

Discussing Main Point and Meaning

1. According to Friedman, women are supposedly "natural mediators"; they are "levelheaded" and know "how to multitask" (para. 3). They are better communicators and "kinder, gentler" leaders (para. 4). Do students agree with these generalizations about women?

2. Women can act like men in a male-dominated business world by being aggressive, demanding, and self-promoting: "if you can't beat the boys' club, join it" (para. 1). Alternately, women can "embrace the idea that powerful women promise to be different, somehow, from powerful men" (para. 3). As Friedman considers the "stalled progress" of women in the working world, she concludes that "neither of these two options is working" (para. 5).

3. Friedman thinks it is a "broad, cultural problem," rather than a matter of any one person's choices: "This is much bigger than women's individual behavior" (para. 7). While she addresses the issue as a writer, Friedman moves beyond abstraction and reporting: "I not only write publicly about

the 'byline gap' between men and women in political journalism—I actively seek out women writers and encourage them to pitch their ideas" (para. 8). Her ultimate goal is to change an "unjust system," rather than compete within it (para. 9).

Examining Sentences, Paragraphs, and Organization

1. The writer lists common presumptions about women's skills and aptitudes. Women are "natural mediators"; they "know how to multitask"; they are "more levelheaded." The repetitions build to the final sentence: "If women ruled the world, it would be more stable, less violent, and color-coordinated." She takes an ironic attitude toward these clichés—a sense heightened by the inclusion of "color-coordinated." For Friedman, the presumption that women are better business leaders than men is just another example of the fallacy that "what's between your legs determines your management style" (para. 4).

2. In paragraph 4, Friedman cites specific authors who believe that women's superior business skills have a biological basis. She lets them speak for themselves; the prominence of their books shows that their views are influential. Friedman wants to move beyond these essentialist arguments, however: These writers only reinforce the notion that "what's between your legs determines your management style" (para. 4). She engages the specific claims and specific language of those she disagrees with. Doing so allows her to show the naivete of a phrase like "responsible femininity" in paragraph 6.

3. Shirky represents the view that women should act more like men—a position Friedman finds unsatisfactory. But more important, his blog post provides a timely occasion for Friedman to make her case. She is not conjuring a controversy out of nowhere or debating straw targets; rather, she is participating in a lively, contentious, and relevant conversation. You might point out to students that writing often comes from responses to other writing—especially when we are active and thoughtful readers.

Thinking Critically

1. Friedman offers her evidence in a single parenthetical phrase about corporate top earners. She implies that the practice of acting more like men or embracing distinctly female aptitudes is ineffective or has even "stalled" women's progress, but she does not demonstrate it conclusively. The writer could provide more substantive proof—statistical trends, etc.—showing that women's progress is at a standstill; then, she would have to demonstrate causal connections between the two approaches (acting like men, embracing femininity) and "stalled" progress.

2. Friedman rejects biological explanations. Instead, she believes that "we are shaped by the society in which we live," and that "there are cultural, structural reasons why men are typically more assertive, more self-promotional, and more successful everywhere from the boardroom

to the op-ed pages to the halls of Congress" (para. 7). Students might reflect on the relationship between internal, biological differences and external, social factors in shaping the fortunes of men and women—professionally and otherwise.

3. Students might have fun with this premise or they might question it altogether (e.g., are there spheres in which women already "rule"?). Friedman focuses on positive stereotypes (e.g., that women are "natural mediators"), but what about more pejorative conceptions of women? There is a serious side to this question as well: Demographic trends indicate that within a few years, the United States will have more living female college graduates than male college graduates. Increasingly, women are primary "breadwinners" for families. Do these trends complicate Friedman's argument?

In-Class Writing Activities

1. The image of the "professional ladder" is a clichéd metaphor that students will most likely agree is still in place. Most professions require that people start from the bottom and work their way up, although there are exceptions to this, especially in more creative professions. Students may note that this idea of a "ladder" is what encourages them to work harder in school; some may say it motivates them to avoid the corporate world altogether because they don't feel comfortable with the concept. Students may also mention clichés here like "glass ceiling," "pulling yourself up by your bootstrap," and the like.
2. Friedman does not cite a specific study, and her word choice ("wary," "high-achieving") is vague. But students can use this prompt to consider their own attitudes about "high-achieving women": Why would they be "wary"? Are such women stereotyped? Do students see this dynamic at work in academic contexts?
3. Students will bring a wide range of aspirations to this prompt. The assignment should give them a chance to consider how "cultural" and "structural" factors (to use Friedman's words) will affect their careers. In some cases—students with athletic ambitions, for example—biology will play a direct role. Other professions might still carry strong gender connotations (nursing, preschool teaching, human resources, carpentry and other trades).

Kim Elsesser

And the Gender-Neutral Oscar Goes To...

[*The New York Times*, March 4, 2010]

Vocabulary/Using a Dictionary

1. *Ceremony* comes from the Latin *ceremonia* or *cærimonia* ("awe, deeply respectful ritual").

2. *Laud* means "to praise." It derives from the Latin *laudere*. It's related to words like *laudatory* and *laudable* and persists in the academic honor *cum laude* ("with praise").

3. Strictly speaking, the English does not have gender in its structure the way languages like German or French do. But since the fourteenth century or so, English has appropriated some feminine French nouns (which use the *-ess* ending) as well as added the French feminine ending to native English words. The suffix has its roots in both Latin and Greek, which use *-issa* for feminine nouns.

Responding to Words in Context

1. "Separate is not equal" carries associations of the civil rights era, particularly the 1954 Supreme Court case, *Brown v. Board of Education of Topeka*. In that decision, the Court ruled that state laws establishing separate public schools for black and white students was unconstitutional. The so-called separate but equal doctrine had been put in place by the Court's 1896 case *Plessy v. Ferguson*. Elsesser draws upon these connotations in making her argument about separate Oscars for men and women.

2. There is no strict definition of a "strong female character," but students should have some ideas about what the phrase means. Such characters might be independent, strong (emotionally, psychologically, physically), active (as opposed to passive), complex, and multidimensional. Usually, they are not helpless victims; they do not need to be "saved" by male characters. Students might provide examples. Following Elsesser's argument, however, you might ask whether we still need a separate category for "strong female characters," rather than just "strong characters."

3. In this context, *genre* would mean that movies are divided by theme, subject, and form—musicals, comedies, dramas. Other categories might include documentaries, action movies, and science fiction films. Ask students if they think this is a better way to divide the awards process.

Discussing Main Point and Meaning

1. The writer compares the awarding of separate Oscars to men and women with the practices of racial segregation—especially the doctrine of "separate but equal." Her use of the words *segregate* and *segregated* also emphasizes this analogy. In Elsesser's view, there is no significant difference between dividing these awards based on gender and giving them based on race.

2. Elsesser points out several upsides. First, she suggests that the gender divisions are inherently wrong, in the same way that racial segregation is wrong. Second, making the Oscars gender-neutral would help eliminate the stereotype that men and women "cannot be evaluated as equals in their professions" (para. 5). Third, this gender neutrality would better reflect the increasing parity between men and women in the Hollywood film industry. Last, it would reduce the length of the Oscar broadcast, "a move that many viewers would laud" (para. 8).

3. Elsesser's attitude seems to be that gender-segregated Oscars are inherently and self-evidently wrong. She also points to general progress toward equality between the genders. But she does not give an extended analysis of why the segregation endures, other than acknowledging that it stems from the early days of the awards, when women "had only recently won the right to vote and were still decades away from equal rights outside the voting booth" (para. 3). She does not take a hostile or angry tone toward the academy: The sexism appears institutional, rather than personal. Her final sentence implies that in the future perhaps having an award for best actress will seem as silly as having an award for best "directress." Would the essay be more persuasive or effective if Elsesser's tone was more indignant? Why or why not?

Examining Sentences, Paragraphs, and Organization

1. Elsesser begins with a hypothetical situation: "Suppose . . . that the Academy of Motion Picture Arts and Sciences presented separate honors for best white actor and best non-white actor . . ." (para. 1). She then moves from this hypothetical to a rhetorical question: "Why, then, is it considered acceptable to segregate nominations by sex . . . ?" (para. 2). In beginning this way, she evokes a response from her reader (repulsion at racially segregated Oscars), then ties that response to the issue of gender segregation. This analogy structures her entire argument.
2. Elsesser addresses a counterargument in paragraph 4: "Perhaps the academy would argue that the separate awards guarantee equity, since men and women have received exactly the same number of best acting Oscars." She also acknowledges that the academy might want to "preserve the number of acting awards" (para. 8). However, Elsesser does not quote any specific counterarguments, nor does she cite anyone with an opposing point of view. This fits the general idea that gender-segregated Oscars are largely a matter of tradition and custom, rather than the deliberate work of people who oppose equality between men and women. Still, she might have contacted the academy to include their view on the issue.
3. Elsesser makes her fullest thesis statement in the last paragraph of the essay: "For next year's Oscars, the academy should modify its ballots so that men and women are finally treated as full equals." When restating or summarizing the thesis, students may want to include the analogy between racial segregation and gender segregation. You might discuss the advantages of placing the thesis statement in the last paragraph. How would the essay be different if this essay began with this concluding paragraph? Would that placement work as well? Better?

Thinking Critically

1. Elsesser implies that women have achieved equality, which may be true in legal contexts. Socially and culturally, however, men and women are still treated differently. Those differences can range from disparities in salaries and glass ceilings for female executives to the persistence of

chivalry and customs of polite behavior toward women. They might also include different expectations about men and women—their roles, potential, aptitudes, behavior. Is it possible to acknowledge gender differences without creating systems of inequality? Does separation always lead to inequality?

2. The writer sees gendered awards at the Oscars as similar to racial segregation. In contrast, she accepts the separation of male and female athletes because of "biological differences" (para. 5). Notice that she does not use the word *segregation* when referring to sports. Do students agree with this standard? Biological differences do not apply to acting skills in the same way that they do in sports. However, what about cases where the distinctions are not so obvious? Several years ago, then Harvard President Lawrence Summers proposed that there might be "issues of intrinsic aptitude" that limited female achievement in math, science, and engineering. How do we distinguish gender differences determined by society and culture from those which are biological or intrinsic?

3. Elsesser emphasizes the analogy of racial segregation. Yet, she does not succeed in making the case that separate Oscars for separate genders is the moral equivalent of racial segregation (in their consequences, for example). You might note that her article appeared during the Oscar season. Is the issue important enough to be covered at some other time of year? Some students may agree that Elsesser evokes the absurdity of this separation—especially in the last line of her essay. Why is "directress" any sillier than "actress"? She also highlights unexamined biases in our popular culture and our language.

In-Class Writing Activities

1. Direct students to examples of gender-neutral language that may be second nature to them: *server* instead of "waiter" or "waitress"; *first-year students* instead of "freshmen"; *police officer* instead of "policeman." They should consider the significance of these changes. Students' responses will vary depending on their use of gender neutrality in their writing. They may bring up confusion with the fact that they are discouraged from using the phrase *his/her* even though gender neutrality seems to be an important issue. They may have examples of how they write around gender, and try to justify which pronouns they tend to use more often.

2. Students' answers will vary depending on the strong female characters that they choose to write about. Some of the attributes that students may discuss are intelligence, resilience, and determination, but they may also talk about more typically feminine attributes like compassion and generosity.

3. Elsesser reads the divided categories as an "insult," which implies that women cannot win otherwise. However, the division leads to a kind of rough equity: Male and female actors each receive the same number of awards. Her example of the "directress" may be questionable, as well.

Acting roles in movies are often determined by gender; women play female characters—mothers and daughters, for example. In contrast, there is no corresponding determination for directors. As students consider what would happen if the academy took Elsesser's advice, they should ask themselves if there are more—and weightier—roles for men in films, would that make it difficult for women to win Oscars?

Shannon Morgan (student essay)

Defending Camelot: Chivalry Is Not Dead

[*Arbiter Online*, Boise State University, February 24, 2010]

Vocabulary/Using a Dictionary

1. *Chivalry* comes from the French *chevalrie* ("horsemanship") and *chevaler* ("knight"); these French terms have their roots in the Latin *caballus* ("pack horse").
2. In this context, to be *patronized* means to be treated in a condescending way. The word ultimately derives from the Latin *pater* ("father"). It is related to words such as *patron, paternity*, and *pattern*.
3. *Antiquated* means old-fashioned, out-of-date, and no longer in use. Synonyms include *obsolete, unfashionable, antique, dated*.

Responding to Words in Context

1. In a literal sense, "weaker" might mean physically weaker. But the phrase connotes emotional and psychological fragility, as well. In this context, Morgan is using the phrase to show that women are not the *lesser* sex.
2. The word *discreet* denotes the practice of being careful and wise when speaking, as well as respecting privacy. Morgan argues that chivalrous people should be careful and thoughtful when offering criticism of their romantic partners; they should also keep such criticism and disagreement private. This fits in with the traditional idea that avoiding scandal is part of chivalry.
3. The writer is using the word *romantic* in the context of romantic relationships. You might note that romance is commonly characterized by a preoccupation with love, but *romantic* and *romance* also carry connotations of impracticality, fancy, idealism, and even a desire for adventure. Romance is associated with passion, too, yet Morgan sees chivalry—which is certainly part of a Romantic literary and historical tradition—as a "check on our urges" and passions (para. 4). Is this paradoxical?

Discussing Main Point and Meaning

1. Morgan wants to redefine chivalry so that it is "gender-neutral" rather than sexist (para. 2). She notes that the idea originates in a medieval

code for knightly men. For contemporary people, however, Morgan argues that chivalry should help both men and women cultivate "rewarding and supportive relationships" (para. 4).

2. Her writing is not specific, as she refers to chivalry as a "compass to ensure we are behaving in ways that cultivate rewarding and supportive relationships" (para. 4). But Morgan seems to mean that chivalric attitudes and behaviors will help us think long-term about our connections with others (support, commitment, affection), rather than following our instincts for more immediate gratification. In the context of romantic relationships, this appears to refer to sexual desire, but she is not specific. Morgan does note, however, that chivalry is not "spontaneous" (para. 4). Spontaneity usually has a good connotation. What problems can it cause? Why would a chivalric code prevent them?

3. Morgan sees chivalry in the attitudes and behaviors that support long-term and committed relationships—fairness, faithfulness, compassion, dependability, strength, kindness, and discretion. She also refers to the small, daily acts, like "brewing coffee in the morning, picking your wet towels up off the floor, or taking time to write a love letter or plan a romantic evening" (para. 4).

Examining Sentences, Paragraphs, and Organization

1. Morgan refers to "some women" and "antiquated gestures of chivalry," which are relatively general. The sentence could be more specific if Morgan had quoted a specific woman or even given brief examples from her own experience to support her statement; doing so would make the purpose and timeliness of her essay clearer to the reader.

2. Morgan lists some "polite gestures," which men and women both make "in situations that extend beyond the pursuit of romance" (para. 2). She then moves to a dictionary definition of *chivalry*. Ask your students what they think the distinction is between "chivalry" and "good manners." Is the difference that chivalry exists only in the context of romantic relationships, while good manners do not? Is the distinction between the superficiality of manners and the depth of chivalry?

3. Morgan's tone is serious and earnest, for the most part (rather than, say, ironic or flippant). She takes chivalry, manners, and romantic relationships seriously; she believes in decorum and discretion. Appropriately, her diction tends to be relatively decorous as opposed to slangy.

   "Chivalry should be a check on our urges, a compass to ensure we are behaving in ways that cultivate rewarding and supportive relationships" (para. 4). You might have students rewrite this sentence in a different register: "Without chivalry, we'd do nothing but hook-up all the time." Morgan wrote her article for Valentine's Day, but she is not preoccupied with the saccharine or passionate aspects of love; rather, she writes about chivalry as "respect for yourself and your lover—and the commitment to serve and honor each other" (para. 4).

Thinking Critically

1. As the writer acknowledges, chivalry has traditionally been linked to a code of male behavior toward women. She also refers to good manners, generally, as something that both sexes can practice. Still, some polite gestures have a gender connotation: giving up a seat on public transportation to a woman, avoiding certain kinds of language around women, standing when women enter a room, etc.

2. This prompt should get students to consider their own views and expectations about gender roles within relationships. For example, do the men see themselves as "protectors" of women, on some level? Do women see themselves as "nurturers"? Morgan refers to "balance": Does balance in a relationship imply equality as well?

3. Students may bring a range of definitions, practices, and expectations to these questions. You might also note the perennial complaint that people are not mannerly anymore or that politeness is a thing of the past. Do they agree? Some might argue that manners can be anachronistic, superficial, false, or inhibiting. But do manners reflect deeper truths or essential rules—about mutual respect, tradition, civilization itself?

In-Class Writing Assignments

1. Of course, people bring a range of attitudes and behaviors to their romantic relationships. But there seem to be enduring customs, codes, and rules. These questions should get students thinking about their own views—and perhaps even the views of their peers. Implicitly, Morgan writes from the standpoint of a person seeking to maintain a long-term and committed relationship. Does this seem like a particularly "feminine" point of view? Are there different "codes" for men and women?

2. While chivalry is most associated with male courtesy toward women, it traditionally includes such qualities as selflessness, religious devotion, obligations toward fellow citizens, care for the poor, and protection of the innocent. Certainly, if society moves toward less formality and more equality (particularly between men and women), that trend would undermine ideals of courtesy and decorum. But chivalry—as evident in much medieval literature, for example—helps bind society and social classes together through rules and customs. Do we have such codes now that encourage us to be selfless or protect the innocent? Where do we find them?

3. This prompt provides an opportunity for students to make their own arguments for—or against—chivalric ideals. Generally, we value qualities such as compassion and kindness, but does it make sense to see them as part of a chivalric code, as Morgan proposes? Does it seem like a practical model for romantic relationships?

Discussing the Unit

Suggested Topic for Discussion

You may want to begin this discussion with Shirky's "rant." Perhaps women are getting ahead because they are adapting "masculine" behaviors and becoming more aggressive at self-promotion. At the same time, the increasing number of women in professional positions and academic institutions might be changing the "system" in fundamental ways, as Friedman prescribes. Biological differences probably make less of a difference in white-collar careers than they do in fields like construction and manufacturing—a distinction that made blue-collar work implicitly masculine. So is it possible that women—with their corresponding stereotypes as good communicators and social connectors—might be better suited to dominate the business and professional world? Conversely, what qualities—whether determined by biology or culture—might be causing men to lag behind?

Preparing for Class Discussion

1. For this prompt, try to get students to move beyond the obvious topical descriptions (e.g., "gender," "men and women") to more subtle inferences and thematic patterns that allow for debate and discussion. For example, the essays address gender differences, but they also investigate the origins of these differences, attempt to highlight the consequences of these differences, and (most important) recommend ways of managing these differences equitably—e.g., Shirky argues that women should act more like men, while Elsesser argues for gender-neutral Oscars as a way eliminating gender disparities. You might also encourage students to look for two essays that might play well off each other. Friedman and Shirky are an obvious choice, but Jacobs's report on romance novels would also pair well with Morgan's analysis of chivalry.

2. In some of the essays, the stereotypes are obvious. Shirky refers to male tendencies toward self-promotion and con artistry; Jacobs tries to analyze the desires of women through the lens of romance novels. Even Morgan's column about chivalry elevates values like long-term commitment, supportive relationships, and nurturing—characteristics that are often associated with women. At the same time, students might quibble with Shirky's assertions: Are there stereotypes of conning, deceitful, or self-aggrandizing women as well?

From Discussion to Writing

1. Students' responses will vary depending on their opinion. Shirky and Friedman both present arguments about what women would have to do in order to achieve workplace equality, and students may base their answers to this question on which author they thought made a more compelling argument. Students who agreed with Shirky may think that equality is attainable as long as women start acting more like men, while those who were more persuaded by Friedman might think that

equality may not be attainable in the near future because her idea—changing the system itself—is more daunting than changing individuals' behavior.

2. Students' answers will vary based on their opinions and their gender. There will most likely be students who do not feel that their gender has limited them in their career choice or path thus far, but that does not mean they will not be affected in the future. Students may want to talk about the gender make-up of their classes, why they chose their major, or even their particular school.

Topics for Cross-Cultural Discussion

1. Gender is already a sensitive topic for students. Religious and ethnic differences can heighten that sensitivity, so approach these questions with respect and care. Remember, suspending judgment and remaining civil does not mean that you cannot hold an opinion—even a strong opinion. But tolerance and open-mindedness require us to test our ideas against contrary ideas and arguments. The point of this prompt is not to arrive at a bland, everyone-is-right consensus or (alternately) elevate a single view of men and women as "correct." Rather, the questions should give students a chance to understand how their opinions and ideas have been formed—and how they may continue to change.

2. The essays provide a range of views on this dichotomy. Friedman, for example, views gender as something "shaped by society" rather than purely biological; Elsesser wants to eliminate the distinction related to awards between male and female actors—and, implicitly, that distinction as it applies to other professions. Jacobs's essay suggests that these differences may be hardwired and "natural." Do writers like Friedman and Elsesser seem to want a "genderless" society? Are there definite "male" and "female" qualities that need to be maintained? Why or why not?

8

Does Our Need for Security Threaten Our Right to Privacy?

The years since the terrorist attacks of September 11, 2001, have brought an increased awareness of safety and security issues. Umar Farouk Abdulmutallab's 2009 unsuccessful attempt to blow up a Northwest Airlines flight from Amsterdam to Detroit, as well as Faisal Shazad's 2010 failed car-bomb attack in Times Square remind us that real threats persist—as do questions about the best way to prevent such attacks. How do we maintain security without infringing on people's privacy or civil liberties? To what degree is the federal government capable of protecting us? What role should ethnic and racial profiling play in our security efforts? How do we distinguish between effective safeguards and mere "security theater"?

That last question animates Jeffrey Rosen's essay "Nude Awakening." He argues that highly touted, new body-scanning machines at airports not only raise major privacy concerns, but also provide a false sense of security: "The next plot rarely looks like the last one. But, if we need to waste money on feel-good technologies that don't make us safer, let's at least make sure they don't unnecessarily reveal us naked." In "New Airport Policy: Grin and Bare It," Connie Schultz takes the opposite view—and a more lighthearted approach. Privacy concerns about these new scanners are overblown, according to Schultz. She sees those who distrust the government's travel-safety measures as a laughable "cast of angry Americans"; for her, their skepticism is unfounded, given that they trust the state to provide safety in so many other areas of their lives.

Student writer Mohammed Khan focuses on the pervasiveness—and ineffectiveness—of racial and ethnic profiling. He notes that such profiling would have likely missed the 2001 "shoe bomber" Richard Reid, as well as Umar Farouk Abdulmutallab. Khan also writes from personal experience, having been detained at Chicago's O'Hare Airport apparently because of his name. He argues that while the "need for safety is paramount," security protocols must adapt to meet a terrorist threat that is always changing and evolving.

Jay Griffiths's "The Tips of Your Fingers" discusses border crossing, biometric identification, and the meaning of privacy. Her essay has a much broader scope than the others in this unit. While Rosen, Schultz, and Khan focus on airport security, Griffiths meditates on individualism, modernity, art, and spirituality. She is less interested in government competence or the nature of terrorist threats than she is in more fundamental questions about identity and the reach of the state.

Jeffrey Rosen

Nude Awakening

[*The New Republic*, February 4, 2010]

Vocabulary/Using a Dictionary

1. *Enthusiastic*, which means passionate, devoted, or excited regarding an interest or pursuit, comes from the Greek entheos (*en*- "in") + (*theos*- "god"): inspired or possessed by a god. In the seventeenth and eighteenth centuries, the word had a negative connotation related to excessive emotion or religious zeal.
2. *Contraband* means illegal goods, especially in the context of trade importation or exportation. It derives from the Latin *contra*- ("against") + the Italian *bando* ("law").
3. *Hypothetical* comes from the Greek *hypo*- ("under") + *thesis* ("proposition"), meaning the basis of an argument, especially something taken as true for the purposes of argument or investigation. It is related to the words *thesis* and *hypothetical*.
4. *Ephemeral* means short-lived and fleeting. It originates from the Greek word *ephemeros*: lasting only one day.

Responding to Words in Context

1. To "mince words" means to sugarcoat, euphemize, or otherwise blunt language so that it remains inoffensive or hides more straightforward facts or truths. Here, Rosen implies that those who support the use of body scanners might downplay or avoid the reality that the scanners are a "virtual strip search," while he (in contrast) is more honest in his assessment.
2. The word *rogue* suggests a person—in this case, a government official—operating outside the bounds of laws or rules. It connotes unpredictability and even destructiveness.
3. The adjective *feel-good* is often used to describe movies that leave viewers with a pleasant feeling. In this context, "feel-good technologies" suggests sophisticated devices that make people feel safe and secure, while not actually providing substantive safety or security.

Discussing Main Point and Meaning

1. Rosen argues that the machines are an example of "security theater," which gives people the "illusion of safety without actually making us

safer" (para. 3). They cannot detect lower-density explosives, nor can they detect explosives hidden in body cavities. In addition to being ineffective, they require people to sacrifice privacy—and pose a "serious threat to the dignity" of many people traveling in the United States (para. 7).

2. According to Rosen, the scanners constitute a "virtual strip search" (para. 7). He cites the customs of certain Muslim sects, which "forbid men from gazing at Muslim women unless they are veiled" (para. 7). His greatest privacy concern, however, is that images may later be leaked (para. 8) or used by "rogue officials" (para. 8). Because the Transportation Security Administration is "free of independent oversight, it's impossible to tell precisely how [the scanners are] being used" (para. 5).

3. There are scanners "with an alternative design that is more sensitive to privacy" (para. 4). They allow images to remain anonymous and ephemeral. Rosen suggests that President Barack Obama—with a "few simple technological and legal fixes"—authorize the use of "blob machines" instead of "naked machines" (para. 9).

Examining Sentences, Paragraphs, and Organization

1. The quotation points to a balance between two competing values: the need for aggressive security measures and the need to respect privacy. In citing the president's specific words, Rosen suggests that Obama needs to institute policies in line with his own stated goals and values. In the context of Rosen's essay, that means requiring the use of "blob machines" instead of "naked machines" (para. 9).

2. Rosen deliberately argues against popular wisdom. He implies that many people are reacting emotionally, especially "in the wake of the failed Christmas bombing of Northwest Flight 253" (para. 2). But according to Rosen, a closer, more rational analysis of the full-body scanning machines and their implications reveals that they are merely "security theater" (para. 3). The main point of his essay is to get readers to think more carefully and thoughtfully about their security and their privacy, rather than reflexively embracing "feel-good technologies" (para. 9).

3. The opening paragraph recounts an airline passenger following the instructions of an airport security officer, even as the passenger remains unaware that "TSA officials in a separate room were staring at a graphic, anatomically correct image of his naked body" (para. 1). The anecdote evokes the themes of unawareness of—and "surrender" to—technological authority continued throughout the essay. But Rosen uses the indignant words of the TSA official at the gate to contrast with the general acceptance of these machines in the wider public: "Someone ought to do something about those machines—it's like we don't have any privacy in this country anymore!" (para. 1). The outburst allows the writer to move from personal observation to the broader issues in the essay.

Thinking Critically

1. Rosen relies on a limited number of sources: polling from *USA Today*, information from the TSA Web site, personal observation, an unnamed member of the British Parliament, and the words of officials and ex-officials such as Barack Obama and former Department of Homeland Security director Michael Chertoff. The writer also seems to be influenced by the thinking of Bruce Schneider, who is quoted but identified only as a "security expert" (para. 3). The article might have benefited from a more thoroughly sourced explanation of how the scanners are a "waste of money" (para. 9), as well as more direct and explicit engagement with those who support the use of the machines.

2. Most people would agree that people's privacy should be protected and that these images should not be "leaked." But Rosen builds his argument on the notion that a celebrity image will inevitably be sold "to the tabloids" (para. 8). He also refers to the possibility of "rogue officials" misusing the scanners' databases, citing the example of Erroll Southers, who searched confidential criminal records to impugn his estranged wife's boyfriend. Despite Rosen's implications to the contrary, however, Southers's example is not directly related to the scanners and may not support his point. Rosen's argument might be more effective if he addressed specific people who are willing to accept the risk to their privacy.

3. Rosen's article presents a skeptical view of the TSA, from the opening paragraph in which a TSA official refuses to describe the image on the scanner, but then blurts out his privacy concerns. He implies that the agency is complicit in the practice of "security theater," which does not actually keep people safe. He also notes that they operate "free of independent oversight," so "it's impossible to tell" exactly how the scanners are being used (para. 5).

In-Class Writing Activities

1. Students' answers will vary depending on their experience and views on privacy, but many may use personal experience to back up their claims. Most students will have experience with airport security, some even with the body-scanners that Rosen describes. It could be interesting to hear their perspective since many students may not have known airports before this heightened level of security.

2. Rosen clearly takes a suspicious and even cynical view of the TSA. This assignment should encourage students to reflect on their own attitude toward government authority in the context of national security: Do they trust officials to make the right choices, act wisely and efficiently, with respect for both the privacy rights of citizens and also our need to remain secure? They may also broaden their scope beyond issues of terrorism and airport security: Do government agencies usually take care of the public interest?

3. Rosen provides no explicit examples in his own essay, but students may be able to propose some of their own—for example, in the contrast between the phrases "necessary security procedures" and "virtual strip searches." They might also consider how people soften or blunt their language when discussing (or arguing about) other potentially controversial subjects: abortion, torture, gay marriage, race, etc.

Connie Schultz

New Airport Policy: Grin and Bare It

[*Cleveland Plain Dealer*, January 10, 2010]

Vocabulary/Using a Dictionary

1. The word *privacy* comes from the Latin *privatus* ("set apart, belonging to the individual rather than the state") and *privare* ("to separate or deprive"). The word is related to terms such as *deprived* and *privilege*.

2. In its contemporary meaning, *visa* refers to an official endorsement on a passport that authorizes the bearer of the passport to enter or travel legally in a country. The term originally comes from the Latin *videre* ("to see") and the French *charta visa* (paper that has been seen).

3. The word *violation* means an infringement or the breaking of a law, but it also connotes desecration, disrespectful treatment, and even sexual violence. It originates in the Latin word *violare* ("to treat with violence") and shares its origins with words such as *violent* and *inviolate*.

Responding to Words in Context

1. We tend to think of a "travel accessory" as some harmless object—a piece of luggage or a child safety seat. Schultz uses understatement and irony to describe hidden explosives as a "travel accessory." She makes light of a serious subject, but then moves in the same sentence to the more substantive claim that such an accessory "probably would not make it through a full-body scanner" (para. 5).

2. The writer argues that the news media sensationalizes the full-body scanners by referring to "graphic images" when the images are (in Schultz's opinion) not graphic at all. Similarly, the "brave" and "courageous" volunteers demonstrating the machines are not actually acting bravely or courageously; rather, they are participating in a manufactured controversy. The quotation marks indicate that the writer is being ironic.

3. In paragraph 2, the word refers to the supposedly controversial and "graphic" images displayed on the full-body scanners in airports. She states (humorously) that the bodies of her readers have "more bumps and bulges than the Appalachian foothills" (para. 3). At the end of the essay, the image remains comic. Rather than referring to the out-of-

shape physiques of airport travelers, however, the humorous image now becomes that of people who trust the government to regulate innumerable other aspects of their lives, but not airport security.

Discussing Main Point and Meaning

1. Schultz believes that the scanners are an improvement over standard metal detectors, which failed to stop Umar Farouk Abdulmutallab. But she also makes a broader argument that we should generally trust the government to provide safety and security. Additionally, most of her essay focuses on the spuriousness—and even absurdity—of arguments against using the new machines.

2. Schultz does not believe the images are truly an invasion of privacy in the first place. But in paragraph 10, she notes that the screener who waves passengers through the scanner is not the same person who sees their computer images; she also points out that the images are immediately deleted and cannot be stored or shared in any way. TSA officials are not allowed to bring cell phones or cameras into the room where the scanning takes place. You might ask students whether these precautions seem thorough enough.

3. Schultz makes several generalizations about those concerned by the new scanners. In paragraph 4, she suggests that those who worry about the images being pornographic have "issues." She refers to the American Civil Liberties Union, which (according to Schultz) argued against the use of the machines by "champion[ing] the rights of celebrities" who "regularly expose themselves for money and attention" and consequently "don't make the best victims" (para. 12). The writer also points to the "usual cast of angry Americans who insist you can't trust the government" (para. 13). According to Schultz, these people trust the government in many other aspects of their lives, so their opposition to the scanners is "curious" and (implicitly) illogical.

Examining Sentences, Paragraphs, and Organization

1. Students should recognize elements in the essay that are informal and comic. For example, Schultz uses a sentence fragment (para. 6) and slangy diction like "c'mon" (para. 15). In addition to her sustained irony, the writer relies on hyperbole: "Now we're talking about how Grandma should be able to keep her waist-highs to herself" (para. 12). She pokes fun at celebrities (who "probably don't make the best victims"), as well as the "usual cast of angry Americans" (para. 13). Schultz even places a would-be terrorist in a comic light: "Not exactly Secret Agent Man" (para. 6). You might ask students if they think the topic deserves a more serious tone.

2. In particular, her choice to use the second person allows her to address the reader directly and conversationally—even in the first sentence of the article. But her transitions are effective as well. After she discusses the "usual cast of angry Americans" who do not trust the government

(para. 13), she shifts to the second-person plural ("We" in paragraph 14), and then asks her readers a question in the second person: "So, c'mon, you're going to stand there and tell me you don't trust the government?" (para. 15). The grammar here carries a sense of immediacy, as well as the implication that it would be absurd to disagree with the writer's logic.

3. The writer addresses implicit claims and counterarguments that the images of "virtually nude, lumpy" (para. 2) airline passengers are prurient or sexually suggestive. She characterizes such views as absurd, suitable only to those whose "sexual fantasies steer toward cartoon characters and robots" (para. 4). This dismissal supports her point that the machines are not a real threat to privacy—and her goal of "making light" of the controversy (para. 4). The sentence also implies that those outraged by—or concerned about—the scanners for such reasons are ridiculous.

Thinking Critically

1. The writer relies upon personal observation. For example, she dismisses the notion that the images are graphic by claiming, "I saw these computer-generated images close-up and personal last summer . . ." (para. 4). Schultz also makes a qualified statement about the effectiveness of the machines, stating that a person carrying explosives (such as Abdulmutallab) "probably would not make it through a full-body scanner" (para. 5). Students might note that more substantive evidence that the machines work better than metal detectors or other devices would improve her argument.

2. Schultz cites no specific counterarguments, choosing instead to generalize—perhaps to the point of engaging in an "Appeal to Ridicule" fallacy. Schultz might have included a particular example of an argument she finds specious or unpersuasive, rather than using such a broad approach. Her characterization of the ACLU's opposition to the scanners appears exaggerated and perhaps unfair as well (para. 12). Students might investigate the degree to which the writer caricatures the organization's position.

3. Schultz uses analogies to get her point across, but often her main purpose seems to be humor. For example, her arguments that "lurking under what's left of your clothing are more bumps and bulges than the Appalachian foothills have" (para. 3) and that the images created by the monitors "are not pornographic unless your sexual fantasies steer toward cartoon characters and robots" (para. 4) serve not only to show that the airport scanners are not dangerous, but that people are severely overreacting to them. She finds humor in a situation that many, like Rosen, find incredibly disturbing. Whether students think these analo gies are successful will vary, but most will probably concede that they are entertaining, whether they agree with Schultz's point or not.

In-Class Writing Activities

1. After September 11, 2001, the threat of terrorism became far more vivid and prominent in our society. The possibility remains a serious and persistent concern; at the same time, the likelihood of any particular American dying in a terrorist attack remains statistically low, compared to other threats (car accidents, etc.). Students' answers will vary depending on their own experiences and beliefs.

2. Schultz generalizes broadly about attitudes toward government competence and its ability to keep us secure. Students should consider her logic carefully: We trust the government when it comes to paving roads or licensing drivers, therefore, we should probably trust it in the case of airport security. This assignment might also be an opportunity to investigate how much trust in the authority of the state is unexamined and taken for granted.

3. This question should encourage students to evaluate how they balance issues of safety, privacy, and trust in the government. Schultz notes that the TSA is ordering hundreds of the scanners over the next year; it appears that they will soon become standard. Do students think that the machines have been adequately evaluated for their effectiveness and their privacy safeguards? What choices would students have if they believed their privacy was being compromised?

Mohammed Khan (student essay)

The Need for Safety Is Paramount

[*The Daily Evergreen*, Washington State University, January 13, 2010]

Vocabulary/Using a Dictionary

1. *Feasible* means capable of being done or accomplished. Its roots are in the Latin *facere* ("to do, perform").

2. *Paramount* means "most important" in Khan's sentence. It comes from Old French, *par* ("by") + *amunt* ("up") and the Latin *per ad montem* ("to the hill"). *Paramount* is sometimes confused with *tantamount*, which means "equivalent."

3. In this context, *protocol* denotes a code of correct conduct or procedures. The word originally comes from the Greek *protokollon* ("first sheet glued onto a manuscript, table of contents"). You might note the prefix *proto* refers to "first" or "primary" in other words, as well: *prototype, protoplasm.*

Responding to Words in Context

1. Even before the attacks of September 11, 2001, these terms were contested. The language we assign to people has consequences: foreign and domestic terrorists or "enemy combatants" may have different legal

status than, say, soldiers from a foreign military. Students will have different ideas of how to define a *terrorist* or *terrorism*, but most will agree that terrorism cannot be directly linked to a recognized state or government.

2. *Racial profiling* refers to the use of a person's race or ethnicity by law enforcement or security officials as a factor in deciding whether to investigate that person or engage in enforcement (search someone at an airport security checkpoint, make a traffic stop or arrest). The term can carry racist connotations, e.g., the presumption that some races are more likely to commit crimes and therefore more likely to be stopped by police.

3. In its precise meaning, *strategy* refers to large-scale, long-range, "big-picture" planning, especially military planning during both peace time and war time. In contrast, *tactics* denotes the deployment of specific troops, devices, or procedures in carrying out such plans. Khan uses the term correctly: Airport screenings are ostensibly a tactic in a broader, strategic campaign to reduce the threat of terrorism.

Discussing Main Point and Meaning

1. Khan argues that racial profiling is ineffective and impractical, and that we must instead emphasize "intelligence-based" tactics such as full-body scanners. Despite concerns about these techniques, the need for security is paramount and must ultimately override concerns about privacy. You might point out that Khan frames his argument in a way that implies a false choice: "An enormous amount of evidence indicates racial profiling is not sufficient to protect us from terrorists" (para. 2). Ask your students: Is anyone arguing that racial profiling—alone—is "sufficient to protect us from terrorists"? Might profiling be just one part of an overall strategy?

2. For Khan, Reid and Abdulmutallab demonstrate that (presumably) conventional ethnic profiling methods are ineffective. Reid is half English, half Jamaican; Abdulmutallab is Nigerian and comes from an affluent English family. Neither fits the ethnic profile of an Arab, Iranian, or Pakistani. Ask students if we can draw broad conclusions about profiling from these two examples.

3. Khan writes that discomfort with "invasive" security procedures is "understandable" (para. 6). After conceding that new protocols must "address people's qualms," he proposes that those who are uncomfortable with body-scanning machines come to the airport early so they can undergo a "thorough search" from security officials. You might note that such searches could raise other privacy concerns. But for Khan, safety, not privacy, is "paramount."

Examining Sentences, Paragraphs, and Organization

1. Khan believes that profiling is part of a "facade": a superficial, illusory, or false appearance of safety and security. Instead, he proposes

"intelligence-based" measures, like full-body scanners. Some students may note that the use of "intelligence" here is ambiguous—Khan could either be referring to being smart and informed, or he could be referring to "intelligence" in its security and military context. This reading could affect how a student answers the question. In terms of a contrast, Khan is trying to illustrate that intelligence, not racial profiling, would have been effective in stopping the Christmas day bombing attempt by Umar Farouk Abdulmautallab—he was not Arab, he was Nigerian, and therefore not targeted for racial profiling.

2. Rather than just referring to "many people" (a generality), Khan could have cited a specific example or quoted a person with a particular privacy concern. A quotation (from a news source, for example) would allow his argument to move from the general to the specific. It could also provide his column with a more explicit connection to the timely and ongoing public conversation about terrorism and security issues.

3. When Khan writes about the ineffectiveness of profiling, he does so from experience. He was held at the airport for two hours—in large part, because of his name. The example supports his overall point. Note that the anecdote is subtle, given its placement: Many arguments against profiling are based on the idea that stereotyping is wrong and dangerous. But Khan focuses on the ineffectiveness of profiling, rather than making a moral argument about racism or civil liberties.

Thinking Critically

1. Khan writes that determining individual religious beliefs is difficult. Additionally, Muslims comprise "more than one-fifth of the world's population" (para. 3). Notice that he emphasizes that profiling all Muslims would be ineffective or impossible, rather than making a moral argument about the "rightness" or "wrongness" of profiling.

2. Khan does not delve deeply into the specifics of privacy concerns or "qualms" about privacy. However, he acknowledges that "privacy infringements" raise "important questions" (para. 6). What might those questions be? What concerns do students have?

3. While he refers to an "enormous amount of evidence," Khan does not cite much of it in his essay. He relies primarily on the examples of Reid, Abdulmutallab, and himself. He could strengthen the argument by citing expert sources, airport security workers, or scholarly research on the subject.

In-Class Writing Activities

1. Students should use this prompt to reflect on their own images and presumptions about terrorists and terrorism. As the backgrounds, goals, nationalities, ethnicities, and religions of terrorists can vary, students may want to explore current research on the topic and measure their assumptions and impressions against more empirical data.

2. Khan's essay provides an excellent basis for a response, either pro or con. If students agree with his claim that racial profiling is not sufficient to protect us, they may want to elaborate on the moral and legal aspects of racial and ethnic profiling. If students disagree, they might highlight the dichotomy implicit in Khan's column: Racial profiling, on its own, is "not sufficient to protect us from terrorists," but perhaps the practice—if used in a limited and careful way—could have some place or value.
3. This prompt will give students the chance to consider their own fears—or lack thereof—in (to use Khan's words) "this age of global terrorism" (para. 1). How did they react, for example, to Faisal Shahzad's failed attempt to attack Times Square with a car bomb? Do they trust the U.S. government to keep citizens safe? Do they agree with Khan's emphasis on safety over privacy?

Jay Griffiths

The Tips of Your Fingers

[*Orion*, January/February 2010]

Vocabulary/Using a Dictionary

1. An *idiosyncrasy* is a characteristic, habit, or mannerism that is peculiar to an individual. Deriving from the Greek *idios* ("one's own"), the word is related to terms such as *idiom* or *idiot*, as Griffiths notes in her seventh paragraph.
2. The writer's usage suggests not only the psychology or mind of a person (which is the common contemporary usage), but also the human spirit or soul. The word comes from Greek and Roman mythology: Psyche was a beautiful girl loved by Cupid. As a Latin and Greek noun, the term means "soul, mind, life, or animating spirit of the body."
3. *Panopticon* derives from the Greek *pan* ("all, everything") + *optikon* ("sight"). It denotes an object that is all-seeing.

Responding to Words in Context

1. Here, *diviners* suggests that fingertips have the power of prophecy, insight, and intuition. The word connotes a god-like power to reveal the self—and achieve a transcendent connection with others.
2. The term *cache* refers to a secret space for hidden valuables. Griffiths is especially tuned to the sound of her words. *Cache* evokes a small, soft, inner "tenderness" or space: the "sh" sound connects it with the word *shelter* in the same sentence, which is an example of consonance.
3. *Individuation* is the act or process whereby social individuals become different from one another. *Individuality* refers to the specific character or qualities that distinguish one person or one thing from others.

Discussing Main Point and Meaning

1. Griffiths sees biometrics and national ID cards as a threat to individuals on different levels. For example, in the context of border protection, she states that practices like identification and tagging are "used to intimidate those at the margins, the borders of society": refugees, political dissidents, protesters, and people who threaten dominant cultures of "intolerant homogeneity" (paras. 4–5). They become a tool for modern surveillance, which encourages conformity and political docility. Such identification and surveillance practices also allow the "state" to cross into the inalienable, idiosyncratic, and personal spaces of our private selves—an "ugly act" (para. 10).

2. The writer sees the "state's assault" as part of larger and interconnected trends toward homogeneity. Such forces support "monoism, destroying variety from biodiversity to linguistic diversity" (para. 5). They range from our food and our politics to our entertainment: "Like the monoculture of Hollywood and the monocrops of agribusiness, the monopolitics of world powers erase the particular . . ." (para. 5). The contrast is between individuality and diversity on one side, and "monoism" on the other.

3. For Griffiths, state intrusions into the "private self" are "ugly," especially when they are enforcing boundaries at the expense of the marginalized and the idiosyncratic. She contrasts such intrusions with a different kind of border crossing: the "self reaching outward," which is an "act of beauty and transcendence" (para. 10). Such acts seek to escape the "confines of the single self" and connect with others (para. 10). Humans find "benevolence" in these border crossings. In Griffiths's view, art, spirituality, environmentalism, and movements for social justice all partake of this benevolent transcendence.

Examining Sentences, Paragraphs, and Organization

1. Students should be able to point to several examples of her stylish, figurative, and sonorous prose. For example, Griffiths uses rhyme to refer to those who stand out for their beliefs, "who poke and provoke with the demeanor of a pitchfork in the cutlery drawer" (para. 4). She is fond of alliteration: "These laws of life agree with the law of love . . ." (para. 14). Such rhetoric can be powerful, persuasive, and even dazzling to readers. At the same time, her claims and arguments can be more poetic and associative than strictly logical; sometimes, they are not clear: Who, exactly, are the "insane with their flashes of specific mind-lightning" (para. 4) and how, exactly, do they pertain to her main point? In a larger sense, a practical reader might also wonder how the "perennial philosophy of a universal oneness" (para. 11) might be reconciled to the more prosaic, real-world concerns of patrolling national borders.

2. Griffiths traces the etymology of the words *private* and *idiot* in paragraphs 6 and 7, respectively. She uses the original meaning of the terms to reinforce the idea that most people today are "deprived of public

life" (para. 6) and must be "purely private persons," as if governments preferred "their subjects to remain idiots, disengaged from the state's process but suffering its intrusions" (para. 7). The etymologies do not "prove" her point on their own, but these linguistic recoveries do reveal and reinforce her notion that citizens are increasingly deprived of connection and political power.

3. Griffiths begins with a practical example of people searing their fingers to get through border checkpoints: Fingertips and fingerprints have obvious associations with identification procedures. But she moves in the next two paragraphs to the other associations of fingertips—with touching, feeling, connecting, idiosyncrasy. As the essay develops, their significance becomes more figurative than literal: "Burning away the signature of individuality, at the borders of those very countries that most profess individualism, is a metaphor of terrible reproach" (para. 5). Indeed, the removal of fingertips becomes a metaphor for the way our society is not "individualistic." She returns to fingertips again in the final paragraph of the essay—the way they delineate an "exquisite uniqueness" in their ability to both reveal ourselves and touch others, even through time.

Thinking Critically

1. Griffiths makes broad generalizations in this essay. In this instance, readers may even have a hard time determining what, exactly, the "dominant culture" and "society" refer to here. Whether or not students agree with her statements will vary. Students may interpret Griffiths's argument as unsupported—she makes many big claims in a short space. Other students might argue that this is exactly what she set out to do, and was successful in her argument.

2. In paragraph 6, Griffiths writes: "A vote every few years does not constitute a political voice." This suggests that citizens are largely voiceless—particularly people who hold idiosyncratic or dissenting points of view. Students may argue that there are many other ways for your political voice to be heard—in polls, rallies, protests, etc.—but that people do not take full advantage of these possibilities. Students may also disagree with Griffiths completely, and think that the current voting process is the best way to maintain a representative democracy. Students may want to discuss how anyone on the "fringe" can be heard, and whether or not they are fairly represented by the current voting process. Griffiths obviously does not think they are, but some students might disagree with her.

3. Students should be able to understand the possible dangers of too much surveillance: invasions of privacy, the implicit presumption of guilt, the reduction of freedom. They might also be familiar with novels like *1984* and other dystopian representations of police states. Yet, on a daily basis, is surveillance always sinister? For example, security cameras in convenience stores or large parking lots? Airport security? Customs procedures? Griffiths seems more concerned about surveillance practiced

by the state: Is there a difference between government surveillance and that practiced in the private sphere (e.g., security cameras in a mall)?

In-Class Writing Activities

1. The words that Griffiths lists—*solidarity, trade unions, co-operatives*, and *collectives*—may be difficult for students to analyze because they may not have much experience with them. Students may think that these words have positive connotations, therefore undermining Griffiths's argument, or students may also think that these concepts are outdated, which somewhat proves Griffiths's point, even though students might not realize it. Students may also take this time to explore their own views on the difference between *individualistic* and *hyper-privatized*—many may not have been aware that there even was a difference, and some might still believe that there isn't.
2. For the writer, true individualism reveals and values the "'this-ness,' the essential specificity of the beloved person" (para. 14). She also associates with the marginalized, the eccentric, and all of those people who urge us to "see it otherwise" (para. 4). Students should be well-versed in the clichés of individualism, so it may be difficult to get them to think beyond platitudes and conventional wisdom. You may want to prompt them with Griffiths's provocative statements. For example, she seems to suggest that all attempts to encourage "normality" within a dominant culture are hostile to individualism. Moreover, she tries to separate individualism from "hyper-privatization": the tendency of people to become atomized, separated, and isolated from one another. Whether or not students agree with her view of individualism will vary.
3. Griffiths chooses the example of solitary television viewing. Students may consider other kinds of entertainment, including new media forms like Internet social networking sites and video games. Do they prefer "hyper-privatized" entertainments to communal ones? Moreover, are online role-playing games or Internet communications "communal" or are they still isolating, even when they do bring people in contact with one another? Is there a significant difference between listening to music on an iPod and going to a concert? What kind of communities are being built around contemporary forms of entertainment (e.g., music file sharing)?

Discussing the Unit

Suggested Topic For Discussion

These essays suggest a range of responses about the role of the state, from Griffiths's deeply philosophical skepticism to Schultz's pragmatic trust. You might also note the government's role in issues less sensational than border security, terrorism, or outbreaks of disease: food safety, day-to-day police protection, traffic laws, etc.

Preparing for Class Discussion

1. Most of us are familiar with the use of fingerprints as a biometric for identity, especially in the context of police procedures. But you might get students to discuss the broader implications of biometrics and biometric identification. For example, one immigration reform proposal in circulation would require a national biometric ID card for employment eligibility and Social Security purposes. Would students agree with this? Do they worry about the "state" crossing the borders of their "private selves" (as Griffiths does), or would the benefits of such a requirement outweigh any possible drawbacks?

2. Encourage students to be specific in their responses and assessments. Do diction and style play any part in their judgment? Each of the essays addresses security issues, but the authors also reveal broader attitudes and assumptions. Griffiths, for example, provides a meditation on identity; Schultz discusses how Americans view the role of government in their lives. Student responses will vary depending on which essay they find most effective.

From Discussion to Writing

1. There are a number of ways into this exercise. Rosen writes from personal observation, and students may want to begin with a specific example from their own lives that helps define the right to privacy. Griffiths notes the old argument that "if you have nothing to hide, you have nothing to fear." Do students accept that point of view? If not, how would they go about refuting it in the interest of privacy? They might also rely on their sense of rights and liberties as enumerated in the U.S. Constitution, although that document does not explicitly name a right to "privacy."

2. Khan gives no definite sense of the official's tone. We do not know whether he or she was being completely serious, flippant, grimly honest, or even sympathetic. The essay does not include his response at the time, either. Students might write about how they would react if they were profiled because of their names or backgrounds.

Questions for Cross-Cultural Discussion

1. Immigration is a perennial controversy in the United States. Griffiths seems to value "universal oneness" and the inviolability of the individual over national and state identities. Immigration and national identity are contested issues in many countries and students views will most likely be varied, and possibly polarized. Students should consider the practical necessity of national borders and border security, in particular.

2. Khan refers to his own experience traveling as a person with an Islamic-sounding name. Rosen points out that new body-scanning machines pose a "serious threat to the dignity" of travelers such as Muslim men, who may be forbidden to view unveiled women. To what degree do people need to sacrifice such cultural, religious, or even individual notions

to participate in contemporary life? Griffiths writes that surveillance "creates conformity," and compares this process to the creation of a docile herd. But is the modern world—airline travel, for example—possible without surveillance, a certain level of conformity, and accepted conventions of behavior?

9

Barack Obama: What Does His Election Mean to America?

Americans' discussion of race has always been fraught and difficult, weighed down by the legacy of slavery and discrimination, and occasionally opting to avoid the painfully difficult question of poverty in the African American community. As the charismatic and wildly popular Barack Obama soared in the polls during the 2008 election cycle, many began to wonder what it would actually mean to have a black president. Would Obama bring a real change to a Washington establishment many Americans felt was out of touch? Or would he just represent a superficial manicure, putting a new face on old ideas and ways of governing? Would he help to defuse racial tensions and bring the country together? Or would his policies—or even vestigial prejudices—widen the race-based rift in American society?

The answers to these questions have become no clearer. Many have faulted the president for failing to live up to his initial promise, while others consider his administration a welcome departure from the past and argue that real change will take real time. In these essays, though, written around the time of Obama's election and inauguration, several writers from several different backgrounds consider the implications of the Obama election to American policy and the American social fabric.

Diane McKinney-Whetstone and John Edgar Wideman observed the election of Obama in November of 2008 from two very different angles: McKinney-Whetstone ("The First Family") watched the actual acceptance ceremony in Grant Park in Chicago, while Wideman ("Street Corner Dreamers") considered a group of African American youths outside an underserved school in New York City, going about their routine as if nothing had changed. Both writers hold out enormous hopes that President Obama will make real changes to the state of black America, symbolized in the smiling faces of his family and the crumbling facade of that school. But both also seem to harbor doubts and concerns.

Student essayist Pearl Wong is more direct: She embraces the more race-blind opinion that Barack Obama must be, as her title asserts, a "President for All," not just black Americans. Wong appreciates the enormous mantle Obama has taken on—he is not only subject to the hopes and fears of critics like McKinney-Whetstone and Wideman, but must actually govern a large and complex country with the interests of all its citizens in mind. Wong suggests the only way to do so is to act without race directly on the agenda and offers a related lesson for the way we can all improve race relations and race dialogue.

The most skeptical essay in the chapter is by critic Christopher Hedges, who derides the notion that Obama will represent a real change on either front, calling him a celebrity brand used to repackage the regressive ideas of the past. In "Celebrity Culture and the Obama Brand," Hedges focuses on the political and policy dimensions of the Obama presidency, but students should keep both of these themes—our policies and our larger discussion of our diverse heritage—in mind throughout the chapter.

Diane McKinney-Whetstone

The First Family

[*Essence,* January 2009]

Vocabulary/Using a Dictionary

1. To know something *intimately* is to know it very closely, as you would know a good friend. One possible opposite would be *sketchily*.
2. *Culminate* is a verb, meaning to finish in a particular state, usually a climax. Typically, a series of events *culminates* in an interesting peak.
3. *Ebullience* is a very bright and optimistic demeanor. It comes from a Latin word meaning "bubbling."

Responding to Words in Context

1. "Norman Rockwellesque" means in the style of Rockwell, an illustrator known for painting scenes of ordinary, wholesome suburban American life in the first half of the twentieth century. A Rockwellesque diner would be one that's clean and well-ordered, most likely in a small town. McKinney-Whetstone implies that the scene was one typical of a loving, intact family unit.
2. *Supplant* is a verb, meaning to replace. It typically means to serve in something's place, and here it means filling in for absent parents.
3. *Buoyant* means afloat, and has come to mean very excited and cheerful, giving off an air of optimism and happiness. We imagine the president-elect smiling widely, moving around, embracing his family, etc.

Discussing Main Point and Meaning

1. McKinney-Whetstone is describing a feeling of solidarity with the Obama family, who achieved great things despite humble beginnings and low expectations, combined with pride that a black family had achieved so much.

2. McKinney-Whetstone implies that many people only see the "fractured part" of the black experience in America — dire poverty and dysfunction in families. The Obamas, by being a loving, intact unit, challenged that notion.

3. The author is referring to African Americans, and particularly to African Americans from families that encouraged them to achieve despite their humble beginnings. She says this group understands the poverty and adversity Barack and Michelle faced—especially the single-parent home in which Barack was raised—but also empathizes with a spirit of perseverance they represent.

Examining Sentences, Paragraphs, and Organization

1. These details show us how much McKinney-Whetstone sees herself in the Obama daughters; we imagine from her description that she owned similar dresses and at least recognizes a hairstyle from Sunday school. (She later refers to being in church as a child.) It also illustrates how carefully she examined every detail of that night, further underscoring how the image of the Obamas on stage was so important to her—as important, perhaps, as the speech the president-elect gave or the policies he backed during the campaign.

2. The paragraph lists the many obstacles the Obamas had to overcome to succeed, obstacles McKinney-Whetstone says are familiar to all African Americans. The long sentences listing these adversities illuminate the depth of their adversity, while the terse final sentence ("And for the Obamas, the moment came.") underlines how triumphant the moment of the election felt.

3. The essay alternates frequently between the two scenes, beginning on stage in Chicago, switching into the homes, we presume, of the black audience, and then back and forth repeatedly. This confusion of the scenes highlights McKinney-Whetstone's main point, which is that the black audience on election night was able to see itself in the Obamas: They are one and the same.

Thinking Critically

1. A good response will address the tensions between American society as a whole and the black community, particularly in terms of America's image of African Americans. Obama has the potential, as McKinney-Whetstone argues, to counter harmful stereotypes of blacks, and particularly of the black family. Another tactic for answering the question is the more race-blind one: The election means very little, because most Americans already encounter a politician like Obama outside of the context of his race.

2. This question asks students to confront the problem of stereotyping, which the essay both attacks and partially relies on. Responses should note that there is a huge diversity—socioeconomically, politically, and otherwise—within black families. But students are likely to divide on

whether a "typical" black family is a useful construct: Some will describe families broken up by poverty and neglect, others strong, vibrant communities bound together by a larger sense of family, and still others will argue that the group is too large to typify, and that doing so borders on the offensive.

3. McKinney-Whetstone wants to avoid entering the political fray directly, especially when writing about a candidate and a president as controversial as Obama. Rather than discussing the issue of his race analytically, she relies on a visual narrative nobody can dispute, one whose images are familiar to all Americans. This makes her point stronger and more compelling than if she were to discuss Obama's significance to the black community from an immediately political or philosophical point of view.

In-Class Writing Activities

1. Responses should focus on the centrality of the family, rather than the politician, throughout the acceptance: the way Michelle and the couple's daughters really are front-and-center. Some students may notice the large bulletproof glass that separates the Obamas, physically and figuratively, from the crowd, and also responds to an atmosphere of danger for the president-elect. This very salient danger is one example of something absent from McKinney-Whetstone's essay.

2. This is likely to be a divisive question that raises some passions. As above, students may argue that the idea of a typical black family is too reductive to be useful and may even be offensive. But some may write that there is an archetype, however many aberrations there may be from it, of a black family in America, and that poverty and dysfunction are facets of it. Some students may blame these hallmarks on endemic American racism that still denies blacks opportunities, and others will argue the community itself is to blame for failing its members. The most important thing to look for in this essay is that students engage Obama's *impact* on relations between blacks and whites. Will an Obama administration, in which a black man both leads the country and absorbs its criticisms, help defuse tensions between blacks and whites who feel alienated from their fellow Americans of other races? Or could he make things worse, particularly for the way whites see the black family?

3. Responses will vary widely, but prompt students to replicate the visuality of McKinney-Whetstone's essay—the way a public figure's posture, clothing, manner of waving, etc.—said more than the words or ideas associated with the event. If students can't come up with such an event in their lifetimes, challenge them to look for one through their study of history: a photo of Lincoln at Gettysburg, for instance, or a video of Kennedy's famous speech at the Berlin Wall.

John Edgar Wideman

Street Corner Dreamers

[*Essence*, January 2009]

Vocabulary/Using a Dictionary

1. To *marginalize* something is to make it feel or appear unimportant—to put it on the margins. Wideman is arguing that America's urban youth has not been a priority for society over the last few decades, that they have essentially been treated as insignificant.
2. *Motley* means mixed in color or fabric, and is used to refer to the many-colored costumes worn by jesters. Wideman uses it to describe the outfits worn by the inner-city kids, which are not coordinated or styled, but patched together.
3. *Amalgamated* means mixed together, related to *amalgam*, a chemistry term meaning a mixture of mercury and another metal.

Responding to Words in Context

1. A *scowl* is an angry expression, typically on a human or even an animal face. Wideman is using the word metaphorically when referring to the facade of a building, indicating just how ugly and unpleasant the broken-down school is to look at.
2. Wideman is continuing the metaphor he started when he referred to the building's "scowl"—comparing its front to a human face. A *facelift* is a surgery that changes a person's face but does not change what's behind it; Wideman is implying that the change to the school may not have improved the education offered within it.
3. A *blight* is most literally a disease of a plant, caused by neglect and decay. Wideman is suggesting by this metaphorical use that society has neglected these youths and thus caused their potential to wither and decompose.

Discussing Main Point and Meaning

1. The students stand for poor, urban youths, who are mostly black. Wideman witnesses these particular students living near their school in New York, but they come to represent, for the author, the "missing ones" throughout the nation.
2. Wideman writes that urban poverty is a product of marginalization—a sense that America decided long ago not to deal with poor, mostly black urban youths, because "we could get along just fine without them, thank you." As a result, these kids are often in prison or dead, and the students who remain don't see themselves as part of America or think they have a real voice within it.
3. Wideman declares he will do no "crystal-ball gazing" to keep the essay in the present, and announces that he has no specific prediction for the

future. But the tone of the essay can be read as either optimistic—especially its last paragraph describing President Obama firmly in charge and willing to do what it takes to improve the lot of these students—or pessimistic—since it gives a large space to describing just how large and apparently insurmountable the problem of urban poverty is.

Examining Sentences, Paragraphs, and Organization

1. Wideman is illustrating the contrast between Washington politics and reality on the street—he doesn't mean to imply that these two things literally happened at the same time, but their *juxtaposition* serves to show us the disconnect politicians can have from the very reasons they do things like, for instance, raise taxes.
2. All three sentences are questions—specifically, rhetorical questions posing difficult problems in the war on poverty. The paragraph therefore advances Wideman's general feeling of exasperation at the problem, and his aspiration to provoke action from his readers, whom he directly engages with the series of questions.
3. The essay begins by describing the rotting front of the Seward Park High School building in Manhattan, giving us a vivid sense of how neglected the children who attend the school have become. The essay gradually shifts from a literal description of the crowd of students exiting the school to an argument about what needs to be done to secure their future. By beginning with something so concrete, Wideman makes his argument more vivid and makes us feel the urgency that underpins it.

Thinking Critically

1. Students should recognize that Wideman's term means not that the children are literally missing, but that they've been ignored—particularly by the media in its depiction of American life and by the government in its allocation of resources. Students are likely to divide on whether they really are ignored, with some placing the blame on black communities themselves for the problems Wideman is describing, and others concurring that the problem of black poverty is one many Americans, and especially the American media, do not want to confront, let alone solve.
2. There are two potential arguments for the positive impact President Obama could have on urban poverty. He could change policy in a way that alleviates it somehow, such as spending more money on urban renewal or education; he could also improve race relations in a way that ultimately benefits blacks. The argument against his influence would be grounded in the empirical evidence of his first few years in office—many critics claim he's had very little impact and has not been active enough in effecting the change his campaign promised.
3. Wideman's comment is not meant to endorse total race-blindness, but students may read it to endorse a society where our traditional racial

identities are less salient in everyday life. Some students may feel we make too much of race, while others are likely to think we as a society, or our government, need to do more to tackle race problems, particularly economic inequalities between the races. Look for all responses to acknowledge the differences between consciousness about race in everyday life—like, say, being conscious of what race someone is when deciding to hire him or her—and consciousness about the racial tensions facing America.

In-Class Writing Activities

1. The most startling facts involve unemployment, which is considerably higher for blacks than for whites. Students will divide on the causes of this disparity—whether racism or inertia is to blame, or whether the community itself has not done enough to bridge the gap. Encourage students to propose solutions that do more than just redistribute wealth: They should be aware of the roles that culture and discrimination play in poverty.
2. Look for responses that stress the visual impact of the school and its surroundings—not just the facade of the building, but how well manicured its lawn and hedges are, how welcoming it looks, what (if anything) is advertised outside. Better maintained schools, of course, suggest that more money is going into them.
3. Again, students will divide between cynicism and optimism about politicians, but look for them to pay particular attention to the special potential of an Obama administration, namely to help improve race relations and bring a major change to the tone and policy of Washington.

Pearl Wong (student essay)

Obama—President for All

[*The Santa Clara*, Santa Clara University, February 25, 2010]

Vocabulary/Using a Dictionary

1. *Dis-* is a general negative prefix. *Discontentment*, in turn, is a lack of satisfaction, which Wong is here ascribing to the African American community.
2. A literal *milestone* is a stone set up on a road to mark an important place or to indicate a distance. Figuratively, which is the way Wong means it, it means an important moment or turning point in time.

Responding to Words in Context

1. Something *conspicuous* is highly visible. Wong is referring to activities like ethnic pride parades and literature and art with an ethnic focus, which are very conscious of heritage and make it very open.

2. To *embody* means to be a visual representation of an abstract idea—literally to become the body of something. Wong is suggesting that the "milestone" in American history is an expanded acceptance of African Americans in public life and that Obama represents that milestone physically.

Discussing Main Point and Meaning

1. Wong is describing a fine line between an overly conspicuous embrace of ethnic identities, which she believes can be showy and divisive, and being ashamed of who we are.
2. Wong says individuals have to act locally in their communities to achieve real change, and that minorities cannot expect politicians, even Obama, to improve their lot.

Examining Sentences, Paragraphs, and Organization

1. "Red pill or blue" refers to *The Matrix* (see gloss), in which it represents an exceedingly difficult choice, where either option has serious downsides. Wong is describing the choice politicians like Obama face between protecting minority groups and representing all Americans. She is emphasizing what a challenge this is for the president and how significant the ramifications are.
2. Wong quotes Obama declaring that he is responsible for all Americans, very directly and literally reiterating her main idea. She also quotes Mother Teresa making a perhaps more profound point, which rounds off the essay by making us think about our responsibility to care for each other without judging each other.

Thinking Critically

1. Some students will argue, against Wong, that individuals can have a racial consciousness without defining themselves entirely by their heritage or ethnicity. Prompt students to think of membership in clubs as a concrete manifestation of this sort of identification: They, or their peers, may be in ethnically based clubs, but does that preclude membership in other clubs as well? Is it the most defining organization one can belong to? Why or why not?
2. Responses should consider thoughtfully and carefully the pros and cons of both local and national efforts. Government attempts to alleviate racial problems include more money for local urban-renewal programs, and large-scale political and social efforts akin to President Clinton's "national conversation on race." Some students will argue that these efforts have often failed in the past, while others will argue that local, individual efforts, while important in their own right, are too small to account for any real change.

In-Class Writing Activities

1. Examples are split into two major categories: 1) reallocation of funds and efforts to projects like urban renewal and education; and 2) defus-

ing racial tensions and working to depolarize Americans psychologically about race. Specific examples will vary widely, but look for students to come up with original ideas that go beyond throwing money at problems.

2. This works well as a group exercise: Have students break into small groups and write out specific proposals for improving race relations locally. Then have the groups critique each others' proposals. The important thing here is specificity: Look for concrete examples like programs to bolster after-school clubs where students of different ethnicities work together on community service projects, rather than "more money for education."

Christopher Hedges

Celebrity Culture and the Obama Brand

[*Tikkun*, January/February 2010]

Vocabulary/Using a Dictionary

1. *Imperial* comes from "empire," and describes actions by one country intended to dominate or rule other parts of the world.
2. *Tilting* means leaning very slightly, in order to change the meaning of these concepts without being conspicuous.
3. A *demagogue* is any politician or leader who appeals more to people's emotions than to their sense of logic or reason. It comes from Greek *demos*, meaning "people," and *agein*, meaning "to lead," and thus originally meant "a leader of people." It has a decidedly negative connotation.

Responding to Words in Context

1. To *grease* someone's *palms* is to bribe him or her, whether directly or, as in this case, simply by offering campaign money in order to secure favorable policy stances, as lobbyists often do to politicians.
2. *Trivia* means anything unimportant, and is familiar to most of us as a designation of quiz-type questions. Here, it refers to the objects of media attention (presumably celebrity gossip and the like) that Hedges considers insignificant.
3. *Deflation* means letting the air out of something, and in this context Hedges is illustrating an advertising strategy that has lost its "hot air," the rhetoric that has puffed it up. In other words, it no longer has an effect on people's opinions.

Discussing Main Point and Meaning

1. *Brand* is an advertising term, meaning a way of thinking about a product controlled by the producer, and not necessarily completely accurate. Hedges considers Obama a brand because his backers are selling the public a particular image of him at odds with reality.

2. Hedges, a liberal, is viciously opposed to the policies of the Bush administration, which he characterizes as lawless and imperial. He points especially to the administration's secrecy laws, suspension of habeas corpus, wars in the Middle East, and neglect of domestic problems. He implies that Obama promised a substantial departure from these policies, but writes that he has not lived up to those promises, extending Bush's policies and altering only the image of the presidency.
3. Hedges says explicitly that corporations "control our politics" (para. 3) and describes our system of government as "corporate" and "consumption-oriented." Hedges believes that the corporate interests that control America have rolled Obama out as a new brand to replace Bush, much as they would replace a failing product with a new one; he does not believe, however, that the new president actually represents a new set of ideas or policies.

Examining Sentences, Paragraphs, and Organization

1. Both of these terms are in scare quotes, representing Hedges's skepticism that they represent the kinds of changes they claim to and casting them as more empty corporate branding. Nuclear energy is not, Hedges says with those quotes, actually green; the bill in question did not reform anything.
2. With these short, choppy sentences, Hedges mimics the workings of a mind that has been numbed to any real nuanced thoughts. All we know is that we feel entertained and happy; and we are ignoring the larger problems that still face our country.
3. Hedges is writing for *Tikkun*, a left-leaning magazine, and seems to presume that his readers share most of his conclusions. To take one example, Hedges faults Obama for expanding the war in Afghanistan, not an effective argument for a reader who believes the war is justified or necessary.

Thinking Critically

1. Hedges's premise is essentially that commerce and politics should be kept separate, and there is certainly a strong philosophical argument to back that premise up. Some students might worry that an expanded commercialism in politics will invite a situation where the candidate who spends the most on branding wins—some may think we're already there. Others may argue, as Hedges does, that a corporatist state will never allow for any real change, since corporations are known to thrive on stasis and inertia. Others, however, may take the position that there's nothing wrong with branding a politician, or that it may be inevitable. We've been trained to think in terms of brands, for better or worse, and a unified sense of who a candidate or leader is and what he or she believes in may be the best avenue Americans have to connect to their government.
2. Answers will vary depending on the way students interpret the given definition of "junk politics," and whether or not they agree that America

is functioning under a junk politics system. The definition given may be a bit confusing, and it might also lead to some debate over what constitutes issues "at home" and "abroad." Politicians have been criticized for downplaying the wars in Iraq and Afghanistan, but those would appear to be the "threats from abroad" that Hedges implies are being magnified. Students may not be able to completely agree or disagree with this definition, simply because the current political and socioeconomic landscapes are so complex.

3. Hedges would likely answer that the dissent, whether its practitioners are aware of it or not, is all "part of the show," an entertaining, competitive contest meant to distract Americans from the way their country is actually being run by both parties. Ask students to consider this point of view, particularly in light of the partisan rancor that was especially vitriolic leading up to the 2010 midterm elections. Are there real differences between Democrats and Republicans?

In-Class Writing Activities

1. Hedges is referring to media coverage of celebrities and minor news events that, while perhaps temporarily interesting, do not do, in his opinion, the media's job of informing the country about what's really going on. Students should give examples of coverage of the latest celebrity breakups or scandals, and consider 1) whether this is really such a bad thing, and 2) whether Hedges's characterization of the media as made up entirely of this sort of triviality is accurate.
2. Prompt students to think of a specific, concrete issue. Health care, for instance, was legally reformed under Obama, but many people claim the reforms did not go nearly far enough or were simply window-dressing on the old policy. Alternatively, ask them to take John Edgar Wideman's approach from earlier in this chapter: Have them measure how much of an impact Obama has had on their communities by looking at the actual, physical landscape of the communities themselves. Has anything really changed on the ground in their towns and cities?
3. The typical meta-image of Obama is one associated with youth, vitality, and an urban spirit of liberalism and friendly cooperation. Do students believe this image matches the reality? Why or why not? Ask them what they think Hedges means by the "erotic appeal" of Obama. Is it just that some people find him good-looking? Or is there something deeper to this claim of eroticism? Do students agree with it?

Discussing the Unit

Suggested Topic for Discussion

You may want to pair this unit with Ira Berlin's essay "Migrations Forced and Free," at the end of Chapter 12. Berlin considers the extraordinary importance the African American narrative—particularly the legacy of slavery and discrimination—still has for black people in this country. To keep the conversation on this controversial topic civil, remind students how hard it is to imagine and access the consciousness of a person with a different heritage, a different ancestral history, and in many cases a completely different way of viewing the world as a result. Many students will disagree with this point itself, of course, preferring to see America as a country where everyone is equal in front of the law and, increasingly, in everyday social standing. Remember to keep the question focused not on what divides the races in this country, but on what binds them together.

Preparing for Class Discussion

1. This question, like many in this chapter, can engender some strong emotions and attitudes, so keep it analytical. Remind students who put more blame on the African American community itself that nobody wants to live in poverty, and also of how long the legacy of inequality was—Isn't it likely to last a lot longer? For students who consider discrimination the sole cause, discuss other groups (including poor whites) that live in similar penury: How do they account for them? The ultimate answer to this question must be that the problem McKinney-Whetstone and Wideman discuss is too complex to have a simple cause—otherwise, it would have a simple answer.

2. Note that Hedges does not dispute the psychological importance that Obama has had in the black community: He would likely acknowledge this importance and consider it a positive. But one of Hedges's main themes is that mass psychology is less important and far easier to manipulate than the real, radical political change he believes is necessary in America. While he might applaud the election of a black president that McKinney-Whetstone and Wideman take such pride in, he would be very skeptical of their hopes that Obama will make any substantial changes that could affect the "street-corner dreamers" Wideman observes in New York City.

From Discussion to Writing

1. Again, it's important to divide the promise both of these authors see in Obama between the political and the psychological. Both seem to believe that Obama can help repair race relations in America, but acknowledge that this will mean a combination of simple inspiration (which few can doubt Obama has on some level achieved) and actual policy change. Have students, if they're able, discuss the latter more substantively here. Based on their reading of the news (have them do

some research if they're behind), what do they think Obama has accomplished? Or do they agree with Hedges that he's the same soup, just reheated?

2. Look for responses that encapsulate the momentous importance of the 2008 election and inauguration itself—encourage the temporary historians to quote McKinney-Whetstone to illustrate the significance of the election for black Americans in particular—but use this question as an opportunity to consider the long-term historical importance the election has had on the population as a whole. Then prompt students to continue their account with either a contrast in tone or a continuation of it, depending on their prognostications for the coming years. Remind them of the ways history has judged previous presidents—Lincoln, Harding, Clinton, George W. Bush—as a template for their own judgments.

Topics for Cross-Cultural Discussion

1. A few examples of groups for fertile discussion are Native Americans, foreign-born citizens (and noncitizens), and even women. Is Obama, as Pearl Wong asserts, "president for all"? How will these groups fare in this administration? Why? Ask students to predict whether a broad selection of ethnic and other minority groups will vote for Obama's reelection or not, and why they make the predictions they do.

2. Ask students who have recently traveled internationally, or have relatives overseas, what the impressions of Obama were in the countries which they visited or to which they have connections. Or ask them to evaluate Obama pretending that they were not Americans but foreigners. Many believe George W. Bush's foreign policy damaged the image of America overseas, casting it as a selfish, bellicose nation callous to the concerns of the rest of the world. Do students agree? How, if at all, do they think Obama has altered the international perspective of America?

10

Social Networking— How Is It Transforming Behavior?

Start this chapter with a quick poll: How many students have used a social-networking site like Facebook or Twitter at some point in their lives? In an American classroom, the odds are extremely good that a large majority, even 100 percent, will raise hands. But see if the result even changes if you replace "at some point in their lives" with "today." Social networking is not an occasional diversion like team sports or movies. It's woven into the day-to-day fabric of life, especially for young Americans. The essays in this chapter raise the question: Is this a good or a bad thing?

Garry Trudeau's cartoon strip "Hi, Dad" opens the chapter neatly by presenting all the problems it will consider: whether social networking is "ruining" the lives of young people—as the daughter in the strip insists, with some irony, that it isn't, for instance—and how the generational gap can lead to a misunderstanding of the Facebook Age and its conventions.

Each of the subsequent essays examines one of those conventions, looking at the way some aspect of everyday life has changed, for better and for worse, since the dawn of the social-networking revolution. In "We Shall Overshare," Mary Katharine Ham discusses the basic ethics of communication (and over-communication) online. In student Brent Baughman's "Growing Older in the Digital Age: An Exercise in Egotism," the author considers the way Facebook has redefined something as basic as celebrating one's birthday. Finally, Professor Elizabeth Stone dissects her students' online responses to the tragic death of one of their peers in "Grief in the Age of Facebook."

This chapter obviously affords instructors ample opportunities to use their students' own lives as background and example: Again, even instructors who are not familiar with the details of social networking will find that almost all of their students are, and in depth. Continue to ask them, however, to see the issues the chapter raises objectively, and in terms larger than Facebook or Twitter.

Garry Trudeau

Hi, Dad

[*Doonesbury, Boston Globe* (syndicated), November 8, 2009]

Vocabulary/Using a Dictionary

1. *Secs* is short for "seconds." The daughter using this abbreviation, and even claiming what she had to do will take only seconds, is ironic considering how involved it turns out to be.
2. Here *blog* is a verb, though we often see it as a noun. It comes from the words "web log" and is just that—an online diary or record of events, usually associated with posting strong opinions or personal narratives online.

Responding to Words in Context

1. To *tag*, particularly on Facebook, is to identify someone in a photo with a link to his or her profile. To *strip* means to remove a tag.
2. Both of these terms are borrowed from corporate brand management and refer to the way a company controls the public's image of it or of its products.

Discussing Main Point and Meaning

1. Trudeau sympathizes with the father in the strip and casts doubt on the daughter's assertion that social networking is not ruining her life. The rigmarole she describes sounds truly painful and horrible, and we are led to agree with the father's befuddlement over why she goes through it.
2. The father is wearing his coat, suggesting he's ready to go outside into the world, a stark contrast with the hermetic, enclosed online life of his daughter. This is important in furthering the contrast between the two generations, and furthering our sympathy for the participant that actually wants to do something presumably more fun and meaningful than untagging photos.

Examining Sentences, Paragraphs, and Organization

1. The strip is set in a generic dorm room, which we can tell from the furniture—the short bookcase and the futon, for instance. This is important because it generalizes the discussion to one between all parents and their college-aged children, many of whom inhabit dorm rooms very similar to the one in the strip.
2. The strip is basically a monologue, with the daughter saying everything except her father's response of "Okay. Sorry." This underlines the strip's central idea that her activity is empty and meaningless compared to spending quality time with her father on parents' weekend—she says so much but none of it registers as personally as the father's short and sincerely perplexed apology.

Thinking Critically

1. Some students may raise issues with Trudeau's specific understanding of the mechanisms of social networking, or with his vocabulary—remind them that Trudeau is writing satire, and his details are unlikely to be perfect. Look for responses that argue for or against the general premise: that Facebook is ruining young people's lives. Do students think there's such a thing as responsible use of sites like Facebook, and do most of their peers (like the generic daughter here) use them responsibly?

2. The best arguments for a positive effect revolve around the binding effects Facebook and other sites have on communities that already exist and its ability to help forge new friendships and professional relationships. Students will likely have examples of occasions when Facebook or other sites have improved their social lives in some way. Others may argue, along the lines of Trudeau, that these sites absorb more time from socialization than they add to it, and that much of the human contact they provide is empty and artificial.

In-Class Writing Activities

1. Facebook estimates that its average user uses the site actively for an hour a day—a relatively enormous commitment of time. Ask students who both do and don't use social networking to break that hour down. How much of it is on a computer at home? How much is on a cell phone? What (if anything) is a waste of time, and what (if anything) is improving users' lives? Ask students to consider what that hour is supplanting: What did people do in that hour before Facebook came along?

2. Younger students will probably have stories of their parents or teachers misunderstanding their activity online: Ask them to elaborate on the causes. Do they just have a different vocabulary than their parents? Or do they approach and relate to technology in a substantially different way—perhaps trusting it as a part of their lives more than their forebears do?

Mary Katharine Ham

We Shall Overshare

[*The Weekly Standard*, June 8, 2009]

Vocabulary/Using a Dictionary

1. A *narcissist* is someone obsessed with him- or herself. It comes from the Greek mythical figure Narcissus, who was transfixed by his own reflection.

2. *Broadcast* is a word from television and radio, meaning to send out something (like a program) so that a wide audience can see it (i.e., send it "broadly"). Ham is making an analogy between her use of social media and a television or radio station sending out its programming over the airwaves.

3. To *cultivate* is to grow, or add culture; the term is originally agricultural. The word in this context means to develop an attitude by nurturing it.

Responding to Words in Context

1. *Erosion* is the process by which natural elements and weather gradually wear away land. Here, Ham is using the word metaphorically to mean the slow but steady diminution of oversharers' dignity.
2. An *antidote* is a medicine that counteracts the effects of a poison. Using it here, of course, implies that oversharing is somewhat poisonous.
3. Ham uses *pioneer* to suggest not only the first people to explore something (like the value of a technology) but bold and intrepid trailblazers like Lewis and Clark. Note that she also uses the word more ironically in paragraph 4.

Discussing Main Point and Meaning

1. Ham says she's more careful about what she posts online knowing it's all public: "It's amazing how reasonably you act when everyone you know (and many you don't) is watching you" (para 6). She's implying that someone with a more private profile on Facebook or Twitter, for instance, might be more casual about publishing something that could prove damning or embarrassing.
2. Ham mentions Facebook's role in raising money for cancer research, and its use by dissidents in Iran for spreading their message. These examples provide a stark contrast to the kind of casual sharing of trivial personal details Ham is criticizing.
3. Ham casts the revolutionaries as fighting a real battle against real tyranny, making the problems her Facebook and Twitter friends complain about seem extremely petty. Note how she sets this off especially against her friend whose status update makes her sound like she's in a gulag—the protesters in Iran actually have a right, Ham implies, to post such messages.

Examining Sentences, Paragraphs, and Organization

1. "We Shall Overcome" was the anthem of the civil rights movement, describing the eventual victory of justice over racial discrimination. Ham's title playfully contrasts the righteous goals and efforts of that era and movement with the inconsequential trifles shared online today.
2. Ham's example sets up the contrast with which the essay as a whole will deal—the contrast between the monumental struggles of the past (the struggles of Russian dissidents against the autocracy of the Soviet Union, for instance) and a culture in which, although we're constantly talking, we have very little of substance to talk about. The example also shows us, however, how well tapped in Ham is to her social network and gives us a preview of how aloof she simultaneously feels from it.
3. Ham juxtaposes throughout the essay to establish the conflict between the past and the present discussed above. Offer paragraph 9 as the

quintessential example of an effective juxtaposition: "When pondering another photo shoot for my profile picture the other day, I couldn't help recalling the Facebook users who raised $800,000 for St. Jude Children's Research Hospital only last week." The example of Alexander Graham Bell, an ossified figure from history, provides an especially stark and comic juxtaposition with the "serial masturbator" story.

Thinking Critically

1. Some students may feel that Ham jumps to a conclusion: Her friend could have been sharing something that, while not as physically harmful as imprisonment in a gulag, was nonetheless a psychological stress. Others may feel that nobody, at least nobody with access to Facebook, could possibly be in a situation that would warrant such a response. Ask whether the lack of context in the status update—notice that the friend explains a mood but does not articulate the circumstances that have brought it about—is in and of itself irresponsible? Is such a status update unusual?
2. Ham does not discuss the positive impact social networking can have on its users' social lives—introducing them to friends or tightening the bonds with friends they already have. Students may also mention academic uses on college campuses—Facebook has proven extremely useful for group studying in many instances—or further examples along Ham's lines, like political organizing or the establishment of volunteer networks.
3. Students should look up the "Twitter Revolution" in Iran in the summer of 2009: Not only were Iranian dissidents organizing their protest and spreading the word on Twitter and Facebook, but the site proved an extraordinary way of highlighting their struggles to the world, after journalists were restricted from the country. Some students may question the power of a resource to which not everyone has access and which the government can easily squash; others may feel that the political power of social networks is awesome and perhaps unrealized.

In-Class Writing Activities

1. *The Weekly Standard* is a conservative magazine; Ham's contention that her use of social networking follows a "quintessentially conservative formula" rests on the idea that she is taking personal responsibility for everything she posts, rather than putting the burden on the larger community. Ask students to imagine what a "liberal" way of using Facebook or Twitter would be.
2. Prompt students to ask what qualifies as "TMI" (too much information) on the Internet, and why. Think in terms beyond social networking—what is it we don't like about people talking about themselves too much? Some students may not mind any level of conversation on their social networks; ask them why. Have them break into groups and write ten sample tweets; then have the other groups vote on which ones count as an "overshare." Why does TMI turn us off in the way it does?

3. Ham makes the analogy on two levels—both she and Lewis and Clark are "pioneers," people at the beginning of a long journey whose destination is not entirely clear. She also notes that Lewis and Clark documented their journeys extensively, while she is doing the same, albeit in a much shorter format. Ham points out that some people on these sites are actual pioneers—like the users in Iran who were temporarily banned—but in terms of her own Twitter use, the analogy is mostly facetious.

Brent Baughman (student essay)

Growing Older in the Digital Age: An Exercise in Egotism

[*The Berkeley Beacon*, Emerson College, February 25, 2010]

Vocabulary/Using a Dictionary

1. *Egotism* comes from the Latin *ego*, meaning "I," and is the quality of self-absorption even to the point of self-worship.
2. An *interface* is the space where two systems meet, and is used especially for the computer users to connect and give commands. An operating system like Windows is the most familiar example of an interface.
3. *Mitigate* comes from the Latin *mitis*, "soft"; to *mitigate* something is to make it milder, easier, or less painful.

Responding to Words in Context

1. A *smirk* is a smile, usually with the connotation of smug satisfaction. The "collective smirk" Baughman mentions refers to a shared idea—here the possibility of revelry and sex on a twenty-first birthday—that is collectively understood but not expressed except by a subtle facial gesture.
2. The word *fester* usually refers to a wound or a sore, and means to suppurate or become septic. Metaphorically it means to rot or simply to become more intense from sitting still. Baughman means that at these bars sexual energy increases over time as young people gather.
3. A *fantasy* can mean a trip of the imagination unfettered by conventional rules, as it's used in music. It can also mean an idea with no basis in reality. Baughman employs both meanings in reference to modern birthdays.

Discussing Main Point and Meaning

1. Baughman writes that a twenty-first birthday is a major milestone, because it frees the celebrant to drink alcohol legally. The natural state of affairs, he argues, would be for subsequent birthdays (at least until another milestone) to be far more subdued. In fact, in the Facebook era, he suggests all birthdays become twenty-first birthdays.

2. Baughman points out superficial differences—on Twitter, for instance, one has to compact the birthday self-promotion into 140 characters and on Facebook he or she can monitor well wishes through e-mail alerts. But he maintains that all of the forms of social-network birthday celebration are essentially bound by self-absorption.

3. Baughman writes that the actual celebratory time with friends is the heart of the birthday and the reason it's celebrated. Today, he complains, a birthday is little more than an opportunity to count congratulatory e-mails and Facebook messages, which for many people has even become its *raison d'être*.

Examining Sentences, Paragraphs, and Organization

1. Throughout his essay, Baughman playfully criticizes his generation's practices online, but then indicates that he's just as guilty as any of his peers. Notice how he does so subtly and playfully, for instance, by calling generic passing birthday wishes "'Happy Birthday Brent!'s." Putting himself in the center of his own satire makes Baughman more relatable and makes his very valid social censure feel less like a direct assault.

2. He is referring to the robots Japanese men take to the movies, a phenomenon to which he alluded earlier in the essay. The comment both ties the essay together humorously and emphasizes the self-centered (even masturbatory) activity of young social networkers, which he equates with a romantic love for technology.

Thinking Critically

1. Baughman's essay is full of jokes—he jokes about the Japanese dating robots, for instance, and "Gmail bold." Ask students whether this style of writing would work if Baughman's subject were more serious than birthdays. Or does the humor perhaps take a subject that is quite serious (our increasing collective narcissism) and make it slightly more relatable? Have students dissect Baughman's joke about Social Security in the first paragraph—how does he connect to his (young) audience with it, and how does it help him set the tone for the rest of the piece?

2. Prompt students to think of examples beyond social networking or even the Internet. Are we addicted to our cell phones, to text messaging, to e-mail on our BlackBerrys? What do these addictions, if they exist, mean? What are they replacing—or could it be that they're just filling a void and improving our means of communicating with our peers? Remind students to think not just of what technology "addicts" are literally doing (staring at a computer screen, typing on a phone all day) but what they might be accomplishing by doing it. Compare it to the world before the technology existed. Is it an improvement?

In-Class Writing Activities

1. Many young people report that Facebook cements new friendships much more quickly than traditional, analog socializing. If your students make

this claim, ask them why: What is the Facebook environment like for meeting and chatting with new people, and how does it differ from the putative "real world"? What about with their existing friends? Is socializing online more or less sincere, more or less intimate, than socializing in a bar or student center? Don't assume the answer to this one is obvious.

2. Have students break into groups and guess which of the other group's messages correspond to which method of delivery. How does the medium direct the message, so to speak?

Elizabeth Stone

Grief in the Age of Facebook

[*The Chronicle Review*, March 5, 2010]

Vocabulary/Using a Dictionary

1. A *paradox* is an apparent contradiction drawn from apparently logical premises, or a statement that contradicts itself. *Paradoxically* is an adjective, meaning that something takes the form of a paradox—or more often, is simply complex and confounding.

2. *Virtually* can be an adverb from *virtual*, applied to something created by software but not in the real world; it can also mean "almost" or "nearly." Stone literally means the latter use here, but the former provides a poignant double entendre.

3. The verb *atomize* means to break down into very small parts, from *atom*, the smallest unit of a chemical element. Stone uses the word with its most popular contemporary meaning—a lifestyle in which there are many small, perhaps unconnected, components.

Responding to Words in Context

1. *Viral* means having the properties of a virus, an infective agent that enters a host and then multiplies. In the context of marketing, to call something *viral* has come to mean that it spreads fast by encouraging people marketed to to send the advertisement to their friends—advertisers achieve this by making the ad especially funny or making it appear that it isn't even really an ad.

2. Of a word, phrase, or speech, *colloquial* means informal and characterized by everyday conversational patterns. One possible antonym would be *formal*. "Hang out with" is a colloquial construction; "commune with" would be a more formal one.

3. *Uncharted* means unmapped, a term from cartography. (Note the shared root *carta*, Latin for "map.") Stone is using the word to mean a space in human relations that is unexplored, whose participants don't know what they're approaching.

Discussing Main Point and Meaning

1. The general tone of Stone's essay is anthropological, describing unfamiliar conventions in an objective, neutral way. But occasionally she sounds perfectly laudatory, or even in awe, of her students—especially those who reposted their profile photos with Casey—suggesting she thinks Facebook mourning may not only be an inevitable change in the social fabric but a healthy one. She also describes the classmates' grieving processes as preferable to the ones prescribed by Sigmund Freud.

2. Stone mentions the problem that initial displays of grief online can spread word of a death too casually and quickly, which is why she praises her students for using the phone to notify each other. She also delineates the issue of when to take down memorials: How soon should profile pictures with the deceased be changed back, for instance, or pages on which mourning has been registered return to their old exuberant uses?

3. Because of the effusion of mourners' expression, Stone learned things about her student that she wouldn't have otherwise known, like her acting talent and her love of horses. The Facebook memorial platform offers far more space, Stone suggests, than the traditional eulogy to bring out and illuminate the character of the deceased.

Examining Sentences, Paragraphs, and Organization

1. The essay is about the way the Millennial generation does things (namely mourns) differently from previous generations, and this idea—of being constantly connected and emitting a constant stream of information and update—is at the heart of that contrast. Because Stone was Casey's journalism professor, the characterization also helps illustrate the bond between teacher and student.

2. Stone wants to convey students' expressions of grief exactly, because it is precisely their colloquialism that distinguishes them from similar expressions in previous generations. Have students note how a Millennial who reads Facebook posts all day would read the wall post as Stone transmits it differently than an older person.

3. Although the essay is an exposition of an issue, it is told as narrative. This is important to bringing across the process of mourning, which even in the Facebook age unfolds gradually and in steps. It also helps us connect with Stone more personally as she undergoes the process.

Thinking Critically

1. Stone's precis of Freud is that we should "detach from the dead." Her experience of Facebook mourners is that they do exactly the opposite—continuing for a period much longer than traditional mourning to reminisce and even addressing the deceased directly. Have students list the potential advantages and disadvantages of each form of mourning, concentrating on the psychological benefits and drawbacks for the mourners themselves.

2. Some students will argue, in line with Stone's essay, that the social-networking revolution makes this kind of mourning inevitable, and that alternate policies—taking the profile down immediately—for instance, would be worse. Others will see this kind of continued intimacy as a psychologically healthier way to exhibit grief. Ask students to formulate other possible policies and compare them to Facebook's.
3. Stone brings us back to the bond she herself had with Casey, as her journalism professor. She reminds us of Casey's prowess as a writer and also furthers the intimacy of the connection she feels to Casey, who would be doing exactly what she (Stone) is doing had she lived.

In-Class Writing Activities

1. Have students with the experience who are comfortable sharing it compare their memories with Stone's essay, particularly focusing on how things would have been different in an age before online social media. Use the experience of another student who is comfortable discussing a pre-Facebook loss to compare the issues the essay raises: How did the bereaved express their grief? Was there anything inappropriate shared online? How long did the mourning last, and was that a good or bad thing?
2. If you're on Facebook, discuss your policy for friending your students and why having a policy is important. Have students consider the pitfalls of a close social connection with their teachers, and particularly those that express themselves in an era of oversharing. Press for specific examples of things Facebook allows us to know about our friends that teachers and their pupils are best off not sharing.
3. Ask students who present their stories to consider how the teacher looks back on the relationship. Are the salient details the same in the memory of both instructor and pupil?

Discussing the Unit

Suggested Topic for Discussion

Throughout this unit, keep in mind, and remind students, of what life was like before the conveniences (and inconveniences) of the modern Internet age. The central question the unit ponders is whether America before social networking was a comparatively impoverished place, yearning for a forum in which people could connect from their homes, or a much simpler, better, easier world to live in. Have Facebook and its peers made life better or worse for the average American?

Preparing for Class Discussion

1. If there are any students in your class who don't use social networking (a remote possibility), ask them to explain why they don't. Do they get along just fine without it, or do they feel its void in their lives? Do students have

friends who are not on Facebook or Twitter? How do they view these friends if so—as hopeless Luddites or as refuseniks who may even be too cool to log in? Ask them to deeply consider what life would be like without their social-networking sites. Perhaps the change would not be as monumental as some imagine.

2. Many critics fault Facebook especially for storing massive amounts of data on its users, data it could (if the site proves unscrupulous) sell to advertisers or otherwise use to betray its loyal users. Other critics also point out (as Ham does) that Facebook and Twitter users have often been caught in a serious jam when a boss, or some other person with whom a social networker is not on entirely open terms, sees something on a profile that person was not meant to see. Defenders counter that nobody is forcing anyone to sign up for social-networking sites, and a person puts everything he puts about himself online voluntarily. Ask students for examples of concerns they've had using Facebook and similar sites. Are they at all concerned about the wrong people seeing their profile? About being stalked? About other privacy concerns?

From Discussion to Writing

1. This question works well as a good, creative assignment and will especially appeal to students with a background in science fiction. Is a world without social networking a horrible dystopia or a pastoral regeneration of a simpler and better time? Prompt students to imagine what life is like in some of the spaces where social networking's impact has been most obvious: in dating, for instance, or, to borrow material from Brett Baughman and Elizabeth Stone, in celebrating a friend's birthday or grieving over a loved one.

2. Some possible areas of focus not covered directly in this chapter are dating and relationships, doing business and networking, learning and education, political and volunteer organization, etc. Notice how almost any aspect of life works for this essay — that in and of itself should provide students with a lesson about the impact social networking has had. Keep students focused on the broader anthropological aspects of the Facebook-age phenomenon they are dissecting.

Topics for Cross-Cultural Discussion

1. Students will likely be familiar with countries in which Facebook is used in much the same way as it is domestically. But have them tease out Ham's distinction: Facebook and other sites have become virtually ubiquitous, but in places where life is harder and more fraught with uncertainty than it is in the United States and Western Europe, the uses of social networking tend to reflect this fact. Students with experience making friends from other countries online, or students who have family members overseas that use social-networking sites, will be especially valuable in this discussion.

2. Some countries have banned or restricted social networks because they fear the large-scale organization these sites so enormously facilitate.

Others, including China, have expressed concerns about the leaks of state secrets on networks where anyone can make any contribution he or she wishes. Consider with students other reasons governments are afraid of Facebook and its peers. What does this censorship say more about—those governments or Facebook?

11

Saving the Planet: Is It Too Late?

The global warming debate is one of the most peculiar in American life: In few other cases is the crux of a divide between Americans the question of whether a scientific conclusion is valid. At issue is simply whether the earth is rapidly warming, whether that poses a danger to human life, and whether human beings are to blame. Ask students to keep these questions in mind as they read the selections in this chapter, but also keep in mind the deeper issues that undergird them: Whether humans (and particularly human industry) can have an immediate impact on the natural environment, and what our responsibilities are as a society to alleviate this impact.

Bill McKibben begins the chapter by addressing one of the most familiar of our environmental responsibilities: recycling. But McKibben argues in "Waste Not Want Not" that it isn't only plastic bottles and rubber tires we're wasting. We live in a culture that epidemically wastes its resources, natural—economic, and even human.

In "Warming Gets Worse," *Rolling Stone* writer Jeff Goodell lays out the case for a state of climate-change emergency, while conservative Cal Thomas disputes both the premises and the conclusions of the argument in "Sinking 'Climate Change.'" Throughout these two essays, have your students consider why liberals and conservatives fall where they do in the divide: What is it about the conservative political disposition that rejects the premises of climate change?

Bill McKibben

Waste Not Want Not

[*Mother Jones*, May/June 2009]

Vocabulary/Using a Dictionary

1. *Hyper-* is a prefix meaning "too much" (as in *hyperactive*), and these terms refer to a social problem of too much consumption and consumer activity.

2. The word *particulates* is related to *particles*, and similarly describes small pieces of matter that float in the air. Particulates are finer than particles, however.

3. *Throughput* is a play on *input* and *output*, and refers to matter as it goes through the system.

Responding to Words in Context

1. Students are likely most familiar with the word describing a character—namely of a deeply unpleasant person. Generally, though, it refers to a sensory unpleasantness that is impossible to ignore, such as the large, visible forms of waste McKibben begins with.

2. *Margin* here is a term borrowed from the world of investing, where it refers to the capital available to an investor taking risks. It is related to the idea of a "margin of error," and thus to the more familiar concept of a border.

3. The word *thrifty* means hesitant to spend money, and *frugality* is the state of thriftiness.

Discussing Main Point and Meaning

1. McKibben argues that other societies (he mentions Tanzania) have enormous and expanding populations without using nearly the amount of energy Americans do. Costco, which sells excessively bulky quantities of consumer goods, is a symbol to McKibben of a kind of waste particular and endemic to Americans.

2. McKibben is referring, ironically, to a waste of human resources—the way a company that wants to lay off employees is likely to phrase its problem. McKibben doesn't believe a human being can be a "waste," and the reference is tongue-in-cheek.

3. The reference to "Harvard graduates" is meant more generally as an allusion to talented people, who McKibben believes are squandering their abilities working in the corporate world, for banks and other entities that add to the waste problem. McKibben would rather see talented youth go into jobs that are sustainable, help the environment, etc.

Examining Sentences, Paragraphs, and Organization

1. McKibben is referring to printed advertisements, particularly in catalogues and mailers. In addition to wasting paper, McKibben believes these ads contribute to our hyperconsumerist culture by fetishizing "stuff"—presenting the goods they're advertising in an almost pornographic way in order to increase Americans' lust for material possessions.

2. The list of forms of waste that literally exhausts McKibben here suggests that there are simply too many to list—he has to give up once he realizes how extensive a problem it is.

3. McKibben begins with the most obvious ("obnoxious," as he says) forms of waste: materials that are clogging the environment. As he moves on, his examples become more counterintuitive, until he is finally discussing social problems like employment and the use of our young people's talents that we would not conventionally place under the umbrella of waste.

Thinking Critically

1. Challenge students to think of the issue two ways: 1) Are the problems McKibben describes really all grouped under the heading of waste; and 2) Is it possible to have a truly less wasteful society? Ask students to imagine an America seriously committed to cutting down all of the forms of waste McKibben delineates. Is it really possible, or just a fantasy?

2. There are examples of humor throughout the essay. For instance, McKibben refers to a hypothetical Neanderthal tribe throwing out water bottles as having "no real effect except someday puzzling anthropologists," and summarizes the SUV craze by writing that "everyone in America thinks he requires the kind of vehicle that might make sense for a forest ranger." Students should note that McKibben isn't being flippant, however, but sardonic. His humor is expressing and encoding a sincere, if somewhat satirical, reproach for his society.

3. Many students will focus on the "waste of talent" argument as particularly ripe for disagreement. Ask them if they aspire to work in an industry McKibben considers wasteful after graduation. Why or why not? Could society function without those jobs and, if not, does that negate defining them as wasteful?

In-Class Writing Activities

1. Have students focus on the specifics here, particularly the ways government action needs to be coordinated with local, individual initiative. How can society encourage individuals—who are ultimately the key to changing large-scale behavior—to make more responsible, less wasteful decisions? How can individuals in turn change the patterns of wastefulness as they occur at higher, governmental levels?

2. McKibben is decidedly a liberal. He mentions wasting the talents of "gay folks," is incensed at environmental despoliation, and takes it for granted that corporations are often acting against the public good these days. Ask students who are more conservatively inclined what they think is wasteful about our society, and how we can fix it.

3. Have students consider whether these movements could make a real impact, especially when most Americans will likely find them incompatible with their lifestyles. Ask students to think up an advertising campaign for a postwaste movement they believe could make a real difference.

Jeff Goodell

Warming Gets Worse

[*Rolling Stone*, November 12, 2009]

Vocabulary/Using a Dictionary

1. *Permafrost* is land that is always frosted over, occurring near the North and South poles. The word has the prefix *perma-* from *permanent*.
2. *Microscopic* means "very small"—so small it requires a microscope to see. *Microscope* comes from Greek words meaning "small" and "see."
3. The noun *glacier* refers to a huge block of ice. The adjective *glacial* has come to mean "very slow," referring to the movement of glaciers in arctic waters.

Responding to Words in Context

1. *Greenhouse gases* are gases introduced into the atmosphere by various forms of pollution, and include carbon dioxide, methane, nitrous oxide, and ozone. They are worrisome because they contribute to the "greenhouse effect": They trap the sun's rays inside the atmosphere and thus raise the surface temperature on earth.
2. *Hosed*, to Jim White, means "completely finished"—or at least in deep trouble.
3. *A feedback loop* is another term for a *vicious* or *virtuous circle*, a process whose result accelerates or worsens the process itself. Familiar examples include the "poverty cycle," in which poor people, because of a lack of educational resources and other disadvantages, are likely to have children who will also be poor.

Discussing Main Point and Meaning

1. A furnace involves a central boiler that releases heat through ducts. Melting the Arctic will release more gases that would exacerbate the greenhouse problem.
2. A rise in sea level would sink low-lying coastal regions. Goodell is especially interested in poorer cities and countries, because they often lack preparedness and response mechanisms.
3. Goodell is likely to answer, besides providing his own numbers, that simple logical analysis of what is happening on the polar caps suggests that the problem will start getting bad soon, if it isn't already.

Examining Sentences, Paragraphs, and Organization

1. Goodell is illustrating just how cataclysmically major the effects of unchecked climate change will be. We shouldn't take this picture literally, but the incongruity of it should shake us—it's a far more effective image than simply citing figures of rising water levels would be.

2. The essay compares or quotes a comparison between the Arctic and a furnace, between the Arctic and a ticking time bomb, and between nature and a timekeeper. The subject of climate change can potentially be very dry, and using metaphor to enliven it is important in creating a reader's sense of urgency and personal investment in the problem.
3. The essay is quite pessimistic, but without fulminating or moralizing: It simply cites facts that read as incontrovertible. The effect of this tone is to make whatever a reader *can* do about the climate crisis seem worthwhile without a second thought.

Thinking Critically

1. The Copenhagen conference was widely regarded as a failure. The delegates did not agree on anything climate scientists regard as a long-term solution. Goodell's first sentence juxtaposes the delegates' meeting—we are tempted to imagine a large, slow bureaucratic process—with the problem they are seeking to address spiraling out of hand. The effect is to prime us to the idea that traditional solutions and approaches to the climate crisis are probably inadequate.
2. Goodell clearly thinks humans are to blame for the climate crisis, but does not feel compelled to argue to defend this point. He takes it for granted that the problem he's describing stems in part from our own policies: "thanks to our failure to reduce greenhouse-gas pollution," he says, "the fuse has already been lit."
3. Goodell clearly thinks reducing fossil fuel emissions is the only potential way to curb the warming of the earth caused by the greenhouse gas effect. But he implies throughout the essay that, because warming is accelerating in a feedback loop that's already in place, even large-scale action may be too late to be effective.

In-Class Writing Activities

1. Have students read this essay closely alongside the arguments of a climate-change skeptic like Cal Thomas (see below). Note how Thomas would regard the tone of Goodell's argument: as excessive, gratuitous fear-mongering. This question provides a good platform for a debate on the central thematic question of this chapter: Should we be afraid of a change in the climate, and why or why not?
2. Climate-change skeptics look to the warming of the earth, and the melting of the ice caps, as part of a cycle of temperature fluctuation that has been occurring on earth since its infancy and has little or nothing to do with human activity. They believe nature ultimately finds equilibrium, and any claims of total cataclysm as a result of the cycle are overblown.
3. Some skeptics have pointed to colder-than-average winters in many parts of the world—and to previous concerns about a "new ice age"—as rhetorical fodder against the existence of "global warming." As a result, environmentalists have adopted "climate change" as a more neutral term representing the irregular, but still catastrophic, changes in the earth's overall weather patterns they believe are caused by human behavior.

Cal Thomas

Sinking "Climate Change"

[*Townhall.com*, June 3, 2010]

Vocabulary/Using a Dictionary

1. A *consensus* is a general agreement within a community, particularly a community of experts on a particular topic. Thomas puts the word in scare quotes because he believes dissenting voices have not had their say.
2. *Domestic* means "at home," and here means within one's own country, as opposed to foreign. Domestic exploration of oil refers to drilling for oil locally, as opposed to importing it from elsewhere.
3. The adjective *dubious* means "doubtful or unlikely."

Responding to Words in Context

1. The word *myth* comes from the Greek word *mythos*, meaning "a story." It has come to mean a story that is widely believed but untrue, which is how Thomas uses it.
2. *Cuddly* means "cute and furry"; putting a cuddly face on the issue of climate change means making it more palatable by using the viscerally lovable image of a polar bear as opposed to colder, more objectively falsifiable statistics. Thomas obviously thinks using wildlife to promote the environmental agenda is a fallacious appeal to emotion.
3. A *cultist* is any member of a cult, a group that is swindled into subscribing on faith to precepts that are often false and promoted by charlatans.

Discussing Main Point and Meaning

1. Thomas believes that scientists and pundits who warn us about climate change are not well informed, but simply giving into a hysteria whose correspondence to reality they can not substantiate. The fact that thirty years ago *Newsweek* warned of global cooling and is now warning of global warming casts its concern as flimsy and malleable, and therefore ungrounded.
2. Most of our energy comes from fossil fuels, which are not renewable and which, when burned, introduce gases into the atmosphere that (people less skeptical than Thomas believe) create a greenhouse effect that is raising the earth's temperature.
3. Thomas believes we should be looking for more oil on our own coasts, which would not only have increased our supply of fossil fuels, but reduced the amount of money we send to oil producing nations in the Middle East that have also been targets of the war on terror.

Examining Sentences, Paragraphs, and Organization

1. Thomas is playing on the concern that the polar ice caps are melting and the water levels on earth are rising, a belief he is ridiculing as false.

2. Thomas wants to establish immediately that he is a conservative and at the same time hopes to link the "liberal" doctrine of anthropogenic climate change to Obama and Pelosi. This helps him appeal to his audience, which has presumably been disappointed by Democrats in Washington, and will connect the fear of climate change to them.

3. The *Focus* article further confuses the causes and effects of climate change, and suggests an alternative explanation for rising temperatures—the meteorological phenomenon El Niño, and not pollution, it suggests, may be the cause of the recent spike in hot years.

Thinking Critically

1. Thomas is suggesting that environmentalists are less concerned with saving the planet from peril and more concerned with increasing the power of government, and particularly of the federal government, at the expense of individual liberties. Notice how this aligns with the rest of Thomas's conservative platform and agenda.

2. Thomas considers the media an arm of the liberal establishment in Washington, and suggests that they are not above fabricating or spinning the facts in order to sell a liberal package of responses to climate change.

3. Students should recognize that climatedepot.com is decidedly conservative and appeals directly to climate–change skeptics like Thomas. Use this question to consider the issue of confirmation bias in the climate debate—both sides favor sources that provide statistics in line with their preconceived views of the causes and seriousness of climate change.

In-Class Writing Activities

1. By now students should understand the breakdown of liberal and conservative positions on climate change and how they relate to the rest of the contemporary political philosophies with which they correspond. Liberals believe human beings should be responsible, on a large scale, for the environment; conservatives believe that environmentalism is an attempt to abridge basic freedoms and rights, particularly those of the businesses accused of polluting the environment. Many students are likely to feel passionate on the issue; those that believe climate change is real in particular may feel that our response should not be a politically divisive issue if the facts bear out that it is happening.

2. Challenge students to consider where they get their information on climate change. Is it possible that they are coming at the issue from a biased perspective? What ulterior motives could those who promote their opinions on the issue have besides the search for scientific truth?

3. There are dozens of examples of inertia in politics. Students may feel passionate about issues ranging from the war in Iraq to the refusal to legalize marijuana. Remind them of the importance of political will and political capital, and especially the amount of each that it requires to contravene a wide consensus and a widely held public feeling.

Yevgeniya Lomakina (student essay)

"Going Green" Misses the Point

[*The Daily Collegian*, University of Massachusetts, April 22, 2010]

Vocabulary/Using a Dictionary

1. An *initiative* is a proposal or an act designed to improve something; it comes from a Latin word meaning "to begin." One example of a green initiative would be a government plan to incentivize reducing auto emissions; another would be handing out more efficient light bulbs in a community.

2. *Novelty* is a noun meaning "newness," from the Latin word for "new." Here it means the relatively untested distribution methods of green products. Note that the relationship of the word to *novel* derives from a time when long-form fiction was a new literary form. Another use of the word *novelty* can refer to any amusing object with no real purpose, which is where the term "novelty shop" originates.

3. An *emission* is a noun, from the Latin for "to put out," referring to anything that is released by a system. *Carbon emissions* are simply the gases released by carbon-burning devices like automobiles.

Responding to Words in Context

1. Lomakina's catchphrase is "going green," and related phrases about the green economy and lifestyle. *Catchphrase* is a relatively pejorative term for a phrase repeated by people and spread by media without concern for its appropriateness to the situation. Another example might be "death panels," in reference to the The Patient Protection and Affordable Care Act. In this case, Lomakina wishes to cast the green movement as somewhat empty.

2. Produce is considered *organic* if it is grown without pesticides, which environmentalists believe have long-term deleterious effects on the environment.

3. *Consumerism* is the attitude of capitalistic covetousness for material goods. Our *consumerist desires*, in Lomakina's construction, are simply our desires for consumer goods.

Discussing Main Point and Meaning

1. Scientists say the emission of carbon dioxide, and other greenhouse gases, traps the sun's heat inside the atmosphere and raises the temperature of the earth, or at least leads to radical temperature fluctuations.

2. Lomakina is criticizing the materialism of the environmental movement, one she associates with the larger pattern of American consumerism. Americans, she writes, are so eager to buy things that their method of getting involved in environmentalism is to purchase more stuff, which, she argues, ultimately has destructive effects on the environment.

3. Lomakina endorses activities that are meaningful on a local level, rather than feeding into a general green fad. Examples could include unplugging cell phone chargers at night and driving less instead of driving more efficient cars. Underlying Lomakina's essay is the theme that traditional green behavior is actually quite easy and a way of placating consumers who need to make more sweeping changes in their overall behavior.

Examining Sentences, Paragraphs, and Organization

1. The implication of this phrase is that green initiatives are only words, not actions. Actions are much harder than slogans and catchphrases, but the environmental movement hasn't gone far enough beyond the surface.
2. Lomakina is setting up a contrast between behavior that will make a real difference in helping to save the environment and behavior that is merely a bandage that makes consumers feel better about themselves. The rhetorical questions, in particular, represent the way the modern consumerist culture addresses environmental issues.
3. Lomakina is suggesting that large environmental action groups like the Sierra Club are out of touch, and more concerned with preserving their own images than with preserving the natural environment. She implies that criticism from within is essential to keeping the environmental movement successful, and succinctly points out that this criticism comes only from individuals, not from nonprofit behemoths.

Thinking Critically

1. Have students compare other movements they're involved in to the environmental movement. They may even think of it outside of the context of activism: Does it make them like a band, or a TV show, any less to know that other fans appreciate it for different reasons? Why should the composition of the tent make any difference to the various committed members inside it?
2. Some students may point to the positive effects celebrities and other public figures can have even on the kind of private behavior Lomakina is describing. Campaigns for conservation and environmental consciousness on the level she advocates often thrive because of how publicly aware they are.
3. The United States emits a massively disproportionate amount of greenhouse gas and other pollutants, due to its inordinate industrialization. Some students will argue that that puts the burden on the U.S. government, or even on individual Americans, to take serious green action; others will likely feel that, as it's a dilemma that faces all human beings, human beings have to work together regardless of boundaries to fix it.

In-Class Writing Activities

1. Break the class into groups and have them assess each other's plans. In a matrix as complex as reversing environmental destruction, there are a number of factors to consider: Are the plans feasible? Will they be effective? Are they an easy way out where a tougher, less palatable course of action may be the only real solution?
2. Have students assess the green initiatives they have witnessed in the mass media. What kinds of large- and small-scale behavior are we taught will save the planet? Are these real solutions or just placebos? How, from our current vantage, can we tell the difference?
3. Look for press releases and strategies that take full advantage of the strengths of social media, namely organizing at the local level. How can students use tools like Facebook and other social networks to get their peers involved in solutions to the climate crisis, and other environmental crises, that require individual participation in large-scale efforts?

Discussing the Unit

Suggested Topic for Discussion

Some students may not fully believe in climate change, while others may be completely convinced of its existence and its severity. Students may want to discuss how public opinion can affect scientific findings think of Copernicus and Galileo—and how politicians have used global warming as a tool for campaigning. Some may see the idea of politicians latching onto global warming as a good thing because it may inspire debate and more funding for research, while others may be skeptical of its place in politics, regardless of whether they believe it is real or not.

Preparing for Class Discussion

1. Conservatives tend to distrust environmentalism, perhaps in part because they see it as hostile to business and private development, issues near to their heart. Culturally, conservatives also tend (with many exceptions) to come from parts of the country closer to agriculture and where conservational sentiment is weaker. You may want to connect this to the debate over drilling for oil in Arctic reserves. Liberals believe in conserving these areas and developing other sources of energy, while conservatives ridicule what they see as a terribly misplaced concern for Alaskan caribou over Americans being squeezed at the gas pump. Remind students, however, that environmentalism is not an exclusively liberal domain: It was a Republican (Teddy Roosevelt) who created our national parks system, and another one (Richard Nixon) who presided over the creation of the Environmental Protection Agency. What is it about our modern political climate, though, that has made conservatives more automatically hostile to the idea that the planet is in trouble and that humans should do something about it?

2. Refer particularly to Jeff Goodell's essay, but turn this into a broader discussion about optimism and pessimism, environmental and otherwise, in America. Are there truly intractable problems, or is there always some solution—even when we're perhaps unwilling to brave it? Connect this question to other units in the book: race, immigration, etc.

From Discussion to Writing

1. McKibben and Goodell take for granted that a solution will come from some combination of government action and individual initiative. We all need to pitch in, but in the end the problem is so large that huge actors like the federal government need to be involved in solving it. Where do students stand on this question? Are their answers based more in their general convictions about the role of government in public and private life or more in their beliefs about what the solution (if one is needed) to climate change will actually be? Challenge the private-sector students to consider the possibility that the answer will involve some massive project, like shooting a cocktail of chemicals into the air. (This has been proposed.) Can the private sector really be trusted to undertake something like that? Conversely, ask students who have faith in the government whether Washington may be too slow and inefficient to deal with a problem essentially caused by inefficiency.

2. Scientists rarely write popular scientific articles, because the actual conclusions of science are far too complex and nuanced for a general audience with a typical attention span to understand and appreciate. Ask students if they think the preponderance of pundits in this chapter, and accordingly in the larger debate, suggests a larger problem in our public discourse. Should we aim to cultivate magazines and newspapers that treat issues of scientific import with more of a scientific approach?

Topics for Cross-Cultural Discussion

1. Many commentators have pointed out the cruel irony that the countries most likely to be affected by climate change are the ones that have contributed the least to its putative anthropogenic causes: poor countries like those in sub-Saharan Africa, South and Southeast Asia. Much of the hard work needed to overcome climate change will also have to come from developing countries like China and India, whose rapid growth comes at the cost of large-scale environmental damage.

2. Students should divide on the causes of American skepticism. Some will consider American optimism in the ability to fix the problems of the world quickly and easily the root of this divide, but others will argue that Americans are the least likely and the least willing to surrender the carbon-burning lifestyle that most scientists say is at least partially to blame for the problem.

12

Immigration: Who Is an American?

In 2010, the state of Arizona raised passions throughout the country to a boiling point when it passed a law authorizing local authorities to ask for documentation from anyone they suspected of being in the state—and the country—illegally. The law, opponents said, not only gave the state a traditionally federal power of enforcing legal immigration, but would inevitably lead to racial profiling.

But the fracas reflected larger issues that remain at the forefront of America's debate over its borders: Who is an American? Who deserves to be in America? What protections, if any, do we owe people who are here illegally? And why, after all, do so many people want to come to the United States—particularly from Latin America?

The chapter begins with a debate on a question that often underlies our discourse on immigration: Are immigrants inherently harder working than native-born Americans, and is there an attendant economic value in having a large immigrant population? Tamar Jacoby answers that immigration does indeed "increase the virtues of hard work and fortitude in the United States," because the hardship of immigration reduces the immigrant population to only the most industrious. Mark Krikorian disputes both claims in his brief response.

"The Crossing," by an undocumented worked pseudonymously named Vicente Martinez, gives a first-person account of what the immigrant experience is really like, supporting Jacoby's view more than Krikorian's. Luis Rodríguez considers the experience of immigrants, legal and otherwise, already past the crossing stage; in "Slurring Spanish" he describes the plight of Spanish-speaking students in American schools and argues for more bilingualism there.

The final two essays in the chapter consider immigration from the angles of other groups affected by the debate. In "Uniting Families" student Elyse Toplin makes an argument for expanding citizenship to gay and lesbian couples with a foreign-born partner, and in "Migrations Forced and Free" Ira Berlin questions whether recent immigrants from Africa and the Caribbean belong to the history-rich African American community.

DEBATE: Does Immigration Increase the Virtues of Hard Work and Fortitude in the United States?

Tamar Jacoby (Yes)

[*In Character*, Spring 2009]

Vocabulary/Using a Dictionary

1. *Winnow* is an agricultural term meaning to separate wheat from chaff with a gust of air. Jacoby is using it with its metaphorical force, meaning to separate the weak from the strong over time.
2. *Norms* are social conventions; American norms include the idea of a two-parent family, a career, home ownership, etc.

Responding to Words in Context

1. Jacoby uses *scrappier* here to mean extremely determined, despite significant obstacles.
2. A *beacon* is a light used for guiding ships, but Jacoby is using it more figuratively to mean a shining example that guides the world and attracts newcomers—it is famous in this sense as a nickname for America, dating back to the Pilgrims.

Discussing Main Point and Meaning

1. Jacoby is trying to establish that immigrants do not come to America in order to leech off of American resources and the American way of life, as many detractors suggest. Nor do they come out of simple whimsical preference for America over their home countries. Rather, true economic exigency and emergency forces their migration. Jacoby uses the economic argument to suggest that we should sympathize with people whose motives are similar to our own.
2. Jacoby is referring to the types of jobs we often associate, usually accurately, with the majority of migrant workers: cleaning, busing tables, working on farms, etc., for very little money. Jacoby reminds us once again that the jobs immigrants take do not represent a threat to the American workforce—few of us would want such jobs. Krikorian, an opponent of immigration, does not focus on these jobs, turning his attention instead to the negative impact immigrants have on social entitlement programs like welfare.

Examining Sentences, Paragraphs, and Organization

1. The third and fourth paragraphs of Jacoby's essay are rich with statistics, but by the end she focuses on the more intangible aspects of immigration. This is an effective way of laying a theoretical groundwork, but bringing the essay overall back to the more specific and personal.
2. Jacoby is suggesting that hardworking immigrants who instill their values in their children should have even more hardworking descendants.

Some students might challenge this premise, preferring to assume that children born in the comfort of the United States, and immune to the vicious struggles of immigration and assimilation Jacoby describes, will be—for lack of a better word—lazier.

Thinking Critically

1. Jacoby is describing a process akin to biological natural selection, in which only the immigrants most suited to the harsh travails of their migration—and therefore the toughest and probably the hardest-working—will survive the ordeal without dying or returning home.

2. Jacoby suggests that immigrants (and particularly undocumented ones) get the advantage of relocating to a better life in America, while we get the advantage of their cheap labor in the short term. The first part is beyond much argument, though some students might wonder whether conditions in America are really worth the hardships required to get and stay here. Other students may argue with the second claim on the basis that it encourages an ugly sort of exploitation that dare not speak its name.

In-Class Writing Activities

1. Ask students to draw on their own experience in answering this question, and compare it to that of their classmates. How long have their families been in America, and where do they rank themselves against their forebears in terms of the "pluck and determination" Jacoby discusses?

2. In the context of the immigration debate, most of us assume "immigrants" are from Latin America. Some students will typify them as hard-working, winnowed as they are by the experience of coming here, and desperate as they are to make a better life for themselves. Other students may see immigrants less romantically, imagining them—more along Krikorian's lines—as somewhat greedy and no more productive than the average legal citizen. Encourage students to be imaginative with this activity, emphasizing the way we perceive immigrants (even visually) and how that perception lines up with reality.

DEBATE: Does Immigration Increase the Virtues of Hard Work and Fortitude in the United States?

Mark Krikorian (No)

[*In Character*, Spring 2009]

Vocabulary/Using a Dictionary

1. *Grit* is a term for small particles of stone or sand like dust. *Gritty* means covered with grit, suggesting hard work and courage. Krikorian puts the word in scare quotes because he disagrees that immigrants automatically deserve the modifier.

2. *Transnationalism* is defined as the philosophy of extending oneself, one's ideas, or one's efforts, across national borders. It comes from the prefix *trans-*, meaning "across."

Responding to Words in Context

1. *Decadence* can mean either moral or cultural downfall or decay, or luxurious self-indulgence. Krikorian uses it in both senses—he is referring to a putative American collapse caused by a collapse in our moral structure, particularly our sense of industry and hard work.

2. A *parasite* is an organism that lives off another; here Krikorian uses the word figuratively to cast immigrants, in the conception of the pundit he's imagining, as leeches living off the hard work of Americans.

Discussing Main Point and Meaning

1. Krikorian is saying that this labor, performed by unskilled workers, is not especially valuable because it's easy to find and commands less money than highly skilled labor.

2. A *miasma* is a deeply unpleasant situation—here Krikorian is referring to the fact that undocumented immigrants must openly break the law in order to survive in American society.

Examining Sentences, Paragraphs, and Organization

1. The essay thrives on a contrast between European immigrants from previous generations, who endured a degree of self-selection and whose labor was uniquely valuable at the time, and immigrants today, whose labor is less valuable and whose conditions of entry to the country obviate the "pluck" inculcated in their forebears.

2. This short paragraph delivers the major thematic punch of the essay: that immigrants do not provide the kind of general utility critics like Jacoby believe they do. Have students observe the rhetorical technique of building up evidence in longer paragraphs and then summarizing the conclusion in a one-sentence paragraph.

Thinking Critically

1. Jacoby's statistics suggest that immigrants take advantage of public welfare programs far less than do Krikorian's. Students may note that Jacoby only argues that illegal immigrants are not eligible for welfare, whereas Krikorian may be accounting for cases of welfare fraud.

2. Krikorian pictures the countries from which the immigrant population is drawn—namely those of Central America—as being without industrial mechanization and the attendant modern social advancement of the United States. Some students may argue this characterization represents a severe exaggeration, and that countries like Mexico are in fact quite advanced industrially and socially. All students should recognize that, because Krikorian's argument rests on the premise that immigrant

labor is not especially useful anymore, the characterization of these societies is central to his point.

In-Class Writing Activities

1. Remind students that Krikorian is writing in a magazine that is consumed almost entirely by middle-class or richer people. Some students might feel that his rhetoric would be different if he were writing with immigrants themselves in his audience; he might, for instance, be more sensitive to the difficulty and peril of the sorts of jobs they do. Have students discuss as a group whether it's possible to bring people into the dialogue —immigrants, the urban poor, etc.—who are central to it but often alienated from it.

2. Break students into teams for a lively debate on this interesting topic. Have them identify the cruces of the debate between Jacoby and Krikorian: whether the immigrant experience hardens and winnows people so that only the hardest working are left; whether immigrants in fact do work harder than native-born Americans; whether their work is valuable because Americans won't do it or relatively cheap because it's so easy to replace workers; and whether it's good and right for us to rely on this hard work to pick our crops and build our cities while immigrants themselves often live in poverty. Encourage them to come up with other main points in their argument.

Vicente Martinez

The Crossing

[*Oregon Humanities*, Fall/Winter 2009]

Vocabulary/Using a Dictionary

1. The word *isolated* comes from the Latin *isola*, meaning "an island"; *isolated* means not connected to other people or things, as an island is unconnected to a continent.

2. *Seep* is a verb from Old English *sipian*, meaning "to leak slowly through small openings." It is almost always used to describe liquids.

3. *Hypothermia* means simply a lack of warmth, from the prefix *hypo-* meaning "too little" and *thermia* meaning "heat." It is a medical condition, usually caused by exposure to the elements, in which a person's body temperature becomes dangerously low.

Responding to Words in Context

1. *Commerce* is the exchange of goods, and the adjective *commercial* means relating to that exchange. We're familiar with it from television commercial advertisements, but a commercial area is a part of a city or town that stands in contrast to a residential one.

2. *Terrain* refers to the topography, or the physical features, of a stretch of land.

3. The *shoulder* of a highway is the lane on either side of it usually reserved for broken-down cars.

Discussing Main Point and Meaning

1. Martinez is older than the typical migrant and slightly frailer; he also has HIV, which makes him weaker yet and also means he has to carry his medication with him.
2. The coyotes are vicious, motivated by profit more than altruism at every turn, and they treat the migrants terribly. One example of many is that they force their human cargo to take off their shoes when they go to the bathroom to discourage them from escaping.
3. The coyotes cover Martinez's head with a blanket to keep him from knowing, he suspects, exactly where they live. This detail reinforces the cruelty and inhumanity of the entire process, and particularly of the coyotes.

Examining Sentences, Paragraphs, and Organization

1. Martinez intends to put his reader directly into the scene visually and objectively. The descriptions of the terrain are a crucial aspect of this objectivity, both painting us a vivid portrait of the crossing—particularly its harsh landscape and brutal temperatures—and stirring sympathy for a man who had to undertake it, whatever our feelings about the legality of the situation.
2. The unbroken, objective narrative is a major facet of this essay's central style, and a reason the essay is so effective. Rather than considering the morality of immigration, the INS, or anything else, Martinez shows us the crossing exactly as he experienced it, and leaves it to us to decide what to make of it. This is a good strategy for an essay on a controversial topic.

Thinking Critically

1. "Undocumented worker" has far less negative connotations than does "illegal immigrant," which implies that the individual him- or herself is illegal. The first term also stresses the work the immigrants do, in contrast with the stereotype of these migrants as lazy drains on the system. Students are likely to divide on which term is more accurate and better roughly along the lines of their feelings on immigration and immigration reform.
2. The scene with the INS checkpoint strongly implies that the system is ineffective as well as unfair—some minor choreography gets Martinez past the checkpoint easily. But Martinez suggests that the checkpoint relies on racial profiling to catch illegal immigrants, checking cars not for papers but for Mexicans.
3. The community is close, tight-knit, and mutually supportive, paying coyotes, hosting big dinners, and generally doing what it can to assure

the survival and comfort, such as it is, of its members. Some students might be surprised to find this contrast to occasional stereotypes of migrant communities as especially competitive, dog-eat-dog populations.

In-Class Writing Activities

1. Martinez's writing style is extremely plain, rarely internalizing, and describing what he's seen and heard as objectively as possible. Most of the scenes in the narrative are especially effective because of this objectivity in making us experience what he went through. For instance, in the scene where the guide scans the horizon, Martinez gives us a few guesses of what he's looking for, but doesn't tell us for sure, because he doesn't know. We feel the uncertainty and confusion that accompanies Martinez's journey far more viscerally here than had he simply and explicitly asserted it.
2. Responses will vary widely, but look for them to draw on Martinez's style, focusing on what actually happened—especially the bitter hardships of the journey—rather than the broader implications or meaning of this journey. Remind students of how much this strategy puts us in the place of the actual immigrant, not just a participant in the debate over immigration.
3. This question offers the best opportunity in the unit for a conventional debate on immigration and immigration reform. Have students break into two groups and pick out points from their essays as cruces of contention for an oral debate. Then ask them to describe how reading Martinez's narrative changed, if at all, their thoughts on the issue.

Luis J. Rodríguez

Slurring Spanish

[*The Progressive*, March 2010]

Vocabulary/Using a Dictionary

1. A *curriculum* was originally a race course, but is now generally used to mean the course of education someone undertakes—that is, the requirements for completing a degree or the materials taught within a degree program.
2. *Bi-* means "two." Other examples include *bicolored, binocular, biennial, bisexual,* etc.
3. *Ramifications* is related to the verb *ramify*, which means "to spread or branch out." The word has come to mean the complex set of consequences some thing or action has.

Responding to Words in Context

1. *Multicultural* simply means embracing many (multi-) cultures. Rodríguez definitely uses the word as a general positive—an attitude we need to adopt more universally.

2. *Derailment* means going off a rail, and its literal meaning applies to trains. Rodríguez is using the word metaphorically.
3. Rodríguez means falling victim to drugs, gang violence, or other misfortunes measured by statistics. This construction suggests such a misfortune renders these young victims nothing more than fodder for analysts.

Discussing Main Point and Meaning

1. Rodríguez says that punishing students for speaking their native language, particularly Spanish, makes them feel marginalized and damages their self-esteem.
2. Rodríguez writes that Spanish-speaking students feel alienated from their education as a result of a single-language system.
3. In the penultimate paragraph of the essay, Rodríguez writes that other countries emphasize "the skill of speaking more than one language," and suggests that all students would benefit from the United States following suit.

Examining Sentences, Paragraphs, and Organization

1. The two narratives have a great deal in common, and Rodríguez is certainly inviting the comparison. In both cases, the students—Rodríguez and Zaragoza—were marginalized for being Spanish speakers. By juxtaposing them, Rodríguez is suggesting that things may have gotten a little better (Zaragoza is not "swatted"), but not nearly enough, since Spanish speakers are still treated as second-class students.
2. The paragraphs are 7, 10, 15, and 19. Rodríguez says he wants to "defer to the wisdom" of Zaragoza, but it's also important for his argument that his readers hear about the plight of Spanish-speaking students from one of them, particularly one who is eloquent and passionate; this lends the argument both a personal touch and some rhetorical gravitas.
3. Rodríguez uses *no problema* as a callback to the phrase that nearly got a student suspended. By repeating it in this upbeat context, he robs it of the negative connotations the near-suspension gave both the phrase and the general practice of speaking Spanish in school. By using a phrase we can all decipher and most of us know, he also illustrates how harmless, and even beneficial, bilingualism can be.

Thinking Critically

1. Students should have a sense of the larger implications of the argument —to what degree English should be treated as an "official" language, and what the implications of that question are for Spanish speakers. Many students are likely to sympathize with foreigners, often poor ones, who are having a hard enough time adapting to life in America without being forced to learn English immediately. Others will make the more pragmatic argument that government (and government services

like public schools) can not run efficiently in multiple languages, and including Spanish means by necessity including every other language as well.

2. Rodríguez mentions his many publications, an impressive feat even for a native English speaker. Ask students to consider how they would gauge their own success if they were forced to live in a country whose language they didn't speak at first. What could they expect to achieve as expatriates, and what do they think is a reasonable goal? With so many Spanish speakers in America, what sorts of standards should we have as a society for their success?

3. One example is Belgium, in which Dutch and French are spoken almost evenly. Canada, in which French is a minority language but appears on all official documents, may also be a familiar example. Both of these countries, of course, harbored speakers of each language before achieving nationhood, while America was principally English speaking through most of its early history. Challenge students to consider whether this really matters. What would it take to make America more like its multilingual peers in the world community?

In-Class Writing Activities

1. Three major arguments against bilingual education are: 1) it keeps Spanish-speaking students from learning English, an essential skill for their success in America; 2) it creates confusion and slows down education for students of all languages; and 3) it is impractical when students may come from countries where a language other than English or Spanish is spoken. Rodríguez would likely answer: 1) Spanish-speaking students will learn English from immersion in America; 2) exposing English speakers to Spanish will actually assure far more bilingual young people, which is good for everyone; 3) practical limits will of course have to be applied, but more exposure to foreign cultures and languages is never a bad thing.

2. When students are finished with this exercise, ask them to evaluate what could have made the difference in making their traits advantages. Were they burdened by them because of their own failures to exercise their potential? By other people's prejudices? Some combination of the two?

3. Students defending English-only laws will likely argue for them as a practical measure—to make things easier at the DMV or in school. The argument against them is typically more philosophical, focusing on giving people the right to live in a society that is not automatically hostile to their way of communicating. Conversely, challenge students to think of the philosophical reasons for having a single language in a country—and the pragmatic advantages of multilingualism.

Elyse Toplin (student essay)

Uniting Families

[*The Hullabaloo*, Tulane University, January 29, 2010]

Vocabulary/Using a Dictionary

1. *Deportation* comes from the prefix *de-* meaning "out of," and the Latin *portare*, meaning "to carry." It means the shipping of something, usually a person, out of a country forcefully.

2. *Homo-* and *hetero-* are Greek prefixes meaning "the same" and "different," respectively. Students should be familiar with the prefixes in the scientific words *homogeneous* (made up of the same material) and *heterogeneous* (made up of different materials).

Responding to Words in Context

1. In the context of law and government, to *introduce* a bill, or proposed law, means to suggest it formally.

2. Toplin is borrowing the phrase from the Declaration of Independence, tying the struggle of gay men and women to that of the struggles to found the country and overcome tyranny.

Discussing Main Point and Meaning

1. Toplin is referring to people who are not really in a relationship with someone pretending to be in one to get him or her citizenship. This is a very common form of fraud for which immigration authorities are constantly on the watch.

2. Toplin lists countries with similar legislation that are considered advanced, developed nations. The long list makes it appear that the United States is truly behind the times and maybe even backwards in its failure to recognize gay couples.

Examining Sentences, Paragraphs, and Organization

1. The first paragraph of the essay lays out a general legal problem theoretically, while the second transitions into a personal, anecdotal example with "Meet Gordon Stewart." Toplin is challenging us with this transition to see the problem of gay couples' citizenship rights not as a vague and hypothetical one, but through the lens of an actual individual struggling to secure his rights.

2. See the answer to Thinking Critically question 2 below—Toplin is characterizing the couple as normal, productive, and unthreatening to the basic American values of family and community.

3. Toplin brings up the fraud counterargument in paragraph 7, but responds cogently by arguing that the problem of defrauding immigration authorities is not a gay or straight one. The paragraph is important, however,

because anticipating one of her opponents' strongest and no doubt most popular arguments gives Toplin an edge and makes her entire essay read as more thoughtful and meticulous.

Thinking Critically

1. The arguments for extending citizenship are chiefly of convenience and encouraging the family unit—giving committed families in which one partner is from overseas the comfort and civil rights that domestically born couples have. The arguments against it are that it is easy to defraud, especially as relationships become more diaphanous, and that it admits lots of new citizens with access to our services. Some students may argue that the best way to control the number of citizens as entitlements increase is to continue to restrict new entrants, even those married to citizens. Indeed, some countries, like Kuwait, take this hard line on citizenship.

2. Toplin characterizes the couples as happy, functional, good citizens—carefully drawing her readers away from the ugly stereotypes of gay people that sometimes pervade the media and our national consciousness. She writes of Tan and Mercado, for instance, that "the family goes to church, the parents are involved in the school, and the kids get good grades." She also stresses that the couples are "tax-paying" and "law-abiding." This picture resembles our standard notion of a happy, productive family, and suggests that gay couples look only to expand this institution, not to corrupt it.

3. Toplin puts aside the well-worn argument over gay marriage and argues only for a modest, basic extension of rights. She lists other countries in which similar recognition already exists, but not all of these countries allow gay marriage. Her argument does not presume gay marriage should be legal, but students should recognize that reactions to Toplin's argument are likely to fall along the same lines as general feelings about gay rights, especially the right to marry.

In-Class Writing Activities

1. Students might guess correctly that immigration authorities must constantly struggle to tell phony relationships arranged for one partner to get a green card apart from sincere, committed ones, and that this is true of heterosexual as well as gay couples. It becomes even more of a problem, in fact, as the nature and variety of relationships change. Ask students to think up solutions that respect the different ways people show commitment but still reduces fraud and makes sure citizenship is extended neither too liberally nor too stingily.

2. Responses will vary widely, but look for recommendations that stress the importance of immigrants to the American workforce but also recognize the need to keep borders secure and reward legal immigration. Encourage students who are drawing a blank to look at both major parties' platforms on immigration, available on their Web sites.

Ira Berlin

Migrations Forced and Free

[*Smithsonian*, February 2010]

Vocabulary/Using a Dictionary

1. An *ideal* is an imaginary state of perfection, and *idealism* is the philosophical disposition that such a state is at least partially achievable. It is usually accompanied by political activity its practitioners believe will help make the world a better place. *Abolitionist idealism*, in turn, casts the efforts of the men and women who worked to abolish slavery in nineteenth-century America as striving for a more perfect future despite the opposition not only of slavery proponents but of cynics.
2. See the answer to In-Class Writing Activity question 2 below: "Collective consciousness" was a term coined by French sociologist Émile Durkheim to refer to the shared ideas and perceptions of a certain group that operate as a force in society.
3. *Disfranchisement* means the loss of an important civil right, especially the right to vote. One's *franchise* is often used to mean one's voting rights.

Responding to Words in Context

1. *Authorship* means being the creator of something, by analogy to writing it. Here Berlin means that the slaves did the work to create their own freedom.
2. Berlin uses *knot*, which here means a heavily congested crowd, to suggest visually a group of people huddled closely together.
3. *Rooted* means "coming from," as a tree comes out of its roots, but the word has further implications and significance here because of the context of our ancestry (or "roots").

Discussing Main Point and Meaning

1. A migration is a movement, particularly of a large group of people—like an ethnic group—from one geographical location to another. The "forced" migration in Berlin's title refers to the triangle trade and slavery; the Africans and Caribbean Americans who have come since slavery, Berlin implies, have had a relatively more "free" migratory experience.
2. Berlin is referring to slavery, and the ensuing segregation and discrimination particular to the Southern United States. Other black people, including those from the Caribbean, have no doubt faced adversity, but they tend not to share in this special history, according to Berlin.
3. Berlin was impressed by how little notionally "black" people understood about the heritage of slavery and discrimination when that her-

itage was not directly linked to their own. He suggests the conversation weighed on his mind so much partially because it occurred in the context of a discussion about the importance of black people in securing their own rights and future. But it led him to consider how important an understanding of one's own ancestral struggles is in confronting the struggles of the future.

Examining Sentences, Paragraphs, and Organization

1. The examples Berlin offers come from a wide variety of ethnic groups, not just blacks; this variety attempts to illustrate how important the celebration of ethnic identity is to all people everywhere.
2. Berlin begins with an anecdote that will illuminate his ultimate expositional point—that history is particularly important to African Americans who were "long denied a past." The anecdote is especially effective because the point is complicated, and best understood by witnessing people from outside the group whose cohesion Berlin is interested in discussing. After this anecdote, Berlin moves through a short history of African Americans and immigration, and how the two are related. He shows the transformation of Black America, giving a truncated history that supports his eventual argument, which he leaves the reader with in the final paragraph. Many students may find that this is an effective method, since he brings the reader into the article with an anecdote, provides ample support for his argument, and then leaves the reader with his final statement, that, as he puts it, "African-American history is, in the end, of one piece" (para. 18).

Thinking Critically

1. This question relies on a basic outline of the history of the Civil War—make sure to give some rudimentary background. Students should recognize the view that slaves were helpless in the physical battle over their emancipation, which was largely fought by white soldiers. Some may argue, however, that there were a number of well-known African American units in the Civil War, which played an outsize role in defeating the institution of slavery. Others might argue, as Berlin probably did on the radio show, that undergoing the horrible cruelty and oppression of slavery, and responding eloquently and peacefully through ambassadors like Frederick Douglass, hastened the end of the institution.
2. Some students will argue that *black* refers only to a color, whether the black person is from Africa, the Americas, or elsewhere. The other extreme view is that the descendants of African slaves are the only real "black" people in America. Ask students to think carefully about counterexamples. Are recent arrivals with dark skin, like the ones Berlin describes, who do not have the cultural memory of the legacy of slavery and discrimination other black people harbor, really part of the same racial equation? On the other hand, isn't a descendant of a recent African immigrant (like, say, Barack Obama) black?

3. Students will likely divide on celebrations like Black History Month—some seeing a ceremonial connection to heritage as an important part of that heritage in a diverse society, and others seeing these celebrations as divisive, arguing that America should celebrate only America. Prompt those advocating a more "race-blind" model to consider large-scale celebrations of their own legacy and tradition, and not only other groups'. Ask those who take the side of such celebrations, on the other hand, to acknowledge ways outsiders might feel alienated by them, and suggest ways of reconciling this feeling.

In-Class Writing Activities

1. Look for students to write not only about the larger group they come from (African, European, etc.) but the smaller subgroups and the specifics of their heritage as they've had it articulated to them. Ask them to consider not only how the vicissitudes of their origin stories have come to define them and the way they think about the world, but whether they feel connected to other people with similar origin stories today.
2. The "collective consciousness," especially as Berlin uses it, refers to the common ideas and principles that underlie the thinking of a group—whether everyone in society or, as used here, a particular ethnic group—such that it appears the group is almost of one mind. Point out that the term comes from sociology—it was coined by Émile Durkheim—but that Berlin is using it here as a measure of shared ideology. Students should divide in their writing between those who argue that individuals within a group, especially a group as large as "black people in mainland North America," are too unique and distinct to share such a consciousness, and those who believe that such a construct is useful or even accurate in describing the way people in groups think and draw their thinking from each other.

Discussing the Unit

Suggested Topic for Discussion

This unit requires students to consider a variety of perspectives on the border. Have them begin by thinking of what the border means—to an undocumented immigrant like Martinez, to an English-speaking activist like Rodríguez, and to Americans like Jacoby and Krikorian. What is the border, and what does it separate—physically as well as figuratively?

Preparing for Class Discussion

1. The twin cruces of the debate in this chapter are 1) how much immigrants add to or subtract from the lives of native-born Americans, and 2) what is the fairest and most humane way to treat recent arrivals. Jacoby and Krikorian, as well as Rodríguez to an extent, are preoccupied with the first question. Ask students which question is more important.

Can we, and should we, rightfully exclude people from our society even if we can say for sure they don't add economic value? Conversely, would a student who opposes immigration on philosophical grounds exclude immigrants even if it could be shown for sure that they do?

2. Conservatives tend to believe that the federal government should be weak—except in matters of the military and border protection. Notice that liberals and conservatives make a similar switch when it comes to international wars: Traditional defenders of smaller government often advocate for more spending on war in Iraq and Afghanistan. Discuss the origin of this apparent contradiction with students: Is it cultural, geographical, or does it not imply an actual contradiction at all?

From Discussion to Writing

1. All of the first four essays in this chapter advance, in some way, an image of a "typical" immigrant. Students should elaborate on those images where they're not as clear. Where is the immigrant from, and what is his or her family and work life like? How do these images relate to the conclusions the authors draw, or imply, about what we should do about our borders as a society? Compare the pictures of immigrants in Jacoby and Krikorian especially. As for the possible racism of such an image, consider with students whether a reductive picture of a member of a particular group can ever be useful in discussing that group as a whole. Think of other examples from outside this debate—of Native Americans, women, or "Wall Street bankers" to give a few examples.

2. Look for policies that address the central problems of the immigration debate: How can we be fair and humane to people trying to achieve a better life without overcrowding the country or diminishing the rule of law? Look for students to use Martinez's testimony about the actual event of crossing the border illegally, Jacoby's and Krikorian's agreement that immigrants come to the country for good, understandable reasons, or (perhaps on the other side of the debate) Toplin's description of the kinds of people waiting for legal citizenship, as evidence.

Topics for Cross-Cultural Discussion

1. Latin American immigrants are rarely claimed to be a threat to national security, but the 9/11 hijackers—some of whom came into the United States illegally through Canada—raise more immediate concerns on that front. Would students who could not stomach racial profiling of the kind Martinez and Ramírez describe perhaps condone it if lives were at stake? Should our immigration policy, in general, stress economic or security concerns, and how can the two be balanced?

2. Students will bring a number of examples to the table, but Western European countries like France and the Netherlands have seen the most acrimonious immigration debates in recent times. Isolate and identify the reasons: To give a few, these countries have traditionally had largely homogeneous populations where ethnic identity was a part of citizenship;

they are also especially secular societies, where very religious, and even fundamentalist, immigrants from the Middle East are seen as a particular threat to the culture and way of life.

7

Gender Roles: Should Women Act More Like Men?

Whether there are real, biologically caused differences between the ways men and women think, act, speak, and behave has remained an important sidebar in the debates over feminism and sexism. If, aside from trifling physical differences, men and women are more or less exactly alike psychologically, doesn't that indicate conclusively that they should be treated alike? But what if they aren't? Take the character traits of aggression and arrogance. In his well-publicized controversial blog "A Rant about Women," Clay Shirky, a New York University communications teacher, worries that even the most talented women fall behind men because they are less willing to be self-assertive and self-promoting: "I sometimes wonder what would happen," he writes, ". . . if my college spent as much effort teaching women self-advancement as self-defense." Responding to Shirky's advice in an *American Prospect* column, "Swagger Like Us," Ann Friedman argues that just acting like men will not alone advance women's professional lives: "It will take a long time—and a lot of conscious effort—to dispel deeply ingrained stereotypes about work and gender."

Workplace gender stereotypes can occur in many industries, even the most glamorous, as Kim Elsesser provocatively maintains in "And the Gender-Neutral Oscar Goes To. . . ." Americans would be outraged, Elsesser claims, if there were separate awards for white and black actors, so why "is it considered acceptable to segregate nominations by sex, offering different Oscars for best actor and best actress?"

For centuries women were considered the "weaker sex," and men were expected to protect, respect, and honor them according to a medieval code known as "chivalry." But with the expansion of feminist ideals and the rise of independent women, the practice of chivalry began to seem quaint and condescending. Writing on the occasion of Valentine's Day, Boise State University student Shannon Morgan decides to take a new look at medieval gender roles. In "Defending Camelot: Chivalry Is Not Dead," she imagines a new chivalry for the twenty-first century: "I propose that modern chivalry should be gender-neutral; it can apply to any sexual orientation, and can cross cultures." Modern chivalry, she suggests, would encourage women to behave more like men and men more like women.

Finally, in our "Spotlight on Research" feature, journalist Tom Jacobs cites a recent study that examines how the titles of popular romance novels help answer the age-old question: "What do women want?"

Clay Shirky

A Rant about Women

[Clay Shirky Blog, *Shirky.com*, January 2010]

BEFORE YOU READ

Do you ever engage in self-promotion? Are men better at promoting themselves than women are? How much do you care about what people think of you? Is it ever okay to lie to get ahead in your career?

WORDS TO LEARN

superlative (para. 1): surpassing or superior to all others (adjective).

incarceration (para. 7): imprisonment, time in jail (noun).

fickle (para. 12): likely to change, unstable, unsteady (adjective).

correlates (para. 20): establishes an orderly connection between; places in a mutual relationship (verb).

So I get email from a good former student, applying for a job and asking for a recommendation. "Sure," I say, "Tell me what you think I should say." I then get a draft letter back in which the student has described their work and fitness for the job in terms so superlative it would make an Assistant Brand Manager blush. 1

So I write my letter, looking over the student's self-assessment and toning it down so that it sounds like it's coming from a person and not a PR department, and send it off. And then, as I get over my annoyance, I realize that, by overstating their abilities, the student has probably gotten the best letter out of me they could have gotten. 2

Now, can you guess the gender of the student involved? 3

Of course you can. My home, the Interactive Telecommunications Program at NYU, is fairly gender-balanced, and I've taught about as 4

Clay Shirky is a specialist in the field of Internet technologies and teaches new media at New York University's Interactive Telecommunications Program. His writing has appeared in the New York Times, *the* Wall Street Journal, Wired, *the* Harvard Business Review, *and other periodicals. His books include* Voices from the Net *(1995) and* Here Comes Everybody: The Power of Organizing without Organizations *(2008).*

many women as men over the last decade. In theory, the gender of my
former student should be a coin-toss. In practice, I might as well have
given him the pseudonym Moustache McMasculine for all the mystery
there was. And I've grown increasingly worried that most of the women
in the department, past or present, simply couldn't write a letter like that.

This worry isn't about psychology; I'm not concerned that women 5
don't engage in enough building of self-confidence or self-esteem. I'm
worried about something much simpler: Not enough women have what
it takes to behave like arrogant self-aggrandizing jerks.

Remember David Hampton, the con artist immortalized in *Six* 6
Degrees of Separation,[1] who pretended he was Sidney Poitier's son? He
lied his way into restaurants and clubs, managed to borrow money, and
crashed in celebrity guest rooms. He didn't miss the fact that he was taking a risk, or that he might suffer. He just didn't care.

It's not that women will be better off being con artists; a lot of con 7
artists aren't better off being con artists either. It's just that until women
have role models who are willing to risk incarceration to get ahead,
they'll miss out on channelling smaller amounts of self-promoting con
artistry to get what they want, and if they can't do that, they'll get less of
what they want than they want.

There is no upper limit to the risks men are willing to take in order 8
to succeed, and if there is an upper limit for women, they will succeed
less. They will also end up in jail less, but I don't think we get the rewards
without the risks.

* * *

When I was 19 and three days into my freshman year, I went to see Bill 9
Warfel, the head of grad theater design (my chosen profession, back in
the day), to ask if I could enroll in a design course. He asked me two
questions. The first was "How's your drawing?" Not so good, I replied. (I
could barely draw in those days.) "OK, how's your drafting?" I realized
this was it. I could either go for a set design or lighting design course, and
since I couldn't draw or draft well, I couldn't take either.

"My drafting's fine," I said. 10

That's the kind of behavior I mean. I sat in the office of someone 11
I admired and feared, someone who was the gatekeeper for something
I wanted, and I lied to his face. We talked some more and then he said,
"OK, you can take my class." And I ran to the local art supply place and
bought a drafting board, since I had to start practicing.

---

[1] *Six Degrees of Separation*: A 1990 play by John Guare, made into a film in 1993.

That got me in the door. I learned to draft, Bill became my teacher 12
and mentor, and four years later I moved to New York and started doing my own design work. I can't say my ability to earn a living in that fickle profession was because of my behavior in Bill's office, but I can say it was because I was willing to do that kind of thing. The difference between me and David Hampton isn't that he's a con artist and I'm not; the difference is that I only told lies I could live up to, and I knew when to stop. That's not a different type of behavior, it's just a different amount.

And it looks to me like women in general, and the women whose edu- 13
cations I am responsible for in particular, are often lousy at those kinds of behaviors, even when the situation calls for it. They aren't just bad at behaving like arrogant self-aggrandizing jerks. They are bad at behaving like self-promoting narcissists, anti-social obsessives, or pompous blowhards, even a little bit, even temporarily, even when it would be in their best interests to do so. Whatever bad things you can say about those behaviors, you can't say they are underrepresented among people who have changed the world.

Now this is asking women to behave 14
more like men, but so what? We ask people to cross gender lines all the time. We're in the middle of a generations-long project to encourage men to be better listeners and more sensitive partners, to take more account of others' feelings and to let out our own feelings more. Similarly, I see colleges spending time and effort teaching women strategies for self-defense, including direct physical aggression. I sometimes wonder what would happen, though, if my college spent as much effort teaching women self-advancement as self-defense.

We ask people to cross gender lines all the time.

* * *

Some of the reason these strategies succeed is because we live in a world 15
where women are discriminated against. However, even in an ideal future, self-promotion will be a skill that produces disproportionate rewards, and if skill at self-promotion remains disproportionately male, those rewards will as well. This isn't because of oppression, it's because of freedom.

Citizens of the developed world have an unprecedented amount of free- 16
dom to choose how we live, which means we experience life as a giant distributed discovery problem: What should I do? Where should I work? Who should I spend my time with? In most cases, there is no right answer, just tradeoffs. Many of these tradeoffs happen in the market; for everything from what you should eat to where you should live, there is a menu of options, and between your preferences and your budget, you'll make a choice.

Some markets, though, are two-sided — while you are weighing your options, those options are also weighing you. People fortunate enough to have those options quickly discover that it's not enough to decide you want to go to Swarthmore, or get money out of Kleiner Perkins.[2] Those institutions must also decide if they will have you. 17

Some of the most important opportunities we have are in two-sided markets: education and employment, contracts and loans, grants and prizes. And the institutions that offer these opportunities operate in an environment where accurate information is hard to come by. One of their main sources of judgment is asking the candidate directly: Tell us why we should admit you. Tell us why we should hire you. Tell us why we should give you a grant. Tell us why we should promote you. 18

In these circumstances, people who don't raise their hands don't get called on, and people who raise their hands timidly get called on less. Some of this is because assertive people get noticed more easily, but some of it is because raising your hand is itself a high-cost signal that you are willing to risk public failure in order to try something. 19

That in turn correlates with many of the skills the candidate will need to actually do the work — to recruit colleagues and raise money, to motivate participants and convince skeptics, to persevere in the face of both obstacles and ridicule. Institutions assessing the fitness of candidates, in other words, often select self-promoters because self-promotion is tied to other characteristics needed for success. 20

It's tempting to imagine that women could be forceful and self-confident without being arrogant or jerky, but that's a false hope, because it's other people who get to decide when they think you're a jerk, and trying to stay under that threshold means giving those people veto power over your actions. To put yourself forward as someone good enough to do interesting things is, by definition, to expose yourself to all kinds of negative judgments, and as far as I can tell, the fact that other people get to decide what they think of your behavior leaves only two strategies for not suffering from those judgments: not doing anything, or not caring about the reaction. 21

* * *

Not caring works surprisingly well. Another of my great former students, now a peer and a friend, saw a request from a magazine reporter doing a tech story and looking for examples. My friend, who'd previously been too quiet about her work, decided to write the reporter and say "My work is awesome. You should write about it." 22

---

[2] *Kleiner Perkins* (para. 17): Well-known venture capital firm that has invested in companies such as Amazon.com and Google.

The reporter looked at her work and wrote back saying, "Your work is indeed awesome, and I will write about it. I also have to tell you you are the only woman who suggested her own work. Men do that all the time, but women wait for someone else to recommend them." My friend stopped waiting, and now her work is getting the attention it deserves. 23

If you walked into my department at NYU, you wouldn't say, "Oh my, look how much more talented the men are than the women." The level and variety of creative energy in the place is still breathtaking to me, and it's not divided by gender. However, you would be justified in saying, "I bet that the students who get famous five years from now will include more men than women," because that's what happens, year after year. My friend talking to the reporter remains the sad exception. 24

Part of this sorting out of careers is sexism, but part of it is that men are just better at being arrogant, and less concerned about people thinking we're stupid (often correctly, it should be noted) for trying things we're not qualified for. 25

Now I don't know what to do about this problem. (The essence of a rant, in fact, is that the ranter has no idea how to fix the thing being ranted about.) What I do know is this: It would be good if more women see interesting opportunities that they might not be qualified for, opportunities which they might in fact fuck up if they try to take them on, and then try to take them on. It would be good if more women got in the habit of raising their hands and saying, "I can do that. Sign me up. My work is awesome," no matter how many people that behavior upsets. 26

VOCABULARY/USING A DICTIONARY

1. In paragraph 4, Shirky says that he might as well have given his former student the "pseudonym Moustache McMasculine." What is a *pseudonym*? What are the word's origins?
2. The writer claims that women "are bad at behaving like self-promoting narcissists . . ." (para. 13). What is a *narcissist*? Where did the term originate?
3. Several times in his essay, Shirky refers to "con artists." What is a *con artist*, and where does the term come from?

RESPONDING TO WORDS IN CONTEXT

1. Shirky recounts a time that he lied to Bill Warfel, a professor who "was the gatekeeper for something I wanted . . ." (para. 11). How is Shirky using the word *gatekeeper* here? What connotation does it have? What is its significance in this context?
2. According to the writer, we live in a market of choices (professional, personal, geographical, etc.). Some markets are one-sided, while others

are "two-sided" (para. 17). What does Shirky mean by a two-sided market? Why is this idea important for his argument?

3. In paragraph 13, Shirky writes, "And it looks to me like women in general, and the women whose educations I am responsible for in particular, are often lousy at those kinds of behaviors, even when the situation calls for it." What sort of word is "lousy"? What does it mean to you? Do you think it's an appropriate word for Shirky to use in this context?

DISCUSSING MAIN POINT AND MEANING

1. In what way is Shirky concerned about women? What distinction does he make in paragraph 5?
2. Shirky discusses the character David Hampton, a con artist in John Guare's 1990 play *Six Degrees of Separation*. How does Shirky distinguish between Hampton's cons and his own?
3. The writer acknowledges that his argument asks "women to behave more like men" (para. 14). Is this a problem? How does he respond to those who might take issue with requiring women to meet a standard set by men?

EXAMINING SENTENCES, PARAGRAPHS, AND ORGANIZATION

1. What is the purpose of paragraphs 9 through 12? How does this story support Shirky's overall argument?
2. Shirky's third paragraph is one sentence long: "Now, can you guess the gender of the student involved?" Is this choice effective? Did you guess the gender of the student? Does it matter if you did or not?
3. The writer's concluding paragraph begins: "Now I don't know what to do about this problem. (The essence of a rant, in fact, is that the ranter has no idea how to fix the thing being ranted about.)" (para. 26). What is a "rant"? Do you accept this disclaimer? Why do you think Shirky placed it here, rather than at the beginning of his essay?

THINKING CRITICALLY

1. Shirky describes a time that he lied to advance his education and career. How do you react to his dishonesty? Do you think he was justified?
2. Shirky refers to qualities like arrogance, narcissism, self-aggrandizement, and pomposity. He writes, "Whatever bad things you can say about those behaviors, you can't say they are underrepresented among people who have changed the world" (para. 13). Do you agree?
3. In evaluating the prospects of women students, Shirky acknowledges that sexism plays a part in the "sorting out of careers" (para. 25). Where do you see sexism? Are you hurt by it? Does it benefit you in any way?

IN-CLASS WRITING ACTIVITIES

1. Shirky wrote his former student a recommendation that sounded like it came "from a person and not a PR department" (para. 2). He notes that applicants for jobs, grants, and other opportunities are often asked directly: "Tell us why we should admit you" (para. 18). How do you respond to situations like this? Is it possible to promote yourself—either in person or in writing—without sounding like a "PR department"? Write a brief "how-to" guide for achieving this balance. What kind of language should you use? What should you avoid?
2. The writer discusses con artists and con artistry in "A Rant about Women." Have you ever been conned? Have you ever conned anyone? Write an essay about the experience.
3. Shirky makes a strong case for the necessity of self-promotion, even if it occasionally requires dishonesty or other kinds of "bad" behavior. Will this essay change the way you "promote" yourself or the way you think about the process? Does your gender play a part in your "self-promotion" skills? Why or why not?

Ann Friedman

Swagger Like Us

[*The American Prospect*, March 2010]

BEFORE YOU READ

Should women act more like men to compete in the business world? Do women have special talents for leadership and management just because they are women? Are men and women's career prospects shaped by cultural attitudes toward gender?

WORDS TO LEARN

refrain (para. 2): a phrase or verse recurring at intervals in a song or poem (noun).

extolling (para. 4): praising highly (verb).

testosterone (para. 5): male sex hormone (noun).

Ann Friedman is the deputy editor of The American Prospect *and a frequent contributor of political commentary to that periodical and others. She holds degrees in journalism and Spanish literature from the University of Missouri, Columbia and currently lives in Washington, D.C.*

Ever since women began making serious workplace gains in the 1970s, there has been a debate about the best way for them to climb the professional ladder. More often than not, the answer has been to "act like a man" — if you can't beat the boys' club, join it. Oversell yourself in job interviews. Ask for more raises. Demand a better title. Be assertive in expressing your opinion. You're gonna make it after all. 1

Women have made only marginal professional and political progress over the last decade, yet this simple refrain — be aggressive! B-E aggressive! — still makes for a convenient, can-do solution. In January, new-media guru Clay Shirky published "A Rant about Women" on his blog, summing up this view: "I sometimes wonder what would happen, though, if my college spent as much effort teaching women self-advancement as self-defense. . . . Now this is asking women to behave more like men, but so what? We ask people to cross gender lines all the time." 2

> **Even after decades of women suiting up in shoulder pads and trying to cross that line, we continue to simultaneously embrace the idea that powerful women promise to be different, somehow, from powerful men.**

Even after decades of women suiting up in shoulder pads and trying to cross that line, we continue to simultaneously embrace the idea that powerful women promise to be different, somehow, from powerful men. Supposedly, women are natural mediators. Women know how to multitask. Women are more levelheaded. If women ruled the world, it would be more stable, less violent, and color-coordinated. 3

The idea that what's between your legs determines your management style is also nothing new. LouAnn Brizendine generated a flurry of style-section articles in 2006 when she released her book, *The Female Brain*, about how every woman is "a lean, mean communicating machine." Antifeminist crusader Christina Hoff Sommers has written that "a practical, responsible femininity could be a force for good in the world beyond the family, through charitable works and more enlightened politics and government." And in December, *The Economist* reported on a new breed of "feminist management theorists" who are extolling the virtues of women's kinder, gentler leadership style. 4

So which is it? Should women be amplifying their aggression to mimic successful men? Or should they try to get ahead by playing up what supposedly makes them different from the testosterone-fueled CEOs who fed one financial bubble after another? The more time you spend thinking about women's stalled progress in the working world — they 5 were only 6.3 percent of corporate top earners last year — the clearer it becomes that neither of these two options is working.

Shirky does not acknowledge that his answer (which says women just need to man up) sets women up for backlash. Women who are loud and proud about their abilities and experience will be declared uppity bitches — or at least privately thought of that way. Studies have shown that employees, both male and female, are wary of working for high-achieving women. And what about women who follow Hoff Sommers' advice (which says women just need to, well, woman up)? They won't even get their applications read, let alone taken seriously. When was the last time you saw "responsible femininity" among desired qualities in a job listing? 6

This is a broad, cultural problem. If, like me, you believe that your biology is not the primary factor in determining your strengths and weaknesses in the workplace, you believe that we are shaped by the society in which we live. Which is to say, there are cultural, structural reasons why men are typically more assertive, more self-promotional, and more successful everywhere from the boardroom to the op-ed pages to the halls of Congress. This is much bigger than women's individual behavior. 7

To use Shirky's own example: Just as self-defense classes are not a solution to the problem of campus rape, self-advancement classes will not, on their own, improve things for women in the professional world. It will take a long time — and a lot of conscious effort — to dispel deeply ingrained stereotypes about work and gender. Women can't do that alone. The burden also falls on people in positions of power — those who are doing the hiring, promoting, recommending, and mentoring — to understand the gender dynamics at play and to push back against them. In my line of work, that means I not only write publicly about the "byline gap" between men and women in political journalism — I actively seek out women writers and encourage them to pitch their ideas. And I'm fairly certain I see more results than an editor who simply professes to care about this issue in the abstract. 8

For decades, we've told women how to get ahead in an unjust system. It's high time we all work to change the system itself. 9

VOCABULARY/USING A DICTIONARY

1. Friedman refers to the common assumption that women are "natural mediators" (para. 3). What is a *mediator*? Where does the word come from? What other words is it related to?
2. According to the writer, "feminist management theorists" extol the "virtues" of women's leadership (para. 4). What is the origin of the word *virtue*? Why might its roots be important in the context of Friedman's essay?
3. The writer claims that assertive women are perceived as "uppity bitches" (para. 6). What does *uppity* mean? What connotations does it have?

RESPONDING TO WORDS IN CONTEXT

1. Friedman concludes her opening paragraph with the sentence, "You're gonna make it after all." What allusion is the writer making here? How does it fit with her overall argument?
2. The writer claims that women have spent decades "suiting up in shoulder pads and trying to cross that line" (para. 3). What is the double meaning in this phrase? How is it related to her main point?
3. According to Friedman, the "idea that what's between your legs determines your management style is also nothing new" (para. 4). Why do you think she chose this specific wording? Is she being euphemistic?
4. The phrase "responsible femininity" appears twice in this essay. How does its meaning change depending on context?

DISCUSSING MAIN POINT AND MEANING

1. What characteristics supposedly distinguish powerful women from powerful men? What "special" skills or talents do women possess?
2. According to Friedman, career-minded women have two choices if they want to compete in the professional world. What are they? What does she think of the two paths?
3. What is Friedman's solution to the problem? What is she doing about it, personally?

EXAMINING SENTENCES, PARAGRAPHS, AND ORGANIZATION

1. How does Friedman use repetition near the end of the third paragraph? What is her tone in these sentences? How is that attitude related to her main point?
2. What is the purpose of paragraph 4? Would the essay be as effective without it? Could she have summarized the paragraph's content more briefly?
3. In paragraph 2, Friedman includes a long quotation from "new media guru" Clay Shirky's blog. Why does she do this? What is the relationship between Shirky's "rant" and "Swagger Like Us"?

THINKING CRITICALLY

1. Friedman writes, "The more time you spend thinking about women's stalled progress in the working world—they were only 6.3 percent of corporate top earners last year—the clearer it becomes that neither of these two options is working" (para. 5). How well does she support her view that women's progress in the working world is "stalled"? What would make her argument more effective?
2. What accounts for the differences between men and women, professionally, according to Friedman? Do you agree? Why or why not?

3. The writer refers to the hypothetical premise "If women ruled the world . . ." (para. 3). She uses the hypothesis to note several common positive stereotypes of women. How would you elaborate on the premise? Do you think the world would be fundamentally different if women "ruled" it?

IN-CLASS WRITING ACTIVITIES

1. Friedman considers debates about the best ways for women to "climb the professional ladder" (para. 1). What does that metaphor mean, exactly? Do you view your current or future career as a ladder? What other figures of speech could you use?
2. According to the writer, "Studies have shown that employees, both male and female, are wary of working for high-achieving women" (para. 6). Does this appear true from your own observations? Explain why you agree or disagree.
3. Do you think your gender will affect your career choices and prospects? How big a role, if any, will it play in shaping your professional life? Will your gender give you any advantages? Any disadvantages?

Kim Elsesser

And the Gender-Neutral Oscar Goes To . . .

[*The New York Times*, March 4, 2010]

BEFORE YOU READ

Why is there an Oscar given for the best "actress," but not for the best "directress"? Are men and women usually evaluated as equals when they work in the same profession? Is gender-neutral language important?

WORDS TO LEARN

segregate (para. 2): to separate (verb).
perpetuate (para. 5): to maintain or preserve (verb).
stereotype (para. 5): a conventional, formulaic, and oversimplified idea, opinion, characterization, or image (noun).

Kim Elsesser is a research scholar at the Center for Study of Women at the University of California, Los Angeles. She specializes in workplace issues.

1 Many hours into the 82nd Academy Awards ceremony this Sunday, the Oscar for best actor will go to Morgan Freeman, Jeff Bridges, George Clooney, Colin Firth or Jeremy Renner. Suppose, however, that the Academy of Motion Picture Arts and Sciences presented separate honors for best white actor and best non-white actor, and that Mr. Freeman was prohibited from competing against the likes of Mr. Clooney and Mr. Bridges. Surely, the academy would be derided as intolerant and out of touch; public outcry would swiftly ensure that Oscar nominations never again fell along racial lines.

2 Why, then, is it considered acceptable to segregate nominations by sex, offering different Oscars for best actor and best actress?

3 Since the first Academy Awards ceremony in 1929, separate acting Oscars have been presented to men and women. Women at that time had only recently won the right to vote and were still several decades away from equal rights outside the voting booth, so perhaps it was reasonable to offer them their own acting awards. But in the twenty-first century women contend with men for titles ranging from the American president to the American Idol. Clearly, there is no reason to still segregate acting Oscars by sex.

4 Perhaps the academy would argue that the separate awards guarantee equity, since men and women have received exactly the same number of best acting Oscars. And the academy is not alone in this regard: the Golden Globes, the Screen Actors Guild, the British Academy of Film and the Independent Spirit Awards all split acting nominees by sex as well.

Just as stewardesses are now called flight attendants, many actresses now prefer to be called actors.

5 But separate is not equal. While it is certainly acceptable for sports competitions like the Olympics to have separate events for male and female athletes, the biological differences do not affect acting performances. The divided Oscar categories merely insult women, because they suggest that women would not be victorious if the categories were combined. In addition, this segregation helps perpetuate the stereotype that the differences between men and women are so great that the two sexes cannot be evaluated as equals in their professions.

6 Today, the number of female-run production companies, female directors and great roles for women continues to increase. Four of the five films represented in this year's best actress category center on strong female characters.

7 As women gain more influence in Hollywood, even the term "actress" is disappearing. Just as stewardesses are now called flight attendants, many actresses now prefer to be called actors. The Screen Actors Guild has eliminated the term "actress" in the presentation of its awards,

instead using "female actor." Perhaps, as the term "actress" falls further out of favor, the award-granting organizations will be forced to acknowledge that male and female actors do indeed have the same occupation.

Collapsing two major categories into one would have the added value of reducing the length of the awards show, a move that many viewers would laud. But if the academy wanted to preserve the number of acting awards, it could easily follow the lead of the Hollywood Foreign Press Association, which has, since 1951, offered genre-based Golden Globe honors, for best performances in dramatic, and comedic and musical roles. 8

For next year's Oscars, the academy should modify its ballots so that men and women are finally treated as full equals, able to compete together in every category, for every nomination. And if the academy insists on continuing to segregate awards, then it should at least remain consistent and create an Oscar for best directress. 9

VOCABULARY/USING A DICTIONARY

1. Where does the word *ceremony* (para. 1) come from?
2. According to Elsesser, many viewers would "laud" (para. 8) the shortening of the Oscar awards show. What does *laud* mean? What are its origins? What words are related to it?
3. The writer notes that "even the term 'actress' is disappearing," much as the word "stewardess" has (para. 7). Where does the practice of adding an "-ess" to the end of a word to denote femininity come from?

RESPONDING TO WORDS IN CONTEXT

1. In paragraph 5, the author says, "but separate is not equal" and later in the paragraph uses the term "segregation." What is the origin of these expressions; in other words, in what context do these terms usually appear? Do you think these terms are being applied here appropriately? Why or why not?
2. Elsesser refers to the high number of Oscar-nominated films with "strong female characters" (para. 6). What is a "strong female character"? Why does she note the prevalence of these characters?
3. The writer proposes that the Oscars follow the format of the Hollywood Foreign Press Association, which gives "genre-based Golden Globe honors" (para. 8). What does "genre-based" mean?

DISCUSSING MAIN POINT AND MEANING

1. Elsesser makes her argument primarily by using an extended analogy. What is the comparison?
2. What are the benefits of eliminating gender-based Oscar awards, according to Elsesser?

3. How would you characterize Elsesser's overall tone? For example, does she sound optimistic in this article? Skeptical? Is there any attitude conveyed in her writing style?

EXAMINING SENTENCES, PARAGRAPHS, AND ORGANIZATION

1. How does Elsesser set up her argument in the first two paragraphs? Is it an effective strategy? Why or why not?
2. Does the writer acknowledge counterarguments? Does she address them effectively?
3. Where is the thesis of this essay? How would you restate it in your own words?

THINKING CRITICALLY

1. Elsesser writes that at the first Oscar ceremony, women "were still several decades away from equal rights outside the voting booth" (para. 3). Do men and women have equal rights now? Where do you see inequality between the sexes? Are some disparities justified?
2. When is gender separation acceptable, according to Elsesser? What is her standard for making this judgment? Do you agree?
3. The writer argues that the Academy of Motion Picture Arts and Sciences should change their ballots so that men and women are treated equally. Does this seem like an important issue? Does Elsesser justify its significance effectively?

IN-CLASS WRITING ACTIVITIES

1. Elsesser notes that the word actress is "disappearing," just as "stewardesses are now called flight attendants" (para. 7). Are you aware of gender in your writing? Do you try to write in "gender-neutral" ways? Do you think it matters? Why or why not?
2. The writer refers to "strong female characters" in films (para. 6). Choose such a character from film or fiction; then, explain how she fits this description. What qualities do you associate with "strong female characters"?
3. According to Elsesser, "the divided Oscar categories merely insult women, because they suggest that women would not be victorious if the categories were combined" (para. 5). Do you agree with her inference? Are there other ways of looking at the separate Oscars? Write a persuasive essay that argues either for or against the divided categories.

Shannon Morgan (student essay)

Defending Camelot: Chivalry Is Not Dead

[*Arbiter Online*, Boise State University, February 24, 2010]

BEFORE YOU READ

How would you define *chivalry*? Should men have a special code of manners and behavior in their relationships with women? What rules guide your behavior in romantic relationships?

WORDS TO LEARN

harking back (para. 3): going back to an origin or source (verb).

medieval (para. 3): referring to the "Middle Ages" in Europe, often dated between 476 and 1453 (adjective).

spontaneous (para. 4): arising from a momentary impulse or circumstance (adjective).

I've heard some women say they don't appreciate being patronized by antiquated gestures of chivalry. Women are not the "weaker sex" and we do not need protecting. I've heard some men say they are afraid to be chivalrous because they don't want to disrespect their partner. These men struggle with wanting to employ a time-honored tradition of chivalry without being sexist. 1

I propose that modern chivalry should be gender-neutral; it can apply to any sexual orientation, and can cross cultures. In honor of Cupid, I'll focus my arguments on the romantic aspects of chivalry, the code of how to treat our intimate partners. If both women and men should strive to be chivalrous, we must first discuss what this means. Chivalry is far more than having good manners. Opening someone's door, helping someone put on a jacket, or picking up the check at dinner are polite gestures, employed by women and men alike, in situations that extend beyond the pursuit of romance. 2

Shannon Morgan is the editor-in-chief of The Arbiter. *She will graduate in 2011 from Boise State University, where she is majoring in communications, with minors in political science and history.*

According to chivalrynow.net, "Chivalry spells out certain ethical standards that foster the development of manhood. Men are called to be: truthful, loyal, courteous to others, helpmates to women, supporters of justice, and defenders of the weak. They are also expected to avoid scandal." Harking back to Camelot,[1] chivalry is rooted in a medieval code of honor for knightly men. Let us bring chivalry into the twenty-first century, and have it serve as a moral and ethical code both sexes can follow to help guide relationships. I appreciate traditional gender roles in relationships (to a degree), but I also believe people should be free to find a partner to balance them in the effort to create a meaningful and supportive bond. Whether we are more comfortable in the role of protector, nurturer, or a combination of the two, we can subscribe to the code of chivalry. 3

> **Let us bring chivalry into the twenty-first century, and have it serve as a moral and ethical code both sexes can follow to help guide relationships.**

Chivalry should be a check on our urges, a compass to ensure we are behaving in ways that cultivate rewarding and supportive relationships. In committed relationships it means we will "avoid scandal" by being faithful, and that we will seek to be just, fair, and discreet with our criticism of our partners. Being chivalrous, in a romantic sense, is intimate. It's affectionate; it's a commitment to being supportive and encouraging of your partner. It is not a spontaneous act, but a concentrated and time-tested effort. It's expressed in small, everyday actions like brewing coffee in the morning, picking your wet towels up off the floor, or taking time to write a love letter or plan a romantic evening. It's also expressed in larger ways, such as being supportive when your partner is in a weakened state. Maybe someone lost a job, or lost a loved one, or experienced a crisis of faith, or suffered a medical catastrophe. Being chivalrous is a commitment to love your partner, not only when it's easy, but when it's hard. It is a commitment to work through problems, to seek to understand before being understood. It's being compassionate, dependable, strong, and kind. Chivalry is about respect. Respect for yourself and for your lover — and the commitment to serve and honor each other. 4

---

[1] *Camelot*: The site of the legendary King Arthur's palace and court, possibly near Exeter, England. Traditionally, it is associated with goodness, beauty, and knightly ideals.

VOCABULARY/USING A DICTIONARY

1. Morgan's article focuses on *chivalry* (para. 1). What are the origins of that word?
2. According to the writer, some women "don't appreciate being patronized by antiquated gestures of chivalry" (para. 1). What does *patronized* mean? What are its roots? What other words are related to it?
3. What does *antiquated* (para. 1) mean? What synonym could Morgan have used in its place?

RESPONDING TO WORDS IN CONTEXT

1. Morgan writes, "Women are not the 'weaker sex' and we do not need protecting" (para. 1). What does she mean, exactly? How do you interpret the phrase "weaker sex"?
2. According to the writer, chivalrous behavior includes being "just, fair, and discreet with our criticism of our partners" (para. 4). What does *discreet* mean in this context? How does it fit in with her definition of chivalry?
3. "Being chivalrous, in a romantic sense, is intimate" (para. 4). What "sense" of the word *romantic* is Morgan using here? What other meanings does that term have? Are any of them applicable here?

DISCUSSING MAIN POINT AND MEANING

1. Morgan wants to bring chivalry "into the twenty-first century" (para. 3). Why do older notions of chivalry need to be revised, according to the writer?
2. According to Morgan, "Chivalry should be a check on our urges" (para. 4). What does that mean? How might chivalric rules restrain "urges"?
3. How might chivalry be expressed, according to the writer?

EXAMINING SENTENCES, PARAGRAPHS, AND ORGANIZATION

1. Morgan begins her essay, "I've heard some women say they don't appreciate being patronized by antiquated gestures of chivalry" (para. 1). Would you describe this sentence as general or specific? How might you improve it as an introduction?
2. According to the writer, "Chivalry is far more than having good manners" (para. 2). Does she clarify this distinction effectively in the second paragraph, or elsewhere in the essay?
3. How would you describe the tone of Morgan's essay? What choices in style and diction contribute to that tone? Does it suit her argument? Why or why not?

THINKING CRITICALLY

1. The writer wants a "gender-neutral" chivalry, as opposed to patronizing, "antiquated," or even chauvinistic chivalry. How do you distinguish between chivalrous behavior and sexist behavior? Where do you draw the line between the two?
2. Morgan writes, "I appreciate traditional gender roles in relationships (to a degree), but I also believe people should be free to find a partner to balance them in the effort to create a meaningful and supportive bond" (para. 3). What part do "traditional gender roles" play in your own romantic relationships? Do you look for "balance"?
3. Do you think good manners are important? How would you define them? What specific practices do they include? What purpose do they serve?

IN-CLASS WRITING ASSIGNMENTS

1. Do you have a "moral and ethical code" that helps you guide your romantic relationships? What is it? Do you have "rules"? Where do they come from? Morgan emphasizes the goal of a "meaningful and supportive bond" (para. 3). Do you share that goal? Does your code reflect that purpose? Do you think your code will change?
2. Morgan cites a definition of *chivalry* from the Web. Research the term on your own. Are there aspects to chivalry that her explanation does not include? Do you think chivalric ideals still persist in our society? If so, where do you see them? What social forces work against them?
3. This essay proposes that we modernize chivalry (para. 3). Do you agree with Morgan? Are her arguments persuasive? Why or why not?

LOOKING CLOSELY

Clearly Expressing the Purpose of Your Essay

In composition, your purpose is your overall goal or aim in writing. It is basically what you hope to accomplish by writing — whether it is to promote or endorse a certain point of view, rally support for a cause, criticize a book or film, or examine the effects of a social trend. Your purpose may or may not be expressed explicitly (in creative writing it rarely is), but in essays and nonfiction it is usually important that the reader understand the purpose behind your writing. An explicitly stated purpose not only helps the reader follow your argument or perspective, but also helps ensure that everything you write reflects that purpose. A carefully expressed purpose will help anchor your essay and keep it from floating aimlessly.

Note how Boise State student Shannon Morgan expresses her purpose in "Defending Camelot: Chivalry Is Not Dead." She begins her Valentine's Day essay by pointing out how men and women feel about chivalric behavior and the difficulties they have with it. Then in paragraph 2 she immediately makes her purpose clear. She is writing the essay to propose a new form of chivalry for our age that benefits both sexes. Note, too, how the remainder of her essay is closely linked to her explicit purpose.

1
Clear statement of purpose

2
Clearly states how the remainder of the essay is linked to her purpose

I propose that modern chivalry should be gender-neutral; it can apply to any sexual orientation, and can cross cultures. (1) In honor of Cupid, I'll focus my arguments on the romantic aspects of chivalry, the code of how to treat our intimate partners. If both women and men should strive to be chivalrous, we must first discuss what this means. (2) Chivalry is far more than having good manners. Opening someone's door, helping someone put on a jacket, or picking up the check at dinner are polite gestures employed by women and men alike, in situations that extend beyond the pursuit of romance.

STUDENT WRITER AT WORK

Shannon Morgan

On Writing "Defending Camelot: Chivalry Is Not Dead"

RA. What inspired you to write this essay? And publish it in your campus paper?

SM. Honestly, I got tired of arguing with my girlfriends about chivalry. It occurred to me that they hadn't thought through what the spirit of chivalry is. My goal was to start a dialogue. History is not static, and our ideas of intimacy, gender roles, and sex have evolved over time. I don't see why attitudes about chivalry can't also.

RA. How long did it take for you to write this piece? Did you revise your work? What were your goals as you revised?

SM. I wrote it over the course of two days and four different drafts. When I finish an article, I send it to editors and friends, and I almost always ask my Facebook and Twitter community if anyone has time to read a draft for me and give me feedback. I like to get at least five different perspectives, mostly just to make sure that the thesis of my article is accurately conveyed to my audience. It's important for me to get it right. There's nothing worse than sending an opinion article to print and getting torn apart in the comments because you have weak arguments. Showing my work to people before it gets published gives me an opportunity to identify weaknesses and fix them.

RA. Are you pursuing a career in which writing will be a component?

SM. I'm not quite sure what I will do for a career yet, but I am certain writing will be a component.

RA. What advice do you have for other student writers?

SM. Be bold. Be curious. Be tenacious. Develop a thick skin early on. Welcome feedback in all forms. Teach yourself as much as you can. Find a mentor. Learn to understand a variety of perspectives and worldviews, especially if they differ from your own. Learn how to listen and communicate effectively. Care about the world and the richness of life all around you. Great writing is a rare thing. It's more than just copying down what people say, or what you see and think. It's about research, accuracy, context, culture . . . so many things. My advice is to get as broad an education as possible because the more you know about the world, the better you are able to write about it.

Spotlight on Research

Tom Jacobs

Romance Novel Titles Reveal Readers' Desires

[*Miller-McCune*, March 2, 2010]

Great thinkers from Sigmund Freud to Mel Gibson have profitably pondered the timeless question "What do women want?" Now, two Canadian researchers — one of each gender — have taken a novel approach to solving this purported puzzle. 1

In a paper titled "The Texas Billionaire's Pregnant Bride," recently published in the *Journal of Social, Evolutionary and Cultural Psychology*, they analyze the titles of Harlequin romance novels. Anthony Cox of the Center of Psychology and Computing and psychologist Maryanne Fisher of St. Mary's University contend these best-selling volumes — and in particular their market-tested titles — provide a unique insight into their buyers' desires. 2

Coming from an evolutionary psychology perspective, they hypothesized these titles would reflect mating preferences that have evolved over the millennia — specifically, a desire for a long-term relationship with a physically fit, financially secure man who will provide the resources needed to successfully raise a family. 3

They found considerable support for this theory, although some of their speculative specifications were spelled out more directly than others. 4

The scholars created a database of just over 15,000 romance novels published between 1949 and 2009. Not surprisingly, they found the most frequently used word in the title was "love," which appeared 840 times. "Bride" was close behind at 835. "Baby" was slightly back at 696, followed by "man" at 672 and "marriage" at 612. 5

These words "clearly suggest long-term commitment and reproduction are important to readers," Cox and Fisher write. Indeed, commitment was the most common theme they discovered, with words like *marriage, wedding, bride, groom* and *honeymoon*. The second-most common was procreation, with words like *baby, child, mommy, daddy* and *pregnant*. 6

The list of frequently used words does not specifically point to a desire for wealth or good looks in a man. Surprisingly, "handsome" turns up only six times, and the word "athletic" does not appear at all. Figuring such desires were coded within the characters, the scholars decided to compile a list of the 20 most frequently occurring professions in these fictional works. 7

Doctor came in at No. 1, with 388 characters practicing medicine. No surprise there: The authors note physicians "take care of others and earn a generous salary," making them something of a two-fer as potential mates go. 8

But who would expect *cowboy* to come in second, at 314? Apparently the archetype of the rugged frontiersman retains its appeal. 9

"We propose that the Western theme might relate to women's preference for attractive mates," the researchers write — "attractive" not in the male-model sense, but rather in the muscular mold. "Cowboys are athletic and have high physical fitness, as their duties primarily involve physical labor," they note. That would presumably make them effective protectors against a variety of physical threats. 10

Nurse was the third most frequent occupation mentioned in the book titles, at 224 (a lot of these stories feature doctors falling in love with nurses). Otherwise unspecified "boss" was fourth at 142 (many feature bosses falling in love with their secretaries). *Prince* was next, at 122 (the Sleeping Beauty myth lives!), followed by *rancher* at 79 (the Western motif returns), *knight* at 77 (there's something about a man who needs his armor polished) and *surgeon*, also at 77 (see *doctor*, above). 11

There is, of course, some danger in assuming women who purchase romance novels are representative of their entire gender. While sales are admittedly huge (almost $1.4 billion in 2007, making it the largest fiction category in the U.S. by far), a significant number of women have no interest in them, and this study does not measure their desires. 12

Nevertheless, this smart, seductive study has inspired us to wonder if we can reposition *Miller-McCune.com* headlines to appeal to what is clearly a huge demographic. Keep an eye out for our coming exposé *The Doctoral Candidate and the Ravishing Researcher*. 13

Discussing the Unit

SUGGESTED TOPIC FOR DISCUSSION

Women now make up the majority of the U.S. workforce, including management and professional positions (they still lag at the highest levels of executive leadership). Additionally, more women than men are earning college degrees. How would you account for these shifts? What do you think the consequences might be — socially, economically, and culturally? Which articles in this unit offer insight into this trend?

PREPARING FOR CLASS DISCUSSION

1. The essays in this unit cover a broad range of topics, from the Academy Awards to the nature of chivalry. What common themes unite the articles? If you had to characterize them in terms of one overriding preoccupation, what would it be?
2. Several of these essays touch upon gender stereotypes, whether directly or indirectly. Which stereotypes can you identify? Do you think they are

valid or "true" in any way? Are any of them pejorative or harmful, or just plain inaccurate? Do you identify with any of the gender stereotypes?

FROM DISCUSSION TO WRITING

1. While women have made enormous gains economically and socially, Friedman notes the "stalled" progress of women at the highest echelons of the business world, where they composed just 6.3 percent of the top earners in 2009. What do you think accounts for this disparity? Do you think that, ultimately, women will achieve parity with men—or even dominance over them? Why or why not?
2. All of these essays suggest that gender remains a significant factor in our society. How has gender shaped your choices in your education and your career ambitions? Has it been a limiting factor in any way? Has it been an advantage? How aware are you of your gender when choosing a particular path, professionally or personally?

TOPICS FOR CROSS-CULTURAL DISCUSSION

1. Unquestionably, our ideas about gender and gender roles are shaped by our culture. What cultural factors—familial, ethnic, religious, racial, or otherwise—have influenced your perceptions of men and women, as well as male and female "roles"? Do your beliefs ever conflict with dominant views of gender and gender roles? Have your views changed in any way? What caused them to change?
2. Do you see the differences between men and women (their behavior, their "roles," their relative places in society, their strengths and weaknesses, etc.) primarily as a matter of unchangeable biology, or do you understand them as culturally constructed? Should people work to eliminate the distinctions between men and women in society, or are such differences fundamental and essential, and therefore in need of preservation?

8

Does Our Need for Security Threaten Our Right to Privacy?

Ever since the attacks of 9/11, Americans have been concerned about balancing two needs—the need for security and the need for privacy. But these needs are not always easily balanced, as many travelers discover routinely at airports every day. As an increase in terror threats is met by new surveillance technologies, many Americans worry that our rights to privacy will become less and less respected. Is it possible to step up security measures while protecting privacy rights, as President Obama claimed when he said that he wants to "aggressively pursue enhanced screening technology . . . consistent with privacy rights and civil liberties"? And when security is at stake and lives are endangered, how much privacy are we willing to sacrifice?

In "Nude Awakening," one of the nation's prominent legal reporters, Jeffrey Rosen, worries that the new full-body scanning machines being rapidly installed at airports across the nation may seriously jeopardize our rights to privacy unless strict efforts are made to blur all personal characteristics. "Let's not mince words about these machines," Rosen argues: "They are a virtual strip search—and an outrage." Yet, not everyone feels so offended by the new airport scanning equipment: "If you think I'm making light of the full-body scanners on order for airports across the country, you're right," says columnist Connie Schultz in

"New Airport Policy: Grin and Bare It," who feels assured that authorities have implemented "numerous precautions to protect your privacy." Since terrorist techniques are constantly evolving, and racial profiling doesn't work, we need "high-tech devices" at airports, maintains Washington State University student Mohammed Khan, himself a victim of such profiling. Although Khan thinks it's understandable that people feel "uncomfortable with these invasive practices," he nevertheless believes, as the title states, that "Safety Is Paramount."

In the final selection, "The Tips of Your Fingers," nature writer Jay Griffiths takes a broader, transcendent look at the meaning of privacy in a surveillance society. She wonders why nations seem so intent on protecting their own borders while showing no respect for those of the individual citizen. "Through the twin prongs of ID cards and surveillance," she writes, "the borders of the private self are invaded."

Jeffrey Rosen

Nude Awakening

[*The New Republic*, February 4, 2010]

BEFORE YOU READ

Are airport security measures too intrusive? Are they effective? Would you submit to new airport scanning machines that create a graphic image of your naked body? How do you balance the need to be secure with the protection of your privacy?

WORDS TO LEARN

blurted (para. 1): uttered suddenly or accidentally (verb).

indignation (para. 2): anger at something considered unjust, offensive, or insulting (noun).

effusive (para. 2): overflowing, lacking hesitation or restraint (adjective).

estranged (para. 8): separated; unfriendly, hostile, or alienated (adjective).

1 Last summer, I watched a fellow passenger at Washington's Reagan National Airport as he was selected to go through a newly installed full-body scanner. These machines — there are now 40 of them spread across 19 U.S. airports — permit officials from the Transportation Security Administration (TSA) to peer through a passenger's clothing in search of explosives and weapons. On the instructions of a security officer, the passenger stepped into the machine and held his arms out in a position of surrender, as invisible millimeter waves surrounded his body. Although he probably didn't know it, TSA officials in a separate room were staring at a graphic, anatomically correct image of his naked body. When I asked the TSA screener whether the passenger's face was blurred, he replied that he couldn't say. But, as I turned to catch my flight, the official blurted,

---

A professor at George Washington University Law School, Jeffrey Rosen is a graduate of Harvard University, Oxford University, and Yale Law School. He comments regularly on legal affairs for The New Republic. *His books include* The Unwanted Gaze: The Destruction of Privacy in America *(2000),* The Most Democratic Branch: How the Courts Serve America *(2006), and* The Supreme Court: The Personalities and Rivalries That Defined America *(2007).*

"Someone ought to do something about those machines — it's like we don't have any privacy in this country anymore!"

2 The officer's indignation was as rare as it was unexpected. In the wake of the failed Christmas bombing of Northwest Flight 253, the public has been overwhelmingly enthusiastic about these scanners. A recent *USA Today* poll found that 78 percent of respondents approved of their use at airports. Western democracies have been no less effusive. President Obama has ordered the Department of Homeland Security (DHS) to install $1 billion in airport screening equipment, and the TSA hopes to include an additional 300 millimeter-wave scanners. Britain, France, Italy, and the Netherlands have all made similar pledges to expand their use.

3 Let's not mince words about these machines. They are a virtual strip search — and an outrage. Body scanners are a form of what security expert Bruce Schneier has called "security theater." That is, they give people the illusion of safety without actually making us safer. A British MP who evaluated the body scanners in a former capacity, as a director at a leading defense technology company, said that they wouldn't have stopped the trouser bomber aboard the Northwest flight. Despite over-hyped claims to the contrary, they simply can't detect low-density materials hidden under clothing, such as liquid, powder, or thin plastics. In other words, the sacrifice these machines require of our privacy is utterly pointless. And, as it happens, it's possible to design and use the body scanners in a way that protects privacy without diminishing security — but the U.S. government has failed to do so.

They give people the illusion of safety without actually making us safer.

4 Millimeter-wave scanners came on the market after September 11 as a way of detecting high-density contraband, such as ceramics or wax, that would be missed by metal detectors when concealed under clothing — while avoiding radiation that could harm humans. The machines also reveal the naked human body far more graphically than a conventional x-ray. But, from the beginning, researchers who developed the millimeter machines at the Pacific Northwest National Laboratory offered an alternative design more sensitive to privacy. They proposed to project any concealed contraband onto a neutral, sexless mannequin while scrambling images of the passenger's naked body into a nondescript blob. But the Bush administration chose the naked machine rather than the blob

machine: Some blob skeptics argue that blotting out private parts would make it harder to detect explosives concealed, for example, in prosthetic genitalia. Of course, neither the blob nor the naked machine would have detected the suicide bombers who have proved perfectly willing to conceal explosives in real body cavities, as a Saudi suicide bomber proved in a failed attempt to assassinate a Saudi prince using explosives planted in a place where the sun doesn't shine.

Former DHS director Michael Chertoff, whose consulting firm now 5
represents the leading vendor of the millimeter machines, Rapiscan, has been a vocal cheerleader for body scanning: He called the Christmas bombing a "very vivid lesson in the value of that machinery." In 2005, under Chertoff's leadership, TSA ordered five scanners from Rapiscan, claiming that its naked images were less graphic than those of competitors. TSA also introduced one additional privacy protection: Agents who review the images of the naked bodies are in a separate room and, therefore, can't see the passengers as they're being scanned. According to the TSA website, the technology blurs all facial features, and, based on some news accounts, private parts have been blurred as well. But because the TSA remains free of independent oversight, it's impossible to tell precisely how they're being used.

Most troubling of all, the TSA website claims that "the machines 6
have zero storage capability" and that "the system has no way to save, transmit or print the image." But documents recently obtained by the Electronic Privacy Information Center reveal that, in 2008, the TSA told vendors that the machines it purchases must have the ability to send or store images when in "test" mode. (The TSA told CNN that the test mode can't be enabled at airports.) Because no regulations prohibit the TSA from storing images, the House (but not the Senate) voted last year to ban the use of body scanning machines for primary screening and to prohibit images from being stored.

As long as the TSA fails to blur images of both faces and private 7
parts, the machines will represent a serious threat to the dignity of some travelers from the 14 countries whose citizens will now be required to go through them (or face intrusive pat-downs) before entering the United States. Some interpretations of Islamic law, for example, forbid men from gazing at Muslim women unless they are veiled. It's also unfortunate that, a year after the Supreme Court declared, 8-1, that strip searches in schools are unreasonable without some suspicion of danger or wrongdoing, virtual strip searches will soon be routine for many randomly selected travelers at airports, rather than reserved for secondary screening of suspicious individuals.

But the greatest privacy concern is that the images may later leak. As soon as a celebrity walks through a naked machine, some creep will want to save the picture and send it to the tabloids. And the danger that rogue officials may troll the database is hardly hypothetical. President Obama's embattled nominee to head the TSA, Erroll Southers, conducted two searches of the confidential criminal records of his estranged wife's boyfriend, downloaded the records, and passed them on to law enforcement, possibly in violation of the Privacy Act, and then gave a misleading account of the incident to Congress. That's why the images should be anonymous and ephemeral, so agents can't save the pictures or connect them to names. 8

Even if the body scanners protected privacy, Schneier insists, they still would be a waste of money: The next plot rarely looks like the last one. But, if we need to waste money on feel-good technologies that don't make us safer, let's at least make sure that they don't unnecessarily reveal us naked. President Obama says that he wants to "aggressively pursue enhanced screening technology . . . consistent with privacy rights and civil liberties." With a few simple technological and legal fixes, he can do precisely that. Blob machine or naked machine — the choice is his. 9

VOCABULARY/USING A DICTIONARY

1. What does the word *enthusiastic* (para. 2) mean, and what are its origins?
2. What are the roots of the word *contraband* (para. 4), and what does it mean?
3. What are the origins of the word *hypothetical* (para. 8)? What other words is it related to?
4. What is the meaning of the word *ephemeral* (para. 8), and what are its origins?

RESPONDING TO WORDS IN CONTEXT

1. In paragraph 3, Rosen writes, "Let's not mince words." What does the phrase "mince words" mean? Why does he use it here?
2. The writer warns of "rogue officials" (para. 8), who might invade people's privacy. What connotations does the word *rogue* have?
3. Rosen describes the body scanners as "feel-good technologies" (para. 9). What does *feel-good* mean in this context?

DISCUSSING MAIN POINT AND MEANING

1. According to Rosen, what are the problems with the full-body scanners now being used in U.S. airports?
2. The writer claims that the scanners constitute a real privacy threat to airline passengers. How, specifically, do the machines threaten privacy and dignity?

3. Rosen argues that it is possible to "use the body scanners in a way that protects privacy without diminishing security" (para. 3). What solution does he propose in his essay?

EXAMINING SENTENCES, PARAGRAPHS, AND ORGANIZATION

1. In the final paragraph of the essay, Rosen quotes specific language from President Barack Obama. How does it support his point?

2. Rosen acknowledges the widespread public and political support for the body scanners in paragraph 2. Why does he include this paragraph, which highlights popular enthusiasm for these machines? In what way does it further his argument?

3. The writer begins his essay with a personal anecdote and observation. Following the first paragraph, how does he transition from his personal experience to the wider focus of his argument?

THINKING CRITICALLY

1. What are Rosen's main sources for his argument? How would you evaluate them?

2. In paragraph 8, Rosen writes that "the greatest privacy concern is that the images may later leak." How does he substantiate this claim? Does he do so effectively? Why or why not?

3. Rosen is writing about the Transportation Security Administration, as well as the body scanners. What view of the TSA comes across in the essay? How does the writer characterize the agency, specifically?

IN-CLASS WRITING ACTIVITIES

1. Rosen describes the TSA's use of body scanners as a "virtual strip search—and an outrage" (para. 3). Do you agree with him? How much privacy are you willing to give up to remain safe? In a response to this essay, explain how you view these issues, particularly with regard to balancing the need for security with the need to protect privacy.

2. The writer is critical of the TSA's "security theater" (para. 3) and the agency's ostensible commitment to "feel-good technologies" (para. 9). Rosen refers to the danger that "rogue officials" pose, citing the example of Erroll Southers (para. 8). Do you agree with Rosen's implicit view of government authority, generally?

3. In presenting his argument, Rosen suggests that, while others may soften their words or deploy euphemisms, he is being honest and candid about the subject. Why might people "mince words" on this issue? What arguments and issues seem to lead to this practice?

Connie Schultz

New Airport Policy: Grin and Bare It

[*Cleveland Plain Dealer*, January 10, 2010]

BEFORE YOU READ

Could airport security measures ever violate your privacy rights? Do you worry about terrorism? How much do you trust the government to keep you safe when you travel—and in other areas of your life?

WORDS TO LEARN

ambled (para. 5): walked at a slow, easy pace (verb).
confounding (para. 7): confusing (adjective).
emit (para. 9): to send forth (verb).
waist-highs (para. 12): panty hose or unfashionable, dated women's underwear (noun).

If you're one of the millions of Americans who resolved to get in shape 1
this year but lack motivation, booking a flight at an airport near you might be just the ticket to push you to feel the burn.

Whenever you fly, you're used to tossing your bags on a conveyor 2
belt and then removing shoes and enough clothing to leave you just this side of bare-naked. Soon you'll get to stand with your arms out and legs spread so that a stranger huddled over a computer can peer at an image of virtually nude, lumpy you.

If you think I'm making light of the full-body scanners on order for airports across the country, you're right.

The stranger doesn't see your face, and 3
you never see the stranger's face. But both of you will know that lurking under what's left of your clothing are more bumps and bulges than the Appalachian foothills have.

If you think I'm making light of the 4
full-body scanners on order for airports across the country, you're right. For one

---

The winner of the 2005 Pulitzer Prize for commentary, Connie Schultz is a nationally syndicated columnist for The Plain Dealer *in Cleveland, Ohio. She is the author of a collection of columns,* Life Happens: And Other Unavoidable Truths *(2006), and* . . . And His Lovely Wife: A Campaign Memoir from the Woman Beside the Man *(2007).*

thing, I saw these computer-generated images up close and personal last summer, after two of the machines were installed at Cleveland's airport. These images are not pornographic unless your sexual fantasies steer toward cartoon characters and robots, in which case "ew" doesn't begin to diagnose your issues.

More importantly, on Christmas Day we allegedly came this close 5
to a would-be terrorist named Umar Farouk Abdulmutallab using plastic explosives sewn in his underwear to blow up a commercial flight headed for America. As I wrote just last summer, anyone wearing this travel accessory probably would not make it through a full-body scanner. But Abdulmutallab — a 23-year-old Nigerian with no coat, no luggage and cash for his ticket — ambled right through the metal detector in Amsterdam and onto Northwest Airlines Flight 253.

Not exactly Secret Agent Man. 6

Abdulmutallab's father had tried to warn American officials about his 7
son. Reportedly, an initial search misspelled his name, so no one discovered he had a multiple-entry visa. This error is confounding to some of us. Enter a misspelled name in a Google search and you immediately are greeted with "Did you mean" in bright red letters, followed by the correct spelling.

It's a little unsettling to think that security systems haven't figured 8
that one out.

The Transportation Security Administration has ordered 130 full- 9
body scanners, which emit low-level X-rays and produce computer images that look like chalk drawings. An additional 300 scanners are on order for next year.

There are numerous precautions to protect your privacy. The TSA 10
screener who waves you through is not the one who sees your computer image, which is deleted as soon as you're cleared. The images can't be stored, printed, or transmitted, and the person scanning the pictures is not allowed to bring a cell phone or camera into the room.

Nevertheless, some insist that these full-body scanners are a vio- 11
lation of privacy. It doesn't help when TV news anchors keep warning viewers about "graphic images" and praising grim-faced male volunteers as "brave" and "courageous" before walking in front of the scanners that pick up every piece of fake contraband they're wearing.

Last year, the American Civil Liberties Union championed the 12
privacy of celebrities who live and work in Los Angeles and fear their computer images could be posted on the Internet. People who regularly expose themselves for money and attention probably don't make the best victims, and so lately we aren't hearing that argument much. Now we're talking about how Grandma should be able to keep her waist-highs to herself.

There are also protests from the usual cast of angry Americans who insist you can't trust the government to make travel any safer. A curious argument coming from an entire population of people who turn the key in the ignition and pull out onto roads paved, painted and policed by — how's this for coincidence? — the government. 13

Think about it. We carry licenses issued by the government, strap on seat belts required by the government and then follow any number of traffic laws passed by the government. We also assume that all the strangers sharing the road with us passed the same driver's test given by the government. 14

So, c'mon, you're going to stand there and tell me you don't trust the government? 15

Now, that's a funny image. 16

VOCABULARY/USING A DICTIONARY

1. What are the roots of the word *privacy* (para. 11)? What terms are related to it?
2. What does the word *visa* (para. 7) mean, and what are its origins?
3. What are the connotations of the word *violation* (para. 11)? What are its roots and related words?

RESPONDING TO WORDS IN CONTEXT

1. Why does the writer use the words "travel accessory" in paragraph 5? How would you characterize the tone of this phrase?
2. In paragraph 11, Schultz places quotation marks around the words "graphic images," "brave," and "courageous." How do the quotation marks affect the way we read the words? What point is she making?
3. How do the meaning and connotation of the word *image* change throughout the essay, especially in the context of the last paragraph?

DISCUSSING MAIN POINT AND MEANING

1. Schultz advocates for the new body-scanning machines. What are her main arguments for their use?
2. According to the writer, the TSA has numerous precautions to protect passenger privacy. What are they?
3. Schultz spends much of her essay describing and addressing opponents of the body-scanning machines. How does she characterize them?

EXAMINING SENTENCES, PARAGRAPHS, AND ORGANIZATION

1. The writer acknowledges that she is "making light" (para. 4) of the controversy around full-body scanners. What specific aspects of her style, tone, and diction demonstrate this attitude? Do they make her argument more persuasive?

2. In her essay, Schultz writes in the first person (both singular and plural), the second person, and the third person. What effects do these different grammatical choices produce? How do they support her main point?
3. What is the purpose of the last sentence in paragraph 4? What do you think she means, specifically? How does this statement fit in with her larger point?

THINKING CRITICALLY

1. Schultz makes an argument in favor of using the full-body scanners in airports. What specific evidence does she use to support her point of view?
2. In paragraph 11, Schultz writes, "some insist that these full-body scanners are a violation of privacy." She also refers to the "usual cast of angry Americans who insist you can't trust the government to make travel any safer" (para. 13). How effectively does she address counterarguments? What would make her position stronger?
3. Where in the essay does Schultz argue by using analogies? How persuasive and effective are these comparisons?

IN-CLASS WRITING ACTIVITIES

1. Schultz consciously makes light of airport security issues and even presents "would-be terrorist" (para. 5) Umar Farouk Abdulmutallab as a comic figure ("Not exactly Secret Agent Man"). How much do you worry about terrorism, in the context of traveling or other aspects of your life? Are people generally too concerned with the possibility of terrorist attacks? Not concerned enough?
2. While Schultz is writing specifically about airport security issues and travel safety, she also considers the role of government more generally. How much do you trust the government?
3. According to the writer, the TSA is taking "numerous precautions" (para. 10) to protect people's privacy. Do you see the scanners as too intrusive? Do the precautions seem thorough enough? Would they change your view of airport security or even your travel habits?

Mohammed Khan (student essay)

The Need for Safety Is Paramount

[*The Daily Evergreen*, Washington State University, January 13, 2010]

BEFORE YOU READ

Should airport security officials and law-enforcement authorities use religious and ethnic profiling to thwart terrorist attacks? Is such profiling effective? What is more important in a time of global terrorism, safety or privacy?

WORDS TO LEARN

ascertaining (para. 3): finding out or learning with certainty (verb).

qualms (para. 7): feelings of uneasiness (noun).

naive (para. 8): lacking worldly experience and unsuspecting; unsophisticated (adjective).

Profiling is an element of airport screening intended to increase security, but it is not the ultimate solution to the problem. In light of what we learned from the attempted airliner bombing over Detroit on Christmas Day [2009], profiling is nowhere near effective in this age of global terrorism. 1

An enormous amount of evidence indicates racial profiling is not sufficient to protect us from terrorists. For instance, Richard Colvin Reid was stopped from igniting a device in his shoe on an American Airlines flight from Paris to Miami on Dec. 22, 2001. Reid, who is currently serving a life sentence in a supermax prison, was born in England and is half English, half Jamaican. 2

Umar Farouk Abdulmutallab, who failed with his Christmas Day bombing attempt over Detroit, is a Nigerian from a relatively rich family in London. Ethnic profiling of Arabs, Iranians, or Pakistanis would not have singled out either Reid or Abdulmutallab for specific attention. Officials could profile all Muslims, but given the difficulty of ascertaining individual religious beliefs and coupled with the fact that Muslims compose more than one-fifth of the world's population, such profiling is not feasible, at least on many international flights. 3

Mohammed Khan is a senior at Washington State University, where he is an opinion columnist for The Daily Evergreen *and majors in electrical engineering.*

4 Upon examining the facts, it is obvious there was a serious security failure in the Detroit case. Abdulmutallab's father warned the United States that his son was a threat. Nonetheless, Abdulmutallab's American visa was not revoked, and he was allowed to board the plane without any extra security measure. The bomb that he carried was undetected.

5 It is becoming increasingly apparent that our system needs to look beyond the facades of profiling and employ tactics that are intelligence based. High-tech devices like full-body scanners have recently come into light. However, privacy advocates are concerned about the machines' capability of virtually stripping people, leaving an image of their nude body on the screen.

6 Many people are uncomfortable with these invasive practices, which is understandable. The issues range from child pornography to obvious privacy infringements, all of them raising important questions. But the need for safety is paramount. Considering al-Qaida's evolving techniques, employing these high-tech devices is the need of the hour.

Considering al-Qaida's evolving techniques, employing these high-tech devices is the need of the hour.

7 New protocols could be adopted to address people's qualms about the devices. Those who are uncomfortable with the machines could arrive at the airport earlier than others. This would give officials time to thoroughly search uneasy passengers. Such a rule would streamline the entire process and improve security while giving people options.

8 It is naive to assume that racial profiling will eliminate any airport security threats. Regardless, profiling inherently exists in our contemporary times. When I first came to the United States in 2005, I was held at the Chicago O'Hare International Airport for two hours, sitting next to a man whose leg was cuffed to the bench. When I asked an official why I was being held, I was told, "With a name like Mohammed Farooq Ali Khan, you are going to be held everywhere."

9 Since my arrival, there have been regular breaches in airport security. Although racial profiling exists to prevent such breaches, it does not work. There is no one solution to this predicament. But one thing is for certain: As al-Qaida is evolving, so must security protocols.

VOCABULARY/USING A DICTIONARY

1. What does the word *feasible* (para. 3) mean? What are the word's origins?
2. According to the writer, the "need for safety is paramount" (para. 6). What does *paramount* mean, and what are its origins? How is its meaning different from that of the term *tantamount*?

3. Khan writes that new security devices could require "new protocols" (para. 7). What does he mean by *protocol*? Where does the word come from?

RESPONDING TO WORDS IN CONTEXT

1. Khan refers to "this age of global terrorism" (para. 1). How would you define the terms *terrorism* and *terrorist*? What characteristics make "terrorism" different from other kinds of crime, military action, or political violence?
2. What is "racial profiling" (para. 2)? What connotations does the term have?
3. According to Khan, security officials must "employ tactics that are intelligence based" (para. 5). What does the word *tactics* mean in this context, and how does it differ from the word *strategy*?

DISCUSSING MAIN POINT AND MEANING

1. How would you phrase Khan's thesis or main point in your own words?
2. Khan refers to Richard Reid and Umar Farouk Abdulmutallab in his essay. What do these two examples demonstrate, according to the writer?
3. How does Khan address privacy concerns in this essay?

EXAMINING SENTENCES, PARAGRAPHS, AND ORGANIZATION

1. According to the writer, "our [airport security] system needs to look beyond the facades of profiling and employ tactics that are intelligence based" (para. 5). What contrast is Khan making here? How is it related to his overall argument?
2. Khan writes, "Many people are uncomfortable with these invasive practices, which is understandable" (para. 6). How could this generalization be supported and made more convincing?
3. Why does Khan include his personal experience in paragraph 8? Would it be as effective if he included it earlier in the essay?

THINKING CRITICALLY

1. Khan suggests that "Officials could profile all Muslims," but then concludes that such a procedure would not be "feasible" (para. 3). Why does he come to this conclusion? What other reasons might make this approach infeasible?
2. Do you have any "qualms" about heightened security measures, such as full-body scanners? How do you respond to Khan's claim that "the need for safety is paramount" (para. 6)?
3. According to Khan, "An enormous amount of evidence indicates racial profiling is not sufficient to protect us from terrorists" (para. 2). Does he substantiate this claim adequately?

IN-CLASS WRITING ACTIVITIES

1. The practice of "racial profiling" (para. 2) implies that terrorists fit a certain profile. What image or stereotype comes to mind for you? Where do these images come from? How accurate is your stereotype? What do you see as the primary factor in creating terrorists?
2. Do you agree with Khan or disagree? Write an argumentative essay that either supports "The Need for Safety Is Paramount" or refutes it.
3. How much do you worry about terrorism in your own life? Where does it rank on your lists of concerns and fears? Do you think people overstate the threat of terrorist attacks? Or have we gotten too complacent about such threats?

LOOKING CLOSELY

Supporting Your Point with Examples

In any discussion or debate, nothing is more persuasive than well-chosen examples. We often use examples to back up a generalization with concrete instances or to support a claim. The examples *show* what we mean. We can see the effective use of appropriate examples in "The Need for Security Is Paramount," an essay by Washington State University student Mohammed Khan. Khan believes that airports should use screening devices because racial profiling does not work. He then offers two examples of would-be terrorists who would not have been stopped by racial profiling because their identities did not fit the ethnic groups being targeted.

1
Khan provides an instance that supports his point about profiling

2
He strengthens his point by adding a second example

An enormous amount of evidence indicates racial profiling is not sufficient to protect us from terrorists. For instance, Richard Colvin Reid was stopped from igniting a device in his shoe on an American Airlines flight from Paris to Miami on Dec. 22, 2001. Reid, who is currently serving a life sentence in a supermax prison, was born in England and is half English, half Jamaican. (1)

Umar Farouk Abdulmutallab, who failed with his Christmas Day bombing attempt over Detroit, is a Nigerian from a relatively rich family in London. Ethnic profiling of Arabs, Iranians, or Pakistanis would not have singled out either Reid or Abdulmutallab for specific attention. (2)

STUDENT WRITER AT WORK

Mohammed Khan

On Writing "The Need for Safety Is Paramount"

RA. What inspired you to write this essay? And publish it in your campus paper?

MK. As a Muslim student of Indian descent, I have far too many times experienced firsthand the extra scrutiny a person receives for belonging to a certain race. During the time I wrote the article, the Christmas bomber was being analyzed and the idea of racial profiling was being debated all over the twenty-four-hour news cycles. I had to make my voice heard as well and so I wrote the article with my perspective.

RA. What do you like to read?

MK. I am an avid fan of the *Huffington Post,* and my favorite magazines range from *National Geographic* to astronomy prints.

RA. What topics most interest you as a writer?

MK. Topics that are hot debates under the sociopolitical umbrella. I like to analyze the story with my perspective and write my opinions on it.

RA. What advice do you have for other student writers?

MK. I believe that writing is a direct result of passion towards a subject. If you really want to be heard, you will develop the skills to not only improve your language, but also the strength of your writing. Nothing can be imposed; it should come from within.

Jay Griffiths

The Tips of Your Fingers

[*Orion*, January/February 2010]

BEFORE YOU READ

What does *individuality* mean? Do you think that the government invades your privacy and your individualism? Does the average citizen have a real political voice? How does our society pressure people to conform?

WORDS TO LEARN

articulate (para. 2): to reveal, make distinct, or give clarity to (verb).

multifold (para. 4): numerous and varied (adjective).

alterity (para. 4): the quality or state of being other or profoundly different (noun).

homogeneity (para. 5): composition of similar parts, elements, or characteristics (noun).

bolsters (para. 5): supports or upholds (verb).

sequestered (para. 6): withdrawn, separated, or isolated (adjective).

biometrics (para. 9): the measurement of physical characteristics, such as fingerprints or DNA, to verify the identity of individuals (noun).

perennial (para. 11): enduring, lasting a long time (adjective).

In the woods near the border checkpoint from France to Britain, several people sit around a fire, pushing iron bars deeper into the flames until the metal is red hot. Taking out the iron, with searing pain they burn their own fingertips, trying to erase their identification. 1

The fingertips are a border checkpoint of the human body, and through them the self reaches out to touch the world. Fingertips are diviners, lovers, poets of the perhaps, emissaries of empathy. They are feelingful, exquisitely sensitive to metal, dough, moss, or splinter. They are also one of the body's places of greatest idiosyncrasy: a fingerprint 2

Jay Griffiths is the award-winning author of two nonfiction books, Pip Pip: A Sideways Look at Time *(2000), and* Wild: An Elemental Journey *(2006), and a short novel about Frida Kahlo,* A Love Letter from a Stray Moon *(2011).*

is the body's signature. Fingertips are at once highly selved and highly sensitive: They articulate difference and they distinguish difference.

Forced to erase the sign of themselves, people scar, burn, stitch, and staple their fingertips at U.S. borders too, and indeed wherever people fear that their identification will be used against them, not because they are criminals but because they are refugees and victims of war, poverty, and neo-imperialism. 3

Border checkpoints bristle with state control, and this control now encroaches within nations. In Britain, already the world leader in surveillance, the state is now pushing for nationwide ID cards. Identification, tagging, and surveillance are used to intimidate those at the margins, the borders of society: Refugees, whose individual stories of blood and horror give the lie to the glossy brochures of foreign policy; the insane with their flashes of specific mind-lightning; those who stand out, eccentrically, for their beliefs, who poke and provoke with the demeanor of a pitchfork in the cutlery drawer; young people at the borders of adulthood; protesters, with their multifold cries of "see it otherwise," demanding political alterity. All are harassed with surveillance. 4

Truly individualistic societies would cherish all such border crossers, not punish them. But the dominant culture is a society of intolerant homogeneity that bolsters racism, ageism, and conformism. It supports monoism, destroying variety from biodiversity to linguistic diversity. Like the monoculture of Hollywood and the monocrops of agribusiness, the monopolitics of world powers erase the particular, searing away the idiomatic dialect of the self, symbolized so specifically by each person's fingertips. Burning away the signature of individuality, at the borders of those very countries that most profess individualism, is a metaphor of terrible reproach. And it tells a deep truth, for ours is not an individualistic society. Rather, it is a hyper-privatized one. 5

The word *private* originally meant to be "deprived of public life," and most people today are so deprived. A vote every few years does not constitute a political voice. Terms for public political life, like *solidarity, trade unions, co-operatives,* or *collectives,* are unwelcome in a world of hyper-privatization. Employees engaged in public protest find their jobs threatened. Citizens are also deprived of public life in nature, fobbed off with parks and that hyper-privatized patch of green, the fenced-in private garden. Entertainment, traditionally a very communal affair, is now hyper-privatized, the individual watching TV in a room alone, where the sequestered self is more vulnerable to advertising. 6

Similarly, the etymology of the word *idiot,* from ancient Greek, refers to a "purely private person" — one who takes no part in public life. In this hyper-privatized world, it is as if governments would prefer their 7 subjects to remain idiots, disengaged from the state's process but suffering its intrusions.

8 Humans need community and public life: we also need the secluded intimacy of privacy, and the latter is threatened by surveillance. Those in favor of surveillance argue that "if you have nothing to hide, you have nothing to fear," but this denies the very significance of privacy — a cache to shelter our tenderness and our name. Telling one's name is a gift. Withholding it is a right.

Telling one's name is a gift. Withholding it is a right.

9 Through the twin prongs of ID cards and surveillance, the borders of the private self are invaded. I am declaring, here, that I am a sovereign state. I do not want alien states to use biometrics to crawl into my eyes like flies. I do not want my identity captured by strangers. But I, who am deprived of the human right to freely roam in my own free land, find that the state can roam freely through the territories of my self, violating the integrity of my borders.

10 When the state crosses the borders into my private self, it is an ugly act. But border crossing the other way — the self reaching outward — is an act of beauty and transcendence. Art, spirituality, environmentalism, and movements for political justice agree, seeking transcendence from the confines of the single self, and it is no surprise that people from backgrounds of faith, activism, and art are those who most vehemently oppose ID cards.

11 The perennial philosophy of a universal oneness suggests a reaching out beyond the ego. So does the traditional posture of fingertips touched together in prayer to set free the spirit, winged for infinity. Movements for political reform take wide, unprivate ideals, the wisest art goes beyond the individual, and at the heart of environmentalism is the extension of the borders of responsibility to encompass lands, times, selves, and species beyond the individual.

12 The human psyche, then, seems to find benevolence in the self transcending its boundaries. By contrast, the psyche finds malevolence in those who invade those boundaries: in the myths and mores of many cultures, people are wary about giving names to strangers. Belief in the Evil Eye is virtually a human universal, embodying the malignity of surveillance. Staring is inherently predatory, and we, as other animals, hate being watched because it is a prelude to attack. Mass surveillance — modernity's Evil Eye — is peculiarly nasty because of its cowardice; the watcher is hidden, unknowable and faceless.

13 Anyone can recognize a sense of guilt merely walking (innocently) through airport customs. Being trailed by a police car provokes a similar

guilt, even when unfounded. Surveillance provokes a pervasive sense of guilt and entrapment and this fusion has a practical history in the invention in 1785 of the Panopticon, the surveillance device designed to watch prisoners without their knowledge. If plans for compulsory ID cards succeed in the UK, we will be carrying our own Panopticons with us, and the protest against these plans is muted. In the U.S., thankfully, there is tougher resistance to ID cards, but a modern Panopticon, the microchip tag within the body, is in use already by an Ohio company (CityWatcher.com) whose business is in providing governments with surveillance tools, and which has inserted microchips under the skin of some of its employees.

Surveillance creates conformity. Anyone queuing at border control 14
attempts to look as "normal" as possible: like any animal under a predatory stare, humans try to fit in with the herd, not to stand out. The glare of surveillance is the opposite of the gaze of love, for under that gaze a person wants to be known, seen especially for themselves, flirting the peacock feathers of otherness, the distinguishing features of the soul. The law of evolution encourages individuation, and diversity is a signature of the vitality of nature. These laws of life agree with the law of love in nurturing true individuality, for the human heart cherishes "this-ness," the essential specificity of the beloved person.

"If you ask me why I loved him," said the Renaissance French human- 15
ist Michel de Montaigne of his friend Étienne de La Boétie, "I can only say: because he was he, and I was I." Delineating an exquisite uniqueness, it is as if their fingertips still touch, after all these centuries, and the fingertips of Montaigne's mind, like all great artists, transcend the borders of self and time to touch minds today with the inalienable signature of love.

VOCABULARY/USING A DICTIONARY

1. What does *idiosyncrasy* (para. 2) mean? What other words is it related to?
2. How does Griffiths use the word *psyche* (para. 12)? What are its origins?
3. In paragraph 13, the writer refers to the development of the Panopticon as a surveillance device to watch prisoners without their knowledge. What are the roots of that word?

RESPONDING TO WORDS IN CONTEXT

1. In paragraph 2, Griffiths writes that "Fingertips are diviners . . ." (para. 2). What does the word *diviners* mean? What connotations does it have in the context of the essay?
2. Griffiths writes that privacy is "a cache to shelter our tenderness and our name" (para. 8). Why did she choose the word *cache* rather than a more common term like *hiding place*?

3. According to the writer, "the law of evolution encourages individuation" (para. 14). What is the difference between *individuation* and *individuality*?

DISCUSSING MAIN POINT AND MEANING

1. The writer argues against the use of "biometrics" (para. 9) and national ID cards. What problems does she see with them?
2. Griffiths criticizes the forces of conformity beyond surveillance and national identification requirements. Where else does she see them at work?
3. According to the writer, "it is no surprise that people from backgrounds of faith, activism, and art are those who most vehemently oppose ID cards" (para. 10). Why would that be the case, in the context of Griffiths's argument?

EXAMINING SENTENCES, PARAGRAPHS, AND ORGANIZATION

1. Griffiths shows a keen awareness of sound and figurative language, from the cadences of her writing and her surprising word choices and metaphors, to her use of rhyme and alliteration: "The fingertips are . . . poets of the perhaps, emissaries of empathy" (para. 2). Point to some specific examples of lyrical or poetical prose within the essay. What are the benefits and drawbacks of writing this way?
2. What purposes do paragraphs 6 and 7 have in the essay? How do they further Griffiths's argument?
3. This article is titled "The Tips of Your Fingers." It begins with a description of people burning their fingertips near a border checkpoint to erase their identities. How does Griffiths use fingertips as an organizing device or theme in her essay?

THINKING CRITICALLY

1. Griffiths writes that genuinely "individualistic societies would cherish all such border crossers . . . [but] the dominant culture is a society of intolerant homogeneity that bolsters racism, ageism, and conformism" (para. 5). How do you interpret these assertions? Do you agree with them?
2. According to the writer, most people today are "deprived of public life" (para. 6). What view does she take of contemporary political participation? Do you agree?
3. Griffiths refers to the "malignity of surveillance" and claims that its widespread presence is "modernity's Evil Eye" (para. 12). Where do you see such surveillance in your own life? Do you share her view of it as a malevolent force?

IN-CLASS WRITING ACTIVITIES

1. According to the writer, most people have no real political voice (para. 6). She then lists several terms for "public political life," which she claims are "unwelcome in a world of hyper-privatization" (para. 6). Choose one or all

of the words, and briefly discuss their meaning and connotations. Do you agree that they are "unwelcome" in our current political and economic climate? Are there other words that designate "public political life" that are just as important?

2. Griffiths writes about the value of—and need for—"true individualism," even as she argues that societies and countries are hostile to individualism. What does "individualism" mean to you? Do you share Griffiths's views?
3. The writer argues that even contemporary amusements are isolating: "Entertainment, traditionally a very communal affair, is now hyper-privatized, the individual watching TV in a room alone, where the sequestered self is more vulnerable to advertising" (para. 6). Consider your own experiences and habits of "entertainment." Do you agree with Griffiths that they generally tend to isolate people rather than connect them? Explain.

Discussing the Unit

SUGGESTED TOPIC FOR DISCUSSION

All the authors in this unit discuss the balance between security and privacy: the need for safety versus the need to guard the boundaries of our personal identities. None of the writers dismiss the real threat of terrorism. But who bears most of the responsibility for protecting us? Rosen is skeptical of "security theater." In contrast, Connie Schultz writes, "So, c'mon, you're going to stand there and tell me you don't trust the government?" To what degree do we need the government to keep us safe? How effective is it at that task? Do you think it should play more of a role in our safety? Less?

PREPARING FOR CLASS DISCUSSION

1. Griffiths writes, "I do not want alien states to use biometrics to crawl into my eyes like flies." Biometrics are the measurement of physical characteristics, such as fingerprints, DNA, or retinal patterns for the use of verifying the identity of individuals. What is your opinion of biometrics? Would you mind being part of a national or international database? Would you object to national ID cards, if they were made mandatory? Why or why not?
2. For Khan and Schultz, security takes precedence over privacy concerns—although Khan has reservations about the use of profiling. Rosen and Griffiths are more concerned with privacy. Which of these four essays do you find the most persuasive and effective? Why?

FROM DISCUSSION TO WRITING

1. Griffiths, Rosen, and Schultz all address privacy rights. How do you define *privacy*? Do you have a "right" to it? What are your own "privacy rights"? How do you balance them against matters of public safety or the interests of the state (e.g., regulating immigration)?
2. Khan writes that during his detention at Chicago's O'Hare airport, an official told him, "With a name like Mohammed Farooq Ali Khan, you are going to be held everywhere." Khan does not include or discuss his response to the official's remark. What is your response? What was the official's tone or goal in making the remark? How would you have responded if you were Khan?

QUESTIONS FOR CROSS-CULTURAL DISCUSSION

1. Griffiths takes a grim view of national and international border controls and checkpoints, which "bristle with state control." What are your own views on border security, immigration, and national identity? Why are these issues often so controversial in the United States?
2. How do cultural and ethnic backgrounds shape attitudes toward privacy rights? Should these considerations be taken into account when, say, formulating policies about airport security? Why or why not?

9

Barack Obama: What Does His Election Mean to America?

The election of America's first African American president filled the country, from left to right, with a momentary euphoria—even those who disagreed with his campaign felt a sense that the boundaries of American life had been suddenly and irreversibly expanded. Barack Obama's opponent, Senator John McCain, even called the election "historic" in his concession speech, telling his Republican supporters that the Democratic president-elect had "achieved a great thing for himself and for his country." The same emotion was felt all over the world: The prime minister of Ukraine declared to Obama, "Your victory is an inspiration for us. That which appeared impossible has become possible."

But as the elation subsided to the anxiety of a country facing two wars and a crippling economic recession, many began to question exactly what Obama's presidency meant—and means. Many observers bristled that despite the inspiring rhetorical power of Obama the candidate, Obama the president would represent more of the same: that he would perpetuate the same Washington policies they felt had failed the country. Moreover, commentators characterized him as a member of the Washington elite, out of touch with ordinary Americans, and particularly with his African American base—poor, uneducated, and powerless—that he had so inspired.

The debate was wide and important enough to spawn an entire issue of *Essence*, the country's premier African American magazine, shortly after Obama's election. In that issue, novelist Diane McKinney-Whetstone summarized the ebullient feeling so many black people had watching the election night ceremony in Chicago's Grant Park—a feeling that the long-promised piece of the American dream was finally really theirs, and that the Obama family members were the best ambassadors they could have asked for. "Barack's story is so familiar to us," she writes. "The child whose father goes away, the single mom struggling on welfare, the grandparents who step in and supplant." Obama represents the shared experience of all African Americans who have struggled through privation and prejudice to reach a purpose in life. "And for the Obamas," she says, "the moment came."

John Edgar Wideman, writing in the same issue of *Essence*, focuses on the realities of life for black children, a reality he sets off against the same pomp and circumstance McKinney-Whetstone celebrates in the election. Wideman describes the ongoing poverty and marginalization of New York's black poor, and wonders, "Is a President Obama too late to help the missing ones?" The problem of urban poverty will not be solved, Wideman argues, simply by having a president with a different skin tone; we have to be willing to actually "listen to our young people on the street corners."

This chapter's student essay, by Santa Clara University's Pearl Wong, agrees that a black president won't be able to fix America's many problems simply by virtue of his ethnicity. "While Obama embodies a milestone in America's history as the first African American president," she writes, "he is not the president of only African Americans." While Wong is skeptical of the specific identity politics she sees in the Obama campaign, Christopher Hedges, writing for *Tikkun*, takes a more generally critical view of Obama. What's interesting about Hedges's essay is that he attacks Obama not from the right but from the left, arguing that he represents a continuation of the conventional policies of the Bush administration, policies he believes are determined and orchestrated by a corporate oligarchy. All Obama's race means, for Hedges, is that the insiders are "rebranding" their message, just as a corporation might rebrand its products. "But like all branded products spun out from the manipulative world of corporate advertising," Hedges writes, "this product is duping us into doing and supporting a lot of things that are not in our interest."

Diane McKinney-Whetstone

The First Family

[*Essence*, January 2009]

BEFORE YOU READ

How do you see the African American family in America today? Is it even possible to think of a "typical" black family, or are all family units marked by too much diversity to entertain such stereotypes? Did the election of Barack Obama change your picture of black families at all? Why or why not?

WORDS TO LEARN

charismatic (para. 1): having a charm that wins people over (adjective).
exude (para. 1): to ooze out (verb).
ebullience (para. 1): energetic cheerfulness (noun).
dysfunction (para. 3): a failure or impairment, especially of a family (noun).
maladjusted (para. 3): unable to fit into a normal social environment (adjective).
intact (para. 3): together (adjective).
fractured (para. 4): broken (adjective).
culminate (para. 4): to reach a certain point in the end (verb).
supplant (para. 4): to replace (verb).
dearth (para. 4): lack (noun).
garner (para. 4): to get (verb).
buoyant (para. 5): staying afloat; optimistic and confident (adjective).

The Obamas made for a stunning visual as they took center stage in Grant Park on election night. When the crowd surged forward, hearts bursting with love and pride, the lens shifted and altered the world's view of the Black family. Here, in President-elect Barack Obama, was a handsome and charismatic father exuding adoration for his daughters; a husband whose affection for his wife was so evident that, as we watched them on the campaign trail, we got the sense that after 16 years of marriage, he still got weak in the knees at the sight of her walking toward him. Here, in Michelle Obama, was a brilliant wife and an attentive mother, eyes trained on her children, protective and strong. And here were the beautiful daughters, Malia and Sasha, in their ebullience and velvet-and-taffeta dresses and their Sunday school hair. 1

Diane McKinney-Whetstone has written five acclaimed novels, the most recent of which is Trading Dreams at Midnight *(2008). The recipient of many awards, she teaches at the University of Pennsylvania.*

President-elect Barack Obama with his family at Grant Park in Chicago, Illinois, November 4, 2008.

As the tears washed down our faces, we flashed on all the moments over the past months that had filled us up, filled us with a recognition of family that has for too long been missing from the public stage: There was Barack, eyes closed for a moment, leaning against his wife in a Norman Rockwell-esque[1] diner, or scooping his daughters into his arms on yet another airport tarmac. And Michelle, exchanging that playful fist dap[2] with her husband, or wiping Malia's brow on a hot summer day, or absently, tenderly, smoothing Sasha's flyaway hair. And there, in family snapshots were the girls, sprawled across their parents, owning them, with perfect assurance that the man who would be president and his first lady were theirs, first and forever; the campaign, the world, everything else, came after. 2

And there, on election night, for all to witness, was the picture-perfect image that the world has not seen enough of because the camera has too often been trained on our dysfunction — the absent father, the hysterical mother and the maladjusted kids. But in Grant Park on that night, we saw an image that could have been lifted from those cardboard fans we used 3

[1] Norman Rockwell (para. 2): (1894–1978) A painter and illustrator famous for scenes of typical family life in the United States.

[2] fist dap (para. 2): A reference to a "fist bump" gesture Barack and Michelle Obama became famous for making on stage in July of 2008.

to sway in church, fans adorned with pictures of the smiling Black parents and their well-appointed children. We saw a family not unlike any number of Black families we know, who live quietly in towns and cities and suburbs throughout the nation. That night, watching the Obamas, even if we didn't leave our seats, inside we were jumping up and down just like the Kenyan relatives.[3] Finally, the world could see what we've always known: Black families can be loving, intact, nurturing worlds that produce confident, talented children.

Finally, the world could see what we've always known.

4 We were moved by the image of the Obamas on that stage for other reasons too. We knew intimately about the fractured pasts and defiant dreams that had culminated in a present that was so wonderfully whole. Barack's story is so familiar to us: the child whose father goes away, the single mom struggling on welfare, the grandparents who step in and supplant. We've lived Michelle's past as well, in the dearth of material privilege, and the sacrifice and the encouragement that never quit. Like Barack and Michelle, many of us were raised by those who would not allow excuses for underachievement. We studied our books and garnered scholarships, and began the quest for a purposeful life. Then there was the miracle of falling in love and partnering with one who had the capacity for compromise. The children came. And for the Obamas, the moment came.

5 It was our moment, too. On the stage at Grant Park the light passed at just the right angle to capture the splendid realness of the Black family. We saw ourselves in the small gestures: Michelle touching Malia's shoulder; Barack sweeping Sasha into the air, the president-elect, buoyant in the presence of his family. And we felt the wonder of the moment, wrought by God's grace, through which even the fractured parts of our history could unfold into such miraculous wholeness. Deep down, we've always known what our families could be. Now with the Obamas' victory, the world knows, too.

VOCABULARY/USING A DICTIONARY

1. What does it mean to know something or someone *intimately* (para. 4)? What would one possible opposite of *intimately* be?
2. What does the word *culminate* (para. 4) mean? What part of speech is it? What does it mean for more than one thing to culminate?
3. What is *ebullience* (para. 1)? What language does it come from, and what did it mean in that language?

[3] Kenyan relatives (para. 3): Barack Obama has an extended family in Kenya, in eastern Africa, whose members were shown on election night celebrating.

RESPONDING TO WORDS IN CONTEXT

1. What exactly does McKinney-Whetstone mean when she refers to a "Norman Rockwell-esque diner" (para. 2)? What does the association the author makes to Rockwell imply about the scene?
2. McKinney-Whetstone refers to "the child whose father goes away, the single mom struggling on welfare, the grandparents who step in and supplant" (para. 4). What does *supplant* mean here?
3. The essay describes President-elect Obama as "buoyant" on the stage in Grant Park (para 5). What does it mean to be *buoyant*? What specific gestures or expressions do you imagine when you hear somebody described as *buoyant*?

DISCUSSING MAIN POINT AND MEANING

1. What is McKinney-Whetstone saying she felt watching the ceremony in Grant Park? How is the feeling related to her childhood?
2. What is the essay implying many people think about black families? How did the image of the Obamas on stage challenge that picture?
3. Who does McKinney-Whetstone mean when she repeatedly says "we" in the essay? (For instance, "We studied our books and garnered scholarships," para. 4.) What does this group have in common with the Obamas?

EXAMINING SENTENCES, PARAGRAPHS, AND ORGANIZATION

1. What is the effect of mentioning Malia and Sasha's "velvet-and-taffeta dresses and their Sunday school hair" in paragraph 1? Why does she include this detail?
2. Paragraph 4 of this essay contains several long sentences and then ends with one short sentence. Study these sentences in context. What is the effect of this organization on the reader?
3. How does the essay switch between its two major scenes—that of the Obamas themselves in Grant Park, and that of the audience? Which one does it start with, when does it transition, and when does it transition back? What is the effect of this back-and-forth motion?

THINKING CRITICALLY

1. What, if anything, do you believe the election of Barack Obama represents for American society? What, if anything, do you think it represents for the image of the black family in America?
2. Do you believe there's such a thing as a "typical" black family? If so, what is it? If not, why not?

3. McKinney-Whetstone focuses entirely on the visual impact of the Obama family, ignoring President Obama's policies and positions. What is the effect of this focus? What does an image of a politician tell us that a political speech or a debate cannot?

IN-CLASS WRITING ACTIVITIES

1. Watch a video of the Grant Park acceptance speech from November of 2008 (available on YouTube.) What is your reaction to President Obama as a public figure, to the Obama family, and to the speech itself? What elements of McKinney-Whetstone's essay resonate with you as you watch the video? Do you think she missed anything or got anything wrong?
2. What do you believe the status, the condition, and the future of the African American family is today? Do you think blacks have overcome the bigotry that has dogged them in the past, or is racism still a problem in America? Do you think the Obama administration will make an impact on race relations, positive or negative? If so, do you think this impact will come from policy decisions or simply from the presence of a black president? Give specific reasons and examples to back up your answer.
3. Describe a moment, like the one McKinney-Whetstone describes, where you saw yourself in a public figure or connected deeply to a person, people, or an idea you encountered in the public sphere, either in person or on TV. What was it about the moment that made such an impact on you? Was it the overall feeling of what was said or done, or was it, as in "The First Family," the details? Give a thorough account of your reaction.

John Edgar Wideman

Street Corner Dreamers

[*Essence*, January 2009]

BEFORE YOU READ

What, if anything, can be done about the crushing problem of poverty in America's cities? What, if anything, will the Obama administration be able to achieve that previous governments have not?

WORDS TO LEARN

scour (para. 1): to clean something by rubbing or wiping it hard (verb).

dour (para. 1): sad and gloomy (adjective).

harbor (para. 1): to have inside (verb).

dire (para. 1): extremely serious (adjective).

droning (para. 1): making a low humming sound (adjective).

predatory (para. 1): planning to attack (adjective).

alienated (para. 2): made to feel apart from (adjective).

phantoms (para. 2): ghosts (noun).

palpable (para. 2): able to be felt (adjective).

jeopardizing (para. 2): putting in danger (verb).

expendable (para. 2): not necessary (adjective).

roiling (para. 3): swirling around (adjective).

exuberance (para. 3): joy and excitement for life (noun).

daunted (para. 3): intimidated or nervous (adjective).

simulate (para. 3): imitate (verb).

motley (para. 3): made of many different colors or fabrics (adjective).

infatuated (para. 4): having a sudden, intense passion for something (adjective).

incarcerated (para. 4): in prison (adjective).

chasm (para. 4): a wide gap, like a cliff (noun).

perilous (para. 5): dangerous (adjective).

intractable (para. 5): unable to be changed or dealt with (adjective).

irrepressible (para. 6): unable to be restrained (adjective).

throng (para. 7): crowd (verb).

One of America's most respected novelists, John Edgar Wideman is the Asa Messer Professor of Africana Studies and Creative Writing at Brown University. He has twice won the prestigious PEN/Faulkner Award and has been a nominee for the National Book Critics Circle Award. His most recent books include a collection of stories, God's Gym *(2005), and a novel,* Fanon *(2008).*

It is the morning after Barack Obama has been elected the forty-fourth president of the United States. In six hours or so, the corner of Grand and Essex, a block from my apartment building on New York's Lower East Side, will fill up with young people exiting Seward Park High School. For more than two years, the city has been sandblasting Seward Park's seven-story exterior walls. As the presidential candidates debated taxes, someone was paid a large chunk of scarce public funds, originally designated for improving education, to clean the building. Unfortunately, the scouring barely altered the dour, dirty gray scowl of the brick and stone. I don't know what was transpiring inside Seward while its outside was being scrubbed, but given the dismal record of public schools educating the poor, I harbor plenty of dire concerns: Has anybody asked the students if they think they're learning more and better after their school's facelift? Are the students being instructed how to survive the droning, predatory streets waiting to eat them up? I want to walk up to one of them and ask, "Do you think your life might be different now that Barack Obama is president? What steps do you believe President Obama will take to improve your life? What steps do you think he should take?" 1

Of course there are many, many young people missing from the corner — in jail, addicted or dead already from violence or neglect, many alienated absolutely from school, citizenship, prospects of jobs and families. Not a lost generation exactly — their bodies survive, though as mere phantoms of what they could have become, could have offered society. They are ghosts whose absence is a palpable presence among the kids on the corner, a shadow haunting and jeopardizing them. How long? Too long. They are the predictable casualties, victims comprising a heartbreakingly high percentage of youth of color, destroyed by marginalization. Why? Because America decided we could get along just fine without them, thank you. Is a President Obama too late to help the missing ones? What higher priority for a nation, for a new president, than to stop the bleeding, to stop the blighting of youth and potential suffered by generation after generation of the colored and poor? Will they continue to be treated as expendable? How will President Barack Obama attempt to seal the cracks they slip through? Not cracks in the pavement of Grand and Essex, but the cracks of broken promises, the cracks that have divided and conquered the will of a nation to treat all citizens equally. 2

Walking the gauntlets of students on the sidewalks surrounding that school, I admit to myself that I've been too busy, too consumed by whatever's on my mind, to ask any of them anything. Though they'd never guess it from my silence as I pass through their ranks, I'm hopelessly in love with them, worry about them, see my nieces, nephews, 3 granddaughter, myself in this unruly, roiling mass of teenagers — young people of amalgamated African, Asian, European descent, every shade of light and dark skin, bushy hair, straight hair, dreads, braids, shaved heads, raw exuberance and noise and eyes hungry only for each other. I am a bit intimidated by them, certainly daunted by the ruthless truth of the vast difference in age and circumstance separating us, overwhelmed finally by the spectacle of their absolute fragility and vulnerability as they pour out onto the streets, exposed by the clothing they wear, clothes manufactured from the cheapest synthetics to simulate expensive flash and flair, colorful clothing brimming with attitude, with confidence and humor and shame and shyness about physically coming of age, bodies sprouting, busting-out young bodies in motley costumes to disguise poverty, clothing calculated to reveal and conceal.

Is there such a thing, really, as a future in young minds infatuated, 4
incarcerated by the present moment? Why would these young people speculate about crossing the gulf between themselves and the future, any future, whether a President Obama's in it or not? How equipped are they to imagine bridging the chasm between a White House in Washington, D.C., and a local, recently scoured public school that serves the Lower East Side's children of color and poverty?

In a classroom inside the building, as a sponsored guest, maybe I 5
could undertake a conversation about who they are, who I am, and the uncertain, unsettling place where we find ourselves at this perilous juncture in our nation's evolution. Perhaps we would explore together the explosive, still almost unbelievable fact that our country finally seized the opportunity to turn away from one deeply rooted, intractable, self-destructive, dead-end understanding of itself as White and Black, finally began to create a new vision of itself, whatever that vision might shake out to be. Will we become a nation converted to a new faith, a new dream, a new political consciousness and commitment, embracing Obama's complex heritage, his courage, his determination, his call for us to be more, collectively, than the sum of our parts?

My vision of what's coming next goes no further. No crystal-ball 6
gazing. I see a swarm of young people congregating down the block, free at last, free at last, of closed rooms, regimented hours, hostility, chaos, good intentions. Young women and men energized by the immediate, compelling hunger and sweetness of being alive. I want to believe that these young people on the corner are not only capable of hearing change, but that they can also be bearers of that change. Do I glimpse that change in the way they walk and talk, the way they occupy space and flash looks at one another, urgent exchanges of joy, anger, longing, understanding, impatience, solidarity, challenge, like

the undeniable, irrepressible reality embodied in singer Sam Cooke's[1] voice when he promises change that must come — music that might be in the general air now or playing just around the corner in the voice of Barack Obama?

Not Barack singing, but President Obama in charge, calling the 7
meeting to order. Putting a finger to his lips: *Quiet, everybody, please.* Let's listen to our young people on the street corners. Let's begin making room for the voices they may not exactly understand they own yet, carve out space for them in this country they may not exactly comprehend belongs to them, too. The president of the United States of America, listening to the words of the young people who throng Grand and Essex, Obama listening to discover what he may do for them, do for us all.

Quiet, everybody, please. Let's listen to our young people on the street corners.

VOCABULARY/USING A DICTIONARY

1. What exactly is *marginalization* (para. 2)? What does Wideman mean by this term, where does it come from, and how does it apply to the "youth of color" to whom he refers?
2. What kind of garments is Wideman describing when he calls them *motley* (para. 3)? To what specific thing did this word once refer, and in what sense is Wideman using it in the essay?
3. What does *amalgamated* (para. 3) mean? What noun is this word related to, and what is its origin?

RESPONDING TO WORDS IN CONTEXT

1. Wideman says that the cleaning of the school building was unable to remove its "scowl" (para. 1). What is a *scowl*, and what do you think he means by the *scowl* of a building?
2. Wideman refers to the "facelift" of the school building in the same paragraph. What is a *facelift*, and what is he implying by using the word in this context?
3. What does Wideman mean when he refers to the "blighting of youth and potential suffered by generation after generation of the colored and poor" (para. 2)? Look up *blighting* in a dictionary. Where does the word come from, and what is its meaning here?

---

[1] Sam Cooke (para. 6): An African American singer killed in 1964. Wideman is referring to his song "A Change Is Gonna Come," released just after his death, which became an anthem for the civil rights movement.

DISCUSSING MAIN POINT AND MEANING

1. What do the students at Seward Park High School stand for? Why is Wideman using them as examples, and how do they represent a larger group?
2. What forces does Wideman blame for the problem he is describing? What exactly is that problem?
3. What does Wideman mean when he says he will do no "crystal-ball gazing" (para. 6)? Do you get the sense that Wideman is optimistic or pessimistic that President Obama will bring real change to the lives of the students at Seward Park?

EXAMINING SENTENCES, PARAGRAPHS, AND ORGANIZATION

1. Wideman writes that "as the presidential candidates debated taxes, someone was paid a large chunk of scarce public funds" (para. 1) to clean the New York school. Why does Wideman point out that these things happened at the same time?
2. What do all the sentences in paragraph 4 have in common? How does this paragraph add to the tone of the essay as a whole?
3. What is the effect of beginning the essay with a descriptive scene? What sort of scene does it set, and how does the image the essay establishes evolve into its argument?

THINKING CRITICALLY

1. Wideman repeatedly invokes the "missing" young people (para. 2), and refers to the black students on the corner of Grand and Essex as "phantoms" and "ghosts." Do you agree that black people, especially young black people, have been ignored in America? If so, why? What forces account for society's lack of attention, and what can be done about it? If not, why do you think Wideman and others believe young black people are "missing"? What can be done to address the problems they raise?
2. Wideman asks why black youths would "speculate about crossing the gulf between themselves and the future, any future, whether a President Obama's in it or not" (para. 4), but stops short of predicting whether in fact they will—or what that future will look like for them. Look into your own crystal ball. Do you think Obama will have an impact on urban poverty? Why or why not?
3. Wideman writes that the best hope for America is to "turn away from one deeply rooted, intractable, self-destructive, dead-end understanding of itself as White and Black" (para. 5). What does he mean by this comment? Is he suggesting that Americans need to ignore racial differences, embrace them, or something in between? How much do you feel race should be a part of our individual identities or of the national conversation? Does it receive too much attention at the moment—or too little?

IN-CLASS WRITING ACTIVITIES

1. Research some statistics on the poverty gap between blacks and whites. What accounts for this disparity? Do you believe there is a solution to the overwhelming imbalance between black and white poverty? If so, detail how you believe this solution could be enacted. If not, why not? What makes the problem, to borrow Wideman's word, so "intractable"?
2. Write a brief description of a public school in your neighborhood or home town following Wideman's example, in which the outward look of the school serves as a metaphor for what kind of education goes on inside it. Is it (and are the students, in turn) suffering from neglect? Or is it a symbol of the class of people who attend it? Show, don't tell.
3. What do you expect President Obama can do for you and your community? Do you feel that politicians have any real impact on the way things stand on the street level anymore, or is it impossible for a disconnected Washington establishment to make any real changes? List three positive changes the federal government could make in your town or city in the next two years, and whether or not you think they will happen. If not, why not?

Pearl Wong (student essay)

Obama—President for All

[*The Santa Clara*, Santa Clara University, February 25, 2010]

BEFORE YOU READ

Have we transcended race in America? If not, will we ever transcend it? How conscious should we be of race in our everyday lives?

WORDS TO LEARN

assailed (para. 2): viciously and repeatedly attacked (adjective).
foundation (para. 3): structure on which something rests (noun).
maintain (para. 3): hold on to (verb).
vulnerable (para. 4): easy to hurt (adjective).

Pearl Wong is an economics major at Santa Clara University. She contributes to the school paper, The Santa Clara, *a few times a year and hopes to make a career out of writing. She expects to graduate in 2012.*

How can one expect others to look past our skin color and ethnic backgrounds if we can't? Now, I'm not talking about being ashamed of one's heritage or about prancing in public with conspicuous banners demanding acceptance. A fine line exists between overtly embracing who we are and quietly concealing our identity. However, by conspicuously identifying themselves with a specific racial group, people essentially allow others to classify them based only on their heritage. 1

Recently, President Barack Obama has been assailed with discontentment from the African American community for not doing enough for black Americans. Of course, black scholars are careful in their criticisms, but the message is clear: They think Obama needs to directly address the issue of race. 2

Although our nation was built on a foundation to protect minority groups, no one ever said one can only help one group of minorities; so, red pill or blue?[1] Rather than focusing on one race, even if it's one particularly close to Obama's heart, the President of the United States must maintain his executive position as a representative of all people residing in America. 3

Addressing the rising grumbling from black scholars, Obama was quoted in the *New York Times*, saying, "I can't pass laws that say I'm just helping black folks. I'm the President of the United States. What I can do is make sure that I am passing laws that help all people, particularly those who are most vulnerable and most in need. That in turn is going to help lift up the African American community." 4

Hence, while Obama embodies a milestone in America's history as the first African American president, he is not the president of only African Americans. In order for true equality to develop, we must begin with ourselves and with each other. Instead of calling for attention, take the opportunity to make positive changes in your local community. 5

In order for true equality to develop, we must begin with ourselves and with each other.

Rather than shaking your heads at the news, ask yourself what you can do to make the world a bit better for minorities. As Mother Teresa said, "If you judge people, you will have no time to love them." 6

VOCABULARY/USING A DICTIONARY

1. What does the prefix *dis-* mean in "discontentment" (para. 2)? What does Wong mean by *discontentment*?

---

[1] red pill or blue (para. 3): A reference to the 1999 film *The Matrix,* in which the choice of pills represents a particularly difficult decision between learning the truth or being happy.

2. What is a *milestone* (para. 5)? What is the literal meaning of the word, and what figurative meaning does the dictionary offer? In which sense is Wong using it here?

RESPONDING TO WORDS IN CONTEXT

1. Wong repeats the word *conspicuous* in paragraph 1, in two different forms. What does this word mean, to what sort of behavior is she referring, and why does she emphasize it?
2. Wong writes that Obama "embodies a milestone in America's history." What does it mean to *embody* something (para. 5)? What is the origin of the word, and how is it used in Wong's essay?

DISCUSSING MAIN POINT AND MEANING

1. Summarize what Wong means by the "fine line" she introduces in paragraph 1. What are the two extremes she is arguing we must avoid?
2. Wong writes that "in order for true equality to develop, we must begin with ourselves and with each other" (para. 5). What do you think she means? What is she suggesting we have to do in order to achieve equality?

EXAMINING SENTENCES, PARAGRAPHS, AND ORGANIZATION

1. What does Wong mean by asking "red pill or blue" in paragraph 3? What two options do the pills represent? Why does she phrase the choice this way, and how does this phrasing enhance her point?
2. Describe how Wong uses quotations in her essay. What two sources does she quote, and what is the effect of each quotation? What is their combined effect?

THINKING CRITICALLY

1. Wong's argument rests in large part on her assertion in paragraph 1 that "by conspicuously identifying themselves with a specific racial group, people essentially allow others to classify them based only on their heritage." Do you agree? Do you think it's possible to make your ethnicity or heritage a major part of your identity without allowing others to judge you based on it?
2. What do you think of Wong's claim that change must come from individual action? What will be more important to solving problems like race relations in America—local efforts by individuals or government intervention? Why? Give specific examples.

IN-CLASS WRITING ACTIVITIES

1. Limited by space, Wong does not offer examples of how black scholars expect President Obama to do more for black Americans, or to "directly address the issue of race (para. 2)." Give three specific examples of actions

black leaders might hope the president would take on behalf of minorities, whether or not you agree he should follow them.

2. Wong challenges us to ask ourselves what we can do "to make the world a bit better for minorities" (para. 6). Do you think this is a reasonable challenge? Should we be considering minorities when we act on a local level, or, following Obama's example, should we simply worry about helping those who need it most, regardless of ethnic group? What do you think is the most useful thing people can do to help the needy in their communities?

LOOKING CLOSELY

Establishing Your Main Point

As you learn to express opinions clearly and effectively, you need to ask yourself a relatively simple question: Will my readers understand my main point? In composition, a main point is sometimes called a thesis or a thesis statement. It is often a sentence that summarizes your central idea or a position. It need not include any factual proof or supporting evidence — that can be supplied in the body of your essay — but it should represent a general statement that clearly shows where you stand on an issue or what exactly your essay is about. Although main points are often found in opening paragraphs, they can also appear later on in an essay, especially when the writer wants to set the stage for his or her opinion by opening with a relevant quotation, a topical reference, an emotional appeal, or a general point.

This is the way Pearl Wong, a student at Santa Clara University, proceeds in "Obama — President for All." She begins with a general point about ethnic identification that prepares the reader for her main point, which is not expressed until the third paragraph, as seen below.

1
In one sentence, Wong states the main point of her essay

Although our nation was built on a foundation to protect minority groups, no one ever said one can only help one group of minorities; so, red pill or blue? Rather than focusing on one race, even if it's one particularly close to Obama's heart, the President of the United States must maintain his executive position as a representative of all people residing in America. (1)

STUDENT WRITER AT WORK

Pearl Wong

On Writing "Obama—President for All"

RA. What was your main purpose in writing this essay?

PW. Writing is my main outlet for my emotions and thoughts. Mainly, that outlet comes from when I feel there is an injustice or a breach in my definition of ethics or when I feel very strongly about a situation in my life.

RA. How long did it take for you to write this piece? Did you revise your work? What were your goals as you revised?

PW. It took me about thirty minutes to write the very first draft. In the end, the final draft was sent after a couple more hours of revision and editing. Whenever I write a first draft, it is a very raw reflection of my viewpoints. I think my revisions usually incorporate more fairness and openness to whatever topic I am working on. I don't like to be biased or narrow-minded. My goals are always to be fair to the other side and understand where they are coming from, even if I don't agree.

RA. What topics most interest you as a writer?

PW. I'm most interested in topics relating to social justice, ethics, business, and international relations.

RA. Are you pursuing a career in which writing will be a component?

PW. Yes, I want to be a writer, but I'm not sure if I want to pursue journalism or be a novelist.

RA. What advice do you have for other student writers?

PW. Write. Write all the time. Keep a journal and let the words flow. Make that journal private — in other words, not a blog — so that you can completely let go of keeping up appearances or trying to be politically or grammatically correct. We all need a place where we do not feel judged, and sometimes that place is actually a physical object like a journal. And that's okay!

Christopher Hedges

Celebrity Culture and the Obama Brand

[*Tikkun*, January/February 2010]

BEFORE YOU READ

Can politicians offer real change, or are their promises more often than not empty? Does President Obama represent a real break from the policies of the past, or is he just part of an elaborate illusion?

WORDS TO LEARN

overlords (para. 1): powerful rulers (noun).
lobbyists (para. 1): people who try to influence government on behalf of an industry or a group (noun).
insolvent (para. 2): unable to pay debts (adjective).
forestalls (para. 2): delays for a little while (verb).
dismantle (para. 2): take down (verb).
inoculates (para. 3): gives someone a vaccine to prevent a disease (verb).
immune (para. 3): unable to be affected by something (adjective).
folksiness (para. 3): the appearance of being ordinary and unpretentious (noun).
artifice (para. 3): fakeness (noun).
precursors (para. 3): something similar that came before (noun).
risqué (para. 3): slightly shocking (adjective).
confound (para. 3): confuse (verb).
predatory (para. 4): attacking like a predator (adjective).
venue (para. 4): a place where something happens (noun).
redress (para. 4): a way of fixing a wrong (noun).
leached (para. 6): dripped (verb).
bequeath (para. 6): leave behind (verb).
reparation (para. 6): making right (noun).
interlocking (para. 6): connecting together (adjective).
braggadocio (para. 6): exaggerated arrogant behavior (noun).
mawkishness (para. 6): being overly sentimental (noun).

The Pulitzer Prize–winning reporter Christopher Hedges spent nearly twenty years as a foreign correspondent. His books include the best-selling War Is a Force That Gives Us Meaning *(2002) and* Empire of Illusion: The End of Literacy and the Triumph of Spectacle *(2009).*

bloating (para. 6): filling to capacity or overflowing (verb).
obliterate (para. 6): completely destroy (verb).
perpetual (para. 8): unending (adjective).
wanton (para. 8): intentional and unprovoked (adjective).
bereft (para. 8): lacking something, especially money (adjective).
potent (para. 8): powerful (adjective).
snuff out (para. 8): kill brutally (verb).

Barack Obama is a brand. And the Obama brand is designed to make us feel good about our government while corporate overlords loot the Treasury, armies of corporate lobbyists grease the palms of our elected officials, our corporate media diverts us with gossip and trivia, and our imperial wars expand in the Middle East. Brand Obama is about being happy consumers. We are entertained. We feel hopeful. We like our president. We believe he is like us. But like all branded products spun out from the manipulative world of corporate advertising, this product is duping us into doing and supporting a lot of things that are not in our interest. 1

What, for all our faith and hope, has the Obama brand given us? His administration has spent, lent, or guaranteed $12.8 trillion in taxpayer dollars to Wall Street[1] and insolvent banks in a doomed effort to re-inflate the bubble economy, a tactic that at best forestalls catastrophe and will leave us broke in a time of profound crisis. Brand Obama has allocated nearly $1 trillion in defense-related spending and the continuation of our doomed imperial projects in Iraq, where military planners now estimate that 70,000 troops will remain for the next fifteen to twenty years. Brand Obama has expanded the war in Afghanistan, increasing the use of drones sent on cross-border bombing runs into Pakistan, which have doubled the number of civilians killed over the past three months. Brand Obama has refused to ease restrictions so workers can organize and will not consider single-payer, not-for-profit health care for all Americans. And Brand Obama will not prosecute the Bush administration for war crimes, including the use of torture, and has refused to dismantle Bush's secrecy laws and restore habeas corpus.[2] 2

[1] Wall Street (para. 2): The location of the financial industry in New York, often used to represent large, wealthy banking interests and the stock market.

[2] habeas corpus (para. 2): The principle that an accused person should be allowed to know the charges against him or her exactly; the Bush administration suspended it during the War on Terror.

Brand Obama offers us an image that appears radically individualistic and new. It inoculates us from seeing that the old engines of corporate power and the vast military-industrial complex continue to plunder the country. Corporations, which control our politics, no longer produce products that are essentially different, but brands that are different. Brand Obama does not threaten the core of the corporate state any more than did Brand George W. Bush. The Bush brand collapsed. We became immune to its studied folksiness. We saw through its artifice. This is a common deflation in the world of advertising. So we have been given a new Obama brand with an exciting and faintly erotic appeal. Benetton and Calvin Klein[3] were the precursors to the Obama brand, using ads to associate themselves with risqué art and progressive politics. This strategy gave their products an edge. But the goal, as with all brands, was to make passive consumers confound a brand with an experience. 3

Obama, who has become a global celebrity, was molded easily into a brand. He had almost no experience, other than two years in the Senate, lacked any moral core, and could be painted as all things to all people. His brief Senate voting record was a miserable surrender to corporate interests. He was happy to promote nuclear power as "green" energy. He voted to continue the wars in Iraq and Afghanistan. He reauthorized the Patriot Act.[4] He would not back a bill designed to cap predatory credit card interest rates. He opposed a bill that would have reformed the notorious Mining Law of 1872.[5] He refused to support the single-payer[6] health care bill HR 676, sponsored by Reps. Dennis Kucinich and John Conyers. He supported the death penalty. And he backed a class-action "reform" bill that was part of a large lobbying effort by financial firms. The law, known as the Class Action Fairness Act, would effectively shut down state courts as a venue to hear most class-action lawsuits and deny redress in many of the courts where these cases have a chance of defying powerful corporate challenges. 4

---

[3] Benneton and Calvin Klein (para. 3): Fashion designers famous for their racy ads, which often feature minority models.

[4] Patriot Act (para. 4): A law passed shortly after 9/11 that expanded the government and, according to some liberals, violated civil liberties, as part of the War on Terror.

[5] Mining Law of 1872 (para. 4): A United States law that oversees prospecting and mining on federal public lands.

[6] single-payer (para. 4): A type of government-provided healthcare coverage in which each taxpayer is automatically enrolled in government health insurance.

Obama's campaign won the vote of hundreds of marketers, agency 5
heads, and marketing-services vendors gathered at the Association of National Advertisers' annual conference in October. The Obama campaign was named *Advertising Age's*[7] marketer of the year for 2008 and edged out runners-up Apple and Zappos.com. Take it from the professionals. Brand Obama is a marketer's dream. President Obama does one thing and Brand Obama gets you to believe another. This is the essence of successful advertising. You buy or do what the advertisers want because of how they can make you feel.

President Obama does one thing and Brand Obama gets you to believe another.

Celebrity culture has leached into every aspect of our culture, includ- 6
ing politics, to bequeath to us what Benjamin DeMott[8] called "junk politics." Junk politics does not demand justice or the reparation of rights. Junk politics personalizes and moralizes issues rather than clarifying them. "It's impatient with articulated conflict, enthusiastic about America's optimism and moral character, and heavily dependent on feel-your-pain language and gesture," DeMott noted. The result of junk politics is that nothing changes — "meaning zero interruption in the processes and practices that strengthen existing, interlocking systems of socioeconomic advantage." Junk politics redefines traditional values, tilting "courage toward braggadocio, sympathy toward mawkishness, humility toward self-disrespect, identification with ordinary citizens toward distrust of brains." Junk politics "miniaturizes large, complex problems at home while maximizing threats from abroad. It's also given to abrupt unexplained reversals of its own public stances, often spectacularly bloating problems previously miniaturized." And finally, it "seeks at every turn to obliterate voters' consciousness of socioeconomic and other differences in their midst."

The old production-oriented culture demanded what the historian 7
Warren Susman termed "character." The new consumption-oriented culture demands what he called "personality." The shift in values is a shift from a fixed morality to the artifice of presentation. The old cultural values of thrift and moderation honored hard work, integrity, and courage. The consumption-oriented culture honors charm, fascination, and likeability. "The social role demanded of all in the new culture of personality

---

[7] *Advertising Age* (para. 5): An industry magazine for advertisers.

[8] Benjamin DeMott (para. 6): American academic, writer, scholar, and cultural critic (1924–2005).

was that of a performer," Susman wrote. "Every American was to become a performing self."

The junk politics practiced by Obama is a consumer fraud. It is about performance. It is about lies. It is about keeping us in a perpetual state of childishness. But the longer we live in illusion, the worse reality will be when it finally shatters our fantasies. Those who do not understand what is happening around them and who are overwhelmed by a brutal reality they did not expect or foresee search desperately for saviors. They beg demagogues to come to their rescue. This is the ultimate danger of the Obama Brand. It effectively masks the wanton internal destruction and theft being carried out by our corporate state. These corporations, once they have stolen trillions in taxpayer wealth, will leave tens of millions of Americans bereft, bewildered, and yearning for even more potent and deadly illusions, ones that could swiftly snuff out what is left of our diminished open society. 8

VOCABULARY/USING A DICTIONARY

1. Hedges twice describes American policy as "imperial" (paras. 1 and 2). What does he mean by *imperial*? What word does *imperial* derive from?
2. What does it mean if junk politics is *tilting* (para. 6) certain virtues toward extreme redefinitions, as Hedges quotes Benjamin DeMott as arguing?
3. Define *demagogue* (para. 8). What language does the word come from, and what does it mean in the original language? Does it have a positive or negative connotation?

RESPONDING TO WORDS IN CONTEXT

1. Based on the passage in which it occurs, what do you think the phrase "grease the palms of" (para. 1) means? Look it up online if necessary. How does Hedges suggest palms are being greased here?
2. Look up the word *trivia* (para. 1). What usages of the word are you familiar with? In what sense does Hedges mean it here?
3. What does Hedges mean by *deflation* (para. 3), judging from the context? What is the literal, dictionary definition of the word?

DISCUSSING MAIN POINT AND MEANING

1. Explain in your own words what Hedges means by a "brand" throughout this essay. What industry does the idea of a brand come from? What does it mean for Barack Obama to be a brand?
2. What does Hedges think of the presidency of George W. Bush? Why? What does he imply Barack Obama promised to do on assuming the presidency, and how does he assess Obama's keeping of those promises?

3. According to Hedges, who really controls American politics and government? How do they do so? How does his argument about "Brand Obama" fit into this assertion?

EXAMINING SENTENCES, PARAGRAPHS, AND ORGANIZATION

1. Why does Hedges put the words *green* and *reform* in quotation marks in paragraph 4? What is he implying, and what does this add to the tone of the essay as a whole?
2. What is the effect of the short, choppy sentences in paragraph 1 ("We are entertained. We feel hopeful," etc.)? What tone is Hedges using to describe our reaction to the Obama presidency?
3. Does Hedges seem to be writing for an audience that agrees or disagrees with his politics? How does he make his political leanings clear throughout the essay? Point out a few places where the author states a premise that some might find controversial but with which he assumes his audience will agree.

THINKING CRITICALLY

1. Should the fact that advertisers admire the Obama campaign—as evinced in *Advertising Age* naming it marketer of the year in 2008—automatically condemn President Obama or his administration? Why or why not? Do you think politicians have an obligation to avoid the sort of tactics and strategies that marketers use, or is some degree of salesmanship unavoidable in electoral politics?
2. Do you agree that we have "junk politics" (para. 6) in America? Describe in your own words what junk politics is, and judge our political system as you know it against this definition. Do politicians stress the right issues in America, or do they, as the essay alleges, aim only to distract voters?
3. Some critics would disagree with Hedges's thesis on the grounds that Barack Obama has been the object of so much severe criticism since taking office—much of it from George W. Bush's Republican Party. Do you think the division between Democrats and Republicans proves that corporations are not in fact pulling the strings behind the scenes of American government, but that the two parties do actually represent real ideological differences? How do you think Hedges would answer this argument?

IN-CLASS WRITING ACTIVITIES

1. What do you think Hedges means by "gossip and trivia" when he describes "corporate" media coverage in paragraph 1 of the essay? Give a few specific examples of gossip and trivia in the media. Do you agree that this kind of media coverage is a bad thing? Do you agree that it

is part of a plot to keep Americans uninformed and unquestioning? Whether or not you feel corporate interests control it, do you think the American media could do a better job of covering politics and government? If so, how?

2. Write a brief assessment of how things have changed, in your experience and research, since Obama entered the White House and Bush left it. Has America changed at all? Or have any changes been, as Hedges claims, superficial and minor?
3. Hedges describes the Obama brand as having an "exciting and faintly erotic appeal" (para. 3). Whether or not you agree with the author's belief that a deliberate effort is behind the Obama brand, offer your own assessment of what this brand is. Start by writing down your immediate associations with President Obama—what do you think of when you hear his name and how do you see him and his administration? What parts of this portrait, if any, may have been planted in your mind by Barack Obama himself or by his supporters? By his opponents?

Discussing the Unit

SUGGESTED TOPIC FOR DISCUSSION

If nothing else, the debate over the significance of the Obama presidency shows us that race is still a prominent and controversial topic in America today. What do you think of the issue of race? Is it overblown—a media invention contrived to keep us arguing about something when we actually live in an increasingly color-blind society? Or do we still live with the vestiges of slavery and discrimination, a civilization fundamentally hampered by our own racial tensions?

PREPARING FOR CLASS DISCUSSION

1. Both Diane McKinney-Whetstone and John Edgar Wideman discuss the nagging problem of black poverty from the vantage point of African Americans with a position of solidarity and conviction that the problem is solvable. What do you think is keeping so many African Americans in poverty in the United States?
2. Compare Christopher Hedges's view of Barack Obama to those of McKinney-Whetstone and Wideman. What would Hedges say about the way these two authors imagine Obama, and why? What do you think?

FROM DISCUSSION TO WRITING

1. Evaluate the Obama administration in terms of what it has done for African Americans. Has President Obama lived up to the promise McKinney-

Whetstone saw in him and his family on election night? Has he done anything about what Wideman calls the "marginalization" (para. 2) of African American youth? How do you perceive his impact on race relations as president?

2. Imagine you're a historian one hundred years from now writing the annals of the Obama administration. How does the presidency begin? How will history see Obama's election — as a significant historic moment, or something else? What are Obama's immediate successes and failures? What does he strive to do for America, and how does he fare?

TOPICS FOR CROSS-CULTURAL DISCUSSION

1. The selections in this chapter focus on racial relations between blacks and whites in America, but this is hardly the end of race as a topic of discussion. What other groups have a significant voice, or pose a significant problem, to our national discussion on race? Should these groups be encouraged by President Obama, or concerned about his administration? Why?
2. Hedges writes that "Brand Obama is a marketer's dream" (para. 5), but mentions only the domestic market — that is, how Obama appeals to Americans. As McKinney-Whetstone points out, Obama's extended family was seen cheering on election night in Kenya, and the Obama brand has certainly sold, for better or worse, overseas. How is the Obama presidency changing the *American* brand in the rest of the world's eyes? Is it a good or a bad change?

10

Social Networking—How Is It Transforming Behavior?

In what ways are social media like Facebook, MySpace, and Twitter transforming our social lives? Are these new forms of instant social connection causing us needless distraction? Do they have a serious impact on how we live today? Even though social media is quickly catching on across generations, many older people view them satirically, believing they are no substitute for traditional methods of communication. In "Hi, Dad," a segment from the popular comic strip *Doonesbury*, Garry Trudeau pokes fun at a college student's total absorption in her online relationships while she ignores her visiting father's presence.

Yet some adults don't mind "oversharing" online, as thirty-year-old journalist and blogger Mary Katharine Ham acknowledges in "We Shall Overshare." Admitting that she is "an enthusiastic user" of Twitter and Facebook, Ham concedes that it is easy to embarrass oneself online: "It's a daily game of public Frogger, hopping frantically to avoid being crushed under the weight of your own narcissism, banality, and plain old stupidity."

Ego is also an issue for Emerson College student Brent Baughman. In "Growing Older in the Digital Age: An Exercise in Egotism," he comically considers how all the new technology comes together when we have a birthday: "Birthdays are the one day of the year when compulsive e-mail checking finally pays off—every five minutes the latest note, e-card, or jotting of affection is waiting there in Gmail bold."

If birthdays provide opportunities to use new social media, what about the deaths of friends? How do we commemorate the loss of loved ones on Facebook? After one of her best students was fatally struck by a van in the summer of 2009, Elizabeth Stone, a Fordham University communications professor, monitored the responses of her many friends on Facebook. In "Grief in the Age of Facebook," she poignantly raises the issue of how social media deals with grief and mourning. She writes: "I've seen how markedly technology has influenced the conventions of grieving among my students, offering them solace but also uncertainty."

Garry Trudeau

Hi, Dad

[*Doonesbury*, *Boston Globe*, November 8, 2009]

BEFORE YOU READ

Are social media and social networking positive or negative forces in your life? Are they bringing you closer to or further from your friends and family?

WORDS TO LEARN

oversharing (panel 2): giving too much personal information (verb).

migrates (panel 8): moves (verb).

curating (panel 8): managing and controlling (verb).

Born in New York City in 1948, Garry Trudeau began publishing comic strips as an undergraduate at Yale University, where he also received an MFA in graphic design. He is best known for Doonesbury, *which was first syndicated in 1970, received a Pulitzer Prize in 1975, and now appears in well over a thousand newspapers across the globe.*

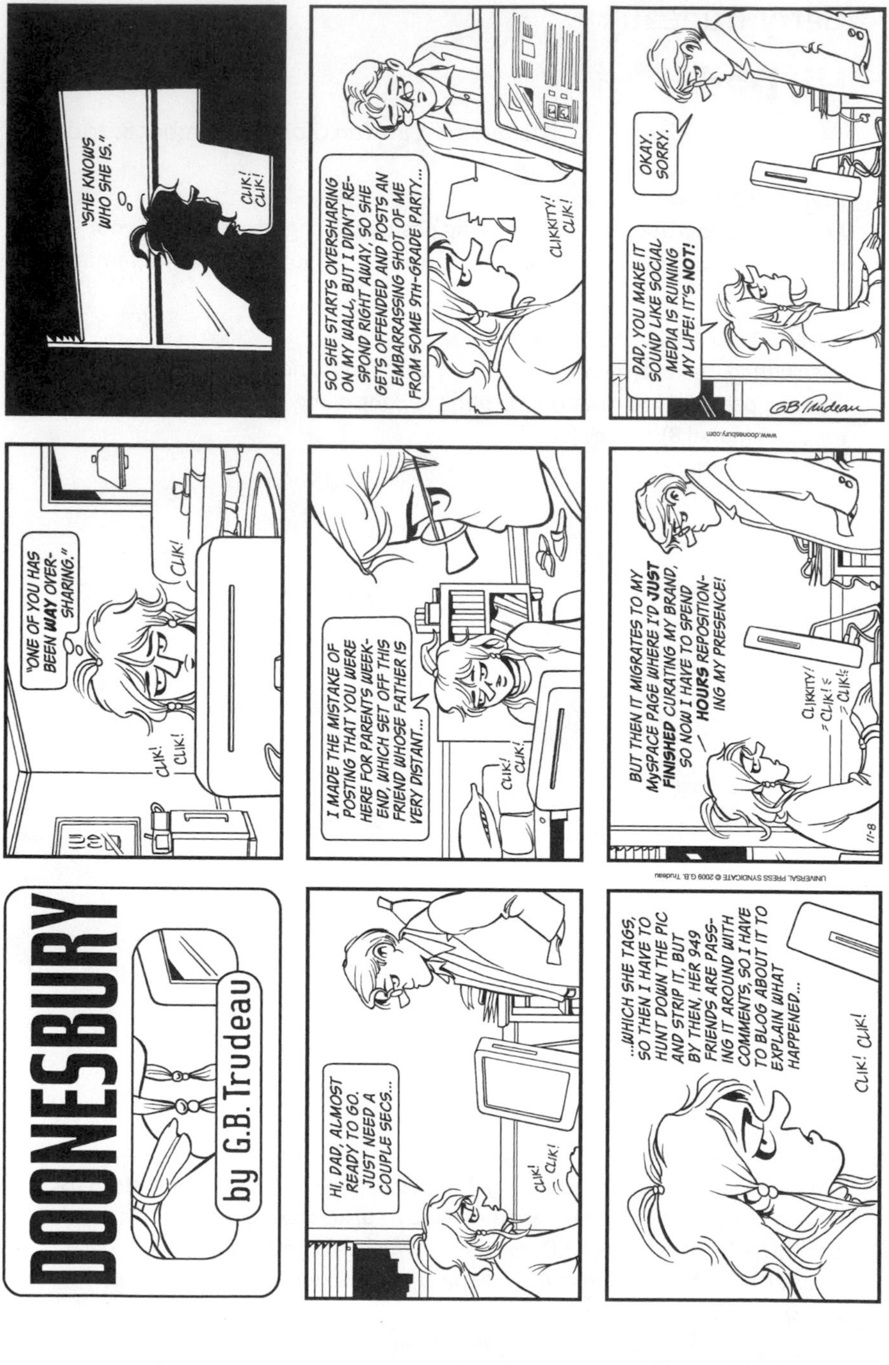
DOONESBURY
by G.B. Trudeau
"ONE OF YOU HAS BEEN WAY OVER-SHARING."
CLIK! CLIK!
CLIK!
"SHE KNOWS WHO SHE IS."
CLIK! CLIK!
HI, DAD, ALMOST READY TO GO. JUST NEED A COUPLE SECS...
CLIK! CLIK!
I MADE THE MISTAKE OF POSTING THAT YOU WERE HERE FOR PARENTS WEEK-END, WHICH SET OFF THIS FRIEND WHOSE FATHER IS VERY DISTANT...
CLIK! CLIK!
SO SHE STARTS OVERSHARING ON MY WALL, BUT I DIDN'T RE-SPOND RIGHT AWAY, SO SHE GETS OFFENDED AND POSTS AN EMBARRASSING SHOT OF ME FROM SOME 9TH-GRADE PARTY...
CLIKKITY! CLIK!
...WHICH SHE TAGS, SO THEN I HAVE TO HUNT DOWN THE PIC AND STRIP IT, BUT BY THEN, HER 949 FRIENDS ARE PASS-ING IT AROUND WITH COMMENTS, SO I HAVE TO BLOG ABOUT IT TO EXPLAIN WHAT HAPPENED...
CLIK! CLIK!
UNIVERSAL PRESS SYNDICATE © 2009 G.B. Trudeau
BUT THEN IT MIGRATES TO MY MySPACE PAGE WHERE I'D JUST FINISHED CURATING MY BRAND, SO NOW I HAVE TO SPEND HOURS REPOSITION-ING MY PRESENCE!
CLIKKITY! CLIK! CLIK!
11-8
www.doonesbury.com
DAD, YOU MAKE IT SOUND LIKE SOCIAL MEDIA IS RUINING MY LIFE! IT'S NOT!
OKAY. SORRY.
G.B. Trudeau

VOCABULARY/USING A DICTIONARY

1. What does *secs* stand for in panel 4 of the strip? Why is the use of the abbreviation here ironic?
2. What does it mean to *blog* (panel 7)? What part of speech is it in this case? What is the origin of this word?

RESPONDING TO WORDS IN CONTEXT

1. You're probably familiar with much of the social-networking vocabulary used in the strip. Look the terms up if you aren't. What does it mean to *tag* (panel 7)? To *strip* (panel 7)?
2. What does the daughter in the strip mean when she says in panel 8 she's *curating* her *brand*? What about *repositioning* her *presence*?

DISCUSSING MAIN POINT AND MEANING

1. What is the main point of the strip? What argument or idea is it advancing? Do you think Trudeau sympathizes more with the daughter or with the father? Defend your answer.
2. What do we assume the father is waiting to do? What clues suggest this to us? Why is this important to the main idea of the strip?

EXAMINING SENTENCES, PARAGRAPHS, AND ORGANIZATION

1. Where is the strip set? How can you tell? How does Trudeau give you hints to the setting without making it obvious, and why is this important?
2. Which character does virtually all of the speaking in the strip? What is the only thing the other character says? What is the effect of this imbalance?

THINKING CRITICALLY

1. Does the daughter's use of social networking resonate with you based on your own experiences? What aspects of it do you think are accurate, and what, if anything, did Trudeau get wrong? Is it an exaggeration, or do you and your friends spend the same amount of time and energy online as the young woman in the strip seems to?
2. Do you agree with the strip that social media could potentially be ruining our lives? Do you think sites like Facebook, MySpace, and Twitter have had an overall positive or negative influence on your life and on the way you work and socialize? Why? Give specific examples.

IN-CLASS WRITING ACTIVITIES

1. Describe in detail the way you use the Internet and social media in particular. How many hours a day do you spend on networking and media sites? What, if anything, do you accomplish by being on them? Do you feel addicted to these sites, or is there a real usefulness to them? If you disagree with Trudeau's premise, defend your use of social media to him. If you agree, explain why it is so worrisome.
2. Regardless of your feelings about social media, do you sympathize more with the daughter or the father in this strip? Why? Describe a time when you experienced the kind of generational gap the strip explores. Were you ever frustrated by someone older than you or befuddled by someone younger? How did it feel? Do you ever worry the situation will be reversed?

Mary Katharine Ham

We Shall Overshare

[*The Weekly Standard*, June 8, 2009]

BEFORE YOU READ

How much is too much when it comes to talking about your personal life online? How do you feel about people who use social media sites as their private diaries? Are they a nuisance or an inevitable part of a more connected world?

WORDS TO LEARN

gulag (para. 2): a Russian prison camp (noun).
tiff (para. 2): a minor fight (noun).
heretofore (para. 3): until now (adverb).
exponentially (para. 3): at a rapidly increasing speed (adverb).
detractors (para. 3): opponents (noun).
scrutiny (para. 3): examination (noun).
spurn (para. 3): hatefully reject (verb).
pictorial (para. 4): a series of related photos (noun).

As a staff writer, Mary Katharine Ham contributes regularly to The Weekly Standard. *She is also a frequent guest on* The O'Reilly Factor. *A journalist and video blogger (see* HamNation*), she is a 2002 graduate of the University of Georgia.*

prowess (para. 4): ability (noun).
banality (para. 5): boringness (noun).
erosion (para. 5): the destruction of something over time (noun).
quintessentially (para. 7): exactly, as the perfect example of (adverb).
cultivate (para. 9): acquire and develop (verb).
ponder (para. 9): consider deeply (verb).
dissidents (para. 10): people who oppose an established political system, religion, organization, etc. (noun).

Allison is "furious. They think they'll break me, but they will only make me fight harder in the end." 1

Either I've got a friend in a gulag somewhere or I've got one who's tripped over one of the potholes of modern life — the overshare. Given that her message didn't arrive via waterborne bottle or scribbled in the margins of a dusty Russian novel, but via her Facebook update, I think it's safe to say that her little tiff at work hasn't placed her in physical danger. 2

It has, however, caused her to illustrate the dangers of living a life online. As millions of us have taken to MySpace, Facebook, and Twitter to connect with friends, share stories, and post pictures at a speed and volume heretofore unknown, we've also exponentially multiplied ways to humiliate ourselves. It's perhaps understandable then that the online life has its detractors. Facebook has been dubbed "mind-numbingly dull" and Twitter a service for "people who need to expose as much of their lives to public scrutiny as possible." As an enthusiastic user of both, I concede that these statements are true. Yet I cannot spurn the new social media. As a result, my online life is a balancing act. 3

Sure, I could settle for a routine in which only traditional social skills are required, but where's the fun in that? I long ago mastered not talking with my mouth full and placing a napkin in my lap, and still felt the world needed people like me — pioneers of electronic propriety — to make tough choices. Is my personal hygiene regimen or lack thereof fit for public consumption? Probably not. What about a pictorial on the proper position for a keg stand? Not a good idea, regardless of my prowess. Does my social circle need to know that the sour cream at Chipotle[1] tastes "a little off"? Tough call. Could be a public health issue. 4

Sure, I could settle for a routine in which only traditional social skills are required, but where's the fun in that?

[1] Chipotle (para. 4): A popular Mexican fast-food chain.

It's a daily game of public Frogger,[2] hopping frantically to avoid being crushed under the weight of your own narcissism, banality, and plain old stupidity. Just as it took Alexander Graham Bell[3] a couple of tries on the telephone to realize that "Hoy! Hoy!" simply wasn't going to work as the standard greeting, so it took a brave South African man to discover that calling your boss a "serial masturbator" on Facebook will get you fired. There are thousands oversharing online as I write, paying the price with a gradual erosion of their dignity, so you don't have to. 5

Ironically, the antidote I've found for my own tendency to overshare online is more sharing online. Everything on my Facebook and Twitter pages is openly available. It's amazing how reasonably you act when everyone you know (and many you don't) is watching you. 6

I make a conscious decision to broadcast my life every day, and I accept the consequences. In a way it's a quintessentially conservative formula: The extent to which you take personal responsibility for your actions dictates the risks and benefits of your online existence. 7

For me, the weird ("Will you send me a picture of your feet?") and embarrassing (thank you to whoever uploaded the middle-school band photos) is outweighed by the rewarding (getting to see my cousins more than once a year). Facebook is such a natural extension of my daily life that it became a fitting public place to memorialize my grandmother with a simple picture when she passed away. What others would do at a gravesite, I did on Facebook. 8

There's another attitude I've resolved to cultivate. Even though the new social technologies are built to feel like they're all about you, it helps to remember they're not. When pondering another photo shoot for my profile picture the other day, I couldn't help recalling the Facebook users who raised $800,000 for St. Jude Children's Research Hospital only last week. 9

Similarly, when I'm tempted to post self-pitying status updates that sound like I'm in prison instead of my condo, it occurs to me that Twitter and Facebook also host actual dissidents. Their status updates were a frightening enough breath of freedom that Iran blocked Facebook 10

[2] Frogger (para. 5): A popular arcade video game from the early 1980s, in which a player must direct frogs to hop out of the way of oncoming traffic.

[3] Alexander Graham Bell (para. 5): (1847–1922) The inventor of the telephone. He originally planned "Hoy! Hoy!" as the proper greeting when picking up the phone, but it was quickly replaced by "Hello."

last week, only to lift the ban days later as Ahmadinejad[4] distanced himself from the unpopular crackdown. Every new technology needs its pioneers. Many are banal, but some are truly brave.

They make me think of other pioneers. The historian Donald Jackson recounts that Lewis and Clark[5] "wrote constantly and abundantly, . . . legibly and illegibly, and always with an urgent sense of purpose." So do I, and almost always in 140 characters or less.[6] 11

VOCABULARY/USING A DICTIONARY

1. Ham describes oversharers as "being crushed under the weight of [their] own narcissism, banality, and plain old stupidity" (para. 5). What is a *narcissist*? What are the origins of the word?
2. What does it mean to *broadcast* one's life, in the sense that Ham uses it when she says she makes a "conscious decision to broadcast" (para. 7) her life every day? From what field does the word come?
3. What does Ham mean when she says she plans to "cultivate" an attitude (para. 9)? What does *cultivate* mean, and what is its origin?

RESPONDING TO WORDS IN CONTEXT

1. Look up the literal meaning of the word *erosion*. In what sense is Ham using it in paragraph 5 of her essay?
2. Ham writes that more online sharing is, "ironically, the antidote I've found for my own tendency to overshare online" (para. 6). What does *antidote* mean, literally? How is Ham using it here? What does its use imply about oversharing?
3. What are the connotations of the word *pioneer* (para. 10) as Ham uses it?

DISCUSSING MAIN POINT AND MEANING

1. Why does Ham say her Facebook and Twitter pages are highly public (para. 6)? What effect does this have on the way she uses them? What is

---

4 Ahmadinejad (para. 10): Mahmoud Ahmadinejad, the president of Iran as of 2010, considered by many in the West to be a corrupt dictator. In the summer of 2009, the Iranian government cracked down on protesters, who kept their message alive on Twitter and other social media sites.

5 Lewis and Clark (para. 11): The team of explorers who surveyed the vast Louisiana Purchase in the early nineteenth century, making careful records and maps along the way.

6 140 characters or less (para. 11): The maximum length of a post (or "tweet") on Twitter.

she implying she might do if she had a smaller audience reading her contributions to social media?

2. What are the advantages of social media and social networking as Ham describes them? What specific examples does she give, and how does this add to her main idea that the danger of these media is overuse?
3. What is the relationship between Ham's general point about the narcissism of oversharers online and her example of the Twitter revolution in Iran? How does she transition between these two points, and how does the organization of her essay accommodate both a slightly playful and a serious argument?

EXAMINING SENTENCES, PARAGRAPHS, AND ORGANIZATION

1. What is the significance of the title of Ham's essay? (Hint: Look up "We Shall Overcome" online.) How does this playful title add to the humor and irony of the essay?
2. Why does Ham start with an example? What is particularly effective about the example she chooses? What does Ham mean by her opening remark ("Either I've got a friend in a gulag somewhere . . .") and how does it combine with paragraph 1 to set the tone for the essay?
3. Discuss the use of juxtaposition—putting together two dissimilar things—in Ham's essay. How does she juxtapose the present use of social media and the ways people communicated in the past? What is the meaning of her sentence comparing Alexander Graham Bell and the unfortunate South African in paragraph 5?

THINKING CRITICALLY

1. Do you agree that the example Ham gives in paragraph 1 is automatically an overshare? Does context matter, or is the category of tweet she is highlighting always a bit ludicrous? Where is the line between sharing something important and serious, and offering too much information?
2. What are the major positive uses of Facebook and Twitter? Give two examples besides those Ham offers.
3. Can social-networking sites really have the sort of political impact Ham describes in paragraph 10? Does hosting dissidents mean that dissent will be more meaningful or effective? Why or why not?

IN-CLASS WRITING ACTIVITIES

1. Look up *The Weekly Standard*—what kind of magazine is it and what are its politics? How does Ham claim her argument fits into *The Weekly Standard*'s mission? (See paragraph 7.) Do you agree? Is there a political dimension to the use of social-networking sites?

2. Give a few examples of oversharing online, either from your experience or your imagination. They might be from Twitter, Facebook, a blog, or any other depository of emotions and narratives you've run into on the Internet. How does oversharing make you feel? Do you greet it as silly but harmless, or do you think it's a real problem? Why?
3. Explain the analogy Ham draws between Twitter users like herself and Lewis and Clark (para 11). Look up more information on the explorers if necessary. To what extent is she being sincere about the analogy and to what extent facetious? Do you think Lewis and Clark might have been oversharers?

Brent Baughman (student essay)

Growing Older in the Digital Age: An Exercise in Egotism

[*The Berkeley Beacon*, Emerson College, February 25, 2010]

BEFORE YOU READ

Is Facebook making us all more egotistical? Are increased opportunities for advertising ourselves making us self-obsessed? How do you react to birthday invitations on Facebook and Twitter? Are they over-the-top?

WORDS TO LEARN

festers (para. 2): becomes worse, like a sore (verb).
collective (para. 2): belonging to all the people in a group (adjective).
interface (para. 4): the computer system a user uses (noun).
mitigate (para. 5): make less bad (verb).
codependence (para. 5): mutual reliance between people (noun).
antique (para. 6): an object held over from a previous age (noun).

Brent Baughman graduated from Emerson College in 2010. He now lives in Washington, D.C., where he works for National Public Radio.

I turned 22 last week. Someone told me it's like Bode Miller[1] from here on out: all downhill. And it might be true. Twenty-two is the last birthday most of us will see in college. The only milestone left to look forward to is qualifying for Social Security, and even that won't exist by the time I'm 65, unless Bill and Melinda Gates[2] get seriously bored. 1

Twenty-one: Now there's a milestone. There's a mischief to turning 21. Everyone makes twinkle-eyed jokes about getting drunk and hitting bars, where all the city's sexual energy apparently festers. There's a cultural connotation, a collective unspoken smirk, that to be a freshly knighted 21-year-old means you can finally be out scoring. It's magnetic, this idea. We pay attention to people turning 21. We wonder what they're doing, where they're going, how they'll celebrate. 2

That sort of attention, however deviant, is what the modern birthday is all about. But with technology in the mix, we're seeking 21-level attention at 22 and beyond. Too far beyond. The modern birthday is a fantasy of attention. On a single day, all the sacred technology we turn to for deliverance from solitude finally makes good on its promises. Birthdays are the one day of the year when compulsive e-mail checking finally pays off—every five minutes the latest note, e-card, or jotting of affection is waiting there in Gmail bold.[3] We never love technology like we do when we see that bold type. It's like being one of those Japanese men who date robots and take them to movies.[4] 3

Birthdays are the one day of the year when compulsive e-mail checking finally pays off.

And Facebook. Oh, Facebook! The trick is setting Facebook updates to arrive in your e-mail. Here's the beauty of it: Your inbox becomes an Eden of wall updates and messages from Zuckerbergland.[5] You click in and out of these messages like candy, each one sweet in its own way. And 4

[1] Bode Miller (para. 1): An American Olympic alpine ski racer.

[2] Bill and Melinda Gates (para. 1): A famous American husband and wife team of philanthropists; Bill cofounded Microsoft in 1975.

[3] Gmail bold (para. 3): New messages in Google's popular e-mail service appear in bold type.

[4] Japanese men . . . movies (para. 3): A recent trend reported in Japan saw men "dating" robotic dolls.

[5] Zuckerbergland (para. 4): Mark Zuckerberg (b. 1984) founded Facebook in 2004.

then — even after you've exhausted your supply of that magic bold — you can still read the same messages on Facebook. It's here they become new again, where all those tokens of affection — even the most impersonal comma-free "Happy Birthday Brent!"s — glisten with new promise in Facebook's interface.

Twitter, on the other hand, presents a challenge. It's more difficult to mask a call for attention in 140 characters. Maybe you mitigate by narrating plans instead of announcing your birthday outright: *Ducking homework. Duck confit and great friends for birthday dinner at Chez Henri.* See? I've publicized my birthday, but I'm not explicitly asking you to acknowledge it. Twitter is cute this way — it lets us project an image of independence upon a screen of codependence. The Twitterverse requires both Tweeters and Followers, but none of the former want to be seen as desperate for the latter. 5

We usually let birthday calls roll into voicemail because the phone call is an antique that violates the virtues of our favorite medium, the text message. It's our modern letter. It allows us to remain sovereign in our own world, while still achieving a degree of connection with someone else. Not too close, not too far, but just right. The joy we feel when our phones light up with the receipt of a new message is a micro-burst of the joy we feel when we open the mailbox to discover we've received a letter. It's a joy of ego. 6

But there's a problem with all this egotism. And no, it's not that we'll drive ourselves to self-worship, into a fire hydrant, and then to sex rehab. It's just generally lame for the people around us who are more than digital strangers. The birthdays we remember are ones that were made special by surprise parties or a perfect gift or a real show of love or friendship. We're missing the point if the first thing we look forward to on our birthday is an over-flowing inbox. 7

But if technology is your biggest priority on your birthday, I have the perfect gift for you. It'll take about two weeks to get here. I'll have to order it from Japan. 8

VOCABULARY/USING A DICTIONARY

1. Look up *interface* (para. 4) and provide a thorough definition. Give an example of an interface.
2. What does *mitigate* mean (para. 5)? What is the origin of the word?
3. Define *egotism* as Baughman uses it in paragraph 7 of his essay. What language does it come from, and what is the meaning of its root?

RESPONDING TO WORDS IN CONTEXT

1. What is a *smirk*? How is it different connotatively from similar expressions? What does Baughman mean when he refers to "a collective unspoken smirk" (para. 2)?

2. What is the literal meaning of the word *fester*? How is Baughman using it when he says that the "city's sexual energy . . . festers" (para. 2)?
3. What does Baughman mean when he calls the modern birthday a "fantasy of attention" (para. 3)? What are two possible meanings of *fantasy* here?

DISCUSSING MAIN POINT AND MEANING

1. Why does Baughman think that twenty-first birthdays are automatically fun and exciting? What does he argue Facebook has done to the practice of celebrating birthdays?
2. What differences does Baughman point to between the ways and conventions of advertising a birthday on various sites? What, however, does he maintain all these sites ultimately have in common?
3. What does Baughman feel is supposed to be really special about celebrating a birthday? What do people look forward to today, according to the essay?

EXAMINING SENTENCES, PARAGRAPHS, AND ORGANIZATION

1. How does Baughman establish that he is just as much a part of the problem he's describing as anyone else? Why is this important to his essay? Give examples from the text of points where he sympathizes with, rather than directly condemning, the foibles of the Digital Era.
2. What gift is Baughman referring to when he says he'll "have to order it from Japan" (para. 8)? How does this joke tie the essay together, and what is he implying about people who rely too much on technology?

THINKING CRITICALLY

1. How does Baughman use humor to advance a serious argument in this essay? Give three examples of jokes from the essay. Do you find them funny? Does the argument rely on the jokes working in order to be effective, or are they simply a way of dressing it up?
2. Do you agree with the spirit of Baughman's piece—that we've become addicted to the machines that are supposed to be making our real lives richer, instead of living those lives? Why or why not? Give specific examples to support your argument.

IN-CLASS WRITING ACTIVITIES

1. Give three concrete examples, besides the birthday invitation, of ways Facebook and Twitter are changing the way you and your friends socialize. What effect do you think these changes are having? Is your generation in fact becoming more self-involved, or are you more conscious of others? Or is it somewhere in between?

2. Try writing an invitation to your birthday party on four media: Facebook, Twitter, e-mail, and—if you can imagine it—a printed, snail-mail letter. What factors affect the content and tone of your message? How are you conscious of the size of your audience, who is seeing it and when, and what kind of atmosphere you want to convey?

LOOKING CLOSELY

Organizing an Essay by Division

One common way to organize the parts of your essay is to break your topic down into categories. For example, someone writing about the dating scene on campus might want to consider several different types of dates and then list each kind with a brief description. Note how Emerson College student Brent Baughman divides his topic into several categories as he proceeds to describe the different ways people receive birthday greetings within our new technology. Observe how in the body of his paper he discusses birthday messages as they are expressed in different media—e-mail, Facebook, Twitter, voicemail, and texting.

1
Baughman divides his essay into five different types of messages

Birthdays are the one day of the year when compulsive e-mail checking finally pays off—every five minutes the latest note, e-card, or jotting of affection is waiting there in Gmail bold. . . .

And Facebook. Oh, Facebook! The trick is setting Facebook updates to arrive in your e-mail. . . .

Twitter, on the other hand, presents a challenge. . . .

We usually let birthday calls roll into voicemail because the phone call is an antique that violates the virtues of our favorite medium, the text message.

STUDENT WRITER AT WORK

Brent Baughman

On Writing "Growing Older in the Digital Age: An Exercise in Egotism"

RA. What was your main purpose in writing this piece?

BB. To highlight an aspect of life I think is under-thought-about by people my age. There's an argument that technology is warping our ability to communicate intimately with each other, and I hope it's clear that I don't agree with that. But I do think it distracts from certain ways we interact socially, and that we need to be conscious about it so we can lessen those distractions before our frontal lobes fuse to the microprocessors in our iPhones. So there's a constant struggle for balance we all face.

RA. Have you read or seen other work on this topic that has interested you?

BB. There's a lot of talk now about how technology is affecting our cranial motherboards. Nicholas Carr wrote an article last summer for *The Atlantic* called "Is Google Making Us Stupid?" that set off more of a mainsteam discussion about things, and he's coming out with a book about the same subject matter. I'm interested and pay attention to this sort of thing as well as I can. People seem to be considering it more thoughtfully as we become more wired, and I find that encouraging.

RA. How long did it take for you to write this piece? Did you revise your work? What were your goals as you revised?

BB. Like most of my columns, I wrote this over the course of a few days. During that time I'd revisit the text, make changes, insert ideas or revisions I'd thought of during off-hours. During revisions I'm looking mostly to make arguments clear, pace my sentences, and be super critical about whether I'm just spewing nonsense. I'd write a sentence and then imagine I was reading it in the paper myself and that I'd never heard of the writer. If it didn't feel true, I'd revise it.

RA. What topics most interest you as a writer?

BB. The way our social brains work, issues of science and technology, literature, and relationships. We'd probably have to sit down for coffee to parse out the Freudian foundation for my interest in these topics.

RA. Are you pursuing a career in which writing will be a component?

BB. I've recently started working at National Public Radio in Washington, D.C. Public radio is really a combination of journalism and creative writing, because they broadcast stories that often require a keen sense of pacing, language, voice, character, and plot. I'll be doing a lot of writing, yes, so I'm thankful for the practice I got in college.

RA: What advice do you have for other student writers?

BB: Actually, I find kind of it comforting to believe that most of us, at this age, are going to be not-very-good for quite a while, and that it just takes patience and practice to become kind-of-good. During my freshman year, I had a fiction professor say something like, "The guy who can lock himself in a room alone for the longest will be the best writer." Trying to emulate the writers you most admire can also work the necessary muscles, I think.

Elizabeth Stone

Grief in the Age of Facebook

[*The Chronicle Review*, March 5, 2010]

BEFORE YOU READ

How have Facebook and other social-networking sites changed the way we mourn when we lose a friend or loved one? It seems beyond argument that these sites will have a lasting effect on the way we communicate—will they (and should they) also change the way we grieve?

WORDS TO LEARN

dogged (para. 1): highly determined (adjective).
whimsical (para. 1): full of imagination (adjective).
markedly (para. 5): with clear indications (adverb).
solace (para. 5): comfort after a loss (noun).
spontaneous (para. 6): sudden and without a direct cause (adjective).
equestrian (para. 8): related to horseback-riding (adjective).
penchant (para. 8): tendency (noun).
uncharted (para. 9): not on a map (adjective).
via (para. 9): through (preposition).
exuberance (para. 9): intense happiness (noun).
prescription (para. 11): piece of advice (noun).
reverberates (para. 12): echoes (verb).

A professor of English, communications, and media studies at Fordham University, Elizabeth Stone is the author of a memoir, A Boy I Once Knew: What a Teacher Learned from Her Student *(2002).*

On July 17 last year, one of my most promising students died. Her name was Casey Feldman, and she was crossing a street in a New Jersey resort town on her way to work when a van went barreling through a stop sign. Her death was a terrible loss for everyone who knew her. Smart and dogged, whimsical and kind, Casey was the news editor of the *The Observer*, the campus paper I advise, and she was going places. She was a finalist for a national college reporting award and had just been chosen for a prestigious television internship for the fall, a fact she conveyed to me in a midnight text message, entirely consistent with her all-news-all-the-time mind-set. Two days later her life ended. 1

I found out about Casey's death the old-fashioned way: in a phone conversation with Kelsey, the layout editor and Casey's roommate. She'd left a neutral-sounding voice mail the night before, asking me to call when I got her message, adding, "It's OK if it's late." I didn't retrieve the message till midnight, so I called the next morning, realizing only later what an extraordinary effort she had made to keep her voice calm. But my students almost never make phone calls if they can help it, so Kelsey's message alone should have raised my antenna. She blogs, she tweets, she texts, and she pings. But voice mail? No. 2

Paradoxically it was Kelsey's understanding of the viral nature of her generation's communication preferences that sent her rushing to the phone, and not just to call boomers[1] like me. She didn't want anyone to learn of Casey's death through Facebook. It was summer, and their friends were scattered, but Kelsey knew that if even one of Casey's 801 Facebook friends posted the news, it would immediately spread. 3

So as Kelsey and her roommates made calls through the night, they monitored Facebook. Within an hour of Casey's death, the first mourner posted her respects on Casey's Facebook wall, a post that any of Casey's friends could have seen. By the next morning, Kelsey, in New Jersey, had reached *The Observer*'s editor in chief in Virginia, and by that evening, the two had reached fellow editors in California, Missouri, Massachusetts, Texas, and elsewhere — and somehow none of them already knew. 4

In the months that followed, I've seen how markedly technology has influenced the conventions of grieving among my students, offering them solace but also uncertainty. The day after Casey's death, several editorial-board members changed their individual Facebook profile pictures. Where there had been photos of Brent, of Kelsey, of Kate, now there were photos of Casey and Brent, Casey and Kelsey, Casey and Kate. 5

---

[1] boomers (para. 3): Short for Baby Boomers, a term for the generation born right after World War II.

6 Now that Casey was gone, she was virtually everywhere. I asked one of my students why she'd changed her profile photo. "It was spontaneous," she said. "Once one person did it, we all joined in." Another student, who had friends at Virginia Tech when, in 2007, a gunman killed 32 people, said that's when she first saw the practice of posting Facebook profile photos of oneself with the person being mourned.

7 Within several days of Casey's death, a Facebook group was created called "In Loving Memory of Casey Feldman," which ran parallel to the wake and funeral planned by Casey's family. Dozens wrote on that group's wall, but Casey's own wall was the more natural gathering place, where the comments were more colloquial and addressed to her: "casey im speechless for words right now," wrote one friend. " i cant believe that just yest i txted you and now your gone . . . i miss you soo much rest in peace."

8 Though we all live atomized lives, memorial services let us know the dead with more dimension than we may have known them during their lifetimes. In the responses of her friends, I was struck by how much I hadn't known about Casey — her equestrian skill, her love of animals, her interest in photography, her acting talent, her penchant for creating her own slang ("Don't be a cow"), and her curiosity — so intense that her friends affectionately called her a "stalker."

> This new, uncharted form of grieving raises new questions.

9 This new, uncharted form of grieving raises new questions. Traditional mourning is governed by conventions. But in the age of Facebook, with selfhood publicly represented via comments and uploaded photos, was it OK for her friends to display joy or exuberance online? Some weren't sure. Six weeks after Casey's death, one student who had posted a shot of herself with Casey wondered aloud when it was all right to post a different photo. Was there a right time? There were no conventions to help her. And would she be judged if she removed her mourning photo before most others did?

10 As it turns out, Facebook has a "memorializing" policy in regard to the pages of those who have died. That policy came into being in 2005, when a good friend and co-worker of Max Kelly, a Facebook employee, was killed in a bicycle accident. As Kelly wrote in a Facebook blog post last October, "The question soon came up: What do we do about his Facebook profile? We had never really thought about this before in such a personal way. How do you deal with an interaction with someone who is no longer able to log on? When someone leaves us, they don't leave our memories or our social network. To reflect that reality, we created

the idea of 'memorialized' profiles as a place where people can save and share their memories of those who've passed."

Casey's Facebook page is now memorialized. Her own postings and lists of interests have been removed, and the page is visible only to her Facebook friends. (I thank Kelsey Butler for making it possible for me to gain access to it.) Eight months after her death, her friends are still posting on her wall, not to "share their memories" but to write to her, acknowledging her absence but maintaining their ties to her—exactly the stance that contemporary grief theorists recommend. To me, that seems preferable to Freud's prescription, in "Mourning and Melancholia," that we should detach from the dead. Quite a few of Casey's friends wished her a merry Christmas, and on the 17th of every month so far, the postings spike. Some share dreams they've had about her, or post a detail of interest. "I had juice box wine recently," wrote one. "I thought of you the whole time :(Miss you girl!" From another: "i miss you. the new lady gaga cd came out, and if i had one wish in the world it would be that you could be singing (more like screaming) along with me in my passenger seat like old times." 11

It was against the natural order for Casey to die at 21, and her death still reverberates among her roommates and fellow editors. I was privileged to know Casey, and though I knew her deeply in certain ways, I wonder—I'm not sure, but I wonder—if I should have known her better. I do know, however, that she would have done a terrific trend piece on "Grief in the Age of Facebook." 12

VOCABULARY/USING A DICTIONARY

1. What is the meaning of *paradoxically* (para. 3)? What part of speech is it? To what word is it related, and what does that word mean?
2. Stone says that with Casey gone, she was "virtually everywhere" (para. 6). What are two meanings of the word *virtually*? Which meaning is Stone using here? (Or could she be using both?)
3. Define *atomized* (para. 8). What is the origin of this word?

RESPONDING TO WORDS IN CONTEXT

1. Stone writes that Kelsey's "understanding of the viral nature of her generation's communications preferences" caused her to call her professor rather than e-mail or text (para. 3). What does *viral* mean in this context? Where does the word come from, and what has it come to mean in communications?
2. Define *colloquial* as Stone uses it in paragraph 7 of the essay. What is a possible antonym of *colloquial*? Give an example of something colloquial and its opposite.

3. What does Stone mean when she refers to an "*uncharted* form of grieving" (para. 9)? What is the origin of the word *uncharted*, and how is it used here?

DISCUSSING MAIN POINT AND MEANING

1. Stone does not come out and say whether she thinks Facebook grieving is a good or bad thing. Which way do you think the essay leans? What is its tone? Give examples from the text.
2. What are two dangers to Facebook mourning that Stone mentions?
3. How did Stone get to know Casey after her death in a way that might not have been possible in another era?

EXAMINING SENTENCES, PARAGRAPHS, AND ORGANIZATION

1. Why does Stone mention Casey's "all-news-all-the-time mind-set" in paragraph 1 of the essay? What is the importance of this detail to the essay as a whole?
2. What is the effect of reproducing Casey's friend's "colloquial" wall post exactly as the friend wrote it in paragraph 7? Why does Stone go to the trouble to preserve the poster's syntax and spelling?
3. How is Stone's essay organized? Is it more of an argument or a narrative? Why did she arrange it this way?

THINKING CRITICALLY

1. What does Stone say Freud's "prescription" for grief was, and what kind of grief does she suggest Facebook mourners are evincing? What do you think is the better, healthier way to express sorrow after a loss—remembrance, detachment, or some combination of the two?
2. How do you feel about Facebook's policy of maintaining the pages of members who pass away as memorials? Does it cheapen the mourning process to do it online, or do Facebook and other sites allow wider access to memorials and expand opportunities to express grief?
3. Discuss the way the essay ends. What is a "trend piece," and why does Stone feel Casey would have written a good one with the same title as her own essay?

IN-CLASS WRITING ACTIVITIES

1. Have you ever witnessed the phenomenon Stone describes? Have you known someone who died whose friends set up a memorial online? If so, describe what it was like. Did the use of the Internet and social media make you feel closer to the person you lost, or give you any sense of closure? If you haven't had the experience, imagine what it might be like.

2. One of the issues the essay highlights is the relationship between students and teachers on social media. Are you friends with your professors on Facebook or other social-networking sites? Why or why not?
3. The essay is in large part about a bond between a teacher and a student, albeit one that occurred after the student's death. Indeed, one of the recurring themes in Stone's writing is what she has learned from her own students. Write about a close relationship you have had with one of your teachers, focusing on what you may have taught the teacher.

Discussing the Unit

SUGGESTED TOPIC FOR DISCUSSION

What will be the lasting impact of social networking on the way we communicate and relate to one another?

PREPARING FOR CLASS DISCUSSION

1. Garry Trudeau implies that Facebook is "ruining" our lives, and Mary Katharine Ham credits it with a near-revolution in Iran. But none of the authors in this chapter considers the possibility that the influence of social-networking sites is overblown. Is this a possibility? Could Facebook and Twitter be nothing more than a passing fad, or are they definitely here to stay for better or worse? Why?
2. The essays in this chapter focus on the impact of social networking on our schedules and our images of ourselves, but don't touch on one of the other major concerns critics have about social networks—their lack of privacy. Are you worried that you have less control over your privacy than you did before the advent of social networks? If so, why? Is your concern based on actual events, anecdotes, or just a lingering fear? If not, explain the concerns some people have about privacy online and why you think those concerns are overblown.

FROM DISCUSSION TO WRITING

1. Imagine a world without social networking: Facebook, MySpace, Bebo, Twitter, and all the rest suddenly disappear tomorrow. What would happen? How would it affect your social life? Would you even have one anymore? Write a short description of the networking apocalypse—do the stock markets crash and millions wander the streets aimlessly? Or does it instantaneously improve everyone's life?
2. Consider Stone's essay "Grief in the Age of Facebook" and write your own "In the Age of Facebook" essay in her style. Consider any aspect of life

Facebook has touched, and compare and contrast it before and after the social-networking revolution. Try to consider both the good and the bad that Facebook has wrought on your area of focus.

TOPICS FOR CROSS-CULTURAL DISCUSSION

1. Ham highlights the effects of Twitter overseas, where she contrasts online heroism with American narcissism and overindulgence. What do you think of this equation? Do you think social media is used more gainfully overseas than it is in the United States? Why or why not? In your experience, how do people from other cultures use sites like Facebook differently than you do?
2. Why do you think some social networks have been banned in several countries, like Syria and the United Arab Emirates? Are these countries paranoid? Are they simply totalitarian? Or are they expressing real concerns for safety and security?

11

Saving the Planet: Is It Too Late?

For at least three decades, leading scientific opinion has held that the earth is getting hotter and that human activity, mostly in the form of carbon emissions, is to blame. But a chorus of skeptics has recently challenged the mainstream view, arguing either that the science behind global warming is faulty or that the threat is overblown. The skeptics were armed with new ammunition in their attack on the mainstream scientists in November 2009, when a hacker uncovered e-mail messages from a number of climate scientists that suggested data had been manipulated.

The chapter opens with one of America's leading environmental authors, Bill McKibben, who cites numerous alarming facts in his essay, "Waste Not Want Not." Concerned by the sheer amount of waste produced by our hyperconsuming nation—"A hundred million trees are cut every year just to satisfy the junk-mail industry"—McKibben persuasively reflects on the way we have constructed an economy that depends on waste. McKibben is not overly optimistic we can recover: "We may have waited too long," he concludes, "we may have wasted our last good chance. It's possible the planet will keep warming and the economy keep sinking no matter what."

McKibben's gloomy statistics and scenarios are confirmed by another influential environmental author, Jeff Goodell. In "Warming Gets Worse," Goodell reports on the speed at which the Arctic is melting and the catastrophe that can result. "The Arctic," he writes, "is melting so quickly that even top ice experts are stunned. Just a few years ago, scientists were assuring us that we wouldn't have an ice-free Arctic until 2100. Now the data suggests that, within a decade or two, there will be sailboats at the North Pole during the summer." But, as is common within the climate change debate, not everyone agrees on the speed or the science. In "Sinking 'Climate Change,'" the prominent conservative columnist Cal Thomas claims (and cites evidence to prove it) that global warming is a myth: "After spending years promoting 'global warming,'" Thomas argues, "the media are beginning to turn in the face of growing evidence that they have been wrong."

University of Massachusetts student Yevgeniya Lomakina has no doubts about the scientific reality of global warming, but she introduces a special twist into the climate change debate. In "'Going Green' Misses the Point," Lomakina objects to the way the environmentalist agenda has actually furthered consumerism. "While saving the planet is a good cause," she says, "carbon dioxide emissions will not decline if one invests in a 'Love planet Earth' T-shirt."

The chapter concludes with a prophetic 1985 warning about climate change from the late Carl Sagan, perhaps America's most popular scientist of his day. At that time, Sagan felt the situation, though real, was not urgent: "Fortunately," he said then, "we have a little time. A great deal can be done in decades." Sagan, it should be noted, believed in the potential of "commercial nuclear fusion power."

Bill McKibben

Waste Not Want Not

[*Mother Jones*, May/June 2009]

BEFORE YOU READ

Do we live in a wasteful society? How much do you waste, and how much waste do you witness in America? Is there anything that can be done about the waste problem?

WORDS TO LEARN

generates (para. 2): creates (verb).
sooty (para. 4): covered in ash (adjective).
exemplifies (para. 5): provides an example of (verb).
manifestly (para. 6): clearly (adverb).
cascade (para. 6): flood (noun).
torque (para. 7): the twisting force involved in car acceleration (noun).
laureate (para. 9): outstanding (adjective).
proximity (para. 9): closeness (noun).
assemblage (para. 11): gathering (noun).
boondoggle (para. 12): wasteful activity (noun).
profligacy (para. 13): wastefulness (noun).
topsoil (para. 14): the top layer of soil, where plants grow (noun).
buffer (para. 14): moderate, hold back (verb).
carnage (para. 15): bloodshed (noun).
commode (para. 15): toilet (noun).
frippery (para. 16): unnecessary showiness (noun).
transfixing (para. 18): holding down (verb).
doldrums (para. 18): depression (noun).

Once a year or so, it's my turn to run recycling day for our tiny town. Saturday morning, 9 to 12, a steady stream of people show up to sort out their plastics (No. 1, No. 2, etc.), their corrugated cardboard (flattened, please), their glass (and their returnable glass, which goes to benefit the elementary school), their Styrofoam peanuts, their paper, their cans. It's quite satisfying — everything in its place. 1

Bill McKibben is one of the nation's best-known environmental writers and activists. A former staff writer for The New Yorker, *he publishes regularly in a wide variety of leading periodicals.*

But it's also kind of disturbing, this waste stream. For one, a town of 550 sure generates a lot — a trailer load every couple of weeks. Sometimes you have to put a kid into the bin and tell her to jump up and down so the lid can close. 2

More than that, though, so much of it seems utterly unnecessary. Not just waste, but wasteful. Plastic water bottles, one after another — 80 million of them get tossed every day. The ones I'm stomping down are being "recycled," but so what? In a country where almost everyone has access to clean drinking water, they define waste to begin with. I mean, you don't have a mug? In fact, once you start thinking about it, the category of "waste" begins to expand, until it includes an alarming percentage of our economy. Let's do some intellectual sorting: 3

There's old-fashioned waste, the dangerous, sooty kind. You're making something useful, but you're not using the latest technology, and so you're spewing: particulates into the air, or maybe sewage into the water. You wish to keep doing it, because it's cheap, and you block any regulation that might interfere with your right to spew. This is the kind of waste that's easy to attack; it's obvious and obnoxious and a lot of it falls under the Clean Air Act and Clean Water Act[1] and so on. There's actually less of this kind of waste than there used to be — that's why we can swim in most of our rivers again. 4

There's waste that comes from everything operating as it should, only too much so. If carbon monoxide (carbon with one oxygen atom) exemplifies pollution of the first type, then carbon dioxide (carbon with two oxygen atoms) typifies the second. Carbon monoxide poisons you in your garage and turns Beijing's[2] air brown, but if you put a catalytic converter[3] on your tailpipe it all but disappears. Carbon dioxide doesn't do anything to you directly — a clean-burning engine used to be defined as one that released only CO_2 and water vapor — but in sufficient quantity it melts the ice caps, converts grassland into desert, and turns every coastal city into New Orleans. 5

[1] Clean Air Act and Clean Water Act (para. 4): Two landmark pieces of environmental legislation in the United States.

[2] Beijing (para. 5): The capital of China, and one of the smoggiest cities in the world.

[3] catalytic converter (para. 5): A device used to reduce the toxicity of emissions from modern car engines.

There's waste that comes from doing something that manifestly doesn't need doing. A hundred million trees are cut every year just to satisfy the junk-mail industry. You can argue about cutting trees for newspapers, or magazines, or Bibles, or symphony scores — but the cascade of stuff-porn that arrives daily in our mailboxes? It wastes forests, and also our time. Which, actually, is precious — we each get about 30,000 days, and it makes one a little sick to calculate how many of them have been spent opening credit card offers. 6

Or think about what we've done with cars. From 1975 to 1985, fuel efficiency for the average new car improved from 14 to 28 miles per gallon. Then we stopped worrying about oil and put all that engineering talent to work on torque. In the mid-1980s, the typical car accelerated from 0 to 60 mph in 14.5 seconds. Today's average (even though vehicles are much heavier) is 9.5 seconds. But it's barely legal to accelerate like that, and it makes you look like an idiot, or a teenager. 7

Then there's the waste that comes with doing something maybe perhaps vaguely useful when you could be doing something actually useful instead. For instance: Congress is being lobbied really, really hard to fork over billions of dollars to the nuclear industry, on the premise that it will fight global warming. There is, of course, that little matter of nuclear waste — but lay that aside (in Nevada[4] or someplace). The greater problem is the wasted opportunity: That money could go to improving efficiency, which can produce the same carbon reductions for about a fifth of the price. 8

Our wasteful habits wouldn't matter much if there were just a few of us — a Neanderthal hunting band could have discarded six plastic water bottles apiece every day with no real effect except someday puzzling anthropologists. But the volumes we manage are something else. Chris Jordan is the photographer laureate of waste — his most recent project, "Running the Numbers," uses exquisite images to show the 106,000 aluminum cans Americans toss every 30 seconds, or the 1 million plastic cups distributed on US airline flights every 6 hours, or the 2 million plastic beverage bottles we run through every 5 minutes, or the 426,000 cell phones we discard every day, or the 1.14 million brown paper supermarket bags we use each hour, or the 60,000 plastic bags we use every 5 seconds, or the 15 million sheets of office paper we use every 5 minutes, or the 170,000 Energizer batteries produced every 15 minutes. The simple amount of stuff it takes — energy especially — to manage this kind of throughput makes it daunting to even think about our waste problem. (Meanwhile, the next 9

[4] Nevada (para. 8): The site of Yucca Mountain, a notorious nuclear waste depository.

"Light Bulbs 2008" by artist Chris Jordan.
Depicts 320,000 light bulbs, equal to the number of kilowatt hours of electricity wasted in the United States every minute from inefficient electricity use.

time someone tells you that population is at the root of our troubles, remind them that the average American uses more energy between the stroke of midnight on New Year's Eve and dinner on January 2 than the average, say, Tanzanian consumes in a year. Population matters, but it *really* matters when you multiply it by proximity to Costco.)

Would you like me to go on? Americans discard enough aluminum 10
to rebuild our entire commercial air fleet every three months — and aluminum represents less than 1 percent of our solid waste stream. We toss 14 percent of the food we buy at the store. More than 46,000 pieces of plastic debris float on each square mile of ocean. And — oh, forget it.

These kinds of numbers get in the way of figuring out how much we 11
really waste. In recent years, for instance, 40 percent of Harvard graduates have gone into finance, consulting, and business. They had just spent four years with the world's greatest library, some of its finest museum collections, an unparalleled assemblage of Nobel-quality scholars, and all they wanted to do was go to lower Manhattan and stare into computer screens. What a waste! And when they got to Wall Street, of course, they figured out extravagant ways to waste the life savings of millions of Americans,

which in turn required the waste of taxpayer dollars to bail them out, money that could have been spent on completely useful things: trains to get us where we want to go — say, new national parks.

Perhaps the only kind of waste we've gotten good at cutting is the kind we least needed to eliminate: An entire industry of consultants survives on telling companies how to get rid of inefficiencies — which generally means people. And an entire class of politicians survives by railing about government waste, which also ends up meaning programs for people: Health care for poor children, what a boondoggle. 12

Want to talk about government waste? We're going to end up spending north of a trillion dollars on the war in Iraq, which will go down as one of the larger wastes of money — and lives — in our history. But we spend more than half a trillion a year on the military anyway, more than the next 10 nations combined. That almost defines profligacy. 13

We've gotten away with all of this for a long time because we had margin, all kinds of margin. Money, for sure — we were the richest nation on Earth, and when we wanted more we just borrowed it from China. But margin in other ways as well: We landed on a continent with topsoil more than a foot thick across its vast interior, so the fact that we immediately started to waste it with inefficient plowing hardly mattered. We inherited an atmosphere that could buffer our emissions for the first 150 years of the Industrial Revolution. We somehow got away with wasting the talents of black people and women and gay folks. 14

But our margin is gone. We're out of cash, we're out of atmosphere, we're out of luck. The current economic carnage is what happens when you waste — when the CEO of Merrill Lynch thinks he needs a $35,000 commode, when the CEO of Tyco[5] thinks it would be fun to spend a million dollars on his wife's birthday party, complete with an ice sculpture of Michelangelo's *David* peeing vodka. The melted Arctic ice cap is what you get when everyone in America thinks he requires the kind of vehicle that might make sense for a forest ranger. 15

> **The melted Arctic ice cap is what you get when everyone in America thinks he requires the kind of vehicle that might make sense for a forest ranger.**

Getting out of the fix we're in — if it's still possible — requires in part that we relearn some very old lessons. We were once famously thrifty: Yankee frugality, straightening bent nails, saving string. We used 16

[5] Tyco (para. 15): An electronics company whose CEO, Dennis Kozlowski, was sentenced to prison for corrupt practices in 2007.

to have a holiday, Thrift Week, which began on Ben Franklin's birthday: "Beware of little expenses; a small leak will sink a great ship," said he. We disapproved of frippery, couldn't imagine wasting money on ourselves, made do or did without. It took a mighty effort to make us what we are today — in fact, it took a mighty industry, advertising, which soaks up plenty more of those Harvard grads and represents an almost total waste.

In the end, we built an economy that depended on waste, and bound- 17
less waste is what it has produced. And the really sad part is, it felt that way, too. Making enough money to build houses with rooms we never used, and cars with engines we had no need of, meant wasting endless hours at work. Which meant that we had, on average, one-third fewer friends than our parents' generation. What waste that! "Getting and spending, we lay waste our powers," wrote Wordsworth.[6] We can't say we weren't warned.

The economic mess now transfixing us will mean some kind of 18
change. We can try to hang on to the status quo — living a Wal-Mart life so we can buy cheaply enough to keep the stream of stuff coming. Or we can say uncle. There are all kinds of experiments in postwaste living springing up: Freecycling,[7] and Craigslisting,[8] and dumpster diving, and car sharing (those unoccupied seats in your vehicle — what a waste!), and open sourcing. We're sharing buses, and going to the library in greater numbers. Economists keep hoping we'll figure out a way to revert — that we'll waste a little more, and pull us out of the economic doldrums. But the psychological tide suddenly runs the other way.

We may have waited too long — we may have wasted our last good 19
chance. It's possible the planet will keep warming and the economy keep sinking no matter what. But perhaps not — and we seem ready to shoot for something nobler than the hyperconsumerism that's wasted so much of the last few decades. Barack Obama said he would "call out" the nation's mayors if they wasted their stimulus[9] money. That's the mood we're in, and it's about time.

[6] Wordsworth (para. 17): (William, 1770–1850) A major English poet. The quotation is from his sonnet "The World Is Too Much with Us."

[7] Freecycling (para. 18): The practice of giving away used consumer items instead of throwing them out.

[8] Craigslisting (para. 18): Using the Web site Craigslist, which allows users to post and respond to ads, often to sell or give away used stuff.

[9] stimulus (para. 19): The 2009 economic stimulus package passed by President Obama to create jobs by giving funds to state and local governments for needed projects.

VOCABULARY/USING A DICTIONARY

1. McKibben refers several times to *hyperconsuming* and *hyperconsumerism* (para. 19). What do these terms refer to? What does the prefix *hyper-* mean?
2. What are *particulates* (para. 4)? To what other words is this one related? What is the difference between *particulates* and *particles*?
3. Explain what McKibben means by *throughput* (para. 9). What more common word is this one related to?

RESPONDING TO WORDS IN CONTEXT

1. What are the various meanings of the word *obnoxious*? How exactly would you characterize the meaning of the word as McKibben uses it in paragraph 4?
2. What does McKibben mean when he says (in paragraph 14) that we've "gotten away with all of this for a long time because we had margin"? What does *margin* mean in this context? How is it related to other meanings of the word in the dictionary?
3. From context, what do the words *thrifty* and *frugality* (para. 16) mean?

DISCUSSING MAIN POINT AND MEANING

1. What is McKibben's answer to critics who say that our expanding population is at the root of our wastefulness? What does he mean when he says, "Population matters, but it *really* matters when you multiply it by proximity to Costco" (para. 9)?
2. What does McKibben say is the only kind of waste we are good at getting rid of? What is he referring to when he makes this point? Does he really believe that this is waste, or is he quoting someone else? If so, whom?
3. How does McKibben feel we're wasting our "Harvard graduates" (para. 11), and who more generally does he mean by that phrase? What would he rather the "Harvard grads" be doing?

EXAMINING SENTENCES, PARAGRAPHS, AND ORGANIZATION

1. What does McKibben mean by "stuff-porn" (para. 6)? How does phrasing it in this way help advance the argument he's making?
2. What is the combined effect of the first and last sentences of paragraph 10? What tone is McKibben trying to set when he asks, "Would you like me to go on?" and ends, "oh, forget it"?
3. Analyze the pattern McKibben employs in his examples of waste. Does he start with one particular kind of example and progress to another kind? How is his organization effective in getting his point across—or how could it be more effective?

THINKING CRITICALLY

1. Do we live in a wasteful society? Does McKibben point out a pattern indicative of some real problems in America, or is his argument overblown? Can anything be done about waste as an epidemic problem, or is some amount of it inevitable?
2. McKibben uses humor throughout his essay. Do you think humor is appropriate for a subject as serious as the one he's broaching? Why or why not? What effect do jokes have in the essay? Pick out two jokes and analyze them — how are they integrated into the essay, what is their function, and how well do they work?
3. What do you think of McKibben's specific examples of American waste? Are they all right on, or are any of them stretches? Pick out one example and provide a counterargument — argue that what McKibben calls waste is necessary, that it can't be helped, or that it doesn't really provide any real peril to our civilization and our environment. Do you think his argument as a whole still stands?

IN-CLASS WRITING ACTIVITIES

1. Write a proposal for eliminating some kind of waste in America. It can be one of the forms of waste McKibben describes or one that you've noticed independently. How can we go about ending the way we misuse resources in the area you choose? Is it even possible? Why or why not? What will it take: individual action, a group effort, government intervention, or some combination of the three?
2. What are McKibben's politics? Where does he fall on the liberal-conservative spectrum? Give some evidence from the text. What effect do his politics have on his view of American waste? Is waste, as McKibben discusses it, a political issue? Or should people on both sides of the left-right debate in America be conscious of what resources we're wasting and be determined to preserve them?
3. McKibben mentions some of the "experiments in postwaste living springing up" (para. 18) and lists Freecycling, Craigslisting, dumpster diving, and car sharing. Research some of these movements and offer an assessment of them. Do any of them have the potential to make a real impact on the way we live? Why or why not?

Jeff Goodell

Warming Gets Worse

[*Rolling Stone*, November 12, 2009]

BEFORE YOU READ

Are you concerned about global warming? Are you ever concerned you might not be concerned enough?

WORDS TO LEARN

fuse (para. 2): the material a flame moves along to explode a bomb (noun).

slab (para. 3): a large, thick, flat stone or piece of material (noun).

organic (para. 3): related to living things (adjective).

amplifying (para. 5): making larger or louder (adjective).

As negotiators prepare to gather in Copenhagen[1] next month to try and reach an agreement to halt climate change, the world's leading scientists have come to an alarming conclusion: Global warming is happening even faster than they thought. 1

The Arctic, it turns out, is melting so quickly that even top ice experts are stunned. Just a few years ago, scientists were assuring us that we wouldn't have an ice-free Arctic until 2100. Now the data suggests that, within a decade or two, there will be sailboats at the North Pole during the summer. The melting Arctic is a ticking time bomb for the Earth's climate — and thanks to our failure to reduce greenhouse-gas pollution, the fuse has already been lit. "It's like man is taking the lid off the northern part of the planet," said Peter Wadhams, an ice expert at the University of Cambridge in England. 2

[1] Copenhagen (para. 1): Danish capital where the UN held a major climate-change conference in 2009; it was widely seen as failing to bring any real, effective resolutions.

A contributing editor to Rolling Stone *magazine, Jeff Goodell writes frequently on energy and the environment. He is the author most recently of* Big Coal: The Dirty Secret behind America's Energy Future *(2006) and* How to Cool the Planet: Geoengineering and the Audacious Quest to Fix Earth's Climate *(2010).*

3 The Arctic is more than just a frozen block of ice — it's more like a frozen block of carbon. Beneath the ice, the region is covered with a slab of permafrost — more than 1,000 feet thick in some places — composed of partially decomposed trees, plants, woolly mammoths and other organic matter that lived in the region thousands of years ago. As it thaws, all that rotting debris sends carbon dioxide into the atmosphere. Worse, the debris is a feast for microscopic bugs that transform it into methane, a greenhouse gas at least 20 times more potent than CO_2. All told, there are some 1 trillion metric tons of carbon buried in the Arctic — the equivalent of the oil, gas and coal reserves on the entire planet. From a planetary perspective, melting the Arctic is like firing up the world's largest furnace — one that will belch catastrophic levels of greenhouse gases into the atmosphere.

Melting the Arctic is like firing up the world's largest furnace.

4 But that's not the worst of it. A similarly huge amount of methane is frozen in the floor of the shallow seas surrounding the Arctic. As the water warms, these blocks of methane ice can bubble to the surface and release millions of tons of methane — more or less cooking the planet overnight. "If that happens," says Jim White, head of the Institute of Arctic and Alpine Research at the University of Colorado, "we are hosed."

5 Even without a sudden release of methane, what's happening in the Arctic has created an ever-accelerating feedback loop that is already speeding up the rate of climate change. As the ice melts, it creates more open water, which absorbs heat faster, which melts ice faster, which warms the water more — and on and on. "One of the biggest questions in climate science is how fast these amplifying feedback loops accelerate," says Ken Caldeira, a climate modeler at the Carnegie Institution. One study found that during periods of rapid sea-ice loss, the land warms three times faster than average, amplifying the feedback loop and further accelerating warming.

6 A warmer Arctic is likely to have a major impact on our weather; some scientists argue that the loss of summer sea ice is already partly responsible for freakish weather events, such as the recent snowstorm in Baghdad. "The Arctic is the global refrigerator for the northern hemisphere," says Mark Serreze, a scientist at the National Snow and Ice Data Center in Colorado. "If you change it, you're likely to see a variety of effects, including drier summers in the southwest United States and wetter winters in the Mediterranean."

7 Even more alarming, rising temperatures in the Arctic threaten to melt the Greenland ice sheets faster than expected. Only two years ago, a United Nations climate report predicted that the seas would likely rise

by no more than 23 inches by 2100. Now, thanks largely to the radical changes in the Arctic in the past few years, scientists believe that even if we take drastic action and cut emissions quickly, we're still likely to see sea levels rise by as much as three feet. And if we don't take action, warns NASA's James Hansen, America's most respected climate scientist, sea levels could rise by as much as nine feet by the end of the century. Such a rise would be catastrophic for many of the world's major cities, including New Orleans, London and Shanghai, as well as the 40 million or so people who live in low-lying areas in poor nations like Bangladesh.

The big question is, is it too late to avert catastrophe? No one knows. 8
"We do not yet have a clear signal of significant methane release from the permafrost," says Ed Dlugokencky, a methane expert with the National Oceanic and Atmospheric Administration. "But we know that as the region heats up, it is inevitable." Once the Arctic is gone, it won't be coming back anytime soon — which is why cutting greenhouse-gas pollution now is so important. As Lonnie Thompson, a glacier expert at Ohio State University, has put it, "Mother Nature is the timekeeper — and nobody can see the clock."

VOCABULARY/USING A DICTIONARY

1. What exactly is *permafrost* (para. 3)? Where does it occur? What is the origin of the word?
2. What are the roots of the word *microscopic* (para. 3)? What does the word mean?
3. What is a *glacier* (para. 8)? What part of speech is it? What does the word *glacial* mean?

RESPONDING TO WORDS IN CONTEXT

1. Goodell warns us that melting the Arctic will release whole new levels of *greenhouse gases* (para. 3) into the atmosphere. What are greenhouse gases, and why are they so worrisome?
2. Based on context, what does Jim White's slang term *hosed* (para. 4) mean?
3. Look up *feedback loop* (para. 5), and provide a thorough definition of it. How is what Goodell is describing in the Arctic an example of a feedback loop? Can you name another example?

DISCUSSING MAIN POINT AND MEANING

1. How does a furnace work, and how, according to Goodell, is melting the Arctic like "firing up the world's largest furnace" (para. 3)?
2. Why would a nine-foot rise in sea level, if it happened, be "catastrophic" for cities like New Orleans and regions like Bangladesh (para. 7)? Why does Goodell single out poor nations like the latter?

3. How do you imagine Goodell would answer skeptics of global warming who say that the current data does not show the earth getting significantly hotter, or that it does not show that any rise in temperature over the next few decades is likely to cause a problem?

EXAMINING SENTENCES, PARAGRAPHS, AND ORGANIZATION

1. Goodell writes that "within a decade or two, there will be sailboats at the North Pole druring the summer" (para. 2). What does he mean by this? Should we take the statement literally?
2. Goodell and the sources he quotes use a number of metaphors—familiar concepts used to illustrate more complicated ones. List all the metaphors you can find in the essay. How do they help a reader understand the complexities of the kind of warming Goodell is explaining?
3. How would you characterize the tone of this short essay? Is Goodell attempting to sound wildly opinionated or precise and factual? Is he optimistic or pessimistic about the future of the Earth's environment?

THINKING CRITICALLY

1. What is the effect of the first sentence of this essay? How does the mention of negotiators gathering at Copenhagen contrast with the new data Goodell will go on to cite about the effects of global warming? How does this contrast help move forward the main point Goodell will be making throughout the essay? Look up a little information on the 2009 Copenhagen conference. Does it sound to you like it was a success?
2. One of the major issues in the climate-change debate is whether any change in the earth's temperature is *anthropogenic*—that is, caused by humans. Where does Goodell fall on this question? Give evidence from the text. Does he argue a case for man-made climate change, or does he appear to assume that his audience accepts it?
3. Goodell asks if it is "too late to avert a catastrophe" such as the one he outlines in the essay (para. 8), but does not explain how we might go about avoiding it. What is Goodell implying humans would need to do in order to stop the vicious cycle of melting in the Arctic? Why might it be too late?

IN-CLASS WRITING ACTIVITIES

1. Are you troubled by reports like this one about the effects of greenhouse gases and climate change? Why or why not? Do you think you'll see the "catastrophic" effects of warming Goodell hints at in your lifetime? Or are numbers and statistics like the ones Goodell lists too vague for you to worry about directly? If you are worried, what, if anything, are you doing about it? If you're not worried, why not?

2. A number of skeptics, including Cal Thomas in the next selection, challenge statistics and conclusions like the ones Goodell presents here. Research some of the specific answers skeptics have to the rapid melting of the Arctic. Why do they think the threat is overblown? Give specifics. Whose evidence do you find more convincing, and why?
3. Goodell uses the terms "global warming" and "climate change" almost interchangeably throughout this essay. What is the difference? Do some research into the history of these terms. Why have scientists and science journalists begun shifting from *global warming* to *climate change* over the last few years? Which term gives the public a more accurate picture of what is happening to the Earth's temperature?

Cal Thomas

Sinking "Climate Change"

[*Townhall.com*, June 3, 2010]

BEFORE YOU READ

Is global climate change really happening? Or is it possible certain forces in government and society just want you to think so?

WORDS TO LEARN

transparent (para. 1): doing things out in the open (adjective).
bickering (para. 4): fighting back and forth (verb).
designation (para. 5): specially declared status (noun).
lamented (para. 6): mourned (noun).
bamboozled (para. 6): tricked (verb).
inhibited (para. 10): stopped from growing (verb).
diversifying (para. 11): making more varied (verb).
underwrite (para. 11): provide financial support for (verb).

Three modern myths have been sold to the American people: the promise of a transparent administration (President Obama); the promise of a more ethical Congress (Speaker Pelosi); and the myth of "global warming," or climate change. 1

Cal Thomas is one of the leading conservative columnists in America. His widely syndicated column appears in over 550 U.S. newspapers and is over 25 years old. Thomas is also a regular presence on radio and television.

The first two are daily proving suspect and now the third is sinking with greater force than melting icebergs — if they were melting, which many believe they are not. 2

After spending years promoting "global warming," the media are beginning to turn in the face of growing evidence that they have been wrong. The *London Times* recently reported: "Britain's premier scientific institution is being forced to review its statements on climate change after a rebellion by members who question mankind's contribution to rising temperatures." 3

It gets worse, or better, depending on your perspective. *Newsweek* magazine, which more than 30 years ago promoted global cooling and a new ice age — and more recently has been drinking the global warming Kool-Aid[1] — headlined a story, "Uncertain Science: Bickering and Defensive, Climate Researchers Have Lost the Public's Trust." *Newsweek* does its best to cling to its increasingly discredited doctrine, but the growing body of contrary evidence only adds to the public's disbelief. 4

In Canada, the polar bear — which has been used by global warming promoters to put a cuddly face on the issue — is in danger of not being endangered any longer. *CBC News* reported that the polar bear's designation as a "species of special concern" has been suspended "while the government reviews the polar bear's status and decides whether to renew the classification or change it." 5

The *New York Times* recently lamented "global warmism's loss of credibility" in a story about hundreds of "environmental activists who met to ponder this question: 'If the scientific consensus on climate change has not changed, why have so many people turned away from the idea that human activity is warming the planet?' " The "consensus" never was a consensus. Most of us may not have gotten an "A" in science, but we can sense when we are being bamboozled. 6

> **The "consensus" never was a consensus.**

The German online news magazine *Focus* recently carried a story, "Warm Times Will Soon Be Over!" Commenting on the "new NASA high temperature record," which may be set, the magazine blames it on El Niño.[2] Meteorologists, like Joe D'Aleo of The 7

[1] drinking . . . the Kool-Aid (para. 4): An expression for accepting an idea blindly, derived from the poisoned Kool-Aid drunk by cult members in the 1978 Jonestown massacre.

[2] El Niño: A complex weather pattern occurring irregularly in the Pacific Ocean and having a widespread effect; La Niña is its "sister system."

Weather Channel, are publicly distancing themselves from the false doctrine of global warming. D'Aleo says, "We'll have La Niña conditions before the summer is over, and it will intensify further through the fall and winter. Thus we'll have cooler temperatures for the next couple of years."

Remember the scare ignited in 2007 by supposed melting Arctic ice caps? The *Star Canada* says a new analysis shows that the apparent change was the result of "shifting winds," while an expedition last year to the North Pole discovered the ice "100 percent thicker than expected." 8

Much of this information — and more — is available at the useful Web site www.climatedepot.com. 9

It is a given that America needs new sources of energy. Environmentalists have inhibited efforts at exploration by supporting policies that have forced some domestic exploration too far offshore (thus increasing chances of an ecological disaster as is occurring in the Gulf of Mexico).[3] 10

Instead of trying to sell us a dubious doctrine at an estimated cost of $100 billion a year worldwide (so far), environmentalists would have done themselves and the world more good had they chosen a different strategy, such as not sending oil money to countries that want to destroy us. This would have increased our patriotic spirit and had the additional benefit of not only diversifying our energy supply, but also depriving our enemies of money they use to underwrite terrorism. 11

Watch for the hardcore "global warming" cultists to continue clinging to their beliefs; but also watch increasing numbers of scientists and eventually politicians to abandon this once "certain" faith and to look for other ways to control our lives. In that pursuit, the left never quits. Rather than acknowledge their error, they will go on to make new mistakes, knowing they will never be held accountable. 12

VOCABULARY/USING A DICTIONARY

1. What is a *consensus*? Why does Thomas put the word in quotation marks when he uses it in paragraph 6?
2. To what does *domestic exploration* (para. 10) refer? What is the opposite of *domestic*?
3. What does *dubious* (para. 11) mean? What part of speech is it?

---

[3] Gulf of Mexico: A reference to the 2010 BP oil spill, the worst ecological disaster in history.

RESPONDING TO WORDS IN CONTEXT

1. Thomas uses the word *myth* throughout the essay. What is the origin of the word? How is it most traditionally used, and what is the precise meaning of the word as he uses it?
2. What does Thomas mean when he says that the polar bear has been used to "put a cuddly face on the issue" (para. 5)? What does *cuddly* mean in this context, and what does its use imply about the way Thomas believes climate change is discussed?
3. What is a *cultist* (para. 12)? From where does that word derive? How does Thomas characterize believers in climate change by calling them cultists?

DISCUSSING MAIN POINT AND MEANING

1. Why does Thomas mention that *Newsweek* magazine "more than 30 years ago promoted global cooling and a new ice age" (para. 4)? Why is *Newsweek*'s history important to Thomas's argument?
2. Thomas says it's "a given that America needs new sources of energy" (para. 10). What do sources of energy have to do with the climate?
3. What strategy does Thomas think environmentalists should have pushed for? What benefits, besides being good for the environment, does he say this strategy would have had?

EXAMINING SENTENCES, PARAGRAPHS, AND ORGANIZATION

1. Explain the joke Thomas makes in his title. Why is it ironic to "sink" climate change?
2. Why does Thomas begin with his other two myths? How are these related to what he considers the "myth" of climate change?
3. What is the function of paragraph 7 in the essay as a whole? How do the conclusions of the German online newsmagazine fit into Thomas's argument?

THINKING CRITICALLY

1. Thomas says that liberals who promote climate change will eventually have to give up their claims and "look for other ways to control our lives." What does he think climate change believers have to gain from their fabrications? Why do they continue to push for changes, in Thomas's mind, when they've been proven wrong on so many things? What is their real agenda?
2. Discuss Thomas's characterization of the media in the essay. Does he consider the media honest and objective? What role does he believe the media play in selling climate change to the public, and why?
3. Take a look at the Web site Thomas recommends, www.climatedepot.com. Does the site look like a useful, objective repository of statistics, as Thomas claims it to be? Or does it have an agenda? If so, what? Do you find its arguments compelling? Why or why not?

IN-CLASS WRITING ACTIVITIES

1. Thomas is writing for *Townhall.com*, a conservative Web site. Why have political conservatives taken up the issue of climate change with such skepticism? Why do liberals promote it? Should climate change be a political issue, or is it something we should approach as a society without politics intruding? Is that possible anymore? Why or why not?
2. Do you believe that climate change is real? Do you feel confident in your answer? How much do you accept your position blindly, and how much of your belief is based on research and evidence? If you are a believer, how do you respond to Thomas's arguments? If you're a skeptic, what would you add to or subtract from Thomas's essay?
3. Thomas writes of climate change believers that "rather than acknowledge their error, they will go on to make new mistakes, knowing they will never be held accountable." Thomas points out a problem that confounds many areas of public life. Give another example of a mistake policy makers cling to even when proven wrong. Why do people persist in errors? What forces keep them going? What does it take to break their resolve?

Yevgeniya Lomakina (student essay)

"Going Green" Misses the Point

[*The Daily Collegian*, University of Massachusetts, April 22, 2010]

BEFORE YOU READ

What can individuals do to curb climate change and fix the environment? Is the burden on big corporations, on governments, or on people like you?

WORDS TO LEARN

amplifies (para. 1): makes louder or more noticeable (verb).
emitting (para. 3): letting out (verb).
suppressed (para. 4): kept quiet (adjective).
spheres (para. 4): areas (noun).
embarked (para. 4): set out (verb).

Yevgeniya Lomakina is a student at the University of Massachusetts.

What is one catchphrase that has recently become more and more popular? The arrival of spring and Earth Day only amplifies its emergence. Occasionally against their will, numerous times a day, unsuspecting consumers are faced with various "Earth-friendly" slogans. 1

Words of affection toward the planet appear on bags, mugs, shirts, pants, cars, buses, buildings and the list can go on. The "green living" movement is here to stay. TV programs encourage viewers to buy Earth-friendly products. Campuses and job facilities boast about their green initiatives. A new market for specifically "green" jobs is on the rise. All these actions are aimed at doing "a little part" at saving the planet from global warming. With such a noble cause in mind, it seems that no price is too high. 2

It can no longer be denied: The Earth is affected by global climate change, which was initiated by humans' misuse of natural resources. The statistics have forced the public to finally acknowledge the problem. In 2002, Colorado and Arizona had their worst wildfire seasons. Extreme heat waves in 2003 caused numerous deaths in Europe and more around the globe. The United States is said to lead the world in pollution, emitting more carbon dioxide than China, India, and Japan combined. Based upon such statistics, it is apparent that action against global climate change was long overdue. 3

While saving the planet is a good cause, carbon dioxide emissions will not decline if one invests in a "Love planet Earth" T-shirt. However, the media create a strong argument for the positive impact of "going" green, at any cost. Those who consent to help "save the environment" are perceived as "Earth-conscious" and their opponents are suppressed. It seems as if suddenly, all spheres of society, from factory owners to private individuals, have embarked upon a massive race for who can be the most green. 4

Green initiatives are as diverse as the people who embrace them.

Green initiatives are as diverse as the people who embrace them. If the planet could be saved based on what kind of cereal a consumer bought, evidently, there would be no problem. The question, however, lies much deeper. 5

Did advertising and popular culture turn a genuine concern for the environment into an easily solvable problem? It seems that the answer to saving the Earth is only one purchase away. Do you want to live green? Buy a mug. Do you want to live greener? Buy a hybrid car. Choosing an environmentally safe product may simply allow the consumer to have a guilt-free conscience, but, in reality, will cost more for the environment. 6

Costs for transportation, packaging, and the novelty of green products must all be taken into account. It is better to spend a lesser amount of money on a regular product, or even better, not to buy any product at all.

Some Earth-friendly initiatives require no spending on the part of the consumer. Instead of buying a hybrid car, a better choice would be taking better care of the currently owned model. To save gas, carpool. Instead of buying newer "green" household electric products, once again, take good care of the ones you already own. Instead of buying organic vegetables at Whole Foods, choose to buy them at a local farm stand. However, these simple ways to reduce carbon emissions and spending do not seem to be "popular" enough. It is assumed that if one's initiatives to be green are not publicly seen, they are not present. 7

It is interesting to note that criticisms of green consumption have only come from individual activists, and not large environmental groups, such as Sierra Club, or Rainforest Action Network.[1] 8

Globalization is on the rise, and more and more countries now produce in surplus quantities and export their products all over the globe. In order to "stop" global warming with any significant rate, every country on the planet needs to play its part in reducing carbon emissions. However, countries outside the United States may not be as easily persuaded to join the green movement, partly due to the common belief that the United States is responsible for global warming. Al Gore expresses it best in his documentary *An Inconvenient Truth* when he says that in order to reduce global warming, every nation needs to contribute its part. Otherwise, individual efforts are meaningless on a worldwide scale. 9

It is only when buyers begin to diminish their consumerist desires that any change will start to take place. If one truly wants to go green, it can be done without expensive purchases. Meanwhile, if the voice of the media remains above the voice of reason, the global warming situation will remain unchanged. 10

VOCABULARY/USING A DICTIONARY

1. Give an example of a *green initiative* (para. 2). Look up the term online if necessary. What does the word *initiative* mean? Where does the word come from?
2. What does *novelty* (para. 6) mean? What is the origin of the word, and what are some other words to which it's related?

---

[1] Sierra Club, Rainforest Action Network (para. 8): Two large nonprofit public-interest environmental groups.

3. Several essays in this chapter refer to *carbon emissions* (paras. 4, 7, and 9). What does the word *emission* mean? What part of speech is it? What are related parts of speech, and what is the word's origin?

RESPONDING TO WORDS IN CONTEXT

1. What is a *catchphrase* (para. 1)? Give an example of a catchphrase besides the one Lomakina gives. What are the connotations of the word, and how does her use of it help to advance her argument?
2. What are *organic* vegetables (para. 7)? Why are they considered an aspect of the environmental movement?
3. What does Lomakina mean when she refers to *consumerist desires* (para. 10)? What is *consumerism*, and what does it mean for something to be *consumerist*?

DISCUSSING MAIN POINT AND MEANING

1. To back her claim that climate change is real, Lomakina writes that the United States emits "more carbon dioxide than China, India, and Japan combined" (para. 3). Explain how the emission of carbon dioxide affects the environment and how scientists say it causes the climate to change.
2. What does Lomakina mean when she writes, sarcastically, that "it seems that the answer to saving the Earth is only one purchase away" (para. 6)? Explain the cultural phenomenon she's criticizing with this assertion.
3. Give a few examples, besides those Lomakina offers, of the types of changes she is encouraging people to make. How do these differ from the behaviors typically encouraged by the "green" movement?

EXAMINING SENTENCES, PARAGRAPHS, AND ORGANIZATION

1. What is the tone of the phrase "words of affection toward the planet" (para. 2)? What is Lomakina implying by using this phrase?
2. Analyze the comparisons and contrasts Lomakina uses in paragraphs 6 and 7. How does the author use rhetorical questions and parallel structures to compare what she considers ineffective and effective ways of saving the planet?
3. What is the function of paragraph 8 in the context of the essay as a whole? Why does Lomakina condemn the groups she mentions in that paragraph by contrasting their behavior with the information she provides in the previous paragraphs?

THINKING CRITICALLY

1. One commenter on the online edition of the *Daily Collegian* writes that he doesn't think the green movement's popularity "necessarily excludes the potential to help the environment. Hey, if the yuppies get on board

because their neighbors do, everybody's happy." One could argue that Lomakina is attacking people's motives for environmentally friendly action in this article, not the actions themselves. Do you agree? If a movement is going in the right direction, does it matter why people join it?

2. Do you agree with Lomakina that the best and most effective methods of saving the environment are the ones that are not "publicly seen" (para. 7)? Are there any possible advantages of public displays of environmental consciousness Lomakina fails to consider?
3. Lomakina writes that "countries outside the United States may not be as easily persuaded to join the green movement, partly due to the common belief that the United States is responsible for global warming" (para. 9). Do you agree that the United States is more responsible for global warming than other countries are? Look up some facts to back your opinion if necessary. Would that matter anyway to the balance of worldwide responsibility for fixing the problem or, as Lomakina asserts, are we all in it together no matter who's at fault?

IN-CLASS WRITING ACTIVITIES

1. Write your own manifesto for how an individual can make a difference in the environment. Is there anything one person can do to save the earth and, if so, what is it? Or do you think, like Lomakina, that it takes large collective action that can't be reduced to a simple set of slogans and pat-yourself-on-the-back actions? Why?
2. One of the themes of Lomakina's essay is that the media has lulled Americans into a sense of complacency about the environment by making them feel that "going green" is really making a difference. Do you agree? Give examples of cases in which the media encourages the view that the environmental crisis is, in Lomakina's words, "an easily solvable problem" (para. 6). Do you think television, the press, and the Internet have had a positive or a negative effect on the way people see environmental issues? Why?
3. Pretend you're organizing a new media campaign to replace the current "green" movement—your job is to educate the public on what it can do locally to save the earth. What, if anything, would you change? How would you get your message across? Write a sample press release detailing three things individuals can do to help curb global warming.

LOOKING CLOSELY

Effective Persuasion: Recommending a Course of Action

The primary purpose of a persuasive essay is to change someone's attitude or course of action. On Election Day, a newspaper editorial will encourage its readers to vote for a particular candidate; in the same paper, a film review may discourage moviegoers from attending a certain film the reviewer finds "pointless, trivial, and embarrassingly dumb." And an opinion column in that paper may try to persuade parents to avoid buying fast food meals for their children. All of these pieces may offer reasons for their views, but they will also urge readers to take some form of action. In "'Going Green' Misses the Point," University of Massachusetts student Yevgeniya Lomakina wants her readers to realize that if they purchase certain items simply because they are advertised or promoted as "green," they may be wasting their time and money. "If one truly wants to go green," she says, "it can be done without expensive purchases." Note how she moves her argument into recommending a course of action by first showing in one paragraph how such "green" purchases defeat their purpose and then in the next paragraph showing what people can do "instead" that would be more effective and cost less or nothing.

Did advertising and popular culture turn a genuine concern for the environment into an easily solvable problem? It seems that the answer to saving the Earth is only one purchase away. Do you want to live green? Buy a mug. Do you want to live greener? Buy a hybrid car. Choosing an environmentally safe product may simply allow the consumer to have a guilt-free conscience, but, in reality, will cost more for the environment. Costs for transportation, packaging, and the novelty of green products must all be taken into account. It is better to spend a lesser amount of money on a regular product, or even better, not to buy any product at all. (1)

1 Lomakina claims that "green" purchases may be environmentally useless

Some Earth-friendly initiatives require no spending on the part of the consumer. Instead of buying a hybrid car, a better choice would be taking better care of the currently owned model. To save gas, carpool. Instead of buying newer "green" household electric products, once again, take good care of the ones you already own. Instead of buying organic vegetables at Whole Foods, choose to buy

2 She then suggests more effective options that may cost nothing

them at a local farm stand. (2) However, these simple ways to reduce carbon emissions and spending do not seem to be "popular" enough. It is assumed that if one's initiatives to be green are not publicly seen, they are not present.

AMERICA THEN . . . 1985

The Warming of the World

In a famous short poem in 1920, Robert Frost wondered whether the earth would end in fire or ice — melted by overheating or turned completely into a frozen wasteland. At the time, it appeared that the future climate of the earth could go in either direction. Many doomsday scenarios, in fact, pictured another Ice Age, with the earth becoming uninhabitable as glaciers expanded and rivers and seas froze over. In the mid-1970s, such predictions grew popular, and they found scientific support in 1981 when a prominent British astronomer, Sir Frederick Hoyle, published his forecast of a new ice age, *Ice: The Ultimate Human Catastrophe.*

But by this time, many scientists were also gathering evidence for an opposing worst-case scenario: The earth was seriously overheating as a result of what was called a "greenhouse effect." The crisis was man-made and attributable to the ever-increasing use of fossil fuels (coal, gas, and oil). In 1985, one of America's leading scientists and a prolific

Astronomer Carl Sagan, 1981. Carl Sagan (1934–1996) was for years one of America's best-known scientists, largely because of such popular books as *The Dragons of Eden: Speculations on the Evolution of Human Intelligence* (1977), *Broca's Brain: Reflections on the Romance of Science* (1979), and the enormously successful TV series he hosted, *Cosmos*. Part of his popularity can be attributed to his respect for the general public he was writing for and speaking to. He once said, "The public is a lot brighter and more interested in science than they're given credit for. . . . They're not numbskulls. Thinking scientifically is as natural as breathing."

scientific writer, Carl Sagan, published a warning in the popular Sunday magazine *Parade*. In "The Warming of the World," Sagan — like Hoyle, an astronomer — explained to his readers how fossil fuels produced dangerous levels of carbon dioxide (CO_2) that were "irreversible." Since the industrial revolution, Sagan wrote, the amount of CO_2 in the atmosphere has been steadily increasing and, unless nothing changes, the surface temperature of the earth will also increase.

One of the earliest proponents of global warming (a term that was first used in 1969), Sagan asked in his *Parade* essay the key questions: At our present rate of fuel consumption, how long will it take before our climate becomes dangerously warmer? And what would be the consequences of a perceptibly warmer earth? But despite the alarming evidence even then, Sagan never sounded panic-stricken and he was optimistic that solutions would be discovered in time. Had this great scientist lived into his late seventies, it would be interesting to see what his attitude towards climate change would be today.

Discussing the Unit

SUGGESTED TOPIC FOR DISCUSSION

How can an issue based in hard science—whether the earth is getting warmer, whether humans are the cause, and how dangerous the effects will be—engender a debate like this one? How did politics get involved in the issue of climate change, and will it finally make real discussion of the issue impossible?

PREPARING FOR CLASS DISCUSSION

1. Bill McKibben's essay, which takes for granted that climate change is real, comes from a liberal magazine; Cal Thomas's, which argues that climate change is invented, comes from a conservative blog. Explain the political side of the global warming debate in concrete terms. Why has this issue become polarized?
2. Could it in fact be too late to do anything about climate change? Or are there always solutions?

FROM DISCUSSION TO WRITING

1. Assuming climate change is a real problem, where will the solution come from? Will it be individual action, the private sector, or massive government intervention? Take the authors in this chapter who believe climate

change is real and truly dangerous, and assess where they think the solution—if there even is a solution—will finally lie.

2. None of the essays in this chapter was written by a scientist. Why has the debate been dominated by pundits, rather than the people who hold the actual data? Does a similar rift exist among scientists? Are their conclusions too complex to relay to the public, or are they just too muddy for a readership that likes clear, easy answers?

TOPICS FOR CROSS-CULTURAL DISCUSSION

1. What countries will be hardest hit by the climate crisis, if it's in fact real, and which countries should be the most responsible for fixing it? Why?
2. America remains the country with the most climate-change skeptics, as well as the loudest. Why is this? Why are other countries sold so much more easily on the idea than the United States is? Is it a reflection of boundless American optimism or foolhardy ignorance?

12

Immigration: Who Is an American?

In April 2010, Arizona's governor signed the strictest anti-illegal immigration law any state has passed in decades. Claiming the federal government had dropped the ball in protecting Arizona's border with Mexico and enforcing its own immigration laws, Arizona authorized local law enforcement to uphold the federal laws. But some provisions gave many both inside and outside Arizona pause: SB 1070 —its moniker was soon famous—made it a misdemeanor for any immigrant to be in public without documentation and allowed law enforcement to ask immigrants for their papers. Critics immediately alleged that the law sanctioned racial profiling and the wholesale harassment of the one minority group it seemed tacitly aimed at: Latin Americans.

Immigration has been and will continue to be one of the most divisive issues facing the nation. The debate can be seen and heard daily on television and radio talk shows and is a regular feature of newspapers and magazines. An example of the debate in miniature appears in "Does Immigration Increase the Virtues of Hard Work and Fortitude in the United States?" The debate, sponsored by *In Character* magazine, features two specialists on the topic of immigration who take opposite sides on the general issue of what immigrants contribute to the United States. The president of Immigration Works USA, Tamar Jacoby, argues affirmatively that new immigrants work harder than native Americans and tend to "rely less on government benefits." But the executive director of the Center for Immigration Studies, Mark Krikorian, sees things differently and points out the high percentage of immigrants receiving welfare. He argues also that in the past, because of the enormous hardship of transportation and relocation, immigrants may have been a more "enterprising" group of people, but that today with the relative ease of travel and communication this is no longer the case.

One wonders how the author of the next selection would feel about Krikorian's assessment that transportation and relocation make immigration today so much easier than in the past. For many undocumented workers who try to enter the United States in the hopes of finding employment, the journey can be difficult, long, expensive, and dangerous. In "The Crossing," Vicente Martinez (the name is fictitious) offers a detailed description of what it was like to get across the Mexican border into California and eventually on to Portland, Oregon, where he felt confident—largely because of his English language skills—that he could find work.

For most people who decide to come to the United States—whether documented or not—one of the greatest obstacles is language. This was especially true for immigrants who, at any time in our history, arrived speaking only their native languages, but it also affected their children who were born in the United States. A large part of the American immigrant narrative is the story of young Americans who grew up trying to learn English in a family where parents only spoke Spanish, Italian, Arabic, Chinese, or any other foreign language. Because of the demands of work and education, quite a few young people eventually lose fluency in the language heard at home; some caught in the conflict of "English Only" standards never reach proficiency in either language. In "Slurring Spanish," noted author Luis J. Rodríguez wonders why in a nation that is the "fifth-largest Spanish-speaking country in the world," speaking Spanish remains a problem.

The daily news shows may make it appear that immigration is an issue only along America's Mexican border, but the problem is much bigger, as the next two selections demonstrate. In "Uniting Families," Tulane University student Elyse Toplin covers pending legislation in

Congress known as the Uniting Americans Family Act that would allow partners of LGBT (lesbian, gay, bisexual, transgender) Americans the same path to citizenship that heterosexual couples enjoy.

Immigration issues also affect our concepts of racial and ethnic identity. This has been especially the case in the African American community, which in the past several decades has experienced unprecedented migrations of people from African nations, the Caribbean, and the Pacific. How has this influx of foreign-born black populations affected the identity of native-born African Americans? In "Migrations Forced and Free," the prominent historian Ira Berlin considers this difficult topic and concludes that all the diverse groups of black Americans share a common experience, "for the migrations that are currently transforming African-American life are directly connected to those that have transformed black life in the past."

The chapter concludes with a 1999 advertisement that views United States immigration policies as a threat to a sustainable future.

DEBATE

Tamar Jacoby

Does Immigration Increase the Virtues of Hard Work and Fortitude in the United States? Yes

[*In Character*, Spring 2009]

BEFORE YOU READ

What effect do illegal immigrants have on the United States? Do they take up resources or provide valuable services? Do we even notice them?

WORDS TO LEARN

fortitude (title): bravery, courage (noun).
pluck (para. 2): spirit of courage (noun).
avail (para. 4): make use of (verb).
assimilate (para. 6): become part of something (verb).

Most migrants make the trip for the opportunity to work. The decision is an economic, not moral one. And like any group, today's newcomers are a mixed bunch, with good and bad apples among them. 1

2 But migration is also a winnowing experience. Those who end up staying in the U.S. despite the hardships are a self-selecting few. Among the qualities that distinguish them are their pluck and determination.

3 Immigrants work harder than native-born Americans. In 2006, before the economic downturn, when 66 percent of native-born men were working or actively looking for work, the rate for males from Mexico was 88 percent, and that for Mexican men in the U.S. illegally

The president of Immigration Works USA, Tamar Jacoby is a widely published writer on the topic of immigration. A 1976 graduate of Yale University, she is the author of Someone Else's House: America's Unfinished Struggle for Integration *(1998) and editor of the anthology* Reinventing the Melting Pot: The New Immigrants and What it Means to Be American *(2004).*

was 94 percent. Immigrants also worked longer hours: At the height of the boom, a typical low-skilled immigrant's work week was a stunning 56 percent longer than a typical low-skilled native's.

4 Newcomers rely less on government benefits. Not even legal immigrants are eligible for federal welfare programs in their first five years in the U.S., and illegal immigrants are ineligible for handouts of any kind. Even when U.S.-born children qualify families for the program most people think of as welfare, Temporary Assistance for Needy Families, only 1 percent of immigrant-headed households avail themselves, compared to 5 percent of households headed by U.S. citizens.

5 Migrants are risk-takers by definition, and uprooted, hungry people are always going to be scrappier than settled folks. Remember the immigrant workers rushing to New Orleans in the wake of Katrina for cleanup and construction jobs. We shouldn't be romantic about this: The jobs immigrants do are often dirty and dangerous, and their eagerness to work under any conditions makes it all too easy for some employers to exploit them. But their drive pays off, both for them and for us, and at both the low and high ends of the economic ladder.

> **Their drive pays off, both for them and for us.**

6 By the third generation, ironically, this determination falls off as immigrant families assimilate to America's far less driven norms. So it has always been, since Ellis Island[1] and before. The good news: By the time the drive gives out, there is another wave of newcomers waiting in the wings, attracted by the beacon that is America and ready to test their spirit in a country they don't know.

VOCABULARY/USING A DICTIONARY

1. What are the various meanings of the verb *winnow* (para. 2), and how has it come to have the meaning Jacoby deploys in her essay?
2. What are *norms* (para. 6)? Give a few examples of America's norms.

RESPONDING TO WORDS IN CONTEXT

1. How would you define *scrappier* as it's used in paragraph 5? How does this word characterize the immigrants Jacoby is talking about?
2. What is a *beacon* (para. 6)? How is Jacoby using the word in this context? Is it meant literally?

---

[1] Ellis Island (para. 6): The immigration center in New York famous for processing many European immigrants in the nineteenth and twentieth centuries.

DISCUSSING MAIN POINT AND MEANING

1. What does Jacoby mean when she writes that the decision to come to America is "an economic, not moral one" (para. 1)? What view is she trying to dispel? How does casting the decision as an economic one support Jacoby's general argument and position?
2. What sorts of jobs is Jacoby referring to when she writes that "the jobs immigrants do are often dirty and dangerous" (para. 5)? Give a few examples. Why does Jacoby dwell on these jobs? You will note in the following selection that Krikorian doesn't mention the sorts of jobs immigrants do at all.

EXAMINING SENTENCES, PARAGRAPHS, AND ORGANIZATION

1. Which of Jacoby's six paragraphs contain statistics? Which do not? How is the pattern of general assertion and hard facts effective in this essay? (Or what could Jacoby have done to make it more effective?)
2. Jacoby writes, "By the third generation, ironically, this determination falls off as immigrant families assimilate to America's far less driven norms" (para. 6). Explain Jacoby's use of the word *ironically* here. How is the diminished work ethic of the grandchildren of immigrants ironic? Do you agree that it is?

THINKING CRITICALLY

1. What exactly does Jacoby mean when she calls migration "a winnowing experience" (para. 2)? What process is she describing? Is her assertion accurate? Does it take "pluck and determination" to make it as a migrant?
2. Central to Jacoby's claim is that immigrants' drive "pays off, both for them and for us" (para. 5). Describe how the drive pays off for them and how it pays off for us, in Jacoby's estimation. Do you agree with either or with both of these claims? Why or why not?

IN-CLASS WRITING ACTIVITIES

1. Do you think Jacoby's assertion that the work ethic of immigrant communities dies off by the third generation is accurate? If so, write a brief essay explaining why exactly you think this happens. If not, how do you think a work ethic is actually apportioned among the generations, and why?
2. Write a short, descriptive essay about what comes to your mind when you hear the word *immigrant*. What country is the person from? What motivates him or her? How does it relate to your views on the political dimension of the issue?

DEBATE

Mark Krikorian

Does Immigration Increase the Virtues of Hard Work and Fortitude in the United States? No

[*In Character*, Spring 2009]

BEFORE YOU READ

Should we tolerate any amount of illegal immigration into the country? How much of your opinion is based on the value you believe immigrants add or subtract from society, and how much is based on ideas of fairness, compassion, or rule of law?

WORDS TO LEARN

enterprising (para. 1): clever and creative in solving problems (adjective).
psychic (para. 1): psychological (adjective).
debunks (para. 2): exposes as false (verb).
succumb (para. 4): give in (verb).
degenerate (para. 4): completely fallen and immoral (adjective).
miasma (para. 5): a very bad atmosphere (noun).

Perhaps in the past there was some self-selection among immigrants; only the most enterprising would dare undertake the long and dangerous journey. But even if that were so, modern transportation and communications technologies have changed things permanently. There is no longer a weeks-long trip in steerage[1] to scare 1

[1] steerage (para. 1): The bottom of a ship, reserved for passengers with the cheapest tickets or with no tickets at all; brings to mind immigrants to America in previous centuries.

The executive director of the Center for Immigration Studies, Mark Krikorian is an advocate for a stricter immigration policy and tougher enforcement of immigration laws. A graduate of Georgetown University, he received a master's degree from the Fletcher School of Law and Diplomacy at Tufts University. A regular contributor to The National Review, *he is the author of* The New Case against Immigration, Both Legal and Illegal *(2008).*

off the weak-willed, nor the prospect of being permanently cut off from contact with home. In fact, in modern conditions, we see the development of transnationalism, where people are essentially able to live in two countries at the same time. This dramatically reduces the psychic and emotional price of departing for America, and is thus less likely to weed out the less "gritty" among potential immigrants.

> **People are essentially able to live in two countries at the same time.**

Welfare use among immigrants debunks the fable of the grit-bearing newcomer. While in 2007 19 percent of households headed by a native-born American used at least one major welfare program (a pretty alarming figure in itself), the number for immigrants was 33 percent. For immigrants who'd lived here twelve years or more, it was 34 percent. And for Mexicans, whose number is equal to the next ten immigrant groups combined, the welfare use rate was more than 50 percent. 2

Not much here to deliver us from our decadence. 3

In trying to understand why the myth of immigrant superiority is false, it's important not to succumb to its flip side, the myth of the "degenerate immigrant," which sees the new arrival as a parasite determined to live off the taxpayer. Instead, immigrants are people like any other, subject to the same temptations and weaknesses, but with an added disadvantage. Immigrants generally come here from pre-industrial societies, with low levels of skill and education, a lot like many of our ancestors a century ago. But unlike our ancestors, these characteristics do not prepare them for life in the America they are entering. 4

This mismatch renders their labor of relatively little worth and plunges them and their children into a moral miasma that we, at least, have had many years to adjust to and evolve with. 5

VOCABULARY/USING A DICTIONARY

1. What do *gritty* (para. 1) and *grit* (para. 2) mean? What is the literal meaning of the noun? Why does Krikorian put the adjective in quotation marks?
2. Explain the word *transnationalism* as Krikorian uses it in paragraph 1. How does your dictionary define it? What does the prefix *trans-* mean in the word? Give another example of this prefix at use in the essay.

RESPONDING TO WORDS IN CONTEXT

1. What does Krikorian mean by our *decadence* in paragraph 3? What is the dictionary definition of the word, and how is it used here?
2. What are the various meanings of the word *parasite* (para. 4)? Which meaning is at work in Krikorian's piece?

DISCUSSING MAIN POINT AND MEANING

1. Why, according to Krikorian, is the labor of recent immigrants "of relatively little worth" (para. 5)? How does Jacoby's position differ?
2. What is the "moral miasma" to which Krikorian refers in paragraph 5? Why are new immigrants unique in having to deal with it?

EXAMINING SENTENCES, PARAGRAPHS, AND ORGANIZATION

1. How does Krikorian tie the end of his essay to its beginning by referencing "our ancestors a century ago" (para. 4)? How do these ancestors provide a thematic backdrop to the entire essay?
2. Why is paragraph 3 so much shorter than the other paragraphs in this brief essay? What effect is Krikorian going for, and why did he select that paragraph to deploy it?

THINKING CRITICALLY

1. Discuss the ways Krikorian's statistics clash with Jacoby's. What is the major issue on which their respective numbers disagree? Whose are you more inclined to believe? Why?
2. Do you think Krikorian's characterization of the societies immigrants are coming from as "pre industrial" (para. 4) is accurate? Or is it an exaggeration? What exactly does the word mean? (Look it up online if you're not sure.) Which societies does he have in mind? How reliant is his argument on the premise that these societies are in fact pre-industrial?

IN-CLASS WRITING ACTIVITIES

1. Notice that Krikorian's essay uses the word "we" (para. 5) to mean non-immigrants—he assumes there are no migrant workers or undocumented aliens reading his argument. Do you think this is a reasonable assumption? Is it a fair one? How do you think his essay, and Jacoby's, would be different if they were writing directly for the immigrants they are writing about?
2. Weigh in on the debate yourself. Do immigrants work harder than native-born citizens in this country? Do they add to or subtract from the nation's total work ethic and output? Is your opinion based on facts, anecdotes, impressions, or some combination? Do you even feel qualified to give a definite answer? Why or why not?

Vicente Martinez

The Crossing

[*Oregon Humanities*, Fall/Winter 2009]

BEFORE YOU READ

Does the often atrocious experience of crossing the border illegally change the way you feel about illegal immigration?

WORDS TO LEARN

inconspicuous (para. 12): not very visible (adjective).
verified (para. 16): made sure (verb).
vulnerable (para. 19): easy to harm (adjective).
traversing (para. 23): traveling across (verb).
hunched (para. 25): crouched with shoulders up (verb).
inclement (para. 29): unpleasant (adjective).
dire (para. 30): serious (adjective).
initially (para. 34): at first (adverb).
potable (para. 35): drinkable (adjective).
wiring (para. 38): sending by telegraph (verb).

On Wednesday, February 4, 2009, I said goodbye to my family. I didn't want to leave, but the thought of getting sick was often on my mind. 1

I'd been looking for work since arriving in Las Calandrias in October. But the economy was in terrible shape, and I wasn't an ideal job candidate. I couldn't do hard labor with my health condition, and I was too old to be considered for most jobs; the cut-off was typically forty, and I was forty-one. I hoped my English language skills might help me find a job with a company that needed bilingual people in Guadalajara — the capital of Jalisco state, where my family lives — but my application was turned down. Ironically, it was far easier for me to find work as an undocumented worker in Portland than as a legal citizen in Mexico. 2

According to Oregon Humanities: *"This essay, adapted from a longer unpublished work, chronicles the fifth border crossing to the United States by Vicente Martinez (a pseudonym).* Oregon Humanities *magazine editorial advisory board member Camela Raymond worked with Martinez on editing this essay for publication. Some names and details have been changed."*

To control my HIV, I needed a regular supply of medicine and periodic blood tests. I could get these for free at a clinic in Portland, but here in Mexico, although I could get my medicine free of charge at a local hospital, I had to pay for my own lab work — 500 pesos every three months. Even if I found a full-time job, which seemed increasingly unlikely, this would be difficult to afford. Minimum wage was 700 pesos a week, barely enough to get by. 3

That Wednesday around noon, I found my mother sitting on her bed. I told her I was going to leave, and she began to cry. The sight of her tears broke my heart. We'd last seen each other almost eighteen years ago, and this recent reunion had lasted only three and a half months. I couldn't tell her the real reason I was leaving. I'd never told my parents I had HIV. I didn't want them to worry. If they knew, they would assume I was suffering; they wouldn't understand that the medicine I was taking would keep me healthy for some time. 4

I kissed my mother, and she kissed me. I assured her that my trip across the border would be easier than it was the first time, when I was twenty-four and walked for days without food. Then I said goodbye to my eighty-one-year old father, who was also very close to crying. It hurt me to leave him, alone and sad. 5

To pay the *coyote*,[1] I'd sold the truck I'd driven from Portland (I'd hoped to give it to my parents, who were one of the few families in Las Calandrias that didn't have a car). So my younger brother Andres drove me to the bus stop about ten miles away in Santa Cruz in our brother Manuel's old car, which broke down all the time. Also with us was Felipe, a young guy in his late twenties, also from Las Calandrias, who was going to cross with me. On the highway at the edge of Santa Cruz, I said goodbye to Andres and told him to behave. 6

Friday morning, after nearly two days on the road, Felipe and I arrived at the Tijuana bus station. I found a pay phone and called Pedro, the *coyote* I'd met in Las Calandrias. About thirty minutes later Pedro pulled up in a white van and took us to his house, which was in a different part of town, on a hill near some railroad tracks. Three dogs guarded the front door from inside a small, walled patio. 7

The house was old, but in decent shape. One guy was sleeping on the living room sofa, another in one of the two bedrooms. Counting Felipe and me, that made four *pollos*[2]— chickens waiting for the *coyote* to take us across. 8

---

[1] *coyote* (para. 6): A smuggler who ferries immigrants across the border from Mexico illegally, usually for a large fee.

---

[2] *pollos* (para. 8): Spanish for "chickens."

I called my cousin Luis in Escondido, California. His wife, Sofia, a U.S. citizen, agreed to drive down to Tijuana and meet me later that night. She'd take the $2,500 I'd set aside to pay the *coyote*, along with my Oregon driver's license and some other important documents, and hold everything in Escondido until I was safely across. 9

Pedro left for a couple of hours and came back loaded with food. He had to attend a funeral in his hometown, he said, and would be gone for two days. Meantime, the four of us would have plenty to eat and were free to do whatever we wanted. This was unfortunate news, but I wasn't too worried; it felt safe at Pedro's house, and I trusted he'd be back. 10

Pedro was supposed to be back on Sunday. On Monday, he still hadn't returned. On Tuesday evening, an associate of Pedro's in his early fifties arrived at the house. He didn't introduce himself, but the dogs knew him; later I found out he was Pedro's stepfather. He told us to get our things. It was time to cross over. 11

Twenty minutes later we arrived at a residential street, not far from the main gate. Pedro's stepfather led us to an inconspicuous spot between two houses. The plan was to cross the border through an underground sewer tunnel; the entrance to the tunnel was being guarded by several border control cars, visible in the near distance. We were to wait here until they moved. 12

Hours went by, and the cars didn't move — unsurprising, I thought. Finally, at about ten-thirty at night, Pedro's stepfather let us have a break. He led us to an abandoned house a few blocks away, gave us a blanket (one for all four of us), and said he'd be back the following morning with food. He left a dog guarding the entrance. 13

I slept for a few hours. It was cold, and there was no working toilet or any running water in the house. In the morning, before Pedro's stepfather returned, I convinced the others to leave. Using some pieces of metal and wood lying in the yard, I trapped the dog against the house. We walked a few blocks to a commercial area, hailed a taxi, and drove back to Pedro's house. His stepfather showed up later, surprised we'd escaped. 14

By Thursday, we had been at Pedro's house for almost a week. Though it felt safe there, it was becoming apparent we were wasting our time. Reluctantly, we decided to go downtown and look for another *coyote*. Within a couple of hours, we found one near the main gate — a tall, chubby guy who called himself Sonora, after the Mexican state. His price was US$1,800, cheaper than Pedro. 15

Sonora's operation moved quickly. Once we got to his house, the *coyotes* (there were two, including Sonora, who appeared to be the big bosses) immediately asked for the phone numbers of our contacts in the 16

United States and verified they'd pick us up and pay our crossing fees. A little later they brought us three blankets to share, roasted chicken for lunch, and more food to take on the road: for each person, two cans of tuna, a loaf of bread, some refried beans, and two bottles of water.

That night, we were taken in a pickup truck to a street corner in Tijuana, where five more *pollos* joined us. An hour or so later, a first-class bus, with a sign that read "Bienvenidos" and flashing lights, arrived. All nine of us, plus a guide, boarded. Soon we arrived at an isolated stretch of highway just east of the city of Tecate, where the driver pulled over. 17

The guide led us across the highway. We walked in single file, carrying no flashlights, which would attract attention, just knapsacks holding our food and blankets. We passed a small village, went through some bushes, and climbed over a five-foot chicken-wire fence. Mostly, though, the terrain was flat and empty. After about four hours, the guide stopped, and we all lay down on the ground and attempted to sleep. 18

Moments later it got very cold, and before long, we were all shaking. Four of us shared three blankets, but the remaining guys had nothing to keep them warm. One of them asked if we'd share ours, but I said no. Though I felt bad refusing him, he was young and healthy; I was older and more vulnerable to getting sick. 19

My body became so cold that night that I thought I wouldn't make it to morning. I spent the hours praying to God, telling Him that if it was my turn to go, He should go ahead and take me. But at the same time, I asked Him to spare me: I had promised my mother I would survive the trip without harm, and the thought that I might die that night filled me with sadness. 20

My body became so cold that night that I thought I wouldn't make it to morning.

Sometime in the middle of the night, the guide stood up and said it was time to get moving again. Before we started walking, though, he asked us to hand over our blankets. With a knife, he cut the three blankets into nine pieces, handing one to each of us. 21

It felt better once we started walking and my body grew warm again. The going was quite easy for a while, with flat ground dotted sparsely with tall bushes. But soon we came to a sign warning of an approaching decline, and we descended into a canyon. At the bottom, the guide told us to wait while he climbed the slope on the other side. He stood at the top of the canyon for at least a half hour, scanning the hills ahead for signs of border patrol — and, perhaps, for *bajadores,* the Mexican bandits who often rob border crossers. Beyond the hills, in the far distance, I could see vehicle lights flashing. 22

After crossing the canyon, we came to a dirt road. The guide asked for our blankets and laid them down on the road so that we wouldn't leave footprints. Then we continued on unmarked terrain, traversing a hill and another canyon. When dawn broke, the guide pointed to some large boulders atop a nearby hill. He was going to go on some unexplained mission. We were to hide among the boulders until he returned. 23

Some hours later the wind began to blow, and I started to shiver again. I pulled a big plastic garbage bag, which the guide had given me, over my entire body, but the wind kept seeping through. Morning passed, then afternoon, and we didn't move except in order to urinate near the edge of the rocks. Some of the others were able to fall asleep, but I couldn't. 24

The guide had given us a code word, and at dusk, we heard him yelling it, and we swiftly packed up our things. Then we continued to walk. We passed over a couple of hills, heading toward the lights of a small town. Suddenly the guide stopped, turned around, and led us back to the top of the nearest hill. We hunched down. I could see people with flashlights, INS[3] agents, combing an area below us. Moments later it started to rain, and we all got inside our plastic bags. After a while the agents left, and we started walking again. 25

We passed straight through the town, avoiding the streets and walking instead through people's yards, climbing over several fences, until we reached a highway marked State Route 94. This indicated not only that we were in U.S. territory, but also that we were nearing the road, Highway 8, where we'd be picked up and delivered to safety. 26

We continued climbing the hills, very high hills this time. My legs almost gave out, but I kept moving. At dawn of the second day we stopped near another large rock. Thankfully, on this day the sun came out. We spent the whole warm, bright day in the shade of the big rock, dozing fitfully, drying out our socks, and eating a little of the remaining food we'd brought. 27

At dusk we started walking again. About four hours later, in the middle of the night, we finally reached Highway 8. We crossed beneath the above-grade roadway through a large drainage tunnel, and as we headed for a grassy shoulder on the other side, the guide ordered the guy at the back of the line to use his piece of blanket to erase the footprints we were leaving in the dirt. Then we proceeded west alongside the freeway, crouching down every time a car passed, until we reached a road sign that marked the place the *coyotes* were supposed to pick us up. 28

---

[3] INS (para. 25): Immigration and Naturalization Services, the federal agency in charge of border patrol.

The guide had already called them on his cell phone. Within moments, a pickup truck arrived. Instead of taking us away in his truck, however, the driver only dropped off some food. We wouldn't be picked up until it rained, our guide explained. According to him, there was an INS checkpoint on the freeway that we had to pass through, and it would probably shut down in inclement weather. 29

We spent the night very close to the freeway. Since the road was built on a high concrete foundation, we weren't visible to the passing cars. Still, there was nothing, not even a rock or a tree, to provide shelter from the cold, and the temperature dropped so low that, once again, all of us shivered badly. The cold made me extremely thirsty, but I had less than a medium-size bottle of water left, and the pickup driver had dropped off only one additional gallon of water for all of us. Sometime in the middle of the night, I took a sip from my bottle, and pieces of ice hit my tongue. I thought I might die from cold again that night; I even planned out how I'd run to the freeway and ask for help if things became truly dire. 30

Before dawn, we moved slightly away from the freeway and lay down under a big tree. Later we moved farther away, hiding in some bushes. There we spent the day, eating a bit of the food left over from what the driver had dropped. 31

Night came, and still we were stranded. Once the rain started, the driver would come, the guide repeated. 32

We were all becoming angry. "What if it doesn't rain for a week?" we said to each other. "Are we going to be stuck here in the cold the whole time, with no food and water?" 33

The *coyotes* had initially told us the entire trip would require only six hours of walking. This estimate wasn't ridiculously far off — we'd spent no more than about ten hours on our feet — but it didn't account for the fact that we'd be walking over a period of three days, and that during that time we wouldn't have enough food, water, and warm clothing. If we died of hypothermia, the *coyotes* wouldn't care, though. They'd just be out a few cans of tuna. The guide was the only one working for his money, and he was clueless; in fact, he was smoking weed day and night. 34

The following day, just before dawn, the guide took our empty bottles and asked one of the other *pollos* to help him fetch some water. When they returned, we drank greedily. We weren't sure where the water came from — presumably some nearby stream — or whether it was potable, but at least it quenched our thirst. 35

Suddenly, a light rain began to fall, and within moments, the guide received a call alerting us that we'd soon be picked up. Once a second call came through, we moved right up beside the freeway, a tall cyclone fence 36 between us and the pavement. When the pickup truck arrived, the same one that had dropped the food the night before, we all jumped the fence and scrambled in. A couple of guys took seats in the cab, and the rest of us lay flat in the open bed. The driver took off speeding.

Within about thirty minutes, we arrived at a house in San Diego. The house was full of people — a group of ten additional border crossers had just arrived; they'd used a route farther east, braving tall hills and snow to avoid the INS checkpoint. The nine from our group were put in the garage. The coyotes brought us plates of warm food — rice, beans, eggs, and tortillas — and immediately began calling our contacts to make arrangements to drop us off. Meantime, they made sure we didn't escape before paying; whenever we used the bathroom, we had to remove our shoes, so as not to be tempted to leave the house through the small bathroom window. 37

It was agreed that instead of wiring my payment, my cousin Luis would pay the *coyotes* in cash once they dropped me at his apartment in Escondido thirty minutes away; I wanted to make sure the *coyotes* really got me all the way there. Before long only four other guys and I were left, and the pickup truck returned for us. Since it was dark, we were allowed to sit upright in the truck bed, but we had to cover our heads with a blanket until we reached the freeway; this, I think, was to prevent us from learning precisely where the *coyotes* lived. 38

We arrived in Escondido, Luis handed over my $1,800, and I was free. Sofia made us a nice, big dinner. It felt good to be with them; Luis was the son of my father's departed sister, and Sofia and I had always been naturally fond of each other. 39

That was Monday night, and I needed to be in Huron, about three hundred miles away, by Wednesday. From there, another cousin would drive me to the Sacramento bus station, where I'd catch a Greyhound to Portland. 40

Tuesday night, Luis and I started out for Huron. The INS checkpoint on Highway 15 didn't ordinarily inspect vehicles, but the traffic started slowing down as we approached the station. We had already passed a couple of INS cars stopped by the side of the road, and Luis, not wishing to take any chances, turned back home. But we immediately returned to the same route, this time with Sofia driving about a mile ahead. Once she passed the checkpoint, she called and reported that it was clear, and Luis and I drove on. 41

That night I stayed with Luis's sister in Huron, and the following evening, my nineteen-year-old nephew Marcos drove me to Sacramento, where yet another cousin gave me a ride to the bus station. 42

The ticket clerks were checking everyone's ID, but when I got to the front of the line, the woman behind the counter noted my Mexican 43 appearance and turned to another female employee. "Do I sell him a ticket?" she asked. "Go ahead," the other woman replied. It was a kind favor, though I had a valid Oregon driver's license in my wallet.

I arrived in the beautiful city of Portland, Oregon, on Thursday afternoon, February 19, 2009. I felt like I was home. 44

VOCABULARY/USING A DICTIONARY

1. What is the meaning of the word *isolated* (para. 17)? What language does the word come from, and what does its root word mean in that language?
2. Define *seep* (para. 24). What part of speech is it, and what is its origin? What is usually described as "seeping"?
3. What is the origin of the word *hypothermia* (para. 34)? What does the prefix *hypo-* mean?

RESPONDING TO WORDS IN CONTEXT

1. What is a *commercial* area (para. 14)? What does the word *commercial* mean, and what does this usage contrast the area with? How is this meaning related to other senses of the word you're familiar with?
2. What exactly does *terrain* mean as Martinez uses it in paragraph 18? How does its meaning differ from *land* or *earth*?
3. What is the meaning of the word *shoulder* in paragraph 28?

DISCUSSING MAIN POINT AND MEANING

1. What specific factors does Martinez mention that make his story especially moving? List three things that made the crossing harder for him than it would be for the typical immigrant.
2. How does Martinez characterize the *coyotes* throughout the essay? What is the picture of these men and their motives you get when Martinez writes "they'd just be out a few cans of tuna" (para. 34)? What other scenes reinforce this characterization?
3. Why was Martinez's head covered with a blanket on the last leg of his journey? Why is this detail important?

EXAMINING SENTENCES, PARAGRAPHS, AND ORGANIZATION

1. Martinez describes much of the landscape of his trip in great detail, as in paragraph 22: "The going was quite easy for a while, with flat ground dotted sparsely with tall bushes." Why does he attempt to paint such a vivid picture of the physical environment he crossed? What effect is this intended to have on the reader?
2. Martinez never breaks from the narrative form in this essay — he never once mentions his opinion on immigration reform, for instance, or

describes what he thinks should be done to improve the condition of undocumented people in the United States. Why is the narrative form of his essay important? Do you think it would be more or less effective if he advanced an argument or used more varied rhetorical forms? Why?

THINKING CRITICALLY

1. Martinez refers to himself as an "undocumented worker" (para. 2), a term used as an alternative to "illegal immigrant." What does each term imply, and why do you think Martinez prefers the first? Which one do you think should be used in most cases, and why?
2. Discuss the activity of the INS as depicted in Martinez's story. How is he trying to characterize their activity? What do you think of the checkpoints they set up on the highway? Do you think that they effectively police the community and enforce the law, or might their presence lead to something more sinister?
3. How does Martinez paint the immigrant community along the Pacific Coast? How does this image fit with your preconceptions of communities of Latin American immigrants in the United States?

IN-CLASS WRITING ACTIVITIES

1. Analyze Martinez's writing style. Is it flowery or plain? Does he attempt to set a visual scene or to make you think about the internal lives of his characters? Pick out an episode or a detail that you especially liked and analyze why it was so effective.
2. Tell another story of crossing over into America — it can be your ancestors', your parents', a friend's, or your own. Take a cue from Martinez and be vivid in your details, even if you're relying on your imagination. Consider as you write what's different about your story and what similarities all immigrant tales have in common.
3. Did reading Martinez's story change the way you think about illegal immigration and migrant workers at all? If so, explain in a brief essay how so. If not, explain your thoughts on undocumented workers and why they held firm against (or with) Martinez's narrative.

Luis J. Rodríguez

Slurring Spanish

[*The Progressive*, March 2010]

BEFORE YOU READ

What do you think of bilingual education? Should students in American schools who speak another language be encouraged to learn English, to grow in their native language, or both?

WORDS TO LEARN

deficit (para. 2): something that is insufficient; a disadvantage (noun).
marginalized (para. 5): made to feel or seem unimportant (adjective).
phenomenon (para. 6): situation or set of events (noun).
barrios (para. 6): Latin American neighborhoods (noun).
fluent (para. 11): able to speak a language with ease and perfect accuracy (adjective).
citing (para. 11): using as evidence (verb).
rescinded (para. 11): took back (verb).
garnered (para. 16): gained (verb).

In 1960, I entered first grade at 109th Street School in Watts[1] speaking only Spanish. I was pushed from one classroom to another. When I finally found a teacher to accept me, I was placed in a corner and told to play with blocks. This lasted for a year. Whenever I spoke Spanish in the classroom or playground, I was yelled at and sometimes swatted. 1

Speaking Spanish, which could have been a valuable tool in my learning, in grasping a new language, in having a healthy social life, instead became a handicap, a social burden, one of the many "deficits" I encountered in my school life during the 1960s and early 1970s. 2

You would think that after years of activism around the country, which secured bilingual education, multicultural curriculums, and a 3

[1] Watts (para. 1): A neighborhood of Los Angeles.

An award-winning poet, novelist, and journalist, Luis J. Rodríguez is a regular contributor to The Progressive, *where "Slurring Spanish" first appeared. An active gang member in his youth, he published his memoir* Always Running: La Vida Loca: Gang Days in L.A. *in 1993. He is also well-known for his successful writing workshops.*

semblance of cultural and racial equity, that this kind of thing wouldn't happen anymore.

But it does. 4

Today, Spanish speakers still remain highly marginalized in most 5
U.S. schools.

Mayra Zaragoza is a nineteen-year-old recent high school graduate. Although 6
Mayra was born in the United States, both her parents spoke only Spanish. Mayra didn't learn English until later, a phenomenon quite common in barrios such as Pacoima in the San Fernando Valley,[2] where she grew up.

"I suffered a lot, and I still suffer now, from starting school with 7
Spanish as my first language," Mayra says. "Spelling and grammar are my biggest weaknesses. At one point, all I wanted to speak was English because I was told in school 'If you only speak English, you will get better at it.'"

Speaking Spanish does not have to be a crisis in the United States.

This made Mayra see Spanish as some- 8
thing bad, something inferior, something that labeled her as a problem student.

In my travels and talks in schools all 9
over the country, Spanish-speaking children are often seen as trouble. Many are forced into speaking English as quickly as possible, often by threat of punishment. Under these kinds of pressures, however, most students don't get good at Spanish or English.

"It's wrong to target Spanish-speaking kids as 'at-risk' only because 10
of their language," Mayra says. "It first happened to me in my English class where I was told to speak only English."

Zach Rubio, sixteen, was suspended in 2005 from a Kansas City school 11
for speaking Spanish. Rubio, a fluent English speaker, apparently said "*no problema*"[3] (often used by English speakers as slang) after a friend asked to borrow money between classes. The school principal promptly suspended Rubio, citing a policy she instituted to outlaw Spanish in the school. The school district, however, rescinded the suspension and the policy, stating that speaking a foreign language was no grounds for suspension, especially outside a classroom.

But I've heard from other students that such punishments continue in 12
their schools.

Speaking Spanish does not have to be a crisis in the United States, 13
which is already the fifth-largest Spanish-speaking country in the world,

---

[2] San Fernando Valley (para. 6): Part of Southern California made up chiefly of Los Angeles.

[3] *no problema* (para. 11): No problem.

with about forty million speakers. Spanish-language speakers can learn English and still maintain their Spanish, a process that favors both languages. But with "English Only" laws, school suspensions, and the derailment of bilingual education programs, Spanish is again being devalued and people who speak it discriminated against.

The ramifications are that millions of school-age children in this country think something is wrong with them for speaking Spanish — the way I felt around fifty years ago. 14

"Culture and roots are important to teach in our schools," Mayra says. "When a Spanish-speaking teenager falls into becoming a social statistic this is mainly due to not having a positive self-identity, of not knowing what their true selves really are. The end result is often drugs, gangs, or violence." 15

With great effort, and despite what schools did to me in my youth, I spent most of my adult life dominating English as well as improving my Spanish. Since then my language skills have garnered me fourteen books in poetry, children's literature, fiction, and nonfiction. I've worked for newspapers and radio. And I'm a regularly requested speaker on campuses, conferences, events, and more. Although the vast majority of my writing and talks are in English, I speak Spanish whenever possible. 16

Today, I wish I could show my books and other recognition to the many teachers I had growing up who told me far too often that I'd "never amount to anything." 17

Again I defer to the wisdom of Mayra Zaragoza. 18

"A bilingual society is needed because we now have more people that speak different languages in this country than ever before — and we all deserve the same opportunity and support as English-only speakers," she declares. "I say we should give more support to classes and workshops that help with bettering our English as well as allowing us to master Spanish." 19

Many countries around the world place great importance on the skill of speaking more than one language. Why shouldn't this be true of the United States, as well? 20

To speak two or more languages. . . . *No problema!* 21

VOCABULARY/USING A DICTIONARY

1. What is the origin of the word *curriculum* (para. 3)? What has the word come to mean today?
2. What does the prefix in the word *bilingual* (para. 3) mean? Find two other words that share this prefix and define them.
3. Define the word *ramifications* (para. 14). What part of speech is it? What verb is it related to?

RESPONDING TO WORDS IN CONTEXT

1. Define the word *multicultural* (para. 3) and explain its origin. Based on the way Rodríguez uses the word, do you think he regards it as a good or a bad way to describe something?
2. What does the word *derailment* mean as Rodríguez uses it in paragraph 13? Where does the term come from, and what process is he referring to here?
3. What does Mayra mean when she refers to "becoming a social statistic" (para. 15)? What exactly does the word *statistic* mean and imply here?

DISCUSSING MAIN POINT AND MEANING

1. What general disciplinary practice does Rodríguez criticize as deeply flawed though widespread in America's schools? What does he say is wrong with it?
2. What attitude does Rodríguez think the American school system instills in students? Why? What does he argue can be done about this?
3. What argument does Rodríguez offer that suggests he believes bilingual education would benefit English as well as Spanish speakers?

EXAMINING SENTENCES, PARAGRAPHS, AND ORGANIZATION

1. The first two sections of the essay begin with narratives, the first Rodríguez's own story, the second that of Mayra Zaragoza. Why does the author structure the opening of his essay in this way? What larger point is he trying to get across by placing these two stories together?
2. Four paragraphs in this essay are almost completely made up of quotations from Mayra. Identify these paragraphs. Why does Rodríguez put so much of the essay directly in Mayra's voice?
3. What is the impact of ending with the phrase *no problema*? How does it tie the essay together, and what effect does it have on the overall tone of the essay?

THINKING CRITICALLY

1. Do you agree that schools should encourage students who speak primarily Spanish—or any other language, for that matter—to grow in their knowledge of their native language and culture? Why or why not?
2. What evidence does Rodríguez give of his own success, despite the school system he was raised in? What do you think of Rodríguez's measure of success? Does he mean to hold himself up as an example of something every Spanish-speaking student in the United States should strive for? How would you judge the ultimate success of an immigrant who comes

to his or her adopted country without knowing the language? Should the standard of success be lower than that for native speakers and citizens? Why or why not?

3. Rodríguez mentions that other countries "place great importance on the skill of speaking more than one language" (para. 20). Look up an example of a country that does so. What factors, if any, are present in that country that make it more conducive to using multiple languages than in America? Could the United States ever really be a multilingual country? Why or why not?

IN-CLASS WRITING ACTIVITIES

1. What are the major arguments *against* bilingual education? Research them online if you need to. List three arguments that proponents of English-only education in American schools might offer, and explain how Rodríguez would likely answer each one.
2. Rodríguez writes poignantly that "speaking Spanish, which could have been a valuable tool in my learning, in grasping a new language, in having a healthy social life, instead became a handicap, a social burden, one of the many 'deficits' I encountered in my school life" (para. 2). Think of another example—not involving language—in which something that should have been an advantage became a social burden to you or someone you knew. Describe what happened and how it felt.
3. Look into some of the "English Only" laws Rodríguez references in paragraph 13. What motivates these laws? Are they sincerely set up to improve the efficiency of society, or is there perhaps a hidden racial element behind them? Write a short essay defending or attacking a hypothetically proposed "English Only" law in your community.

Elyse Toplin (student essay)

Uniting Families

[*The Hullabaloo*, Tulane University, January 29, 2010]

BEFORE YOU READ

Should citizenship be automatically extended to the partners of LGBT citizens? What about to the straight ones?

WORDS TO LEARN

visa (para. 2): a temporary allowance for an immigrant to live or work in a country legally (noun).

contingent (para. 5): depending on (adjective).

unfounded (para. 7): without any reason (adjective).

comprehensive (para. 9): complete (adjective).

In his State of the Union address Wednesday night [January 27, 2010], President Barack Obama said, "We should continue the work of fixing our broken immigration system . . . and ensure that everyone who plays by the rules can contribute to our economy and enrich our nation." A problem in the LGBT [lesbian, gay, bisexual, and transgender] community is a great example of where we can start. Under current laws, gay citizens aren't allowed to transfer citizenship to immigrant spouses like straight couples. This is an example of "our broken immigration system" and the passage of the Uniting American Families Act would be a great first step to fix it. 1

Meet Gordon Stewart. Stewart is an American citizen who currently lives in the United Kingdom with his partner of more than nine years, Renato. Renato lived with Stewart in 2003 while he was studying in the United States, but had to return to his home in Brazil when his visa expired. He was unable to get it renewed, and Stewart could not sponsor his partner because they were not married or otherwise related. 2

After years of continuing their relationship on two continents, the couple decided to move to the United Kingdom, where they could live 3

Elyse Toplin is a junior at Tulane University. At The Hullabaloo *she is a member of the managing editorial board and serves as the chief copyeditor of the paper.*

together. However, in his testimony before Congress in June, Stewart (who traveled to testify alone because Renato is still unable to get so much as a tourist visa to the United States) explained the reality of this situation.

4 "I am furious that we can not visit or live together in the U.S.," Stewart said. "Despite the fact that I am a tax-paying, law-abiding and voting citizen, I feel discrimination from my government. . . . I would like to be able to come home; I should have the right to come with my partner to visit or to live; but we can't."

"Despite the fact that I am a tax-paying, law-abiding and voting citizen, I feel discrimination from my government."

5 Sadly, Stewart's story is not unique. Shirley Tan, whose stay in the United States is currently contingent on the existence of a private bill by Senators Dianne Feinstein and Barbara Boxer, is dealing with the same situation, and faces deportation to the Philippines if the Uniting American Families Act does not pass while the 111th Congress is in session. Tan has lived in the United States for more than two decades, and she and her partner [Jay Mercado] have two sons. The family goes to church, the parents are involved in the school, and the kids get good grades. Essentially, they are exactly the type of person that most Americans would want in this country. However, because Tan and Mercado cannot get married, Mercado cannot sponsor Tan for citizenship.

6 The Uniting American Families Act would right these injustices, as well as rescue the lives of thousands of Americans who risk deportation because they cannot get married. UAFA would change the wording of the Immigration and Nationality Act, adding the words "permanent partner" and "permanent partnership" after the words "spouse" and "marriage" to relevant parts of the bill. This would allow immigrants who are in long-term committed relationships to have a pathway to citizenship in the same way that heterosexual couples can, and those who violate the law would face the same penalties as their heterosexual counterparts, including up to five years imprisonment or a fine of $250,000.

7 Though some may think that fraud would increase with the passage of UAFA, it is not unfounded to believe that many homosexual couples could prove — just as their heterosexual counterparts can — that they are part of a committed, long-term relationship. After Renato was denied entry to the United States, for example, Stewart commuted to Brazil from New York every other weekend for more than a year. When the financial burden of this task became too much to bear, the couple moved to England, where they could still be together. Though most heterosexual

couples are never asked to do things this extreme, the strength of their commitment is never questioned.

The United States would not be unique in providing immigration rights for homosexuals with the passage of UAFA. Eighteen countries have similar laws, and these countries include Australia, Canada, Israel, the United Kingdom, Spain, South Africa, Germany, and France. 8

UAFA has been introduced in every Congress since 2000, and has never made it out of the Senate Judiciary Committee.[1] This bill affects far too many people for it to fail again, and must either pass on its own or be included in any comprehensive immigration reforms considered by the 111th Congress. 9

Gordon Stewart is an American citizen. He votes in elections, abides by laws, and pays taxes from abroad. As such, he is guaranteed the unalienable rights of life, liberty, and the pursuit of happiness. So is Jay Mercado, Shirley Tan's partner of over twenty years. Neither of them, however, will have the right to the pursuit of happiness until the passage of the Uniting American Families Act. 10

VOCABULARY/USING A DICTIONARY

1. What is the origin of the word *deportation* (para. 6)?
2. What do the prefixes *homo-* and *hetero-* mean in *homosexual* and *heterosexual*? Give another example of a pair of English words with these prefixes.

RESPONDING TO WORDS IN CONTEXT

1. Explain the meaning of *introduced* as Toplin uses it in paragraph 9. What kind of context is it used in, and what does it mean in that context?
2. To what is Toplin alluding when she refers to the couples' "unalienable rights of life, liberty, and the pursuit of happiness" (para. 10)? Look up the phrase if it's not familiar. How does this reference strengthen her point?

DISCUSSING MAIN POINT AND MEANING

1. Explain what Toplin means by "fraud" in paragraph 7. How might some people use legislation such as UAFA to perpetrate fraud?
2. What is the point of listing countries with similar laws in paragraph 8? How does this list add to Toplin's argument?

---

[1] Senate Judiciary Committee (para. 9): A standing committee, or special group, of U.S. senators that considers bills related to judicial matters; to "make it out" of the committee means a proposal gets a vote in the full Senate.

EXAMINING SENTENCES, PARAGRAPHS, AND ORGANIZATION

1. Discuss the transition between the first two paragraphs. What is the function of the first sentence of paragraph 2, and how does it shift the focus and strategy of the essay? Do you think it's an effective way to begin the essay?
2. Why does Toplin mention, of Shirley Tan's family, that "the family goes to church, the parents are involved in the school, and the kids get good grades" (para. 5)? What does she mean to communicate about the family with this sentence?
3. Identify a point in the essay in which Toplin brings up a counterargument and answers it. What case does she anticipate opponents of UAFA will bring up? How does she respond? How does bringing the issue up improve the argumentative force of her essay?

THINKING CRITICALLY

1. Toplin appeals to our sense of equal rights for gay and lesbian couples, but never questions the fundamental idea that the partner of a citizen should get citizenship rights. Do you think this widely accepted notion is right? What are some possible arguments against extending citizenship to any foreign spouses of citizens—gay or straight? How do you come down on these arguments, and why?
2. How does Toplin characterize the various gay couples she mentions (like Gordon Stewart and Renato)? What image do you have of these couples? Why is this image important to Toplin's essay?
3. Does Toplin's argument presume that gay marriage should be legal? Are you for or against gay marriage? Why? Do you think it's possible to accept Toplin's premise that gay couples deserve the same protections straight couples get when it comes to immigration without believing in gay marriage? Why or why not?

IN-CLASS WRITING ACTIVITIES

1. One of the problems this essay touches on is how immigration authorities can separate couples in "long-term committed relationships" (para. 6) from those attempting to defraud the system and gain citizenship with a phony relationship. Write an essay describing some of the problems you imagine authorities have making this distinction. What solution, or set of solutions, would you propose to the challenges?
2. Toplin introduces the UAFA as a "great example of where we can start" fixing the immigration system (para. 1). What else do you think President Obama means when he says he wants to give everyone who is law-abiding a chance to "contribute to our economy and enrich our nation"? Give a few examples of immigration reforms you think would improve our system and our economy.

LOOKING CLOSELY

The Art of Argument — Anticipating Opposition

When you take a position you think will be unpopular or controversial, an effective strategy is to anticipate the opposition you may receive. In this way, you indicate that you have thought carefully about your position, and you make it more difficult for those who resist your argument to reject your claims outright. In nearly all effective argument and debate, the writer or speaker will attempt to preempt arguments likely to be made by the other side by dealing with them first. This doesn't mean, of course, that you have answered those opposing arguments satisfactorily, but it does mean that the opposing side will need to take into account your awareness of its position.

In "Uniting Families," Tulane University student Elyse Toplin realizes that one objection readers may have to her position on the Uniting American Families Act is that the legislation, if passed, could open the door to fraud — that is, people might lie about the strength of a relationship to gain citizenship. That is why she acknowledges this possibility directly in paragraph 7. By mentioning that "some may think that fraud would increase with the passage of UAFA," she shows she is aware of this opposing argument. She then answers the objection by saying that same-sex relationships can be as committed as those of heterosexuals and uses her earlier example of such a relationship to reinforce her point.

1
Toplin anticipates the argument that opponents of her position may make

Though some may think that fraud would increase with the passage of UAFA, it is not unfounded to believe that many homosexual couples could prove — just as their heterosexual counterparts can — that they are part of a committed, long-term relationship. (1) After Renato was denied entry to the United States, for example, Stewart commuted to Brazil from New York every other weekend for more than a year. When the financial burden of this task became too much to bear, the couple moved to England, where they could still be together. Though most heterosexual couples are never asked to do things this extreme, the strength of their commitment is never questioned.

STUDENT WRITER AT WORK

Elyse Toplin

On Writing "Uniting Families"

RA. What inspired you to write this essay? And publish it in your campus paper?

ET. I was inspired to write this essay after attending a hearing on UAFA for my summer internship at the Hebrew Immigrant Aid Society in 2009. The hearing, where I heard testimony from Shirley Tan and Gordon Stewart, made me aware of the challenges faced by LGBT couples as they navigate our complicated immigration system. Publication in the campus newspaper was almost by accident. I had written the essay for a class and then showed it to one of my friends on the newspaper, who then showed it to an editor, and he decided to publish it that week.

RA. What response have you received to this piece? Has the feedback you have received affected your views on the topic you wrote about?

ET. I received many positive responses after the article was published online. I was told that it was the only "Views" article that the *Hullabaloo* has ever run that received only positive feedback. The article was also picked up by several blogs, and many people responded to the article with their own stories. The feedback strengthened my opinion that the United States has a flawed immigration policy that needs to be changed.

RA. How long did it take for you to write this piece? Did you revise your work? What were your goals as you revised?

ET. I wrote the original essay for my class in a few hours, and then I revised it to make the point stronger and to adhere to the 750-word limit that my professor had included in the assignment. Once we decided to include the article in the paper, I revised it again and rewrote the introduction, and then the article was further revised before the newspaper was published. My goals while revising were to make my point stronger and more coherent, and I rewrote the introduction to make it more relevant to the student readers. I did this by tying in the recent State of the Union address.

RA. What magazines and newspapers do you like to read?

ET. The magazines and newspapers I read the most frequently are *The Washington Post, Express by the Washington Post, BBC News Online, Time* magazine, and *People*. I also read a lot of magazines related to health and fitness, including *Shape, Self,* and *Runner's World*.

RA. Are you pursuing a career in which writing will be a component?

ET. I definitely plan to have writing play a key role in any career I choose; however, I don't know what I want to be when I grow up and therefore I don't know what exactly that role will be.

RA. What advice do you have for other student writers?

ET. My best advice for other student writers is to read a lot, and become informed about topics that interest you. This will help to form opinions about issues that you are passionate about, and writing about those issues is far easier than writing about issues that you aren't interested in. Also, never stop writing, because if you constantly write and get feedback you will become a more confident writer and then a better writer by being responsive to constructive criticism.

Ira Berlin

Migrations Forced and Free

[*Smithsonian*, February 2010]

BEFORE YOU READ

Does being black in America mean only sharing a part of the history of slavery and segregation, or are recent immigrants from Africa and the Caribbean part of the African American community?

WORDS TO LEARN

interplay (para. 1): the effect two things have on each other (noun).
abolitionist (para. 1): opposing slavery (adjective).
emancipation (para. 1): freeing, especially of a slave (noun).
articulated (para. 3): stated (adjective).
turmoil (para. 3): trouble (noun).
warrant (para. 4): make necessary (verb).

One of the leading historians of the African American experience, Ira Berlin is a distinguished professor at the University of Maryland and the author of numerous books, including Many Thousands Gone: The First Two Centuries of Slavery in North America *(1998), which received the prestigious Bancroft Prize, and the prize-winning* Generations of Captivity: A History of African American Slaves *(2003).*

Some years ago, I was interviewed on public radio about the meaning of the Emancipation Proclamation.[1] I addressed the familiar themes of the origins of that great document: the changing nature of the Civil War, the Union army's growing dependence on black labor, the intensifying opposition to slavery in the North and the interplay of military necessity and abolitionist idealism. I recalled the longstanding debate over the role of Abraham Lincoln, the Radicals in Congress, abolitionists in the North, the Union army in the field and slaves on the plantations of the South in the destruction of slavery and in the authorship of legal freedom. And I stated my long-held position that slaves played a critical role in securing their own freedom. The controversy over what was sometimes called "self-emancipation" had generated great heat among historians, and it still had life. 1

As I left the broadcast booth, a knot of black men and women — most of them technicians at the station — were talking about emancipation and its meaning. Once I was drawn into their discussion, I was surprised to learn that no one in the group was descended from anyone who had been freed by the proclamation or any other Civil War measure. Two had been born in Haiti, one in Jamaica, one in Britain, two in Ghana, and one, I believe, in Somalia. Others may have been the children of immigrants. While they seemed impressed — but not surprised — that slaves had played a part in breaking their own chains, and were interested in the events that had brought Lincoln to his decision during the summer of 1862, they insisted it had nothing to do with them. Simply put, it was not their history. 2

The conversation weighed upon me as I left the studio, and it has since. Much of the collective consciousness of black people in mainland North America — the belief of individual men and women that their own fate was linked to that of the group — has long been articulated through a common history, indeed a particular history: centuries of enslavement, freedom in the course of the Civil War, a great promise made amid the political turmoil of Reconstruction and a great promise broken, followed by disfranchisement, segregation and, finally, the long struggle for equality. 3

In commemorating this history—whether on Martin Luther King Jr.'s birthday, during Black History Month or as current events warrant — African-Americans have rightly laid claim to a unique identity. Such celebrations—their memorialization of the past — are no different 4

[1] The Emancipation Proclamation (para. 1): The document President Abraham Lincoln wrote in 1862 and issued in 1863, freeing most of the slaves in the United States.

from those attached to the rituals of Vietnamese Tet[2] celebrations or the Eastern Orthodox Nativity Fast,[3] or the celebration of the birthdays of Christopher Columbus or Casimir Pulaski;[4] social identity is ever rooted in history. But for African-Americans, their history has always been especially important because they were long denied a past.

And so the "not my history" disclaimer by people of African descent 5
seemed particularly pointed — enough to compel me to look closely at how previous waves of black immigrants had addressed the connections between the history they carried from the Old World and the history they inherited in the New.

In 1965, Congress passed the Voting Rights Act, which became a 6
critical marker in African-American history. Given opportunity, black Americans voted and stood for office in numbers not seen since the collapse of Reconstruction almost 100 years earlier. They soon occupied positions that had been the exclusive preserve of white men for more than half a century. By the beginning of the twenty-first century, black men and women had taken seats in the United States Senate and House of Representatives, as well as in state houses and municipalities throughout the nation. In 2009, a black man assumed the presidency of the United States. African-American life had been transformed.

Within months of passing the Voting Rights Act, Congress passed a 7
new immigration law, replacing the Johnson-Reed Act of 1924, which had favored the admission of northern Europeans, with the Immigration and Nationality Act. The new law scrapped the rule of national origins and enshrined a first-come, first-served principle that made allowances for the recruitment of needed skills and the unification of divided families.

This was a radical change in policy, but few people expected it to 8
have much practical effect. It "is not a revolutionary bill," President Lyndon Johnson intoned. "It does not affect the lives of millions. It will not reshape the structure of our daily lives."

But it has had a profound impact on American life. At the time it was 9
passed, the foreign-born proportion of the American population had fallen to historic lows — about 5 percent — in large measure because of

[2] Tet (para. 4): The Vietnamese New Year festival.

[3] Eastern Orthodox Nativity (para. 4): The holiday celebrating Jesus' birth in the Eastern Orthodox Church, a branch of Christianity centered in Eastern Europe and Asia.

[4] Casimir Pulaski (para. 4): A Polish-American cavalry officer (1745–1779) during the time of the Revolutionary War who saved George Washington's life; he is honored by Polish-Americans, particularly in Illinois, on Casimir Pulaski Day.

the old immigration restrictions. Not since the 1830s had the foreign-born made up such a tiny proportion of the American people. By 1965, the United States was no longer a nation of immigrants.

During the next four decades, forces set in motion by the Immigra- 10
tion and Nationality Act changed that. The number of immigrants entering the United States legally rose sharply, from some 3.3 million in the 1960s to 4.5 million in the 1970s. During the 1980s, a record 7.3 million people of foreign birth came legally to the United States to live. In the last third of the 20th century, America's legally recognized foreign-born population tripled in size, equal to more than one American in ten. By the beginning of the twenty-first century, the United States was accepting foreign-born people at rates higher than at any time since the 1850s. The number of illegal immigrants added yet more to the total, as the United States was transformed into an immigrant society once again.

Black America was similarly transformed. Before 1965, black peo- 11
ple of foreign birth residing in the United States were nearly invisible. According to the 1960 census, their percentage of the population was to the right of the decimal point. But after 1965, men and women of African descent entered the United States in ever-increasing numbers. During the 1990s, some 900,000 black immigrants came from the Caribbean; another 400,000 came from Africa; still others came from Europe and the Pacific rim. By the beginning of the twenty-first century, more people had come from Africa to live in the United States than during the centuries of the slave trade. At that point, nearly one in ten black Americans was an immigrant or the child of an immigrant.

African-American society has begun to reflect this change. In New 12
York, the Roman Catholic diocese has added masses in Ashanti and Fante, while black men and women from various Caribbean islands march in the West Indian-American Carnival and the Dominican Day Parade. In Chicago, Cameroonians celebrate their nation's independence day, while the DuSable Museum of African American History hosts a Nigerian Festival. Black immigrants have joined groups such as the Egbe Omo Yoruba (National Association of Yoruba Descendants in North America), the Association des Sénégalais d'Amérique and the Fédération des Associations Régionales Haïtiennes à l'Étranger rather than the NAACP or the Urban League.

To many of these men and women, Juneteenth celebrations — the 13
commemoration of the end of slavery in the United States — are at best an afterthought. The new arrivals frequently echo the words of the men and women I met outside the radio broadcast booth. Some have struggled over the very appellation "African-American," either shunning it — declaring themselves, for instance, Jamaican-Americans

or Nigerian-Americans — or denying native black Americans' claim to it on the ground that most of them had never been to Africa. At the same time, some old-time black residents refuse to recognize the new arrivals as true African-Americans. "I am African and I am an American citizen; am I not African-American?" a dark-skinned, Ethiopian-born Abdulaziz Kamus asked at a community meeting in suburban Maryland in 2004. To his surprise and dismay, the overwhelmingly black audience responded no. Such discord over the meaning of the African-American experience and who is (and isn't) part of it is not new, but of late has grown more intense.

> **African-American history might best be viewed as a series of great migrations.**

After devoting more than 30 years of my career as a historian to the study of the American past, I've concluded that African-American history might best be viewed as a series of great migrations, during which immigrants — at first forced and then free — transformed an alien place into a home, becoming deeply rooted in a land that once was foreign, even despised. After each migration, the newcomers created new understandings of the African-American experience and new definitions of blackness. Given the numbers of black immigrants arriving after 1965, and the diversity of their origins, it should be no surprise that the overarching narrative of African-American history has become a subject of contention. 14

That narrative, encapsulated in the title of John Hope Franklin's classic text *From Slavery to Freedom,* has been reflected in everything from spirituals to sermons, from folk tales to TV docudramas. Like Booker T. Washington's *Up from Slavery,* Alex Haley's *Roots* and Martin Luther King Jr.'s "I Have a Dream" speech, it retells the nightmare of enslavement, the exhilaration of emancipation, the betrayal of Reconstruction, the ordeal of disfranchisement and segregation, and the pervasive, omnipresent discrimination, along with the heroic and ultimately triumphant struggle against second-class citizenship. 15

This narrative retains incalculable value. It reminds men and women that a shared past binds them together, even when distance and different circumstances and experiences create diverse interests. It also integrates black people's history into an American story of seemingly inevitable progress. While recognizing the realities of black poverty and inequality, it nevertheless depicts the trajectory of black life moving along what Dr. King referred to as the "arc of justice," in which exploitation and coercion yield, reluctantly but inexorably, to fairness and freedom. 16

Yet this story has had less direct relevance for black immigrants. Although new arrivals quickly discover the racial inequalities of American life for themselves, many—fleeing from poverty of the sort rarely experienced even by the poorest of contemporary black Americans and tyranny unknown to even the most oppressed—are quick to embrace a society that offers them opportunities unknown in their homelands. While they have subjected themselves to exploitation by working long hours for little compensation and underconsuming to save for the future (just as their native-born counterparts have done), they often ignore the connection between their own travails and those of previous generations of African-Americans. But those travails are connected, for the migrations that are currently transforming African-American life are directly connected to those that have transformed black life in the past. The trans-Atlantic passage to the tobacco and rice plantations of the coastal South, the nineteenth-century movement to the cotton and sugar plantations of the Southern interior, the twentieth-century shift to the industrializing cities of the North and the waves of arrivals after 1965 all reflect the changing demands of global capitalism and its appetite for labor. 17

New circumstances, it seems, require a new narrative. But it need not—and should not—deny or contradict the slavery-to-freedom story. As the more recent arrivals add their own chapters, the themes derived from these various migrations, both forced and free, grow in significance. They allow us to see the African-American experience afresh and sharpen our awareness that African-American history is, in the end, of one piece. 18

VOCABULARY/USING A DICTIONARY

1. What is *idealism* (para. 1)? Explain how it is related to the word *ideal*. To what does *abolitionist idealism* refer?
2. What exactly does the phrase *collective consciousness* mean as Berlin uses it in paragraph 3?
3. Define *disfranchisement* (para. 3). Explain its origin and the meaning of the related word *franchise*.

RESPONDING TO WORDS IN CONTEXT

1. What does Berlin mean by the word *authorship* in paragraph 1? How were slaves the *authors* of their legal freedom, literally and figuratively?
2. Berlin describes seeing a "knot of black men and women" (para. 2) in the radio station office. What does *knot* mean here? What image does the word give you?

3. Explain the use of the word *rooted* in paragraph 4. What does it mean for social identity to be "rooted in history"? What further connotation does the word have here?

DISCUSSING MAIN POINT AND MEANING

1. To what does Berlin's title, "Migrations Forced and Free," refer? What is a migration, and which are the forced and free ones in his essay? How does this title frame the themes of the short essay?
2. What exactly is it about the history and identity of black people in the United States that Berlin considers "unique" (para. 4)? Why does he argue that the consciousness of African Americans is different from that of other ethnic groups?
3. Explain, in your own words, why the conversation of the technicians at the station weighed on Berlin so much. How did their feelings about emancipation lead to Berlin's conclusion in the final paragraph of the essay?

EXAMINING SENTENCES, PARAGRAPHS, AND ORGANIZATION

1. What is the purpose of the examples listed in paragraph 4 ("Vietnamese Tet celebrations . . . Casimir Pulaski")? What do these examples illustrate? What sort of examples has Berlin attempted to select?
2. Discuss the overall organization of this short essay. What modes of writing does Berlin start with, and how does he conclude? Do you think it's effective? Why or why not?

THINKING CRITICALLY

1. What does Berlin mean by his "long-held position that slaves played a critical role in securing their own freedom" (para. 1)? Why might this be considered a controversial position, and what evidence did Berlin offer in its defense on the public radio show? Based on your research and knowledge of American history, how—if at all—do you think slaves achieved freedom for themselves?
2. What makes someone black in America? Are immigrants from Ghana and the Caribbean who came to North America after the abolishment of slavery still part of the African American community and experience? Why or why not?
3. Berlin elevates celebrations rooted in ethnic heritage, like Black History Month. How do you feel about official celebrations that focus on the contributions and history of one group? Give specific examples. Why does Berlin feel these celebrations are so important? Do you agree? Or do you see them as divisive?

IN-CLASS WRITING ACTIVITIES

1. Discuss the relationship you have to your own ethnic heritage and identity. Was where your family came from an important part of how you were taught to define yourself? Why or why not? To what extent, if any, does your racial, ethnic, and national heritage define you? Why?
2. Berlin refers to "the collective consciousness of black people in mainland North America" (para. 3). Give a few examples of what a collective consciousness is and does. Do you believe the collective consciousness—whether of a society, a nation, a race, or even a family—is a real thing? Why or why not?

The Census Bureau projects that there will be 400 million people in the U.S. by 2050.

Remember when this was heavy traffic?

Ask any of your neighbors – things have changed over the past few years. Traffic has gotten worse and schools more crowded. Large developments, eight-lane highways and shopping centers have replaced open fields and wooded areas. Our suburban communities are overwhelmed by the demands of a larger population.

According to the Census Bureau, the U.S. population will grow from 273 million today to over 400 million within the next fifty years – with mass immigration accounting for over 60% of that growth. Every year, our outdated immigration policy brings over 1,000,000 people to the United States. If immigration and population growth continue at these unsustainable levels, a livable America will become a thing of the past.

Yes, I want to help NPG work for environmentally sound national and global population policies. Here is my tax-deductible contribution.

❑ $30 ❑ $50 ❑ $100 ❑ Other

Name ....

Address ....

City .... State .... Zip ....

Please mail to: NR-180

Negative Population Growth
P.O. Box 53249 • Washington, DC 20009 • (202) 667-8950

For more information about immigration, population growth and the environment, please visit NPG's home on the internet at **www.npg.org**

NPG

Courtesy Negative Population Growth. www.npg.org. Used by permission.

Negative Population Growth (NPG) was founded in 1972. The national organization is committed to reducing America's population growth. One of the significant ways to do this, the organization proposes, is to drastically cut back on immigration. According to its Web page, the organization's goal is "to educate the American public and political leaders about the detrimental effects of overpopulation on our environment, resources, and quality of life. NPG advocates a smaller and truly sustainable United States population accomplished through smaller families and lower, more traditional immigration levels."

Recently, NPG commended the former director of the United Nation's Population Division and current research director at the Center for Migration Studies, Joseph Chamie, who has stated: "Contrary to popular thought, the dominant force fueling America's demographic growth is not natural increase, but immigration." NPG then goes on to say: "Statistics show that U.S. population growth would have stabilized in about 1970 if it were not for the tremendous number of immigrants entering our country after the passage of the Immigration Act of 1965. To make matters even worse, the U.S. Census Bureau estimates that the vast majority of our future population growth will be driven by immigration. In order to halt and eventually reverse our population growth, we absolutely must reduce our current immigration rates."

In 1999, NPG released the print advertisement shown here, which appeared in major magazines nationwide. The ad addresses the issue of overcrowding and what Americans can do about it.

Discussing the Unit

SUGGESTED TOPIC FOR DISCUSSION

What can be done about America's borders, particularly its border with Central America? Should we close it up and attempt to police it more tightly? Or do we need an immigration policy that addresses the root causes of immigration and that deals with the problems immigrants themselves face in the United States?

PREPARING FOR CLASS DISCUSSION

1. How does the debate between Tamar Jacoby and Mark Krikorian in this chapter summarize our immigration debate? Do you think it's the right one to be having? Should it even matter if immigrants are harder

working than native-born Americans? Or, as Luis Rodríguez suggests, is there an inherent value in populating a country with people of different values and traditions?

2. Consider why conservatives, who often believe in less government, and liberals, who traditionally advocate for more, switch sides on this issue. Liberals like Jacoby want less enforcement of the border and of immigration laws, while conservatives argue for a crackdown on what they term illegal immigrants. How does this line up with the rest of the left-right dichotomy in America now? Does your position on immigration match the rest of your politics in this way? Why or why not?

FROM DISCUSSION TO WRITING

1. Discuss the image of the immigrant as described by two of the authors in the chapter, and compare it with the first-person image Vicente Martinez portrays. How do native-born Americans portray immigrants, even when they're sympathetic to their plight? Is talking about a typical immigrant reductive, or even ethnocentric or racist?
2. Write out your own immigration policy to submit to President Obama. Who should get into America, who shouldn't, and how should those in the country illegally be managed? Cite at least two of the essays in this chapter as expert testimony.

TOPICS FOR CROSS-CULTURAL DISCUSSION

1. Four of the essays in this chapter deal with immigration from Latin America, but since 9/11, immigration from other nations around the world has become a national priority for security reasons. Describe the new immigration challenges the country faces as a result of the threat of terrorism. How are these challenges similar to the ones described in this chapter, and how are they different?
2. While our immigration problem seems daunting, America is hardly the only country facing the issue—it's been a headline topic in countries like Denmark, the Netherlands, and even Kuwait. Research another country's immigration debate. What does it have in common with America's? How is it different?

Continued from page ii

Brittany Bergstrom. "The Fighting Sioux: The End of a Legacy?" from *The Spectrum,* The University of North Dakota, September 29, 2009. Reprinted by permission of the author.

Ira Berlin. "Migrations Forced and Free" (*Smithsonian Magazine,* February 2010), from *The Making of African America* by Ira Berlin, copyright © 2010 by Ira Berlin. Used by permission of Viking Penguin, a division of Penguin Group (USA) Inc.

Liz Breslin. "Does a Family Need to Share a Surname? Yes." Reprinted from *Brain, Child,* Winter 2009, by permission of the author.

Chris Clarke. "How to Write an Incendiary Blog Post" from *Boston.com,* February 14, 2010. Reprinted by permission of the author.

Amy Domini. "Why Investing in Fast Food May Be a Good Thing" from *Ode Magazine,* Volume 7, Issue 2. Reprinted by permission of the publisher.

Kim Elsesser. "And the Gender-Neutral Oscar Goes To . . ." from *The New York Times,* March 4, 2010. Copyright © 2010 by The New York Times. All rights reserved. Used by permission and protected by the Copyright Laws of the United States. The printing, copying, redistribution, or retransmission of the material without express written permission is prohibited.

Barbara Fredrickson. Interview with Angela Winter, "The Science of Happiness" from *The Sun,* May 2009. Reprinted by permission of Angela Winter.

Ann Friedman. "Swagger Like Us" reprinted with permission from *The American Prospect,* March 2010. Volume 21, Issue 2. http://www.prospect.org. *The American Prospect,* 1710 Rhode Island Avenue, NW, 12th Floor, Washington, DC 20036. All rights reserved.

Daniel Gilbert. "What You Don't Know Makes You Nervous" from *The New York Times,* May 21, 2009. Copyright © 2009 by The New York Times. All rights reserved. Used by permission and protected by the Copyright Laws of the United States. The printing, copying, redistribution, or retransmission of the material without express written permission is prohibited.

Jeff Goodell. "Warming Gets Worse" from *In Character,* Spring 2009. Reprinted by permission of the John Templeton Foundation.

Jay Griffiths. "The Tips of Your Fingers" from *Orion,* January/February 2010. Reprinted by permission of the author.

Rob Haggart. "This Photo Is Lying to You" by Rob Haggart from *Outside,* September 2009. Reprinted by permission of the author.

Mary Katharine Ham. "We Shall Overshare" from *The Weekly Standard,* June 8, 2009. Reprinted by permission of the publisher.

Aprille Hanson. "Stop Relying on Bloggers for News" from *The Echo,* The University of Central Arkansas, April 7, 2010. Reprinted by permission of the author.

Christopher Hedges. "Celebrity Culture and the Obama Brand" reprinted by permission of International Creative Management, Inc. Copyright © 2010 by Christopher Hedges. First appeared in *Tikkun,* January/February 2010.

Tom Hewitt. "Learning From Tison" from *The Sun Star,* University of Alaska, Fairbanks, December 15, 2009. Reprinted by permission of the author.

Tom Jacobs. "Romance Novel Titles Reveal Readers' Desires," *Miller-McCune,* March 2, 2010. Reprinted by permission of the publisher.

Tamar Jacoby. "Does Immigration Increase the Virtues of Hard Work and Fortitude in the U.S.? Yes." From *In Character,* Spring 2009. Reprinted by permission of the John Templeton Foundation.

Mohammed Khan. "The Need for Safety Is Paramount" from *The Daily Evergreen,* Washington State University, January 13, 2010. Reprinted by permission of the author.

Mark Krikorian. "Does Immigration Increase the Virtues of Hard Work and Fortitude in the U.S.? No." From *In Character,* Spring 2009. Reprinted by permission of the John Templeton Foundation.

Steven D. Levitt and Stephen J. Dubner. Adaptation of an excerpt from *Superfreakonomics* by Steven D. Levitt and Stephen J. Dubner. Copyright © 2009 by Steven D. Levitt and Stephen J. Dubner. Reprinted by permission of HarperCollins Publishers.

Yevgeniya Lomakina. "'Going Green' Misses the Point" from *The Daily Collegian,* April 22, 2010. Reprinted by permission of the publisher.

Vicente Martinez. "The Crossing" from *Oregon Humanities,* Fall/Winter 2009. Reprinted by permission of Oregon Humanities Magazine.

Erin McKean. "Redefining Definition: How the Web Could Help Change What Dictionaries Do" from *The New York Times Magazine,* December 20, 2009. Copyright © 2009 by *The New York Times.* All rights reserved. Used by permission and protected by the Copyright Laws of the United States. The printing, copying, redistribution, or retransmission of the material without express written permission is prohibited.

Bill McKibben. "Waste Not Want Not" by Bill McKibben from *Mother Jones,* May/June 2009. Copyright © 2009, Foundation for National Progress.

Diane McKinney-Whetstone. "The First Family" by Diane McKinney-Whetstone from *Essence,* January 2009. Copyright © 2009. Reprinted by permission.

Rebecca Mead. "What Do You Call It?" by Rebecca Mead. Copyright © 2010 Condé Nast. All rights reserved. Originally published in *The New Yorker.* Reprinted by permission.

Shannon Morgan. "Defending Camelot: Chivalry Is Not Dead" from *The Arbiter,* February 24, 2010. Boise State University. Reprinted by permission.

Walter Mosley. "Get Happy" is reprinted with permission from the October 5, 2009 issue of *The Nation.*

Patrick Olsen. "Does Your Pickup Truck Have a Nickname?" by Patrick Olsen. Copyright 2010 Cars.com, a division of Classified Ventures, LLC. Reprinted by permission.

Jed Perl. "Picture Imperfect" from *The New Republic: A Journal of Politics and the Arts* by Jed Perl. Copyright 2009 by TNR II, LLC. Reproduced with permission of TNR II, LLC in the format Textbook via Copyright Clearance Center.

Luis J. Rodríguez. "Slurring Spanish" copyright © 2010 by Luis J. Rodríguez. First published in *The Progressive,* March 1, 2010. Reprinted by permission of Susan Bergholz Literary Services, New York, NY, and Lamy, NM. All rights reserved.

Jeffrey Rosen. "Nude Awakening" copyright Jeffrey Rosen. This article first appeared in *The New Republic,* February 4, 2010, and is reprinted by permission.

Rebecca J. Rosen. "This Is Your Brain on the Web" reprinted with permission from *The Wilson Quarterly,* Autumn 2009. Copyright © 2009 by the Woodrow Wilson International Center for Scholars.

Warwick Sabin. "The Rich Get Thinner, the Poor Get Fatter" by Warwick Sabin from *The Oxford American,* 68, 2010. Reprinted by permission of the author.

Irwin Savodnik. "All Crisis, All the Time" by Irwin Savodnik from *The Weekly Standard,* November 2, 2009. Reprinted by permission of the author.

Connie Schultz. "New Airport Policy: Grin and Bare It" from *The Cleveland Plain Dealer,* January 10, 2010. Reprinted by permission of the publisher, through the Copyright Clearance Center.

Clay Shirky. "A Rant about Women" from www.shirky.com/weblog. Reprinted by permission of the author.

Brian Jay Stanley. "Confessions of a Carnivore" from *The North American Review,* September/October 2009. Reprinted by permission of the author.

Elizabeth Stone. "Grief in the Age of Facebook" from *The Chronicle Review,* March 5, 2010. Reprinted by permission of the author.

Elizabeth Svokos. "Head to Head — Print Photographs" from *The Bi-College News,* Bryn Mawr College/Haverford College, November 18, 2009. Reprinted by permission of the author.

Jacob Swede. "Remembering Johnny Appleseed" from *The Minnesota Daily,* March 10, 2010. Reprinted by permission of the publisher.

Cal Thomas. "Sinking 'Climate Change'" by Cal Thomas, *Townhall.com*, June 3, 2010. Reprinted by permission.

Clive Thompson. "The New Literacy" by Clive Thompson. First published in *Wired*, September 2009. Copyright © 2010 Clive Thompson. Reprinted by permission of Featurewell.com.

Elyse Toplin. "Uniting Families" from *The Hullabaloo*, Tulane University, January 29, 2010. Reprinted by permission of the author.

John Edgar Wideman. "Street Corner Dreamers" from *Essence*, January 2009. Reprinted by permission of the author.

Laura Williamson. "Does a Family Need to Share a Surname? No." Reprinted from *Brain, Child*, Winter 2009, by permission of the author.

Pearl Wong. "Obama—President For All" from *The Santa Clara*, Santa Clara University, February 25, 2010. Reprinted by permission of the author.

Erica Zucco. "Quit Living in Swine Fear" from *The Maneater*, University of Missouri, Columbia, September 4, 2009. Reprinted by permission of the publisher.

Index of Authors and Titles